Flemming Nielson · David Sands (Eds.)

Principles of Security and Trust

8th International Conference, POST 2019
Held as Part of the European Joint Conferences on Theory and Practice of Software, ETAPS 2019
Prague, Czech Republic, April 6–11, 2019
Proceedings

Editors
Flemming Nielson
Technical University of Denmark
Kongens Lyngby, Denmark

David Sands
Chalmers University of Technology
Gothenburg, Sweden

https://doi.org/10.1007/978-3-030-17138-4

LNCS Sublibrary: SL4 – Security and Cryptology

ETAPS Foreword

Welcome to the 22nd ETAPS! This is the first time that ETAPS took place in the Czech Republic in its beautiful capital Prague.

ETAPS 2019 was the 22nd instance of the European Joint Conferences on Theory and Practice of Software. ETAPS is an annual federated conference established in 1998, and consists of five conferences: ESOP, FASE, FoSSaCS, TACAS, and POST. Each conference has its own Program Committee (PC) and its own Steering Committee (SC). The conferences cover various aspects of software systems, ranging from theoretical computer science to foundations to programming language developments, analysis tools, formal approaches to software engineering, and security.

Organizing these conferences in a coherent, highly synchronized conference program enables participation in an exciting event, offering the possibility to meet many researchers working in different directions in the field and to easily attend talks of different conferences. ETAPS 2019 featured a new program item: the Mentoring Workshop. This workshop is intended to help students early in the program with advice on research, career, and life in the fields of computing that are covered by the ETAPS conference. On the weekend before the main conference, numerous satellite workshops took place and attracted many researchers from all over the globe.

ETAPS 2019 received 436 submissions in total, 137 of which were accepted, yielding an overall acceptance rate of 31.4%. I thank all the authors for their interest in ETAPS, all the reviewers for their reviewing efforts, the PC members for their contributions, and in particular the PC (co-)chairs for their hard work in running this entire intensive process. Last but not least, my congratulations to all authors of the accepted papers!

ETAPS 2019 featured the unifying invited speakers Marsha Chechik (University of Toronto) and Kathleen Fisher (Tufts University) and the conference-specific invited speakers (FoSSaCS) Thomas Colcombet (IRIF, France) and (TACAS) Cormac Flanagan (University of California at Santa Cruz). Invited tutorials were provided by Dirk Beyer (Ludwig Maximilian University) on software verification and Cesare Tinelli (University of Iowa) on SMT and its applications. On behalf of the ETAPS 2019 attendants, I thank all the speakers for their inspiring and interesting talks!

ETAPS 2019 took place in Prague, Czech Republic, and was organized by Charles University. Charles University was founded in 1348 and was the first university in Central Europe. It currently hosts more than 50,000 students. ETAPS 2019 was further supported by the following associations and societies: ETAPS e.V., EATCS (European Association for Theoretical Computer Science), EAPLS (European Association for Programming Languages and Systems), and EASST (European Association of Software Science and Technology). The local organization team consisted of Jan Vitek and Jan Kofron (general chairs), Barbora Buhnova, Milan Ceska, Ryan Culpepper, Vojtech Horky, Paley Li, Petr Maj, Artem Pelenitsyn, and David Safranek.

The ETAPS SC consists of an Executive Board, and representatives of the individual ETAPS conferences, as well as representatives of EATCS, EAPLS, and EASST. The Executive Board consists of Gilles Barthe (Madrid), Holger Hermanns (Saarbrücken), Joost-Pieter Katoen (chair, Aachen and Twente), Gerald Lüttgen (Bamberg), Vladimiro Sassone (Southampton), Tarmo Uustalu (Reykjavik and Tallinn), and Lenore Zuck (Chicago). Other members of the SC are: Wil van der Aalst (Aachen), Dirk Beyer (Munich), Mikolaj Bojanczyk (Warsaw), Armin Biere (Linz), Luis Caires (Lisbon), Jordi Cabot (Barcelona), Jean Goubault-Larrecq (Cachan), Jurriaan Hage (Utrecht), Rainer Hähnle (Darmstadt), Reiko Heckel (Leicester), Panagiotis Katsaros (Thessaloniki), Barbara König (Duisburg), Kim G. Larsen (Aalborg), Matteo Maffei (Vienna), Tiziana Margaria (Limerick), Peter Müller (Zurich), Flemming Nielson (Copenhagen), Catuscia Palamidessi (Palaiseau), Dave Parker (Birmingham), Andrew M. Pitts (Cambridge), Dave Sands (Gothenburg), Don Sannella (Edinburgh), Alex Simpson (Ljubljana), Gabriele Taentzer (Marburg), Peter Thiemann (Freiburg), Jan Vitek (Prague), Tomas Vojnar (Brno), Heike Wehrheim (Paderborn), Anton Wijs (Eindhoven), and Lijun Zhang (Beijing).

I would like to take this opportunity to thank all speakers, attendants, organizers of the satellite workshops, and Springer for their support. I hope you all enjoy the proceedings of ETAPS 2019. Finally, a big thanks to Jan and Jan and their local organization team for all their enormous efforts enabling a fantastic ETAPS in Prague!

February 2019

Joost-Pieter Katoen
ETAPS SC Chair
ETAPS e.V. President

Preface

This volume contains the papers presented at POST 2019, the 8th Conference on Principles of Security and Trust, held April 11, 2019, in Prague, Czech Republic, as part of ETAPS. Principles of Security and Trust is a broad forum related to all theoretical and foundational aspects of security and trust, and thus welcomes papers of many kinds: new theoretical results, practical applications of existing foundational ideas, and innovative approaches stimulated by pressing practical problems; as well as systemization-of-knowledge papers, papers describing tools, and position papers. POST was created in 2012 to combine and replace a number of successful and long-standing workshops in this area: Automated Reasoning and Security Protocol Analysis (ARSPA), Formal Aspects of Security and Trust (FAST), Security in Concurrency (SecCo), and the Workshop on Issues in the Theory of Security (WITS). A subset of these events met jointly as an event affiliated with ETAPS 2011 under the name “Theory of Security and Applications” (TOSCA).

There were 27 submissions to POST 2019. Each submission was reviewed by at least three Program Committee members, who in some cases solicited the help of outside experts to review the papers. We employed a double-blind reviewing process with a rebuttal phase. Electronic discussion was used to decide which papers to select for the program. The committee decided to accept ten papers (37%). The papers are organized in topical sections named: Covert Channels and Information Flow; Privacy and Protocols; Distributed Systems.

We would like to thank the members of the Program Committee, the additional reviewers, the POST Steering Committee, the ETAPS Steering Committee, and the local Organizing Committee, who all contributed to the success of POST 2019. We also thank all authors of submitted papers for their interest in POST and congratulate the authors of accepted papers.

February 2019

Flemming Nielson
David Sands

Organization

Program Committee

Owen Arden	UC Santa Cruz, USA
Aslan Askarov	Aarhus University, Denmark
Musard Balliu	KTH Royal Institute of Technology, Sweden
Chiara Bodei	University of Pisa, Italy
Veronique Cortier	CNRS, Loria, France
Pierpaolo Degano	University of Pisa, Italy
Dieter Gollmann	Hamburg University of Technology, Germany
Joshua Guttman	Worcester Polytechnic Institute, USA
Justin Hsu	University of Pennsylvania, USA
Michael Huth	Imperial College London, UK
Heiko Mantel	TU Darmstadt, Germany
Fabio Martinelli	IIT-CNR, Italy
Flemming Nielson	Technical University of Denmark, Denmark
Christian W. Probst	Unitec Institute of Technology, New Zealand
Peter Ryan	University of Luxembourg, Luxembourg
Andrei Sabelfeld	Chalmers University of Technology, Sweden
David Sands	Chalmers University of Technology, Sweden
Carsten Schürmann	IT University of Copenhagen, Denmark
Alwen Tiu	The Australian National University, Australia
Mingsheng Ying	University of Technology, Sydney, Australia

Additional Reviewers

Bartoletti, Massimo
Beckert, Bernhard
Busi, Matteo
Callia D'Iddio, Andrea
Costa, Gabriele
Dietrich, Sven
Galletta, Letterio
Gheri, Lorenzo
Hamann, Tobias
Isemann, Raphael
Jacomme, Charlie
Lallemand, Joseph
Liu, Junyi
Lluch Lafuente, Alberto
Mercaldo, Francesco
Mestel, David
Miculan, Marino
Pedersen, Mathias
Rafnsson, Willard
Rakotonirina, Itsaka
Saracino, Andrea
Vazquez Sandoval, Itzel
Wang, Qisheng
Weber, Alexandra
Yautsiukhin, Artsiom
Zheng, Haofan
Zhou, Li

Contents

Foundations for Parallel Information Flow Control Runtime Systems

Marco Vassena[1(✉)], Gary Soeller[2], Peter Amidon[2], Matthew Chan[3], John Renner[2], and Deian Stefan[2(✉)]

[1] Chalmers University, Gothenburg, Sweden
vassena@chalmers.se
[2] UC San Diego, San Diego, USA
deian@cs.ucsd.edu
[3] Awake Security, Sunnyvale, USA

Abstract. We present the foundations for a new dynamic information flow control (IFC) parallel runtime system, LIO_{PAR}. To our knowledge, LIO_{PAR} is the first dynamic language-level IFC system to (1) support deterministic parallel thread execution and (2) eliminate both internal- and external-timing covert channels that exploit the runtime system. Most existing IFC systems are vulnerable to external timing attacks because they are built atop vanilla runtime systems that do not account for security—these runtime systems allocate and reclaim shared resources (e.g., CPU-time and memory) *fairly* between threads at different security levels. While such attacks have largely been ignored—or, at best, mitigated—we demonstrate that extending IFC systems with parallelism leads to the *internalization* of these attacks. Our IFC runtime system design addresses these concerns by hierarchically managing resources—both CPU-time and memory—and making resource allocation and reclamation explicit at the language-level. We prove that LIO_{PAR} is secure, i.e., it satisfies progress- and timing-sensitive non-interference, even when exposing clock and heap-statistics APIs.

1 Introduction

Language-level dynamic information flow control (IFC) is a promising approach to building secure software systems. With IFC, developers specify application-specific, data-dependent security policies. The language-level IFC system—often implemented as a library or as part of a language runtime system—then enforces these policies automatically, by tracking and restricting the flow of information throughout the application. In doing so, IFC can ensure that different application components—even when buggy or malicious—cannot violate data confidentiality or integrity.

This work was supported in part by the CONIX Research Center, one of six centers in JUMP, a Semiconductor Research Corporation program sponsored by DARPA and by gifts from Cisco and Fujitsu. This work was partly done while Marco Vassena and Matthew Chan were at UCSD.

F. Nielson and D. Sands (Eds.): POST 2019, LNCS 11426, pp. 1–28, 2019.
https://doi.org/10.1007/978-3-030-17138-4_1

The key to making language-level IFC practical lies in designing real-world programming language features and abstractions without giving up on security. Unfortunately, many practical language features are at odds with security. For example, even exposing language features as simple as `if`-statements can expose users to timing attacks [42,64]. Researchers have made significant strides towards addressing these challenges—many IFC systems now support real-world features and abstractions safely [10,15,20,34,43,50,51,54,55,59,60,62,67,68]. To the best of our knowledge, though, no existing language-level dynamic IFC supports parallelism. Yet, many applications rely on parallel thread execution. For example, modern Web applications typically handle user requests in parallel, on multiple CPU cores, taking advantage of modern hardware. Web applications built atop state-of-the-art dynamic IFC Web frameworks (e.g., Jacqueline [67], Hails [12,13], and LMonad [45]), unfortunately, do not handle user requests in parallel—the language-level IFC systems that underlie them (e.g., Jeeves [68] and LIO [54]) do not support parallel thread execution.

In this paper we show that extending most existing IFC systems—even concurrent IFC systems such as LIO—with parallelism is unsafe. The key insight is that most IFC systems *do not* prevent sensitive computations from affecting public computations; they simply prevent public computations from *observing* such sensitive effects. In the sequential and concurrent setting, such effects are only observable to attackers *external* to the program and thus outside the scope of most IFC systems. However, when computations execute in parallel, they are essentially external to one another and thus do not require an observer external to the system—they can observe such effects internally.

Consider a program consisting of three concurrent threads: two public threads—p_0 and p_1—and a secret thread—s_0. On a single core, language-level IFC can ensure that p_0 and p_1 do not learn anything secret by, for example, disallowing them from observing the return values (or lack thereof) of the secret thread. Systems such as LIO are careful to ensure that public threads cannot learn secrets even indirectly (e.g., via covert channels that abuse the runtime system scheduler). But, secret threads *can* leak information to an external observer that monitors public events (e.g., messages from public threads) by influencing the behavior of the public threads. For example, s_0 can terminate (or not) based on a secret and thus affect the amount of time p_0 and p_1 spend executing on the CPU—if s_0 terminated, the runtime allots the whole CPU to public threads, otherwise it only allots, say, two thirds of the CPU to the public threads; this allows an external attacker to trivially infer the secret (e.g., by measuring the rate of messages written to a public channel). Unfortunately, such *external timing attacks* manifest *internally* to the program when threads execute in parallel, on multiple cores. Suppose, for example, that p_0 and s_0 are co-located on a core and run in parallel to p_1. By terminating early (or not) based on a secret, s_0 affects the CPU time allotted to p_0, which can be measured by p_1. For example, p_1 can count the number of messages sent from p_0 on a public channel—the number of p_0 writes indirectly leaks whether or not s_0 terminated.

We demonstrate that such attacks are feasible by building several proof-of-concept programs that exploit the way the runtime system allocates and reclaims *shared* resources to violate LIO's security guarantees. Then, we design a new dynamic parallel language-level IFC runtime system called LIO_{PAR}, which extends LIO to the parallel setting by changing how *shared* runtime system resources—namely CPU-time and memory—are managed. Ordinary runtime systems (e.g., GHC for LIO) *fairly* balance resources between threads; this means that allocations or reclamations for secret LIO threads directly affect resources available for public LIO threads. In contrast, LIO_{PAR} makes resource management *explicit* and *hierarchical*. When allocating new resources on behalf of a thread, the LIO_{PAR} runtime does not "fairly" steal resources from all threads. Instead, LIO_{PAR} demands that the thread requesting the allocation explicitly gives up a portion of its own resources. Similarly, the runtime does not automatically relinquish the resources of a terminated thread—it requires the parent thread to explicitly reclaim them.

Nevertheless, automatic memory management is an integral component of modern language runtimes—high-level languages (e.g., Haskell and thus LIO) are typically garbage collected, relieving developers from manually reclaiming unused memory. Unfortunately, even if memory is hierarchically partitioned, some garbage collection (GC) algorithms, such as GHC's stop-the-world GC, may introduce timing covert channels [46]. Inspired by previous work on real-time GCs (e.g., [3,5,6,16,44,48]), we equip LIO_{PAR} with a per-thread, interruptible garbage collector. This strategy is agnostic to the particular GC algorithm used: our hierarchical runtime system only demands that the GC runs within the memory confines of individual threads and their time budget.

In sum, this paper makes three contributions:

- ▶ We observe that several external timing attacks *manifest internally* in the presence of parallelism and demonstrate that LIO, when compiled to run on multiple cores, is vulnerable to such attacks (Sect. 2).
- ▶ In response to these attacks, we propose a novel parallel runtime system design that safely manages shared resources by enforcing explicit and *hierarchical* resource allocation and reclamation (Sect. 3). To our knowledge, LIO_{PAR} is the first parallel language-level dynamic IFC runtime system to address both internal and external timing attacks that abuse the runtime system scheduler, memory allocator, and GC.
- ▶ We formalize the LIO_{PAR} hierarchical runtime system (Sect. 4) and prove that it satisfies *progress- and timing-sensitive non-interference* (Sect. 5); we believe that this is the first general purpose dynamic IFC runtime system to provide such strong guarantees in the parallel setting [64].

Neither our attack nor our defense is tied to LIO or GHC—we focus on LIO because it already supports concurrency. We believe that extending any existing language-level IFC system with parallelism will pose the same set of challenges—challenges that can be addressed using explicit and hierarchical resource management.

2 Internal Manifestation of External Attacks

In this section we give a brief overview of LIO and discuss the implications of shared, finite runtime system resources on security. We demonstrate several external timing attacks against LIO that abuse two such resources—the thread scheduler and garbage collector—and show how running LIO threads in parallel internalizes these attacks.

2.1 Overview of the Concurrent LIO Information Flow Control System

At a high level, the goal of an IFC system is to track and restrict the flow of information according to a security policy—almost always a form of *non-interference* [14]. Informally, this policy ensures *confidentiality*, i.e., secret data should not leak to public entities, and *integrity*, i.e., untrusted data should not affect trusted entities.

To this end, LIO tracks the flow of information at a coarse-granularity, by associating *labels* with threads. Implicitly, the thread label classifies all the values in its scope and reflects the sensitivity of the data that it has inspected. Indeed, LIO "raises" the label of a thread to accommodate for reading yet more sensitive data. For example, when a *public* thread reads *secret* data, its label is raised to *secret*—this reflects the fact that the rest of the thread computation may depend on sensitive data. Accordingly, LIO uses the thread's *current label* or *program counter label* to restrict its communication. For example, a *secret* thread can only communicate with other *secret* threads.

In LIO, developers can express programs that manipulate data of varying sensitivity—for example programs that handle both *public* and *secret* data—by forking multiple threads, at run-time, as necessary. However, naively implementing concurrency in an IFC setting is dangerous: concurrency can amplify and internalize the *termination covert channel* [1,58], for example, by allowing public threads to observe whether or not secret threads terminated. Moreover, concurrency often introduces *internal timing covert channels* wherein secret threads leak information by influencing the scheduling behavior of public threads. Both classes of covert channels are high-bandwidth and easy to exploit.

Stefan et al. [54] were careful to ensure that LIO does not expose these termination and timing covert channels *internally*. LIO ensures that even if secret threads terminate early, loop forever, or otherwise influence the runtime system scheduler, they cannot leak information to public threads. But, secret threads *do* affect public threads with those actions and thus expose timing covert channels *externally*—public threads just cannot detect it. In particular, LIO disallows public threads from (1) directly inspecting the return values (and thus timing and termination behavior) of secret threads, without first raising their program counter label, and (2) observing runtime system resource usage (e.g., elapsed time or memory availability) that would indirectly leak secrets.

LIO prevents public threads from measuring CPU-time usage directly—LIO does not expose a clock API—and indirectly—threads are scheduled fairly in a round-robin fashion [54]. Similarly, LIO prevents threads from measuring memory usage directly—LIO does not expose APIs for querying heap statistics—and indirectly, through garbage collection cycles (e.g., induced by secret threads) [46]—GHC's stop-the-world GC stops all threads. Like other IFC systems, the security guarantees of LIO are weaker in practice because its formal model does not account for the GC and assumes memory to be infinite [54,55].

2.2 External Timing Attacks to Runtime Systems

Since secret threads can still influence public threads by abusing the scheduler and GC, LIO is vulnerable to *external timing and termination attacks*, i.e., attacks that leak information to external observers. To illustrate this, we craft several LIO programs consisting of two threads: a public thread p that writes to the external channel observed by the attacker and a secret thread s, which abuses the runtime to influence the throughput of the public thread. The secret thread can leak in many ways, for example, thread s can:

1. *fork bomb*, i.e., fork thousands of secret threads that will be interleaved with p and thus decrease its write throughput;
2. terminate early to relinquish the CPU to p and thus double its write throughput;
3. exhaust all memory to crash the program, and thus stop p from further writing to the channel;
4. force a garbage collection which, because of GHC's stop-the-world GC, will intermittently stop p from writing to the channel.

These attacks abuse the runtime's automatic *allocation* and *reclamation* of shared resources, i.e., CPU time and memory. In particular, attack 1 hinges on the runtime *allocating* CPU time for the new secret threads, thus reducing the CPU time allotted to the public thread. Dually, attack 2 relies on it *reclaiming* the CPU time of terminated threads—it reassigns it to public threads. Similarly, attacks 3 and 4 force the runtime to allocate all the available memory and preemptively reassign CPU time to the GC, respectively.

These attacks are not surprising, but, with the exception of the GC-based attack [46], they are novel in the IFC context. Moreover these attacks are not exhaustive—there are other ways to exploit the runtime system—nor optimized—our implementation leaks sensitive data at a rate of roughly 2bits/second[1]. Nevertheless, they are feasible and—because they abuse the runtime—they are effective against language-level external-timing mitigation techniques, including [54,71]. The attacks are also feasible on other systems—similar attacks that abuse the GC have been demonstrated for both the V8 and JVM runtimes [46].

[1] A more assiduous attacker could craft similar attacks that leak at higher bit-rates.

Core c_0		**Core c_1**
Secret Thread (s_0)	Public Thread (p_0)	Public Thread (p_1)
if secret then terminate else forever skip	forever (write chan p_0)	for [1..n] (write chan p_1) ms <- read chan w_0 <- count p_0 ms w_1 <- count p_1 ms return (w_0 < w_1)

Fig. 1. In this attack three threads run in parallel, colluding to leak secret `secret`. The two public threads write to a *public* output channel; the relative number of messages written on the channel by each thread directly leaks the secret (as inferred by p_1). To affect the rate that p_0 can write, s_0 conditionally terminates—which will free up time on core c_0 for p_0 to execute.

2.3 Internalizing External Timing Attacks

LIO, like almost all IFC systems, considers external timing out of scope for its attacker model. Unfortunately, when we run LIO threads on multiple cores, in parallel, the allocation and reclamation of resources on behalf of secret threads is indirectly observable by public threads. Unsurprisingly, some of the above external timing attacks manifest internally—a thread running on a parallel core acts as an "external" attacker. To demonstrate the feasibility of such attacks, we describe two variants of the aforementioned scheduler-based attacks which leak sensitive information internally to public threads.

Secret threads can leak information by relinquishing CPU time, which the runtime reclaims and *unsafely* redistributes to public threads running on the same core. Our attack program consists of three threads: two public threads—p_0 and p_1—and a secret thread—s_0. Figure 1 shows the pseudo-code for this attack. Note that the threads are secure in isolation, but leak the value of *secret* when executed in parallel, with a round robin scheduler. In particular, threads p_0 and s_0 run concurrently on core c_0 using half of the CPU time each, while p_1 runs in parallel alone on core c_1 using all the CPU time. Both public threads repeatedly write their respective thread IDs to a *public channel*. The secret thread, on the other hand, loops forever or terminates depending on *secret*. Intuitively, when the secret thread terminates, the runtime system redirects its CPU time to p_0, causing both p_1 and p_0 to write at the same rate. In converse, when the secret thread does not terminate early, p_0 is scheduled in a round-robin fashion with s_0 on the same core and can thus only write half as fast as p_1. More specifically:

- If `secret = true`, thread s_0 terminates and the runtime system assigns all the CPU time of core c_0 to public thread p_0, which then writes at the same rate as thread p_1 on core c_1. Then, p_0 writes as many times as p_1, which then returns `true`.

- ▶ If `secret = false`, secret thread s_0 loops and public thread p_0 shares the CPU time on core c_0 with it. Then, p_0 writes messages at roughly half the rate of thread p_1, which writes more often—it has all the CPU time on c_1—and thus returns `false`.[2]

Secret LIO threads can also leak information by allocating many secret threads on a core with public threads—this reduces the CPU-time available to the public threads. For example, using the same setting with three threads from before, the secret thread forks a spinning thread on core c_1 by replacing command `terminate` with command `fork (forever skip)` c_1 in the code of thread s_0 in Fig. 1. Intuitively, if `secret` is `false`, then p_1 writes more often than p_0 before, otherwise the write rate of p_1 decreases—it shares core c_1 with the child thread of s_0—and p_0 writes as often as p_1.

Not all external timing attacks can be internalized, however. In particular, GHC's approach to reclaiming memory via a stop-the-world GC simultaneously stops all threads on *all* cores, thus the relative write rate of public threads remain constant. Interestingly, though, implementing LIO on runtimes (e.g., Node.js as proposed by Heule et al. [17]) with modern parallel garbage collectors that do not always stop the world would internalize the GC-based external timing attacks. Similarly, abusing GHC's memory allocation to exhaust all memory crashes all the program threads and, even though it cannot be internalized, it still results in information leakage.

3 Secure, Parallel Runtime System

To address the external and internal timing attacks, we propose a new dynamic IFC runtime system design. Fundamentally, today's runtime systems are vulnerable because they automatically allocate and reclaim resources that are shared across threads of varying sensitivity. However, the automatic allocation and reclamation is not in itself a problem—it is only a problem because the runtime steals (and grants) resources from (and to) differently-labeled threads.

Our runtime system, LIO_{PAR}, explicitly partitions CPU-time and memory among threads—each thread has a fixed CPU-time and memory *budget* or *quota*. This allows resource management decisions to be made locally, for each thread, independent of the other threads in the system. For example, the runtime scheduler of LIO_{PAR} relies on CPU-time partitioning to ensure that threads always run for a fixed amount of time, irrespective of the other threads running on the same core. Similarly, in LIO_{PAR}, the memory allocator and garbage collector rely on memory partitioning to be able to allocate and collect memory on behalf of a thread without being influenced or otherwise influencing other threads in the system. Furthermore, partitioning resources among threads enables fine-grained control of resources: LIO_{PAR} exposes secure primitives to (i) measure resource usage (e.g., time and memory) and (ii) elicit garbage collection cycles.

---

[2] The attacker needs to empirically find parameter n, so that p_1 writes roughly twice as much as thread p_0 with half CPU time on core c_0.

The LIO_{PAR} runtime does not automatically balance resources between threads. Instead, LIO_{PAR} makes resource management explicit at the language level. When forking a new thread, for example, LIO_{PAR} demands that the parent thread give up part of its CPU-time and memory budgets to the children. Indeed, LIO_{PAR} even manages core ownership or *capabilities* that allow threads to fork threads across cores. This approach ensures that allocating new threads does not indirectly leak any information externally or to other threads. Dually, the LIO_{PAR} runtime does not re-purpose unused memory or CPU-time, even when a thread terminates or "dies" abruptly—parent threads must explicitly kill their children when they wish to reclaim their resources.

To ensure that CPU-time and memory can always be reclaimed, LIO_{PAR} allows threads to kill their children at any time. Unsurprisingly, this feature requires restricting the LIO_{PAR} floating-label approach more than that of LIO—LIO_{PAR} threads cannot raise their current label if they have already forked other threads. As a result, in LIO_{PAR} threads form a *hierarchy*—children threads are always at least as sensitive as their parent—and thus it is secure to expose an API to *allocate* and *reclaim* resources.

Attacks Revisited. LIO_{PAR} enforces security against *reclamation-based attacks* because secret threads cannot automatically relinquish their resources. For example, our hierarchical runtime system stops the attack in Fig. 1: even if secret thread s_0 terminates (`secret = true`), the throughput of public thread p_0 remains constant—LIO_{PAR} does not reassign the CPU time of s_0 to p_0, but keeps s_0 spinning until it gets killed. Similarly, LIO_{PAR} protects against *allocation-based attacks* because secret threads cannot steal resources owned by other public threads. For example, the *fork-bomb* variant of the previous attack fails because LIO_{PAR} aborts command `fork (forever skip)` c_1—thread s_0 does not own the core capability c_1—and thus the throughput of p_1 remains the same. In order to substantiate these claims, we first formalize the design of the *hierarchical* runtime system (Sect. 4) and establish its security guarantees (Sect. 5).

Trust Model. This work addresses attacks that exploit runtime system resource management — in particular memory and CPU-time. We do not address attacks that exploit other shared runtime system state (e.g., event loops [63], lazy evaluation [7,59]), shared operating system state (e.g., file system locks [24], events and I/O [22,32]), or shared hardware (e.g., caches, buses, pipelines and hardware threads [11,47]) Though these are valid concerns, they are orthogonal and outside the scope of this paper.

4 Hierarchical Calculus

In this section we present the formal semantics of LIO_{PAR}. We model LIO_{PAR} as a security monitor that executes simply typed λ-calculus terms extended with *LIO* security primitives on an abstract machine in the style of Sestoft [53]. The security monitor reduces secure programs and aborts the execution of leaky programs.

$$
\begin{array}{lll}
\text{Label} & \ell, pc, cl \in \mathscr{L} \\
\text{Cores} & k \in \{1..\kappa\}, K \in \mathcal{P}(\{1..\kappa\}) \\
\text{Thread Id} & n \in \mathbb{N}, N \in \mathcal{P}(\mathbb{N})
\end{array}
\qquad
\begin{array}{ll}
\text{Params.} & \mu ::= (h, cl) \\
\text{Heap} & \Delta \in Var \rightharpoonup Term \\
\text{Budgets} & h, b \in \mathbb{N}
\end{array}
$$

$$
\begin{array}{lll}
\text{Type} & \tau & ::= () \mid \tau_1 \to \tau_2 \mid Bool \mid \mathscr{L} \mid LIO\ \tau \mid Labeled\ \tau \\
 & & \quad \mid TId \mid Core \mid \mathcal{P}(\{1..\kappa\}) \mid \mathbb{N} \\
\text{Value} & v & ::= () \mid \lambda x.t \mid True \mid False \mid \ell \mid return\ t \mid Labeled\ \ell\ t^{\circ} \mid n \mid k \mid K \\
\text{Term} & t & ::= v \mid x \mid t_1\ t_2 \mid \textbf{if}\ t_1\ \textbf{then}\ t_2\ \textbf{else}\ t_3 \mid t_1 \gg\!= t_2 \mid label\ t_1\ t_2 \\
 & & \quad \mid unlabel\ t \mid fork\ t_1\ t_2\ t_3\ t_4\ t_5 \mid spawn\ t_1\ t_2\ t_3\ t_4\ t_5 \mid kill\ t \\
 & & \quad \mid size \mid time \mid wait\ t \mid send\ t_1\ t_2 \mid receive \\
\text{CTerm} & t^{\circ} & ::= t \text{ such that } fv(t) = \varnothing \\
\text{Cont.} & C & ::= x \mid \textbf{then}\ t_2\ \textbf{else}\ t_3 \mid \gg\!= t_2 \mid label\ t \mid unlabel \mid fork\ t_1\ t_2\ t_3\ t_4 \\
 & & \quad \mid spawn\ t_1\ t_2\ t_3\ t_4 \mid kill \mid send\ t \\
\text{Stack} & S & ::= [] \mid C : S \\
\text{State} & s & ::= (\Delta, pc, N \mid t, S)
\end{array}
$$

(APP$_1$)

$$\frac{|\Delta| < \mu.h \qquad \text{fresh}(x)}{(\Delta, pc, N \mid t_1\ t_2, S) \rightsquigarrow_{\mu} (\Delta[x \mapsto t_2], pc, N \mid t_1, x : S)}$$

(APP$_2$)

$$(\Delta, pc, N \mid \lambda y.t, x : S) \rightsquigarrow_{\mu} (\Delta, pc, N \mid t\ [x \ /\ y], S)$$

(VAR)

$$\frac{x \mapsto t \in \Delta}{(\Delta, pc, N \mid x, S) \rightsquigarrow_{\mu} (\Delta, pc, N \mid t, S)}$$

(BIND$_1$)

$$(\Delta, pc, N \mid t_1 \gg\!= t_2, S) \rightsquigarrow_{\mu} (\Delta, pc, N \mid t_1, \gg\!= t_2 : S)$$

(BIND$_2$)

$$(\Delta, pc, N \mid return\ t_1, \gg\!= t_2 : S) \rightsquigarrow_{\mu} (\Delta, pc, N \mid t_2\ t_1, S)$$

(LABEL$_1$)

$$(\Delta, pc, N \mid label\ t_1\ t_2, S) \rightsquigarrow_{\mu} (\Delta, pc, N \mid t_1, label\ t_2 : S)$$

(LABEL$_2$)

$$\frac{pc \sqsubseteq \ell \sqsubseteq \mu.cl \qquad t^{\circ} = \Delta^{*}(t)}{(\Delta, pc, N \mid \ell, label\ t : S) \rightsquigarrow_{\mu} (\Delta, pc, N \mid return\ (Labeled\ \ell\ t^{\circ}), S)}$$

(UNLABEL$_1$)

$$(\Delta, pc, N \mid unlabel\ t, S) \rightsquigarrow_{\mu} (\Delta, pc, N \mid t, unlabel : S)$$

(UNLABEL$_2$)

$$\frac{pc \sqcup \ell \sqsubseteq \mu.cl}{(\Delta, pc, N \mid Labeled\ \ell\ t, unlabel : S) \rightsquigarrow_{\mu} (\Delta, pc \sqcup \ell, N \mid return\ t, S)}$$

Fig. 2. Sequential LIO$_{\text{PAR}}$.

Semantics. The state of the monitor, written $(\Delta, pc, N \mid t, S)$, stores the state of a thread under execution and consists of a heap Δ that maps variables to terms, the thread's program counter label pc, the set N containing the identifiers of the thread's children, the term currently under reduction t and a stack of continuations S. Figure 2 shows the interesting rules of the sequential small-step operational semantics of the security monitor. The notation $s \rightsquigarrow_{\mu} s'$ denotes a transition of the machine in state s that reduces to state s' in one step with thread parameters $\mu = (h, cl)$.[3] Since we are interested in modeling a system with *finite* resources, we parameterize the transition with the maximum heap size $h \in \mathbb{N}$. Additionally, the clearance label cl represents an upper bound over the sensitivity of the thread's floating counter label pc. Rule [APP_1] begins a function application. Since our calculus is call-by-name, the function argument is saved as a *thunk* (i.e., an unevaluated expression) on the heap at fresh location x and the indirection is pushed on the stack for future lookups.[4] Note that the rule allocates memory on the heap, thus the premise $|\Delta| < h$ forbids a heap overflow, where the notation $|\Delta|$ denotes the size of the heap Δ, i.e., the number of bindings that it contains.[5] To avoid overflows, a thread can measure the size of its own heap via primitive *size* (Sect. 4.2). If t_1 evaluates to a function, e.g., $\lambda y.t$, rule [APP_2] starts evaluating the body, in which the bound variable y is substituted with the heap-allocated argument x, i.e., $t\ [x\ /\ y]$. When the evaluation of the function body requires the value of the argument, variable x is looked up in the heap (rule [VAR]). In the next paragraph we present the rules of the basic security primitives. The other sequential rules are available in the extended version of this paper.

Security Primitives. A labeled value *Labeled* $\ell\ t^{\circ}$ of type *Labeled* τ consists of term t of type τ and a label ℓ, which reflects the sensitivity of the content. The annotation t° denotes that term t is *closed* and does not contain any free variable, i.e., $fv(t) = \varnothing$. We restrict the syntax of labeled values with closed terms for security reasons. Intuitively, LIO_{PAR} allocates free variables inside a secret labeled values on the heap, which then leaks information to public threads with its size. For example, a public thread could distinguish between two secret values, e.g., *Labeled* $H\ x$ with heap $\Delta = [x \mapsto 42]$, and *Labeled* H 0 with heap $\Delta = \varnothing$, by measuring the size of the heap. To avoid that, labeled values are closed and the size of the heap of a thread at a certain security level, is not affected by data labeled at different security levels. A term of type *LIO* τ is a secure computation that performs side effects and returns a result of type τ. Secure computations are structured using standard monadic constructs *return* t, which embeds term t in the monad, and *bind*, written $t_1 \gg\!= t_2$, which sequentially

[3] We use record notation, i.e., $\mu.h$ and $\mu.cl$, to access the components of μ.

[4] The calculus does not feature lazy evaluation. Laziness, because of *sharing*, introduces a covert channel, which has already been considered in previous work [59].

[5] To simplify reasoning, our generic memory model is basic and assumes a uniform size for all the objects stored in the heap. We believe that it is possible to refine our generic model with more accurate memory models (e.g., GHC's tagless G-machine (STG) [23], the basis for GHC's runtime [39]), but leave this to future work.

composes two monadic actions, the second of which takes the result of the first as an argument. Rule [BIND$_1$] deconstructs a computation $t_1 \gg\!= t_2$ into term t_1 to be reduced first and pushes on the stack the continuation $\gg\!= t_2$ to be invoked after term t_1.[6] Then, the second rule [BIND$_2$] pops the topmost continuation placed on the stack (i.e., $\gg\!= t_2$) and evaluates it with the result of the first computation (i.e., $t_2\ t_1$), which is considered complete when it evaluates to a monadic value, i.e., to syntactic form *return* t_1. The runtime monitor secures the interaction between computations and labeled values. In particular, secure computations can construct and inspect labeled values exclusively with monadic primitives *label* and *unlabel* respectively. Rules [LABEL$_1$] and [UNLABEL$_1$] are straightforward and follow the pattern seen in the other rules. Rule [LABEL$_2$] generates a labeled value at security level ℓ, subject to the constraint $pc \sqsubseteq \ell \sqsubseteq cl$, which prevents a computation from labeling values below the program counter label pc or above the clearance label cl.[7] The rule computes the closure of the content, i.e., closed term t°, by recursively substituting every free variable in term t with its value in the heap, written $\Delta^{*}(t)$. Rule [UNLABEL$_2$] extracts the content of a labeled value and taints the program counter label with its label, i.e., it rises it to $pc \sqcup \ell$, to reflect the sensitivity of the data that is now in scope. The premise $pc \sqcup \ell \sqsubseteq cl$ ensures that the program counter label does not float over the clearance cl. Thus, the run-time monitor prevents the program counter label from floating above the clearance label (i.e., $pc \sqsubseteq cl$ always holds).

The calculus also includes concurrent primitives to allocate resources when forking threads (*fork* and *spawn* in Sect. 4.1), reclaim resources and measure resource usage (*kill*, *size*, and *time* in Sect. 4.2), threads synchronization and communication (*wait*, *send* and *receive* in the extended version of this paper).

4.1 Core Scheduler

In this section, we extend LIO$_{\text{PAR}}$ with concurrency, which enables (i) *interleaved* execution of threads on a single core and (ii) *simultaneous* execution on κ cores. To protect against attacks that exploit the automatic management of shared *finite* resource (e.g., those in Sect. 2.3), LIO$_{\text{PAR}}$ maintains a resource budget for each running thread and updates it as threads allocate and reclaim resources. Since κ threads execute at the same time, those changes must be coordinated in order to preserve the consistency of the resource budgets and guarantee *deterministic parallelism*. For this reason, the hierarchical runtime system is split in two components: (i) the *core scheduler*, which executes threads on a single core, ensures that they respect their resource budgets and performs security checks, and (ii) the top-level *parallel scheduler*, which synchronizes the execution on multiple cores and reassigns resources by updating the resource budgets according to the instructions of the core schedulers. We now introduce the core scheduler and describe the top-level parallel scheduler in Sect. 4.3.

---

6 Even though the stack size is unbounded in this model, we could account for its memory usage by explicitly allocating it on the heap, in the style of Yang et al. [66].

7 The labels form a security lattice $(\mathscr{L}, \sqcup, \sqsubseteq)$.

$$\begin{array}{llll}
\text{Thread Map} & T \in \mathit{TId} \rightharpoonup \mathit{State} & \text{Global State} & \Sigma ::= (T, B, H, \theta, \omega) \\
\text{Time Map} & B \in \mathit{TId} \rightharpoonup \mathbb{N} & \text{Core Queue} & Q ::= \langle n^{b} \rangle \mid \langle Q_1 \mid Q_2 \rangle \\
\text{Size Map} & H \in \mathit{TId} \rightharpoonup \mathbb{N} & \text{Event} & e ::= \epsilon \mid \mathbf{fork}(\Delta, n, t, b, h) \\
\text{Core Map} & \theta \in \mathit{TId} \rightharpoonup \mathcal{P}(\{1 \,..\, \kappa\}) & & \quad \mid \mathbf{spawn}(\Delta, n, t, K) \\
\text{Clock} & \omega \in \mathbb{N} & & \quad \mid \mathbf{kill}(n) \mid \mathbf{send}(n, t)
\end{array}$$

STEP

$$\frac{\Sigma.T(n) = s \qquad \mu = (\Sigma.H(n), n.cl) \qquad s \rightsquigarrow_{\mu} s'}{Q[\langle n^{1+b} \rangle] \xrightarrow{(n, s', \epsilon)}_{\Sigma} Q[\langle n^{b} \rangle]}$$

FORK

$$\frac{\begin{array}{c}\Sigma.T(n) = (\Delta, pc, N \mid b_2, \mathit{fork}\ \ell_{\mathrm{L}}\ \ell_{\mathrm{H}}\ h_2\ t : S) \\ pc \sqsubseteq \ell_{\mathrm{L}} \qquad n' \leftarrow \mathsf{fresh}^{\mathit{TId}}(\ell_{\mathrm{L}}, \ell_{\mathrm{H}}, n.k) \\ s = (\Delta, pc, \{n'\} \cup N \mid \mathit{return}\ n', S) \qquad \Delta' = \{x \mapsto \Delta(x) \mid x \in \mathit{fv}^{*}(t, \Delta)\} \\ \Sigma.H(n) = h_1 + h_2 \qquad |\Delta| \leqslant h_1 \quad |\Delta'| \leqslant h_2\end{array}}{Q[\langle n^{1+b_1+b_2} \rangle] \xrightarrow{(n, s, \mathbf{fork}(\Delta', n', t, b_2, h_2))}_{\Sigma} Q[\langle \langle n^{b_1} \rangle | \langle n'^{b_2} \rangle \rangle]}$$

SPAWN

$$\frac{\begin{array}{c}\Sigma.T(n) = (\Delta, pc, N \mid k, \mathit{spawn}\ \ell_{\mathrm{L}}\ \ell_{\mathrm{H}}\ K_1\ t : S) \\ \Sigma.\theta(n) = \{k\} \cup K_1 \cup K_2 \qquad pc \sqsubseteq \ell_{\mathrm{L}} \qquad n' \leftarrow \mathsf{fresh}^{\mathit{TId}}(\ell_{\mathrm{L}}, \ell_{\mathrm{H}}, k) \\ s = (\Delta, pc, \{n'\} \cup N \mid \mathit{return}\ n', S) \qquad \Delta' = \{x \mapsto \Delta(x) \mid x \in \mathit{fv}^{*}(t, \Delta)\}\end{array}}{Q[\langle n^{1+b} \rangle] \xrightarrow{(n, s, \mathbf{spawn}(\Delta', n', t, K_1))}_{\Sigma} Q[\langle n^{b} \rangle]}$$

STUCK

$$\frac{\begin{array}{c}\Sigma.T(n) = s \qquad \mathit{MaxHeapSize}(s, \Sigma.H(n)) \vee \mathit{UnlabelStuck}(n, \Sigma.T) \vee \\ \mathit{ForkStuck}(n, \Sigma.H, \Sigma.T) \vee \mathit{SpawnStuck}(s, \theta(n)) \vee \mathit{ValueStuck}(s) \vee \\ \mathit{WaitStuck}(n, T) \vee \mathit{ReceiveStuck}(s) \vee \mathit{KillStuck}(s)\end{array}}{Q[\langle n^{1+b} \rangle] \xrightarrow{(n, s, \epsilon)}_{\Sigma} Q[\langle n^{b} \rangle]}$$

CONTEXTSWITCH

$$\frac{s_{\circ} = ([\,], \bot, \varnothing \mid \mathit{return}\ (), [\,])}{Q[\langle n^{0} \rangle] \xrightarrow{(\circ, s_{\circ}, \epsilon)}_{\Sigma} Q[\langle n_1^{\Sigma.B(n_1)} \rangle, \ldots, \langle n_{|Q|}^{\Sigma.B(n_{|Q|})} \rangle]}$$

Fig. 3. Concurrent $\mathrm{LIO_{PAR}}$.

Syntax. Figure 3 presents the core scheduler, which has access to the global state $\Sigma = (T, B, H, \theta, \omega)$, consisting of a thread pool map T, which maps a thread id to the corresponding thread's current state, the time budget map B, a memory budget map H, core capabilities map θ, and the global clock ω. Using these maps, the core scheduler ensures that thread n: (i) performs $B(n)$ uninterrupted steps until the next thread takes over, (ii) does not grow its heap above its maximum heap size $H(n)$, and (iii) has exclusive access to the *free* core capabilities $\theta(n)$. Furthermore, each thread id n records the *initial* current label when the thread was created ($n.pc$), its clearance ($n.cl$), and the core where it runs ($n.k$), so that the runtime system can enforce security. Notice that thread ids are *opaque* to threads—they cannot forge them nor access their fields.

Hierarchical Scheduling. The core scheduler performs *deterministic* and *hierarchical* scheduling—threads lower in the hierarchy are scheduled first, i.e., parent threads are scheduled before their children. The scheduler manages a core run queue Q, which is structured as a binary tree with leaves storing thread ids and residual time budgets. The notation n^b indicates that thread n can run for b more steps before the next thread runs. When a new thread is spawned, the scheduler creates a subtree with the parent thread on the left and the child on the right. The scheduler can therefore find the thread with the highest priority by following the left spine of the tree and backtracking to the right if a thread has no residual budget.[8] We write $Q[\langle n^b \rangle]$ to mean the first thread encountered via this traversal is n with budget b. As a result, given the slice $Q[\langle n^{1+b} \rangle]$, thread n is the next thread to run, and $Q[\langle n^0 \rangle]$ occurs only if *all* threads in the queue have zero residual budget. We overload this notation to represent tree updates: a rule $Q[\langle n^{1+b} \rangle] \rightarrow Q[\langle n^b \rangle]$ finds the next thread to run in queue Q and decreases its budget by one.

Semantics. Figure 3 formally defines the transition $Q \xrightarrow{(n,s,e)}_{\Sigma} Q'$, which represents an execution step of the *core scheduler* that schedules thread n in core queue Q, executes it with global state $\Sigma = (T, B, H, \theta, \omega)$ and updates the queue to Q'. Additionally, the core scheduler informs the parallel scheduler of the final state s of the thread and requests on its behalf to update the global state by means of event message e. In rule [Step], the scheduler retrieves the next thread in the schedule, i.e., $Q[\langle n^{1+b} \rangle]$ and its state in the thread pool from the global state, i.e., $\Sigma.T(n) = s$. Then, it executes the thread for one sequential step with its memory budget and clearance, i.e., $s \rightsquigarrow_{\mu} s'$ with $\mu = (\Sigma.H(n), n.cl)$, sends the empty event ϵ to the parallel scheduler, and decrements the thread's residual budget in the final queue, i.e., $Q[\langle n^b \rangle]$. In rule [Fork], thread n creates a new thread t with initial label ℓ_{L} and clearance ℓ_{H}, such that $\ell_{\text{L}} \sqsubseteq \ell_{\text{H}}$ and $pc \sqsubseteq \ell_{\text{L}}$. The child thread runs on the same core of the parent thread, i.e., $n.k$, with fresh id n', which is then added to the set of children, i.e., $\{n'\} \cup N$. Since parent and child threads do not share memory, the core scheduler must copy the portion of the parent's private heap reachable by the child's thread, i.e., Δ'; we do this by copying the bindings of the variables that are transitively reachable from t, i.e., $fv^*(t, \Delta)$, from the parent's heap Δ. The parent thread gives h_2 of its memory budget $\Sigma.H(n)$ to its child. The conditions $|\Delta| \leqslant h_1$ and $|\Delta'| \leqslant h_2$, ensure that the heaps do not overflow their new budgets. Similarly, the core scheduler splits the residual time budget of

[8] When implemented, this procedure might introduce a timing channel that leaks the number of threads running on the core. In practice, techniques from real time schedulers can be used to protect against such timing channels. The model of LIOPAR does not capture the execution time of the runtime system itself and thus this issue does not arise in the security proofs.

the parent into b_1 and b_2 and informs the parallel scheduler about the new thread and its resources with event **fork**$(\Delta', n', t, b_2, h_2)$, and lastly updates the tree Q by replacing the leaf $\langle n^{1+b_1+b_2} \rangle$ with the two-leaves tree $\langle \langle n^{b_1} \rangle | \langle n'^{b_2} \rangle \rangle$, so that the child thread will be scheduled immediately after the parent has consumed its remaining budget b_1, as explained above. Rule [SPAWN] is similar to [FORK], but consumes core capability resources instead of time and memory. In this case, the core scheduler checks that the parent thread owns the core where the child is scheduled and the core capabilities assigned to the child, i.e., $\theta(n) = \{k\} \cup K_1 \cup K_2$ for some set K_2, and informs the parallel scheduler with event **spawn**(Δ', n', t, K_1). Rule [STUCK] performs busy waiting by consuming the time budget of the scheduled thread, when it is *stuck* and cannot make any progress—the premises of the rule enumerate the conditions under which this can occur (see the extended version of this paper for details). Lastly, in rule [CONTEXTSWITCH] all the threads scheduled in the core queue have consumed their time budget, i.e., $Q[\langle n^0 \rangle]$ and the core scheduler resets their residual budget using the budget map $\Sigma.B$. In the rule, the notation $Q[\langle n_i^b \rangle]$ selects the i-th leaf, where $i \in \{1..|Q|\}$ and $|Q|$ denotes the number of leaves of tree Q and symbol $\circ$ denotes the thread identifier of the core scheduler, which updates a dummy thread that simply spins during a context-switch or whenever the core is unused.

4.2 Resource Reclamation and Observations

The calculus presented so far enables threads to manage their time, memory and core capabilities hierarchically, but does not provide any primitive to reclaim their resources. This section rectifies this by introducing (i) a primitive to kill a thread and return its resources back to the owner and (ii) a primitive to elicit a garbage collection cycle and reclaim unused memory. Furthermore, we demonstrate that the runtime system presented in this paper is robust against timing attacks by exposing a timer API allowing threads to access a global clock.[9] Intuitively, it is secure to expose this feature because LIO$_{\text{PAR}}$ ensures that the time spent executing high threads is fixed in advanced, so timing measurements of low threads remain unaffected. Lastly, since memory is hierarchically partitioned, each thread can securely query the current size of its *private heap*, enabling fine-grained control over the garbage collector.

Kill. A parent thread can reclaim the resources given to its child thread n', by executing *kill* n'. If the child thread has itself forked or spawned other threads, they are transitively killed and their resources returned to the parent thread. The concurrent rule [KILL$_2$] in Fig. 4 initiates this process, which is completed by the parallel scheduler via event **kill**(n'). Note that the rule applies only when the thread killed is a *direct* child of the parent thread—that is when the parent's children set has shape $\{n'\} \cup N$ for some set N. Now that threads can unrestrictedly reclaim resources by killing their children, we must revise the primitive

[9] An *external* attacker can take timing measurements using network communications. An attacker equipped with an *internal* clock is equally powerful but simpler to formalize [46].

$$\textsc{Kill}_2\quad \frac{\Sigma.T(n) = (\Delta, pc, \{n'\} \cup N \mid n', kill : S) \qquad s = (\Delta, pc, N \mid return\ (), S)}{Q[\langle n^{1+b}\rangle] \xrightarrow{(n,s,\mathbf{kill}(n'))}_{\Sigma} Q[\langle n^{b}\rangle]}$$

$$\textsc{Unlabel}_2\quad \frac{pc \sqcup \ell \sqsubseteq \mu.cl \qquad \forall n \in N \,.\, pc \sqcup \ell \sqsubseteq n.pc}{(\Delta, pc, N \mid Labeled\ \ell\ t, unlabel : S) \rightsquigarrow_{\mu} (\Delta, pc \sqcup \ell, N \mid return\ t, S)}$$

$$\textsc{GC}\quad \frac{R = fv^{*}(t, \Delta) \cup fv^{*}(S, \Delta) \qquad \Delta' = \{x \mapsto \Delta(x) \mid x \in R\}}{\langle \Delta, pc, N \mid gc\ t, S\rangle \rightsquigarrow_{\mu} \langle \Delta', pc, N \mid t, S\rangle}$$

$$\textsc{App-GC}\quad \frac{|\Delta| \equiv \mu.h}{\langle \Delta, pc, N \mid t_1\ t_2, S\rangle \rightsquigarrow_{\mu} \langle \Delta, pc, N \mid gc\ (t_1\ t_2), S\rangle}$$

$$\textsc{Size}\quad \langle \Delta, pc, N \mid size, S\rangle \rightsquigarrow_{\mu} \langle \Delta, pc, N \mid return\ |\Delta|, S\rangle$$

$$\textsc{Time}\quad \frac{\Sigma.T(n) = (\Delta, pc, N \mid time, S) \qquad s = (\Delta, pc, N \mid return\ \Sigma.\omega, S)}{Q[\langle n^{1+b}\rangle] \xrightarrow{(n,s,\epsilon)}_{\Sigma} Q[\langle n^{b}\rangle]}$$

Fig. 4. LIO$_{\text{PAR}}$ with resource reclamation and observation primitives.

unlabel, since the naive combination of *kill* and *unlabel* can result in information leakage. This will happen if a public thread forks another public thread, then reads a secret value (raising its label to secret), and based on that decides to kill the child. To close the leak, we modify the rule [UNLABEL$_2$] by adding the highlighted premise, causing the primitive *unlabel* to fail whenever the parent thread's label would float above the *initial* current label of one of its children.

Garbage Collection. Rule [GC] extends LIO$_{\text{PAR}}$ with a *time-sensitive hierarchical* garbage collector via the primitive *gc t*. The rule elicits a garbage collection cycle which drops entries that are no longer needed from the heap, and then evaluates t. The sub-heap Δ' includes the portion of the current heap that is (transitively) *reachable* from the free variables in scope (i.e. those present in the term, $fv^*(t, \Delta)$ or on the stack $fv^*(S, \Delta)$). After collection, the thread resumes and evaluates term t under compacted private heap Δ'.[10] In rule [APP-GC], a collection is *automatically* triggered when the thread's next memory allocation would overflow the heap.

[10] In practice a garbage collection cycle takes time that is proportional to the size of the memory used by the thread. That does not hinder security as long as the garbage collector runs on the thread's time budget.

Resource Observations. All threads in the system share a global fine-grained clock ω, which is incremented by the parallel scheduler at each cycle (see below). Rule [TIME] gives all threads unrestricted access to the clock via monadic primitive *time*.

4.3 Parallel Scheduler

This section extends LIO_{PAR} with *deterministic parallelism*, which allows to execute κ threads simultaneously on as many cores. To this end, we introduce the top-level parallel scheduler, which coordinates simultaneous changes to the global state by updating the resource budgets of the threads in response core events (e.g., fork, spawn, and kill) and ticks the global clock.

Queue Map $\Phi \in \{1..\kappa\} \rightarrow \mathit{Queue}$ Configuration $c ::= \langle T, B, H, \theta, \omega, \Phi \rangle$

PARALLEL

$$\frac{\forall\, i \in \{1..\kappa\}.\Phi(i) \xrightarrow{(n_i, s_i, e_i)}_{\Sigma} Q_i \quad T' = \Sigma.T[n_i \mapsto s_i] \quad \Phi' = \Phi[i \mapsto Q_i] \quad c = \langle T', B, H, \theta, \Sigma.\omega + 1, \Phi' \rangle \quad \langle \Sigma', \Phi'' \rangle = \langle\!\langle \mathit{sort}\ [(n_1, e_1), ..., (n_\kappa, e_\kappa)] \rangle\!\rangle^{c}}{\langle \Sigma, \Phi \rangle \hookrightarrow \langle \Sigma', \Phi'' \rangle}$$

$$\begin{aligned}
&\mathit{next}(_, \epsilon, c) = c\\
&\mathit{next}(n_1, \mathbf{fork}(\Delta, n_2, t, b, h), c)\\
&\quad = \langle T', B'[n_2 \mapsto b], H'[n_2 \mapsto h], \theta', \omega, \Phi \rangle\\
&\quad \mathbf{where}\ \langle T, B, H, \theta, \omega, \Phi \rangle = c\\
&\qquad s = (\Delta, n_2.pc, \varnothing \mid t, [\,])\\
&\qquad T' = T[n_2 \mapsto s]\\
&\qquad B' = B[n_1 \mapsto B(n_1) - b]\\
&\qquad H' = H[n_1 \mapsto H(n_1) - h]\\
&\qquad \theta' = \theta[n_2 \mapsto \varnothing]
\end{aligned}$$

$$\begin{aligned}
&\mathit{next}(n_1, \mathbf{spawn}(\Delta, n_2, t, K), c)\\
&\quad = \langle T', B', H', \theta'[n_2 \mapsto K], \omega, \Phi' \rangle\\
&\quad \mathbf{where} \langle T, B, H, \theta, \omega, \Phi \rangle = c\\
&\qquad s = (\Delta, n_2.pc, \varnothing \mid t, [\,])\\
&\qquad T' = T[n_2 \mapsto s]\\
&\qquad B' = B[n_2 \mapsto B_0]\\
&\qquad H' = H[n_2 \mapsto H_0]\\
&\qquad \theta' = \theta[n_1 \mapsto \theta(n_1) \setminus \{n_2.k\} \cup K]\\
&\qquad \Phi' = \Phi[n_2.k \mapsto \langle n_2^{B_0} \rangle]
\end{aligned}$$

$$\begin{aligned}
&\mathit{next}(n, \mathbf{kill}(n'), \langle T, B, H, \theta, \omega, \Phi \rangle)\\
&\quad \mid n \notin \mathit{Dom}(T) = \langle T, B, H, \theta, \omega, \Phi \rangle\\
&\quad \mid n \in \mathit{Dom}(T) = \langle T \setminus N, B' \setminus N, H' \setminus N, \theta' \setminus N, \omega, \Phi' \rangle\\
&\quad \mathbf{where}\ N = [\![\{n'\}]\!]^{T}\\
&\qquad B' = B[n \mapsto B(n) + \textstyle\sum_{i \in N, i.k = n.k} B(i)]\\
&\qquad H' = H[n \mapsto H(n) + \textstyle\sum_{i \in N, i.k = n.k} H(i)]\\
&\qquad \theta' = \theta[n \mapsto \theta(n) \cup \textstyle\bigcup_{i \in N} \theta(i) \cup \{i.k \mid i \in N, i.k \neq n.k\}]\\
&\qquad \Phi' = \lambda k.\Phi[k \mapsto \Phi(k) \setminus N]
\end{aligned}$$

Fig. 5. Top-level parallel scheduler.

Semantics. Figure 5 formalizes the operational semantics of the parallel scheduler, which reduces a configuration $c = \langle \Sigma, \Phi \rangle$ consisting of global state Σ and core map Φ mapping each core to its run queue, to configuration c' in one step, written $c \hookrightarrow c'$, through rule [PARALLEL] only. The rule executes the threads scheduled on each of the κ cores, which all step at once according to the concurrent semantics presented in Sects. 4.1–4.2, with the same current global state Σ. Since the execution of each thread can change Σ *concurrently*, the top-level parallel scheduler reconciles those actions by updating Σ *sequentially* and *deterministically*.[11] First, the scheduler updates the thread pool map T and core map Φ with the final state obtained by running each thread in isolation, i.e., $T' = \Sigma.T[n_i \mapsto s_i]$ and $\Phi' = \Phi[i \mapsto Q_i]$ for $i \in \{1..\kappa\}$. Then, it collects all concurrent events generated by the κ threads together with their thread id, sorts the events according to type, i.e., *sort* $[(n_1, e_1), ..., (n_\kappa, e_\kappa)]$, and computes the updated configuration by processing the events in sequence.[12] In particular, new threads are created first (event **spawn**$(\cdot)$ and **fork**$(\cdot)$), and then killed (event **kill**$(\cdot)$)—the ordering between events of the same type is arbitrary and assumed to be fixed. Trivial events (ϵ) do not affect the configuration and thus their ordering is irrelevant. The function $\langle\!\langle es \rangle\!\rangle^c$ computes a final configuration by processing a list of events in order, accumulating configuration updates ($next(\cdot)$ updates the current configuration by one event-step): $\langle\!\langle (n, e) : es \rangle\!\rangle^c = \langle\!\langle es \rangle\!\rangle^{next(n,e,c)}$. When no more events need processing, the configuration is returned $\langle\!\langle [\,] \rangle\!\rangle^c = c$.

Event Processing. Figure 5 defines function $next(n, e, c)$, which takes a thread identifier n, the event e that thread n generated, the current configuration and outputs the configuration obtained by performing the thread's action. The empty event ϵ is trivial and leaves the state unchanged. Event $(n_1, \textbf{fork}(\Delta, n_2, t, b, h))$ indicates that thread n_1 forks thread t with identifier n_2, sub-heap Δ, time budget b and maximum heap size h. The scheduler deducts these resources from the parent's budgets, i.e., $B' = B[n_1 \mapsto B(n_1) - b]$ and $H' = H[n_1 \mapsto H(n_1) - h]$ and assigns them to the child, i.e., $B'[n_2 \mapsto b]$ and $H'[n_2 \mapsto h]$.[13] The new child shares the core with the parent—it has no core capabilities i.e., $\theta' = \theta[n_2 \mapsto \varnothing]$—and so the core map is left unchanged. Lastly, the scheduler adds the child to the thread pool and initializes its state, i.e., $T[n_2 \mapsto (\Delta, n_2.\ell_{\mathrm{L}}, \varnothing \mid t, [\,])]$. The scheduler handles event $(n_1, \textbf{spawn}(\Delta, n_2, t, K))$ similarly. The new thread t gets scheduled on core $n_2.k$, i.e., $\Phi[n_2.k \mapsto \langle n_2^{B_0} \rangle]$, where the thread takes all the time and memory resources of the core, i.e., $B[n_2 \mapsto B_0]$ and $H[n_2 \mapsto H_0]$, and extra core capabilities K, i.e., $\theta'[n_2 \mapsto K]$. For simplicity, we assume that all cores execute B_0 steps per-cycle and feature a memory of size H_0. Event $(n, \textbf{kill}(n'))$ informs the scheduler that thread n wishes to kill thread n'. The scheduler leaves the global state unchanged if the parent thread has already been killed by the time this event is handled, i.e., when the guard $n \notin Dom(T)$ is true—the resources of the child n' will have been reclaimed by another ancestor.

---

[11] Non-deterministic updates would make the model vulnerable to refinement attacks [40].

[12] Since the clock only needs to be incremented, we could have left it out from the configuration $c = \langle T', B, H, \theta, \Sigma.\omega + 1, \Phi' \rangle$; function $\langle\!\langle es \rangle\!\rangle^c$ does not use nor change its value.

[13] Notice that $|\Delta| < h$ by rule [FORK].

Otherwise, the scheduler collects the identifiers of the descendants of n' that are *alive* ($N = [\![\{n'\}]\!]^T$)—they must be killed (and reclaimed) *transitively*. The set N is computed recursively by $[\![N]\!]^T$, using the thread pool T, i.e., $[\![\varnothing]\!]^T = \varnothing$, $[\![\{n\}]\!]^T = \{n\} \cup [\![T(n).N]\!]^T$ and $[\![N_1 \cup N_2]\!]^T = [\![N_1]\!]^T \cup [\![N_2]\!]^T$. The scheduler then increases the time and memory budget of the parent with the sum of the budget of all its descendants scheduled on the *same* core, i.e., $\sum_{i \in N, i.k = n.k} B(i)$ (resp. $\sum_{i \in N, i.k = n.k} H(i)$)—descendants running on other cores do not share those resources. The scheduler reassigns to the parent thread their core capabilities, which are split between capabilities explicitly assigned but not in use, i.e., $\bigcup_{i \in N} \theta(i)$ and core capabilities assigned and in use by running threads, i.e., $\{i.k \mid i \in N, i.k \neq n.k\}$. Lastly, the scheduler removes the killed threads from each core, written $\Phi(i) \setminus N$, by pruning the leaves containing killed threads and reassigning their leftover time budget to their parent, see the extended version of this paper for details.

5 Security Guarantees

In this section we show that LIO$_{\text{PAR}}$ satisfies a strong security condition that ensures timing-agreement of threads and rules out timing covert channels. In Sect. 5.1, we describe our proof technique based on *term erasure*, which has been used to verify security guarantees of functional programming languages [30], IFC libraries [8,17,54,56,61], and an IFC runtime system [59]. In Sect. 5.2, we formally prove security, i.e., *progress- and timing-sensitive non-interference*, a strong form of non-interference [14], inspired by Volpano and Smith [64]—to our knowledge, it is considered here for the first time in the context of parallel runtime systems. Works that do not address external timing channels [59,62] normally prove *progress-sensitive* non-interference, wherein the number of execution steps of a program may differ in two runs based on a secret. This condition is insufficient in the parallel setting: both public and secret threads may step simultaneously on different cores and any difference in the number of execution steps would introduce *external* and *internal* timing attacks. Similar to previous works on secure multi-threaded systems [36,52], we establish a *strong* low-bisimulation property of the parallel scheduler, which guarantees that attacker-indistinguishable configurations execute in lock-step and remain indistinguishable. Theorem 1 and Corollary 1 use this property to ensure that any two related parallel programs execute in exactly the same number of steps.

5.1 Erasure Function

The term erasure technique relies on an *erasure function*, written $\varepsilon_L(\cdot)$, which rewrites secret data above the attacker's level L to special term $\bullet$, in all the syntactic categories: values, terms, heaps, stacks, global states and configurations.[14] Once the erasure function is defined, the core of the proof technique

[14] For ease of exposition, we use the two-point lattices $\{L, H\}$, where $H \not\sqsubseteq L$ is the only disallowed flow. Neither our proofs nor our model rely on this particular lattice.

consists of proving an essential *commutativity* relationship between the erasure function and reduction steps: given a step $c \hookrightarrow c'$, there must exist a reduction that *simulates* the original reduction between the erased configurations, i.e., $\varepsilon_L(c) \hookrightarrow \varepsilon_L(c')$. Intuitively, if the configuration c leaked secret data while stepping to c', that data would be classified as public in c' and thus would remain in $\varepsilon_L(c')$— but such secret data would be erased by $\varepsilon_L(c)$ and the property would not hold. The erasure function leaves ground values, e.g., $()$, unchanged and on most terms it acts homomorphically, e.g., $\varepsilon_L(t_1\ t_2) = \varepsilon_L(t_1)\ \varepsilon_L(t_2)$. The interesting cases are for labeled values, thread configurations, and resource maps. The erasure function removes the content of secret labeled values, i.e., $\varepsilon_L(\mathit{Labeled}\ H\ t^\circ) = \mathit{Labeled}\ H\ \bullet$, and erases the content recursively otherwise, i.e., $\varepsilon_L(\mathit{Labeled}\ L\ t^\circ) = \mathit{Labeled}\ L\ \varepsilon_L(t)^\circ$. The state of a thread is erased per-component, homomorphically if the program counter label is public, i.e., $\varepsilon_L(\Delta, L, N, \mid t, S) = (\varepsilon_L(\Delta), L, N \mid \varepsilon_L(t), \varepsilon_L(S))$, and in full otherwise, i.e., $\varepsilon_L(\Delta, H, N, \mid t, S) = (\bullet, \bullet, \bullet \mid \bullet, \bullet)$.

Resource Erasure. Since LIO$_{\text{PAR}}$ manages resources explicitly, the simulation property above requires to define the erasure function for resources as well. The erasure function should *preserve* information about the resources (e.g., time, memory, and core capabilities) of *public threads*, since the attacker can explicitly assign resources (e.g., with *fork* and *swap*) and measure them (e.g., with *size*). But what about the resources of secret threads? One might think that such information is secret and thus it should be erased—intuitively, a thread might decide to assign, say, half of its time budget to its secret child depending on secret information. However, public threads can also assign (public) resources to a secret thread when forking: even though these resources currently belong to the secret child, they are *temporary*—the public parent might reclaim them later. Thus, we cannot associate the sensitivity of the resources of a thread with its program counter label when resources are managed *hierarchically*, as in LIO$_{\text{PAR}}$. Instead, we associate the security level of the resources of a secret thread with the sensitivity of its parent: the resources of a secret thread are *public* information whenever the program counter label of the parent is public and *secret* information otherwise. Furthermore, since resource reclamation is transitive, the erasure function cannot discard secret resources, but must rather redistribute them to the hierarchically closest set of public resources, as when *killing* them.

Time Budget. First, we project the identifiers of *public* threads from the thread pool T : $\mathit{Dom}_L(T) = \{n_L \mid n \in \mathit{Dom}(T) \wedge T(n).pc \equiv L\}$, where notation n_L indicates that the program counter label of thread n is public. Then, the set $P = \bigcup_{n \in \mathit{Dom}_L(T)} \{n\} \cup T(n).N$ contains the identifiers of all the public threads and their immediate children.[15] The resources of threads $n \in P$ are public information. However, the program counter label of a thread $n \in P$ is not necessarily public, as explained previously. Hence P can be disjointly partitioned

[15] The id of the spinning thread on each free core is also public, i.e., $\circ_k \in P$ for $k \in \{1..\kappa\}$.

by program counter label: $P = P_L \cup P_H$, where $P_L = \{ n_L \mid n \in P \}$ and $P_H = \{ n_H \mid n \in P \}$. Erasure of the budget map then proceeds on this partition, leaving the budget of the public threads untouched, and summing the budget of their secret children threads to the budgets of their descendants, which are instead omitted. In symbols, $\varepsilon_L(B) = B_L \cup B_H$, where $B_L = \{ n_L \mapsto B(n_L) \mid n_L \in P_L \}$ and $B_H = \{ n_H \mapsto B(n_H) + \sum_{i \in [\![\{ n_H \}]\!]^T} B(i) \mid n_H \in P_H \}$.

Queue Erasure. The erasure of core queues follows the same intuition, preserving public and secret threads $n \in P$ and trimming all other secret threads $n_H \notin P$. Since queues annotate thread ids with their residual time budgets, the erasure function must reassign the budgets of all *secret* threads $n'_H \notin P$ to their closest ancestor $n \in P$ on the same core. The ancestor $n \in P$ could be either (i) another *secret* thread on the same core, i.e., $n_H \in P$, or, (ii) the spinning thread of that core, $\circ \in P$ if there is no other thread $n \in P$ on that core—the difference between these two cases lies on whether the original thread n' was *forked* or *spawned* on that core. More formally, if the queue contains no thread $n \in P$, then the function replaces the queue altogether with the spinning thread and returns the residual budgets of the threads to it, i.e., $\varepsilon_L(Q) = \langle \circ^B \rangle$ if $n_i \notin P$ and $B = \sum b_i$, for each leaf $Q[\langle n_i^{b_i} \rangle]$ where $i \in \{1..|Q|\}$. Otherwise, the core contains at least a thread $n_H \in P$ and the erasure function returns the residual time budget of its secret descendants, i.e., $\varepsilon_L(Q) = Q \downarrow_L$ by combining the effects of the following mutually recursive functions:

$$\langle n^b \rangle \downarrow_L = \langle n^b \rangle \qquad\qquad \langle n_{1H}^{b_1} \rangle \curlyvee \langle n_{2H}^{b_2} \rangle = \langle n_{1H}^{b_1+b_2} \rangle$$

$$\langle Q_1, Q_2 \rangle \downarrow_L = (Q_1 \downarrow_L) \curlyvee (Q_2 \downarrow_L) \qquad\qquad Q_1 \curlyvee Q_2 = \langle Q_1, Q_2 \rangle$$

The interesting case is $\langle n_{1H}^{b_1} \rangle \curlyvee \langle n_{2H}^{b_2} \rangle$, which reassigns the budget of the child (the right leaf $\langle n_{2H}^{b_2} \rangle$) to the parent (the left leaf $\langle n_{1H}^{b_1} \rangle$), by rewriting the subtree into $\langle n_{1H}^{b_1+b_2} \rangle$.

5.2 Timing-Sensitive Non-interference

The proof of progress- and timing-sensitive non-interference relies on two fundamental properties, i.e., *determinacy* and *simulation* of parallel reductions. Determinacy requires that the reduction relation is deterministic.

Proposition 1 (Determinism). *If* $c_1 \hookrightarrow c_2$ *and* $c_1 \hookrightarrow c_3$ *then* $c_2 \equiv c_3$.

The equivalence in the statement denotes alpha-equivalence, i.e., up to the choice of variable names. We now show that the parallel scheduler preserves L-equivalence of parallel configurations.

Definition 1 (L-equivalence). *Two configurations* c_1 *and* c_2 *are indistinguishable from an attacker at security level* L*, written* $c_1 \approx_L c_2$*, if and only if* $\varepsilon_L(c_1) \equiv \varepsilon_L(c_2)$.

Proposition 2 (Parallel simulation). *If* $c \hookrightarrow c'$*, then* $\varepsilon_L(c) \hookrightarrow \varepsilon_L(c')$.

By combining *determinism* (Proposition 1) and *parallel simulation* (Proposition 2), we prove *progress-insensitive non-interference*, which assumes progress of both configurations.

Proposition 3 (Progress-insensitive non-interference). *If* $c_1 \hookrightarrow c_1'$, $c_2 \hookrightarrow c_2'$ *and* $c_1 \approx_L c_2$, *then* $c_1' \approx_L c_2'$.

In order to lift this result to be progress-sensitive, we first prove *timing-sensitive progress*. Intuitively, if a *valid* configuration steps then any low equivalent parallel configuration also steps.[16]

Proposition 4 (Timing-sensitive progress). *Given a valid configuration* c_1 *and a parallel reduction step* $c_1 \hookrightarrow c_1'$ *and* $c_1 \approx_L c_2$, *then there exists* c_2', *such that* $c_2 \hookrightarrow c_2'$.

Using progress-insensitive non-interference, i.e., Proposition 3 and timing-sensitive progress, i.e., Proposition 4 in combination, we obtain a *strong L-bisimulation* property between configurations and prove *progress- and timing-sensitive non-interference.*

Theorem 1 (Progress- and timing-sensitive non-interference). *For all valid configurations* c_1 *and* c_2, *if* $c_1 \hookrightarrow c_1'$ *and* $c_1 \approx_L c_2$, *then there exists a configuration* c_2', *such that* $c_2 \hookrightarrow c_2'$ *and* $c_1' \approx_L c_2'$.

The following corollary instantiates the non-interference security theorem from above for a given LIO_{PAR} parallel program, that explicitly rules out leaks via timing channels. In the following, the notation $\hookrightarrow_u$ denotes u reduction steps of the parallel scheduler.

Corollary 1. *Given a well-typed* LIO_{PAR} *program* t *of type* $\textit{Labeled}\ \tau_1 \rightarrow \textit{LIO}\ \tau_2$ *and two closed secrets* $t_1^\circ, t_2^\circ :: \tau_1$, *let* $s_i = ([\,], L, \varnothing, \mid t\ (\textit{Labeled}\ H\ t_i^\circ), [\,])$, $c_i = (T_i, B, H, \theta, 0, \Phi_i)$, *where* $T_i = [n_L \mapsto s_i, \circ_j \mapsto s_\circ]$, $B = [n_L \mapsto B_0, \circ_j \mapsto 0]$, $H = [n_L \mapsto H_0, \circ_j \mapsto H_0]$, $\theta = [n_L \mapsto \{2\,..\,\kappa\}, \circ_j \mapsto \varnothing]$, $\Phi_i = [1 \mapsto \langle s_i \rangle, 2 \mapsto \langle \circ_2 \rangle, ..., \kappa \mapsto \langle \circ_\kappa \rangle]$, *for* $i \in \{1, 2\}$, $j \in \{1\,..\,\kappa\}$ *and thread identifier* n_L *such that* $n.k = 1$ *and* $n.cl = H$. *If* $c_1 \hookrightarrow_u c_1'$, *then there exists configuration* c_2', *such that* $c_2 \hookrightarrow_u c_2'$ *and* $c_1' \approx_L c_2'$.

To conclude, we show that the *timing-sensitive* security guarantees of LIO_{PAR} extend to concurrent *single-core* programs by instantiating Corollary 1 with $\kappa = 1$.

6 Limitations

Implementation. Implementing LIO_{PAR} is a serious undertaking that requires a major redesign of GHC's runtime system. Conventional runtime systems freely

[16] A configuration is valid if satisfies several basic properties, e.g., it does not contain special term •. See the extended version of this paper for details.

share resources among threads to boost performance and guarantee fairness. For instance, in GHC, threads share heap objects to save memory space and execution time (when evaluating expressions). In contrast, LIO_{PAR} strictly partitions resources to enforce security—threads at different security labels cannot share heap objects. As a result, the GHC memory allocator must be adapted to isolate threads' private heap, so that allocation and collection can occur independently and in parallel. Similarly, the GHC "fair" round robin scheduler must be heavily modified to keep track of and manage threads' time budget, to preemptively perform a context switch when their time slice is up.

Programming Model. Since resource management is explicit, building applications atop LIO_{PAR} introduces new challenges—the programmer must explicitly choose resource bounds for each thread. If done poorly, threads can spend excessive amounts of time sitting idle when given too much CPU time, or garbage collecting when not given enough heap space. The problem of tuning resource allocation parameters is not unique to LIO_{PAR}—Yang and Mazières' [66] propose to use GHC profiling mechanisms to determine heap size while the real-time garbage collector by Henriksson [16] required the programmer to specify the worst case execution time, period, and worst-case allocation of each high-priority thread. Das and Hoffmann [9] demonstrate a more automatic approach—they apply machine learning techniques to statically determine upper bounds on execution time and heap usage of OCaml programs. Similar techniques could be applied to LIO_{PAR} in order to determine the most efficient resource partitions. Moreover, this challenge is not unique to real-time systems or LIO_{PAR}; choosing privacy parameters in differential privacy, for example, shares many similarities [21,29].

The LIO_{PAR} programming model is also likely easier to use in certain application domains—e.g., web applications where the tail latency of a route can inform the thread bounds, or embedded systems where similar latency requirements are the norm. Nevertheless, in order to simplify programming with LIO_{PAR}, we intend to introduce privileges (and thus declassification) similar to LIO [12,56] or COWL [57].

Coarse-grained, floating-label systems such as LIO and LIO_{PAR} can suffer *label creep*, wherein the current computation gets tainted to a point where it cannot perform any useful writes [55]. Sequential LIO [56] addresses label creep through a primitive, `toLabeled`, which executes a computation (that may raise the current label) in a separate context and restores the current label upon its termination. Similar to concurrent LIO [54], LIO_{PAR} relies on fork to address label creep and not `toLabeled`—the latter exposes the termination covert-channel [54]. Even though LIO_{PAR} has a more restricted floating-label semantics than concurrent LIO, LIO_{PAR} also supports parallel execution, garbage collection, and new APIs for getting heap statistics, counting elapsed time, and killing threads.

7 Related Work

There is substantial work on language-level IFC systems [10,15,20,34,43,50,51, 54,55,67,68]. Our work builds on these efforts in several ways. Firstly, LIO_{PAR} extends the concurrent LIO IFC system [54] with parallelism—to our knowledge, this is the first *dynamic* IFC system to support parallelism and address the internalization of external timing channels. Previous static IFC systems implicitly allow for parallelism, e.g., Muller and Chong's [41], several works on IFC π-calculi [18,19,25], and Rafnsson et al. [49] recent foundations for composable timing-sensitive interactive systems. These efforts, however, do not model runtime system resource management. Volpano and Smith [64] enforce a timing agreement condition, similar to ours, but for a static concurrent IFC system. Mantel et al. [37] and Li et al. [31] prove non-interference for static, concurrent systems, using rely-guarantee reasoning.

Unlike most of these previous efforts, our hierarchical runtime system also eliminates classes of resource-based external timing channels, such as memory exhaustion and garbage collection. Pedersen and Askarov [46], however, were the first to identify automatic memory management to be a source of covert channels for IFC systems and demonstrate the feasibility of attacks against both V8 and the JVM. They propose a sequential static IFC language with labeled-partitioned memory and a label-aware timing-sensitive garbage collector, which is vulnerable to *external timing* attacks and satisfies only *termination-insensitive* non-interference.

Previous work on language-based systems—namely [35,66]—identify memory retention and memory exhaustion as a source of denial-of-service (DOS) attacks. Memory retention and exhaustion can also be used as covert channels. In addressing those covert channels, LIO_{PAR} also addresses the DOS attacks outlined by these efforts. Indeed, our work generalizes Yang and Mazières' [66] region-based allocation framework with region-based garbage collection and hierarchical scheduling.

Our LIO_{PAR} design also borrows ideas from the secure operating system community. Our explicit hierarchical memory management is conceptually similar to HiStar's container abstraction [69]. In HiStar, containers—subject to quotas, i.e., space limits—are used to hierarchically allocate and deallocate objects. LIO_{PAR} adopts this idea at the language-level and automates the allocation and reclamation. Moreover, we hierarchically partition CPU-time; Zeldovich et al. [69], however, did observe that their container abstraction can be repurposed to enforce CPU quotas. Deterland [65] splits time into ticks to address internal timing channels and mitigate external timing ones. Deterland builds on Determinator [4], an OS that executes parallel applications deterministically and efficiently. LIO_{PAR} adopts many ideas from these systems—both the deterministic parallelism and ticks (semantic steps)—to the language-level. Deterministic parallelism at the language-level has also been explored previous to this work [27,28,38], but, different from these efforts, LIO_{PAR} also hierarchically manages resources to eliminate classes of external timing channels.

Fabric [33,34] and DStar [70] are distributed IFC systems. Though we believe that our techniques would scale beyond multi-core systems (e.g., to data centers), LIO$_{PAR}$ will likely not easily scale to large distributed systems like Fabric and DStar. Different from Fabric and DStar, however, LIO$_{PAR}$ addresses both internal and external timing channels that result from running code in parallel.

Our hierarchical resource management approach is not unique—other countermeasures to external timing channels have been studied. Hu [22], for example, mitigates both timing channels in the VAX/VMM system [32] using "fuzzy time"—an idea recently adopted to browsers [26]. Askarov et al.'s [2] mitigate external timing channels using predicative black-box mitigation, which delays events and thus bound information leakage. Rather than using noise as in the fuzzy time technique, however, they predict the schedule of future events. Some of these approaches have also been adopted at the language-level [46,54,71]. We find these techniques largely orthogonal: they can be used alongside our techniques to mitigate timing channels we do not eliminate.

Real-time systems—when developed with garbage collected languages [3,5,6,16]—face similar challenges as this work. Blelloch and Cheng [6] describe a real-time garbage collector (RTGC) for multi-core programs with *provable* resource bounds—LIO$_{PAR}$ *enforces* resource bounds instead. A more recent RTGC created by Auerbach et al. [3] describes a technique to "tax" threads into contributing to garbage collection as they utilize more resources. Henricksson [16] describes a RTGC capable of enforcing hard and soft deadlines, once given upper bounds on space and time resources used by threads. Most similarly to LIO$_{PAR}$, Pizlo et al. [48] implement a hierarchical RTGC algorithm that independently collects partitioned heaps.

8 Conclusion

Language-based IFC systems built atop off-the-shelf runtime systems are vulnerable to resource-based external-timing attacks. When these systems are extended with thread parallelism these attacks become yet more vicious—they can be carried out internally. We presented LIO$_{PAR}$, the design of the first dynamic IFC hierarchical runtime system that supports deterministic parallelism and eliminate s both resource-based internal- and external-timing covert channels. To our knowledge, LIO$_{PAR}$ is the first parallel system to satisfy progress- and timing-sensitive non-interference.

References

1. Askarov, A., Hunt, S., Sabelfeld, A., Sands, D.: Termination-insensitive noninterference leaks more than just a bit. In: Jajodia, S., Lopez, J. (eds.) ESORICS 2008. LNCS, vol. 5283, pp. 333–348. Springer, Heidelberg (2008). https://doi.org/10.1007/978-3-540-88313-5_22
2. Askarov, A., Zhang, D., Myers, A.C.: Predictive black-box mitigation of timing channels. In: Proceedings of the 17th ACM Conference on Computer and Communications Security, pp. 297–307. ACM (2010)

3. Auerbach, J., et al.: Tax-and-spend: democratic scheduling for real-time garbage collection. In: Proceedings of the 8th ACM International Conference on Embedded Software, pp. 245–254. ACM (2008)
4. Aviram, A., Weng, S.-C., Hu, S., Ford, B.: Efficient system-enforced deterministic parallelism. Commun. ACM **55**(5), 111–119 (2012)
5. Baker Jr., H.G.: List processing in real time on a serial computer. Commun. ACM **21**(4), 280–294 (1978)
6. Blelloch, G.E., Cheng, P.: On bounding time and space for multiprocessor garbage collection. ACM SIGPLAN Not. **34**, 104–117 (1999)
7. Buiras, P., Russo, A.: Lazy programs leak secrets. In: Riis Nielson, H., Gollmann, D. (eds.) NordSec 2013. LNCS, vol. 8208, pp. 116–122. Springer, Heidelberg (2013). https://doi.org/10.1007/978-3-642-41488-6_8
8. Buiras, P., Vytiniotis, D., Russo, A.: HLIO: mixing static and dynamic typing for information-flow control in Haskell. In: ACM SIGPLAN International Conference on Functional Programming. ACM (2015)
9. Das, A., Hoffmann, J.: ML for ML: learning cost semantics by experiment. In: Legay, A., Margaria, T. (eds.) TACAS 2017. LNCS, vol. 10205, pp. 190–207. Springer, Heidelberg (2017). https://doi.org/10.1007/978-3-662-54577-5_11
10. Fernandes, E., Paupore, J., Rahmati, A., Simionato, D., Conti, M., Prakash, A.: FlowFence: practical data protection for emerging IoT application frameworks. In: USENIX Security Symposium, pp. 531–548 (2016)
11. Ge, Q., Yarom, Y., Cock, D., Heiser, G.: A survey of microarchitectural timing attacks and countermeasures on contemporary hardware. J. Cryptographic Eng. **8**, 1–27 (2016)
12. Giffin, D.B., et al.: Hails: protecting data privacy in untrusted web applications. J. Comput. Secur. **25**(4–5), 427–461 (2017)
13. Giffin, D.B., et al.: Hails: protecting data privacy in untrusted web applications. In: Proceedings of the Symposium on Operating Systems Design and Implementation. USENIX (2012)
14. Goguen, J.A., Meseguer, J.: Unwinding and inference control, pp. 75–86, April 1984
15. Hedin, D., Birgisson, A., Bello, L., Sabelfeld, A.: JSFlow: tracking information flow in JavaScript and its APIs. In: Proceedings of the 29th Annual ACM Symposium on Applied Computing, pp. 1663–1671. ACM (2014)
16. Henriksson, R.: Scheduling garbage collection in embedded systems. Ph.D. thesis, Department of Computer Science (1998)
17. Heule, S., Stefan, D., Yang, E.Z., Mitchell, J.C., Russo, A.: IFC inside: retrofitting languages with dynamic information flow control. In: Focardi, R., Myers, A. (eds.) POST 2015. LNCS, vol. 9036, pp. 11–31. Springer, Heidelberg (2015). https://doi.org/10.1007/978-3-662-46666-7_2
18. Honda, K., Vasconcelos, V., Yoshida, N.: Secure information flow as typed process behaviour. In: Smolka, G. (ed.) ESOP 2000. LNCS, vol. 1782, pp. 180–199. Springer, Heidelberg (2000). https://doi.org/10.1007/3-540-46425-5_12
19. Honda, K., Yoshida, N.: A uniform type structure for secure information flow. ACM Trans. Program. Lang. Syst. (TOPLAS) **29**(6), 31 (2007)
20. Hritcu, C., Greenberg, M., Karel, B., Pierce, B.C., Morrisett, G.: All your IFCException are belong to us. In: 2013 IEEE Symposium on Security and Privacy (SP), pp. 3–17. IEEE (2013)
21. Hsu, J., et al.: Differential privacy: an economic method for choosing epsilon. In: Proceedings of the 2014 IEEE 27th Computer Security Foundations Symposium, CSF 2014, pp. 398–410. IEEE Computer Society, Washington, DC (2014)

22. Hu, W.-M.: Reducing timing channels with fuzzy time. J. Comput. Secur. **1**(3–4), 233–254 (1992)
23. Jones, S.L.P.: Implementing lazy functional languages on stock hardware: the spineless tagless G-machine. J. Funct. Program. **2**, 127–202 (1992)
24. Kemmerer, R.A.: Shared resource matrix methodology: an approach to identifying storage and timing channels. ACM Trans. Comput. Syst. (TOCS) **1**(3), 256–277 (1983)
25. Kobayashi, N.: Type-based information flow analysis for the π-calculus. Acta Informatica **42**(4–5), 291–347 (2005)
26. Kohlbrenner, D., Shacham, H.: Trusted browsers for uncertain times. In: USENIX Security Symposium, pp. 463–480 (2016)
27. Kuper, L., Newton, R.R.: LVars: lattice-based data structures for deterministic parallelism. In: Proceedings of the 2nd ACM SIGPLAN Workshop on Functional High-Performance Computing, pp. 71–84. ACM (2013)
28. Kuper, L., Todd, A., Tobin-Hochstadt, S., Newton, R.R.: Taming the parallel effect zoo: extensible deterministic parallelism with LVish. ACM SIGPLAN Not. **49**(6), 2–14 (2014)
29. Lee, J., Clifton, C.: How much is enough? Choosing ϵ for differential privacy. In: Lai, X., Zhou, J., Li, H. (eds.) ISC 2011. LNCS, vol. 7001, pp. 325–340. Springer, Heidelberg (2011). https://doi.org/10.1007/978-3-642-24861-0_22
30. Li, P., Zdancewic, S.: Arrows for secure information flow. Theoret. Comput. Sci. **411**(19), 1974–1994 (2010)
31. Li, X., Mantel, H., Tasch, M.: Taming message-passing communication in compositional reasoning about confidentiality. In: Chang, B.-Y.E. (ed.) APLAS 2017. LNCS, vol. 10695, pp. 45–66. Springer, Cham (2017). https://doi.org/10.1007/978-3-319-71237-6_3
32. Lipner, S., Jaeger, T., Zurko, M.E.: Lessons from VAX/SVS for high-assurance VM systems. IEEE Secur. Priv. **10**(6), 26–35 (2012)
33. Liu, J., Arden, O., George, M.D., Myers, A.C.: Fabric: building open distributed systems securely by construction. J. Comput. Secur. **25**(4–5), 367–426 (2017)
34. Liu, J., George, M.D., Vikram, K., Qi, X., Waye, L., Myers, A.C.: Fabric: a platform for secure distributed computation and storage. In: Proceedings of the ACM SIGOPS 22nd Symposium on Operating Systems Principles. ACM (2009)
35. Liu, J., Myers, A.C.: Defining and enforcing referential security. In: Abadi, M., Kremer, S. (eds.) POST 2014. LNCS, vol. 8414, pp. 199–219. Springer, Heidelberg (2014). https://doi.org/10.1007/978-3-642-54792-8_11
36. Mantel, H., Sabelfeld, A.: A unifying approach to the security of distributed and multi-threaded programs. J. Comput. Secur. **11**(4), 615–676 (2003)
37. Mantel, H., Sands, D., Sudbrock, H.: Assumptions and guarantees for compositional noninterference. In: 2011 IEEE 24th Computer Security Foundations Symposium, pp. 218–232, June 2011
38. Marlow, S., Newton, R., Peyton Jones, S.: A monad for deterministic parallelism. ACM SIGPLAN Not. **46**(12), 71–82 (2012)
39. Marlow, S., Peyton Jones, S.: Making a fast curry: push/enter vs. eval/apply for higher-order languages. J. Funct. Program. **16**(4–5), 415–449 (2006)
40. McCullough, D.: Specifications for multi-level security and a hook-up. In: 1987 IEEE Symposium on Security and Privacy (SP), p. 161, April 1987
41. Muller, S., Chong, S.: Towards a practical secure concurrent language. In: Proceedings of the 25th Annual ACM SIGPLAN Conference on Object-Oriented Programming Languages, Systems, Languages, and Applications, pp. 57–74. ACM Press, New York, October 2012

42. Myers, A.C., Zheng, L., Zdancewic, S., Chong, S., Nystrom, N.: Jif 3.0: Java information flow, July 2006
43. Nadkarni, A., Andow, B., Enck, W., Jha, S.: Practical DIFC enforcement on android. In: USENIX Security Symposium, pp. 1119–1136 (2016)
44. North, S.C., Reppy, J.H.: Concurrent garbage collection on stock hardware. In: Kahn, G. (ed.) FPCA 1987. LNCS, vol. 274, pp. 113–133. Springer, Heidelberg (1987). https://doi.org/10.1007/3-540-18317-5_8
45. Parker, J.L.: LMonad: information flow control for Haskell web applications. Ph.D. thesis, University of Maryland, College Park (2014)
46. Pedersen, M.V., Askarov, A.: From trash to treasure: timing-sensitive garbage collection. In: Proceedings of the 38th IEEE Symposium on Security and Privacy. IEEE (2017)
47. Percival, C.: Cache missing for fun and profit (2005)
48. Pizlo, F., Hosking, A.L., Vitek, J.: Hierarchical real-time garbage collection. In: Proceedings of the 2007 ACM SIGPLAN/SIGBED Conference on Languages, Compilers, and Tools for Embedded Systems, LCTES 2007, pp. 123–133. ACM, New York (2007)
49. Rafnsson, W., Jia, L., Bauer, L.: Timing-sensitive noninterference through composition. In: Maffei, M., Ryan, M. (eds.) POST 2017. LNCS, vol. 10204, pp. 3–25. Springer, Heidelberg (2017). https://doi.org/10.1007/978-3-662-54455-6_1
50. Roy, I., Porter, D.E., Bond, M.D., McKinley, K.S., Witchel, E.: Laminar: practical fine-grained decentralized information flow control, vol. 44. ACM (2009)
51. Russo, A.: Functional pearl: two can keep a secret, if one of them uses Haskell. ACM SIGPLAN Not. **50**, 280–288 (2015)
52. Sabelfeld, A., Sands, D.: Probabilistic noninterference for multi-threaded programs. In: Proceedings of the 13th IEEE Workshop on Computer Security Foundations, CSFW 2000, p. 200. IEEE Computer Society, Washington, DC (2000)
53. Sestoft, P.: Deriving a lazy abstract machine. J. Funct. Program. **7**(3), 231–264 (1997)
54. Stefan, D., Russo, A., Buiras, P., Levy, A., Mitchell, J.C., Mazières, D.: Addressing covert termination and timing channels in concurrent information flow systems. In: International Conference on Functional Programming (ICFP). ACM SIGPLAN, September 2012
55. Stefan, D., Russo, A., Mazières, D., Mitchell, J.C.: Flexible dynamic information flow control in the presence of exceptions. J. Funct. Program. **27** (2017)
56. Stefan, D., Russo, A., Mitchell, J.C., Mazières, D.: Flexible dynamic information flow control in Haskell. In: Haskell Symposium. ACM SIGPLAN, September 2011
57. Stefan, D., et al.: Protecting users by confining JavaScript with COWL. In: USENIX Symposium on Operating Systems Design and Implementation. USENIX Association (2014)
58. Tsai, T.-C., Russo, A., Hughes, J.: A library for secure multi-threaded information flow in Haskell. In: 20th IEEE Computer Security Foundations Symposium, CSF 2007, pp. 187–202. IEEE (2007)
59. Vassena, M., Breitner, J., Russo, A.: Securing concurrent lazy programs against information leakage. In: 30th IEEE Computer Security Foundations Symposium, CSF 2017, Santa Barbara, CA, USA, 21–25 August 2017, pp. 37–52 (2017)
60. Vassena, M., Buiras, P., Waye, L., Russo, A.: Flexible manipulation of labeled values for information-flow control libraries. In: Askoxylakis, I., Ioannidis, S., Katsikas, S., Meadows, C. (eds.) ESORICS 2016. LNCS, vol. 9878, pp. 538–557. Springer, Cham (2016). https://doi.org/10.1007/978-3-319-45744-4_27

61. Vassena, M., Russo, A.: On formalizing information-flow control libraries. In: Proceedings of the 2016 ACM Workshop on Programming Languages and Analysis for Security, PLAS 2016, pp. 15–28. ACM, New York (2016)
62. Vassena, M., Russo, A., Buiras, P., Waye, L.: MAC a verified static information-flow control library. J. Log. Algebraic Methods Program. (2017)
63. Vila, P., Köpf, B.: Loophole: timing attacks on shared event loops in chrome. In: USENIX Security Symposium (2017)
64. Volpano, D., Smith, G.: Eliminating covert flows with minimum typings. In: Proceedings of the 10th IEEE Workshop on Computer Security Foundations, CSFW 1997, p. 156. IEEE Computer Society, Washington, DC (1997)
65. Wu, W., Zhai, E., Wolinsky, D.I., Ford, B., Gu, L., Jackowitz, D.: Warding off timing attacks in Deterland. In: Conference on Timely Results in Operating Systems, Monterey, CS, US (2015)
66. Yang, E.Z., Mazières, D.: Dynamic space limits for Haskell. In: Proceedings of the 35th ACM SIGPLAN Conference on Programming Language Design and Implementation, PLDI 2014, pp. 588–598. ACM, New York (2014)
67. Yang, J., Hance, T., Austin, T.H., Solar-Lezama, A., Flanagan, C., Chong, S.: Precise, dynamic information flow for database-backed applications. ACM SIGPLAN Not. **51**, 631–647 (2016)
68. Yang, J., Yessenov, K., Solar-Lezama, A.: A language for automatically enforcing privacy policies. ACM SIGPLAN Not. **47**, 85–96 (2012)
69. Zeldovich, N., Boyd-Wickizer, S., Kohler, E., Mazières, D.: Making information flow explicit in HiStar. In: Proceedings of the 7th Symposium on Operating Systems Design and Implementation, pp. 263–278. USENIX Association (2006)
70. Zeldovich, N., Boyd-Wickizer, S., Mazieres, D.: Securing distributed systems with information flow control. NSDI **8**, 293–308 (2008)
71. Zhang, D., Askarov, A., Myers, A.C.: Predictive mitigation of timing channels in interactive systems. In: Proceedings of the 18th ACM Conference on Computer and Communications Security, pp. 563–574. ACM (2011)

A Formal Analysis of Timing Channel Security via Bucketing

Tachio Terauchi[1(✉)] and Timos Antonopoulos[2]

[1] Waseda University, Tokyo, Japan
terauchi@waseda.jp

[2] Yale University, New Haven, USA
timos.antonopoulos@yale.edu

Abstract. This paper investigates the effect of *bucketing* in security against timing channel attacks. Bucketing is a technique proposed to mitigate timing-channel attacks by restricting a system's outputs to only occur at designated time intervals, and has the effect of reducing the possible timing-channel observations to a small number of possibilities. However, there is little formal analysis on when and to what degree bucketing is effective against timing-channel attacks. In this paper, we show that bucketing is in general insufficient to ensure security. Then, we present two conditions that can be used to ensure security of systems against adaptive timing channel attacks. The first is a general condition that ensures that the security of a system decreases only by a limited degree by allowing timing-channel observations, whereas the second condition ensures that the system would satisfy the first condition when bucketing is applied and hence becomes secure against timing-channel attacks. A main benefit of the conditions is that they allow *separation of concerns* whereby the security of the regular channel can be proven independently of concerns of side-channel information leakage, and certain conditions are placed on the side channel to guarantee the security of the whole system. Further, we show that the bucketing technique can be applied compositionally in conjunction with the constant-time-implementation technique to increase their applicability. While we instantiate our contributions to timing channel and bucketing, many of the results are actually quite general and are applicable to any side channels and techniques that reduce the number of possible observations on the channel.

1 Introduction

Side-channel attacks aim to recover a computer system's secret information by observing the target system's side channels such as cache, power, timing and electromagnetic radiation [11,15–17,21,23–25,31,36]. They are well recognized as a serious threat to the security of computer systems. *Timing-channel* (or simply *timing*) *attacks* are a class of side-channel attacks in which the adversary makes observations on the system's running time. Much research has been done to detect and prevent timing attacks [1,3,4,6,7,9,18,20,22,26,27,30,41].

F. Nielson and D. Sands (Eds.): POST 2019, LNCS 11426, pp. 29–50, 2019.
https://doi.org/10.1007/978-3-030-17138-4_2

Bucketing is a technique proposed for mitigating timing attacks [7,14,26,27,41]. It restricts the system's outputs to only occur at designated time intervals. Therefore, bucketing has the effect of reducing the possible timing-channel observations to a small number of possibilities. This is at some cost of system's performance because outputs must be delayed to the next bucket time. Nonetheless, in comparison to the *constant-time implementation* technique [1,3,6,9,20,22] which restricts the system's running time to be independent of secrets, bucketing is often said to be more efficient and easier to implement as it allows running times to vary depending on secrets [26,27].[1] For example, bucketing may be implemented in a blackbox-style by a monitor that buffers and delays outputs [7,41].

In this paper, we formally study the effect of bucketing on security against *adaptive* timing attacks. To this end, first, we give a formal notion of security against adaptive side-channel-observing adversaries, called *(f, ϵ)-security*. Roughly, (f, ϵ)-security says that the probability that an adversary can recover the secret by making at most $f(n)$ many queries to the system is bounded by $\epsilon(n)$, where n is the security parameter.

Next, we show that bucketing alone is in general insufficient to guarantee security against adaptive side-channel attacks by presenting a counterexample that has only two timing observations and yet is efficiently attackable. This motivates a search for conditions sufficient for security. We present a condition, called *secret-restricted side-channel refinement* (SRSCR), which roughly says that a system is secure if there are sufficiently large subsets of secrets such that (1) the system's side channel reveals no more information than the regular channel on the subsets and (2) the system is secure on the subsets against adversaries who only observe the regular channel. The degree of security (i.e., f and ϵ) is proportional to that against regular-channel-only-observing adversaries and the size of the subsets.

Because of the insufficiency of bucketing mentioned above, applying bucketing to an arbitrary system may not lead to a system that satisfies SRSCR (for good f and ϵ). To this end, we present a condition, called *low-input side-channel non-interference* (LISCNI). We show that applying bucketing to a system that satisfies the condition would result in a system that satisfies SRSCR. Therefore, LISCNI is a sufficient condition for security under the bucketing technique. Roughly, LISCNI says that (1) the side-channel observation does not depend on attacker-controlled inputs (but may depend on secrets) and (2) the system is secure against adversaries who only observe the regular channel. The degree of security is proportional to that against regular-channel-only-observing adversaries and the granularity of buckets. A main benefit of the conditions SRSCR and LISCNI is that they allow *separation of concerns* whereby the security of the regular channel can be proven independently of concerns of side-channel

[1] Sometimes, the terminology "constant-time implementation" is used to mean even stricter requirements, such as requiring control flows to be secret independent [3,9]. In this paper, we use the terminology for a more permissive notion in which only the running time is required to be secret independent.

information leakage, and certain conditions are placed on the side channel to guarantee the security of the whole system.

Finally, we show that the bucketing technique can be applied in a compositional manner with the constant-time implementation technique. Specifically, we show that when a system is a sequential composition of components in which one component is constant-time and the other component LISCNI, the whole system can be made secure by applying bucketing only to the non-constant-time part. We show that the combined approach is able to ensure security of some non-constant-time systems that cannot be made secure by applying bucketing to the whole system. We summarize the main contributions below.

- A formal notion of security against adaptive side-channel-observing adversaries, called (f, ϵ)-security. (Sect. 2)
- A counterexample which shows that bucketing alone is insufficient for security against adaptive side-channel attacks. (Sect. 2.1)
- A condition SRSCR which guarantees (f, ϵ)-security. (Sect. 3.1)
- A condition LISCNI which guarantees that the system satisfying it becomes one that satisfies SRSCR and therefore becomes (f, ϵ)-secure after suitable bucketing is applied. (Sect. 3.2)
- A compositional approach that combines bucketing and the constant-time technique. (Sect. 3.3)

While the paper focuses on timing channels and bucketing, many of the results are actually quite general and are applicable to side channels other than timing channels. Specifically, aside from the compositional bucketing result that exploits the "additive" nature of timing channels (cf. Sect. 3.3), the results are applicable to any side channels and techniques that reduce the number of possible side-channel observations

The rest of the paper is organized as follows. Section 2 formalizes the setting, and defines (f, ϵ)-security which is a formal notion of security against adaptive side-channel attacks. We also show that bucketing is in general insufficient to guarantee security of systems against adaptive side-channel attacks. Section 3 presents sufficient conditions for ensuring (f, ϵ)-security: SRSCR and LISCNI. We show that they facilitate proving the security of systems by allowing system designers to prove the security of regular channels separately from the concern of side channels. We also show that the LISCNI condition may be used in combination with the constant-time implementation technique in a compositional manner so as to prove the security of systems that are neither constant-time nor can be made secure by (globally) applying bucketing. Section 4 discusses related work. Section 5 concludes the paper with a discussion on future work.

2 Security Against Adaptive Side-Channel Attacks

Formally, a *system* (or, *program*) is a tuple $(\mathsf{rc}, \mathsf{sc}, \mathcal{S}, \mathcal{I}, \mathcal{O}^{\mathsf{rc}}, \mathcal{O}^{\mathsf{sc}})$ where rc and sc are indexed families of functions (indexed by the security parameter) that represent the regular-channel and side-channel input-output relation of the system, respectively. $\mathcal{S}$ is a security-parameter-indexed family of sets of *secrets* (or, *high inputs*) and $\mathcal{I}$ is a security-parameter-indexed family of sets of *attacker-controlled inputs* (or, *low inputs*). A *security parameter* is a natural number that represents the size of secrets, and we write $\mathcal{S}_n$ for the set of secrets of size n and $\mathcal{I}_n$ for the set of corresponding attacker-controlled inputs. Each indexed function rc_n (respectively sc_n) is a function from $\mathcal{S}_n \times \mathcal{I}_n$ to $\mathcal{O}^{\mathsf{rc}}_n$ (resp. $\mathcal{O}^{\mathsf{sc}}_n$), where $\mathcal{O}^{\mathsf{rc}}$ and $\mathcal{O}^{\mathsf{sc}}$ are indexed families of sets of possible regular-channel and side-channel outputs, respectively. For $(s, v) \in \mathcal{S}_n \times \mathcal{I}_n$, we write $\mathsf{rc}_n(s, v)$ (resp. $\mathsf{sc}_n(s, v)$) for the regular-channel (resp. side-channel) output given the secret s and the attacker-controlled input v.[2] For a system $C = (\mathsf{rc}, \mathsf{sc}, \mathcal{S}, \mathcal{I}, \mathcal{O}^{\mathsf{rc}}, \mathcal{O}^{\mathsf{sc}})$, we often write $\mathsf{rc}\langle C\rangle$ for rc, $\mathsf{sc}\langle C\rangle$ for sc, $\mathcal{S}\langle C\rangle$ for $\mathcal{S}$, $\mathcal{I}\langle C\rangle$ for $\mathcal{I}$, $\mathcal{O}^{\mathsf{rc}}\langle C\rangle$ for $\mathcal{O}^{\mathsf{rc}}$, and $\mathcal{O}^{\mathsf{sc}}\langle C\rangle$ for $\mathcal{O}^{\mathsf{sc}}$. We often omit "$\langle C\rangle$" when it is clear from the context.

For a system C and $s \in \mathcal{S}_n$, we write $C_n(s)$ for the *oracle* which, given $v \in \mathcal{I}_n$, returns a pair of outputs $(o_1, o_2) \in \mathcal{O}^{\mathsf{rc}}_n \times \mathcal{O}^{\mathsf{sc}}_n$ such that $\mathsf{rc}_n(s, v) = o_1$ and $\mathsf{sc}_n(s, v) = o_2$. An *adversary* $\mathcal{A}$ is an algorithm that attempts to discover the secret by making some number of oracle queries. As standard, we assume that $\mathcal{A}$ has the full knowledge of the system. For $i \in \mathbb{N}$, we write $\mathcal{A}^{C_n(s)}(i)$ for the adversary $\mathcal{A}$ that makes at most i oracle queries to $C_n(s)$. We impose no restriction on how the adversary chooses the inputs to the oracle. Importantly, he may choose the inputs based on the outputs of previous oracle queries. Such an adversary is said to be *adaptive* [25].

Also, for generality, we intentionally leave the computation class of adversaries unspecified. The methods presented in this paper work for any computation class, including the class of polynomial time randomized algorithms and the class of resource-unlimited randomized algorithms. The former is the standard for arguing the security of cryptography algorithms, and the latter ensures information theoretic security. In what follows, unless specified otherwise, we assume that the computation class of adversaries is the class of resource-unlimited randomized algorithms.

As standard, we define security as the bound on the probability that an adversary wins a certain game. Let f be a function from $\mathbb{N}$ to $\mathbb{N}$. We define $Win_{\mathcal{A}}(n, f)$ to be the event that the following game outputs true.

$$\begin{array}{l} s \leftarrow \mathcal{S}_n \\ s' \leftarrow \mathcal{A}^{C_n(s)}(f(n)) \\ \mathsf{Output}\ s = s' \end{array}$$

Here, the first line selects s uniformly at random from $\mathcal{S}_n$. We note that, while we restrict to deterministic systems, the adversary algorithm $\mathcal{A}$ may be probabilistic and also the secret s is selected randomly. Therefore, the full range of probabilities is possible for the event $Win_{\mathcal{A}}(n, f)$. Now, we are ready to give the definition of (f, ϵ)-security.

---

[2] We restrict to deterministic systems in this paper. Extension to probabilistic systems is left for future work.

Definition 1 (**(f, ϵ)-security**)**.** Let $f : \mathbb{N} \to \mathbb{N}$ and $\epsilon : \mathbb{N} \to \mathbb{R}$ be such that $0 < \epsilon(n) \leq 1$ for all $n \in \mathbb{N}$. We say that a system is *(f, ϵ)-secure* if there exists $N \in \mathbb{N}$ such that for all adversaries $\mathcal{A}$ and $n \geq N$, it holds that $\Pr[\mathit{Win}_{\mathcal{A}}(n, f)] < \epsilon(n)$.

Roughly, (f, ϵ)-secure means that, for all sufficiently large n, there is no attack that is able to recover secrets in $f(n)$ number of queries with the probability of success $\epsilon(n)$.

By abuse of notation, we often implicitly treat an expression e on the security parameter n as the function $\lambda n{\in}\mathbb{N}.e$. Therefore, for example, (n, ϵ)-secure means that there is no attack that is able to recover secrets in n many queries with the probability of success $\epsilon(n)$, and $(f, 1)$-secure means that there is no attack that makes at most $f(n)$ number of queries and is always successful. Also, by abuse of notation, we often write $\epsilon \leq \epsilon'$ when $\epsilon(n) \leq \epsilon'(n)$ for all sufficiently large n, and likewise for $\epsilon < \epsilon'$.

```
i = 0;
while (i < n) {
  if (pass[i] != guess[i]) return false;
  i++;
}
return true;
```

Fig. 1. Timing insecure login program

Example 1 (Leaky Login). Consider the program shown in Fig. 1 written in a C-like language. The program is an abridged version of the timing insecure login program from [6]. Here, `pass` is the secret and `guess` is the attacker-controlled input, each represented as a length n bit array. We show that there is an efficient adaptive timing attack against the program that recovers the secret in a linear number of queries.

We formalize the program as the system C where for all $n \in \mathbb{N}$,

- $\mathcal{S}_n = \mathcal{I}_n = \{0, 1\}^n$;
- $\mathcal{O}^{\mathsf{rc}}_n = \{\mathtt{true}, \mathtt{false}\}$ and $\mathcal{O}^{\mathsf{sc}}_n = \{i \in \mathbb{N} \mid i \leq n\}$;
- For all $(s, v) \in \mathcal{S}_n \times \mathcal{I}_n$, $\mathsf{rc}_n(s, v) = \mathtt{true}$ if $s = v$ and $\mathsf{rc}_n(s, v) = \mathtt{false}$ if $s \neq v$; and
- For all $(s, v) \in \mathcal{S}_n \times \mathcal{I}_n$, $\mathsf{sc}_n(s, v) = (\operatorname{argmax}_i s{\restriction_i} = v{\restriction_i})$.

Here, $a{\restriction_i}$ denotes the length i prefix of a. Note that sc expresses the timing-channel observation, as its output corresponds to the number of times the loop iterated.

For a secret $s \in \mathcal{S}_n$, the adversary $\mathcal{A}^{C_n(s)}(n)$ efficiently recovers s as follows. He picks an arbitrary $v_1 \in \mathcal{I}_n$ as the initial guess. By seeing the timing-channel output $\mathsf{sc}_n(s, v_1)$, he would be able to discover at least the first bit of s, $s[0]$, because $s[0] = v_1[0]$ if and only if $\mathsf{sc}_n(s, v_1) > 0$. Then, he picks an arbitrary

$v_2 \in \{0,1\}^n$ satisfying $v_2[0] = s[0]$, and by seeing the timing-channel output, he would be able to discover at least up to the second bit of s. Repeating the process n times, he will recover all n bits of s. Therefore, the system is not (n, ϵ)-secure for any ϵ. This is an example of an adaptive attack since the adversary crafts the next input by using the knowledge of previous observations. ▲

Example 2 (Bucketed Leaky Login). Next, we consider the security of the program from Example 1 but with bucketing applied. Here, we assume a constant number of buckets, k, such that the program returns its output at time intervals $i \cdot n/k$ for $i \in \{j \in \mathbb{N} \mid j \leq k\}$.[3] (For simplicity, we assume that n is divisible by k.) The bucketed program can be formalized as the system where

- rc, sc, $\mathcal{I}$, $\mathcal{O}^{\mathsf{rc}}$ are as in Example 1;
- For all $n \in \mathbb{N}$, $\mathcal{O}^{\mathsf{sc}}_n = \{i \in \mathbb{N} \mid i \leq k\}$; and
- For all $n \in \mathbb{N}$ and $(s,v) \in \mathcal{S}_n \times \mathcal{I}_n$, $\mathsf{sc}_n(s,v) = \mathit{bkt}(\text{argmax}_i\, s{\restriction}_i = v{\restriction}_i, n/k)$

where $\mathit{bkt}(i,j)$ is the smallest $a \in \mathbb{N}$ such that $i \leq a \cdot j$. It is easy to see that the system is not constant-time for any $k > 1$. Nonetheless, we can show that the system is (f, ϵ)-secure where $f(n) = 2^{n/k} - (N+1)$ and $\epsilon(n) = 1 - \frac{N-1}{2^{n/k}}$ for any $1 \leq N < 2^{n/k}$. Note that as k approaches 1 (and hence the system becomes constant-time), f approaches $2^n - (N+1)$ and ϵ approaches $1 - \frac{N-1}{2^n}$, which match the security bound of the ideal login program that only leaks whether the input guess matched the password or not. We will show that the approach presented in Sect. 3.1 can be used to derive such a bound. ▲

2.1 Insufficiency of Bucketing

We show that bucketing is in general insufficient to guarantee the security of systems against adaptive side-channel attacks. In fact, we show that bucketing with even just two buckets is insufficient. (Two is the minimum number of buckets that can be used to show the insufficiency because having only one bucket implies that the system is constant-time and therefore is secure.) More generally, our result applies to any side channels, and it shows that there are systems with just two possible side-channel outputs and completely secure (i.e., non-interferent [19,37]) regular channel that is efficiently attackable by side-channel-observing adversaries.

Consider the system such that, for all $n \in \mathbb{N}$,

- $\mathcal{S}_n = \{0,1\}^n$ and $\mathcal{I}_n = \{i \in \mathbb{N} \mid i \leq n\}$;
- $\mathcal{O}^{\mathsf{rc}}_n = \{\bullet\}$ and $\mathcal{O}^{\mathsf{sc}}_n = \{0,1\}$;
- For all $(s,v) \in \mathcal{S}_n \times \mathcal{I}_n$, $\mathsf{rc}_n(s,v) = \bullet$; and
- For all $(s,v) \in \mathcal{S}_n \times \mathcal{I}_n$, $\mathsf{sc}_n(s,v) = s[v]$.

Note that the regular channel rc only has one possible output and therefore is non-interferent. The side channel sc has just two possible outputs. The side channel, given an attacker-controlled input $v \in \mathcal{I}_n$, reveals the v-th bit of s.

[3] A similar analysis can be done for any strictly sub-linear number of buckets.

It is easy to see that the system is linearly attackable. That is, for any secret $s \in \mathcal{S}_n$, the adversary may recover the entire n bits of s by querying with each of the n-many possible attacker-controlled inputs. Therefore, the system is not (n, ϵ)-secure for any ϵ. Note that the side channel is easily realizable as a timing channel, for example, by having a branch with the branch condition "$s[v] = 0$" and different running times for the branches.

We remark that the above attack is not adaptive. Therefore, the counterexample actually shows that bucketing can be made ineffective by just allowing multiple non-adaptive side-channel observations. We also remark that the counterexample shows that some previously proposed measures are insufficient. For example, the *capacity* measure [5,28,33,39] would not be able to detect the vulnerability of the example, because the measure is equivalent to the log of the number of possible outputs for deterministic systems.

3 Sufficient Conditions for Security Against Adaptive Side-Channel Attacks

In this section, we present conditions that guarantee the security of systems against adaptive side-channel-observing adversaries. The condition SRSCR presented in Sect. 3.1 guarantees that systems that satisfy it are secure, whereas the condition LISCNI presented in Sect. 3.2 guarantees that systems that satisfy it become secure once bucketing is applied. We shall show that the conditions facilitate proving (f, ϵ)-security of systems by separating the concerns of regular channels from those of side channels. In addition, we show in Sect. 3.3 that the LISCNI condition may be used in combination with constant-time implementation techniques in a compositional manner so as to prove the security of systems that are neither constant-time nor can be made secure by (globally) applying bucketing.

3.1 Secret-Restricted Side-Channel Refinement Condition

We present the *secret-restricted side-channel refinement* condition (SRSCR). Informally, the idea here is to find large subsets of secrets $S' \subseteq \mathcal{P}(\mathcal{S}_n)$ such that for each $S'' \in S'$, the secrets are difficult for an adversary to recover by only observing the regular channel, and that the side channel reveals no more information than the regular channel for those sets of secrets. Then, because S' is large, the entire system is also ensured to be secure with high probability. We adopt *refinement order* [29,38], which had been studied in quantitative information flow research, to formalize the notion of "reveals no more information". Roughly, a channel C_1 is said to be a refinement of a channel C_2 if, for every attacker-controlled input, every pair of secrets that C_2 can distinguish can also be distinguished by C_1.

We write $\mathcal{O}^\bullet$ for the indexed family of sets such that $\mathcal{O}^\bullet_n = \{\bullet\}$ for all $n \in \mathbb{N}$. Also, we write $\mathsf{sc}^\bullet$ for the indexed family of functions such that $\mathsf{sc}^\bullet_n(s, v) = \bullet$ for all $n \in \mathbb{N}$ and $(s, v) \in \mathcal{S}_n \times \mathcal{I}_n$. For $C = (\mathsf{rc}, \mathsf{sc}, \mathcal{S}, \mathcal{I}, \mathcal{O}^{\mathsf{rc}}, \mathcal{O}^{\mathsf{sc}})$, we write $C^\bullet$ for the system $(\mathsf{rc}, \mathsf{sc}^\bullet, \mathcal{S}, \mathcal{I}, \mathcal{O}^{\mathsf{rc}}, \mathcal{O}^\bullet)$. We define the notion of *regular-channel security*.

Definition 2 (Regular-channel (f, ϵ)-security). We say that the C is *regular-channel (f, ϵ)-secure* if $C^\bullet$ is (f, ϵ)-secure.

Roughly, regular-channel security says that the system is secure against attacks that only observe the regular channel output.

Let us fix a system $C = (\mathsf{rc}, \mathsf{sc}, \mathcal{S}, \mathcal{I}, \mathcal{O}^{\mathsf{rc}}, \mathcal{O}^{\mathsf{sc}})$. For an indexed family of sets of sets of secrets S' (i.e., $S'_n \subseteq \mathcal{P}(\mathcal{S}_n)$ for each n), we write $S'' \prec S'$ when S'' is an indexed family of sets of secrets such that $S''_n \in S'_n$ for each n. Note that such S'' satisfies $S''_n \subseteq \mathcal{S}_n$ for each n. Also, for $S'' \prec S'$, we write $C|_{S''}$ for the system that is equal to C except that its secrets are restricted to S'', that is, $(\mathsf{rc}, \mathsf{sc}, S'', \mathcal{I}, \mathcal{O}^{\mathsf{rc}}, \mathcal{O}^{\mathsf{sc}})$. Next, we formalize the SRSCR condition.

Definition 3 (Secret-Restricted Side-Channel Refinement). Let $f : \mathbb{N} \to \mathbb{N}$, $\epsilon : \mathbb{N} \to (0, 1]$, and $0 < r \leq 1$. We say that the system $C = (\mathsf{rc}, \mathsf{sc}, \mathcal{S}, \mathcal{I}, \mathcal{O}^{\mathsf{rc}}, \mathcal{O}^{\mathsf{sc}})$ satisfies the *secret-restricted side-channel refinement* condition with f, ϵ, and r, written $\mathsf{SRSCR}(f, \epsilon, r)$, if there exists an indexed family of sets of sets of secrets S^{res} such that $S^{res}_n \subseteq \mathcal{P}(\mathcal{S}_n)$ for all $n \in \mathbb{N}$, and:

(1) For all $n \in \mathbb{N}$, $r \leq |\bigcup S^{res}_n|/|\mathcal{S}_n|$;
(2) For all $S'' \prec S^{res}$, $C|_{S''}$ is regular-channel (f, ϵ)-secure; and
(3) For all $n \in \mathbb{N}$, $S \in S^{res}_n$, $v \in \mathcal{I}_n$ and $s_1, s_2 \in S$, it holds that $\mathsf{sc}_n(s_1, v) \neq \mathsf{sc}_n(s_2, v) \Rightarrow \mathsf{rc}_n(s_1, v) \neq \mathsf{rc}_n(s_2, v)$.

Condition (2) says that the system is regular-channel (f, ϵ)-secure when restricted to any subset of secrets $S'' \prec S^{res}$. Condition (3) says that the system's side channel reveals no more information than its regular channel for the restricted secret subsets. Condition (1) says that the ratio of the restricted set over the entire space of secrets is at least r.[4]

We informally describe why SRSCR is a sufficient condition for security. The condition guarantees that, for the restricted secrets S^{res}, the attacker gains no additional information by observing the side-channel compared to what he already knew by observing the regular channel. Then, because r is a bound on the probability that a randomly selected secret falls in S^{res}, the system is secure provided that r is suitably large and the system is regular-channel secure. The theorem below formalizes the above intuition.

Theorem 1 (SRSCR Soundness). *Suppose C satisfies* $\mathsf{SRSCR}(f, \epsilon, r)$. *Then, C is (f, ϵ')-secure, where $\epsilon' = 1 - r(1 - \epsilon)$.*

Proof. Let S^{res} be an indexed family of sets of secret subsets that satisfies conditions (1), (2), and (3) of $\mathsf{SRSCR}(f, \epsilon, r)$. By condition (2), for all sufficiently large n and adversaries $\mathcal{A}$, $\Pr[Win^{\bullet,res}_{\mathcal{A}}(n, f)] < \epsilon(n)$ where $Win^{\bullet,res}_{\mathcal{A}}(n, f)$ is the modified game in which the oracle $C_n(s)$ always outputs $\bullet$ as its side-channel output and the secret s is selected randomly from $\bigcup S^{res}_n$ (rather than from $\mathcal{S}_n$).

[4] It is easy to relax the notion to be asymptotic so that the conditions need to hold only for $n \geq N$ for some $N \in \mathbb{N}$.

For any n, the probability that a randomly selected element from $\mathcal{S}_n$ is in $\bigcup S_n^{res}$ is at least r by condition (1). That is, $\Pr[s \in \bigcup S_n^{res} \mid s \leftarrow \mathcal{S}_n] \geq r$. Also, $\Pr[\neg\, Win_{\mathcal{A}}^{\bullet;res}(n,f)] > 1 - \epsilon(n)$ (for sufficiently large n) for any $\mathcal{A}$ by the argument above. Therefore, by condition (3), for sufficiently large n,

$$\Pr[\neg\, Win_{\mathcal{A}}(n,f)] \geq \Pr[s \in S_n^{res} \mid s \leftarrow \bigcup \mathcal{S}_n] \cdot \Pr[\neg\, Win_{\mathcal{A}}^{\bullet;res}(n,f)] > r \cdot (1 - \epsilon(n))$$

Therefore, $\Pr[Win_{\mathcal{A}}(n,f)] < 1 - r(1 - \epsilon(n))$ for sufficiently large n. □

As a special case where the ratio r is 1, Theorem 1 implies that if a system satisfies $\mathsf{SRSCR}(f,\epsilon,1)$ then it is (f,ϵ)-secure.

Example 3. Recall the bucketed leaky login program from Example 2. We show that the program satisfies the SRSCR condition. For each n, $a \in \{0,1\}^n$, and $0 \leq i < k$, let $S_n^{a,i} \subseteq \mathcal{S}_n$ be the set of secrets whose sub-bits from $i \cdot n/k$ to $(i+1) \cdot n/k - 1$ may differ but the remaining $n - n/k$ bits are a (and therefore same). That is,

$$\begin{aligned} S_n^{a,i} = \{s \in \mathcal{S}_n \mid\ & s[0,\ldots,i \cdot n/k - 1] = a[0,\ldots,i \cdot n/k - 1] \\ & \text{and } s[(i+1) \cdot n/k,\ldots,n-1] = a[(i+1) \cdot n/k,\ldots,n-1]\} \end{aligned}$$

Let S^{res} be the indexed family of sets of sets of secrets such that $S_n^{res} = \{S_n^{a,i} \mid a \in \{0,1\}^n\}$ for some i. Then, the system satisfies conditions (1), (2), and (3) of $\mathsf{SRSCR}(f,\epsilon,r)$ with $r = 1$, $f(n) = 2^{n/k} - (N+1)$, and $\epsilon = 1 - \frac{N-1}{2^{n/k}}$ for any $1 \leq N < 2^{n/k}$. Note that (1) is satisfied with $r = 1$ because $\mathcal{S}_n = \bigcup S_n^{res}$, and (2) is satisfied because $|S_n^{a,i}| = 2^{n/k}$ and (f,ϵ) matches the security of the ideal login program without side channels for the set of secrets of size $2^{n/k}$. To see why (3) is satisfied, note that for any $v \in \mathcal{I}_n$ and $s \in S_n^{a,i}$, $\mathsf{sc}_n(s,v) = i$ if $s \neq v$, and $\mathsf{sc}_n(s,v) = k$ if $s = v$. Hence, for any $v \in \mathcal{I}_n$ and $s_1, s_2 \in S_n^{a,i}$, $\mathsf{sc}_n(s_1,v) \neq \mathsf{sc}_n(s_2,v) \Rightarrow \mathsf{rc}_n(s_1,v) \neq \mathsf{rc}_n(s_2,v)$. Therefore, by Theorem 1, it follows that bucketed leaky login program is (f,ϵ)-secure. Note that the bound matches the one given in Example 2. ▲

To effectively apply Theorem 1, one needs to find suitable subsets of secrets S^{res} on which the system's regular channel is (f,ϵ)-secure and the side channel satisfies the refinement relation with respect to the regular channel. As also observed in prior works [29,38], the refinement relation is a 2-safety property [13,35] for which there are a number of effective verification methods [2,6,10,32,34]. For instance, self-composition [3,4,8,35] is a well-known technique that can be used to verify arbitrary 2-safety properties.

We note that a main benefit of Theorem 1 is *separation of concerns* whereby the security of regular channel can be proven independently of side channels, and the conditions required for side channels can be checked separately. For instance, a system designer may prove the regular-channel (f,ϵ)-security by an elaborate manual reasoning, while the side-channel conditions are checked, possibly automatically, by established program verification methods such as self composition.

Remarks. We make some additional observations regarding the SRSCR condition. First, while Theorem 1 derives a sound security bound, the bound may not be the tightest one. Indeed, when the adversary's error probability (i.e., the "ϵ" part of (f, ϵ)-security) is 1, the bucketed leaky login program can be shown to be actually $(k(2^{n/k} - 2), 1)$-secure, whereas the bound derived in Example 3 only showed that it is $(2^{n/k} - 2, 1)$-secure. That is, there is a factor k gap in the bounds. Intuitively, the gap occurs for the example because the buckets partition a secret into k number of n/k bit blocks, and while an adversary needs to recover the bits of every block in order to recover the entire secret, the analysis derived the bound by assessing only the effort required to recover bits from one of the blocks. Extending the technique to enable tighter analyses is left for future work.

Secondly, the statement of Theorem 1 says that when regular channel of the system is (f, ϵ)-secure for certain subsets of secrets, then the whole system is (f, ϵ')-secure under certain conditions. This may give an impression that only the adversary-success probability parameter (i.e., ϵ) of (f, ϵ)-security is affected by the additional consideration of side channels, leaving the number of oracle queries parameter (i.e., f) unaffected. However, as also seen in Example 2, the two parameters are often correlated so that smaller f implies smaller ϵ and vice versa. Therefore, Theorem 1 suggests that the change in the probability parameter (i.e., from ϵ to ϵ') may need to be compensated by a change in the degree of security with respect to the number of oracle queries.

Finally, condition (2) of SRSCR stipulates that the regular channel is (f, ϵ)-secure for each restricted family of sets of secrets $S'' \prec S^{res}$ rather than the entire space of secrets $\mathcal{S}$. In general, a system can be less secure when secrets are restricted because the adversary has a smaller space of secrets to search. Indeed, in the case when the error probability is 1, the regular channel of the bucketed leaky login program can be shown to be $(2^n - 2, 1)$-secure, but when restricted to each $S'' \prec S^{res}$ used in the analysis of Example 3, it is only $(2^{n/k} - 2, 1)$-secure. That is, there is an implicit correlation between the sizes of the restricted subsets and the degree of regular-channel security. Therefore, finding S^{res} such that each $S'' \in S^{res}_n$ is large and satisfies the conditions is important for deriving good security bounds, even when the ratio $|\bigcup S^{res}_n|/|\mathcal{S}_n|$ is large as in the analysis of the bucketed leaky login program.

3.2 Low-Input Side-Channel Non-Interference Condition

While SRSCR facilitates proving security of systems by separating regular channels from side channels, it requires one to identify suitable subsets of secrets S^{res} that satisfy the conditions. This can be a hurdle to applying the proof method. To this end, this section presents a condition, called *low-input side-channel non-interference* (LISCNI), which guarantees that a system satisfying it becomes secure after applying bucketing (or other techniques) to reduce the number of side-channel outputs. Unlike SRSCR, the condition does not require identifying secret subsets. Roughly, the condition stipulates that the regular channel is secure (for the entire space of secrets) and that the side-channel outputs are independent of attacker-controlled inputs.

We show that the system satisfying the condition becomes a system satisfying SRSCR once bucketing is applied, where the degree of security (i.e., the parameters f, ϵ, r of SRSCR) will be proportional to the degree of regular-channel security and the granularity of buckets. Roughly, this holds because for a system whose side-channel outputs are independent of attacker-controlled inputs, bucketing is guaranteed to partition the secrets into a small number of sets (relative to the bucket granularity) such that for each of the sets, the side channel cannot distinguish the secrets in the set, and the regular-channel security transfers to a certain degree to the case when the secrets are restricted to the ones in the set.

As we shall show next, while the condition is not permissive enough to prove security of the leaky login program (cf. Examples 1, 2 and 3), it covers interesting scenarios such as fast modular exponentiation (cf. Example 4). Also, as we shall show in Sect. 3.3, the condition may be used compositionally in combination with the constant-time implementation technique [1,3,9,22] to further widen its applicability.

Definition 4 (Low-Input Side-Channel Non-Interference). Let $f : \mathbb{N} \rightarrow \mathbb{N}$ and $\epsilon : \mathbb{N} \rightarrow (0, 1]$. We say that the system C satisfies the *low-input side-channel non-interference* condition with f and ϵ, written $\mathsf{LISCNI}(f, \epsilon)$, if the following conditions are satisfied:

(1) C is regular-channel (f, ϵ)-secure; and
(2) For all $n \in \mathbb{N}$, $s \in \mathcal{S}_n$, and $v_1, v_2 \in \mathcal{I}_n$, it holds that $\mathsf{sc}_n(s, v_1) = \mathsf{sc}_n(s, v_2)$.

Condition (2) says that the side-channel outputs are independent of low inputs (i.e., attacker-controlled inputs). We note that this is *non-interference* with respect to low inputs, whereas the usual notion of non-interference says that the outputs are independent of high inputs (i.e., secrets) [19,37].[5]

The LISCNI condition ensures the security of systems after bucketing is applied. We next formalize the notion of "applying bucketing".

Definition 5 (Bucketing). Let C be a system and $k \in \mathbb{N}$ such that $k > 0$. The system C after *k-bucketing* is applied, written $Bkt_k(C)$, is a system C' that satisfies the following:

(1) $\mathsf{rc}\langle C' \rangle = \mathsf{rc}\langle C \rangle$, $\mathcal{S}\langle C' \rangle = \mathcal{S}\langle C \rangle$, $\mathcal{I}\langle C' \rangle = \mathcal{I}\langle C \rangle$, and $\mathcal{O}^{\mathsf{rc}}\langle C' \rangle = \mathcal{O}^{\mathsf{rc}}\langle C \rangle$;
(2) For all $n \in \mathbb{N}$, $\mathcal{O}^{\mathsf{sc}}\langle C' \rangle_n = \{\star_1, \ldots, \star_k\}$ where $\star_i \neq \star_j$ for each $i \neq j$; and
(3) For all $n \in \mathbb{N}$, $s_1, s_2 \in \mathcal{S}_n$ and $v_1, v_2 \in \mathcal{I}_n$, $\mathsf{sc}\langle C \rangle_n(s_1, v_1) = \mathsf{sc}\langle C \rangle_n(s_2, v_2) \Rightarrow \mathsf{sc}\langle C' \rangle_n(s_1, v_2) = \mathsf{sc}\langle C' \rangle_n(s_2, v_2)$.

Roughly, k-bucketing partitions the side channel outputs into k number of buckets. We note that our notion of "bucketing" is quite general in that it does not specify how the side channel outputs are partitioned into the buckets. Indeed, as we shall show next, the security guarantee derived by LISCNI only requires the fact that side channel outputs are partitioned into a small number of buckets.

[5] As with SRSCR, it is easy to relax the notion to be asymptotic so that condition (2) only needs to hold for large n.

This makes our results applicable to any techniques (beyond the usual bucketing technique for timing channels [7,14,26,27,41]) that reduce the number of possible side-channel outputs.

Below states that a system satisfying the LISCNI condition becomes one that satisfies the SRSCR condition after suitable bucketing is applied.

Theorem 2 (LISCNI Soundness). *Suppose that C satisfies* $\mathsf{LISCNI}(f,\epsilon)$*. Let $k > 0$ be such that $k \cdot \epsilon \leq 1$. Then, $Bkt_k(C)$ satisfies* $\mathsf{SRSCR}(f, k \cdot \epsilon, 1/k)$.

Proof. Let $C' = Bkt_k(C)$. By condition (2) of k-bucketing and condition (2) of $\mathsf{LISCNI}(f,\epsilon)$, we have that for all $n \in \mathbb{N}$, $s \in \mathcal{S}_n$ and $v_1, v_2 \in \mathcal{I}_n$, $\mathsf{sc}\langle C' \rangle_n(s, v_1) = \mathsf{sc}\langle C' \rangle_n(s, v_2)$. Therefore, by k-bucketing, there must be an indexed family of sets of secrets S' such that for all n, (a) $S'_n \subseteq \mathcal{S}_n$, (b) $|S'_n| \geq |\mathcal{S}_n|/k$, and (c) for all $s_1, s_2 \in S'_n$ and $v_1, v_2 \in \mathcal{I}_n$, $\mathsf{sc}\langle C' \rangle_n(s_1, v_1) = \mathsf{sc}\langle C' \rangle_n(s_2, v_2)$. Note that such S' can be found by, for each n, choosing a bucket into which a maximal number of secrets fall. We define an indexed family of sets of sets of secrets S^{res} to be such that S^{res}_n is the singleton set $\{S'_n\}$ for each n.

We show that C' satisfies conditions (1), (2), and (3) of $\mathsf{SRSCR}(f, k \cdot \epsilon, 1/k)$ with the restricted secret subsets S^{res} defined above. Firstly, (1) is satisfied because $|S'_n| \geq |\mathcal{S}_n|/k$. Also, (3) is satisfied because of property (c) above (i.e., the side channel is non-interferent for the subset).

It remains to show that (2) is satisfied. That is, $C'|_{S'}$ is regular-channel $(f, k \cdot \epsilon)$-secure. For contradiction, suppose that $C'|_{S'}$ is not regular-channel $(f, k \cdot \epsilon)$-secure, that is, there exists a regular-channel attack $\mathcal{A}$ that queries (the regular channel of) $C'|_{S'}$ at most $f(n)$ many times and successfully recovers the secret with probability at least $k \cdot \epsilon(n)$. Then, we can construct a regular-channel adversary for C which simply runs $\mathcal{A}$ (on any secret from $\mathcal{S}_n$). Note that the adversary makes at most $f(n)$ many queries. We argue that the probability that the adversary succeeds in recovering the secret is at least ϵ. That is, we show that $\Pr[Win^{\bullet}_{\mathcal{A}}(n,f)] \geq \epsilon(n)$ (for sufficiently large n) where $Win^{\bullet}_{\mathcal{A}}(n,f)$ is the modified game in which the oracle always outputs $\bullet$ as its side-channel output.

To see this, note that the probability that a secret randomly selected from $\mathcal{S}_n$ is in S'_n is at least $1/k$, that is, $\Pr[s \in S'_n \mid s \leftarrow \mathcal{S}_n] \geq 1/k$. Also, $\mathcal{A}$'s regular-channel attack succeeds with probability at least $k \cdot \epsilon$ given a randomly chosen secret from S'_n, that is, $\Pr[Win^{\bullet;res}_{\mathcal{A}}(n,f)] \geq k \cdot \epsilon(n)$ where $Win^{\bullet;res}_{\mathcal{A}}(n,f)$ is the modified game in which the oracle always outputs $\bullet$ as its side-channel output and the secret is selected randomly from S'_n (rather than from $\mathcal{S}_n$). Therefore, for sufficiently large n, we have:

$$\Pr[Win^{\bullet}_{\mathcal{A}}(n,f)] \geq \Pr[s \in S'_n \mid s \leftarrow \mathcal{S}_n] \cdot \Pr[Win^{\bullet;res}_{\mathcal{A}}(n,f)] \geq 1/k \cdot (k \cdot \epsilon(n)) = \epsilon(n)$$

This contradicts condition (1) of $\mathsf{LISCNI}(f,\epsilon)$ which says that C is regular-channel (f,ϵ)-secure. Therefore, $C'|_{S'}$ is regular-channel $(f, k \cdot \epsilon)$-secure. □

As a corollary of Theorems 1 and 2, we have the following.

Corollary 1. *Suppose that C satisfies* $\mathsf{LISCNI}(f,\epsilon)$*. Let $k > 0$ be such that $k \cdot \epsilon \leq 1$. Then, $Bkt_k(C)$ is (f,ϵ')-secure where $\epsilon' = 1 - 1/k + \epsilon$.*

Note that as k approaches 1 (and hence the system becomes constant-time), the security bound of $Bkt_k(C)$ approaches (f, ϵ), matching the regular-channel security of C. As with Theorem 1, Theorem 2 may give an impression that the conditions only affect the adversary-success probability parameter (i.e., ϵ) of (f, ϵ)-security, leaving the number of queries parameter (i.e., f) unaffected. However, as also remarked in Sect. 3.1, the two parameters are often correlated so that a change in one can affect the other. Also, like SRSCR, LISCNI separates the concerns regarding regular channels from those regarding side channels. A system designer may check the security of the regular channel while disregarding the side channel, and separately prove the condition on the side channel.

```
i = 0;
a = 1;
while (i < n) {
  if (x[i] == 1) {
    r = (a * y) % m;
  } else {
    r = a;
  }
  a = (r * r) % m;
  i++;
}
return r;
```

Fig. 2. Fast modular exponentiation

Example 4 (Fast Modular Exponentiation). Fast modular exponentiation is an operation that is often found in cryptography algorithms such as RSA [23,30]. Figure 2 shows its implementation written in a C-like language. It computes $\mathtt{y}^{\mathtt{x}}$ `mod m` where `x` is the secret represented as a length `n` bit array and `y` is an attacker controlled-input. The program is not constant-time (assuming that then and else branches in the loop have different running times), and effective timing attacks have been proposed for the program [23,30].

However, assuming that running time of the operation `(a * y) % m` is independent of `y`, it can be seen that the program satisfies the LISCNI condition.[6] Under the assumption, the program can be formalized as the system C where, for all $n \in \mathbb{N}$,

- $\mathcal{S}_n = \mathcal{I}_n = \{0,1\}^n$;
- $\mathcal{O}_n^{\mathsf{rc}} = \mathcal{O}_n^{\mathsf{sc}} = \mathbb{N}$;
- For all $(s, v) \in \mathcal{S}_n \times \mathcal{I}_n$, $\mathsf{rc}_n(s, v) = v^s \, mod \, \mathtt{m}$; and
- For all $(s, v) \in \mathcal{S}_n \times \mathcal{I}_n$, $\mathsf{sc}_n(s, v) = time_{\mathtt{t}} \cdot num(s, 1) + time_{\mathtt{f}} \cdot num(s, 0)$.

[6] This is admittedly an optimistic assumption. Indeed, proposed timing attacks exploit the fact that the running time of the operation can depend on `y` [23,30]. Here, we assume that the running time of the operation is made independent of `y` by some means (e.g., by adopting the constant-time implementation technique).

Here, $num(s, b) = |\{i \in \mathbb{N} \mid i < n \wedge s[i] = b\}|$ for $b \in \{0, 1\}$, and $time_{\mathtt{t}}$ (resp. $time_{\mathtt{f}}$) is the running time of the then (resp. else) branch.

Let the computation class of adversaries be the class of randomized polynomial time algorithms. Then, under the standard computational assumption that inverting modular exponentiation is hard, one can show that C satisfies $\mathsf{LISCNI}(f, \epsilon)$ for any f and negligible ϵ. This follows because the side-channel outputs are independent of low inputs, and the regular-channel is (f, ϵ)-secure for any f and negligible ϵ under the assumption.[7] Therefore, it can be made (f, ϵ)-secure for any f and negligible ϵ by applying bucketing. ▲

Remarks. We make some additional observations regarding the LISCNI condition. First, similar to condition (3) of SRSCR, the low-input independence condition of LISCNI (condition (2)) is a 2-safety property and is amenable to various verification methods proposed for the class of properties. In fact, because the condition is essentially side-channel non-interference but with respect to low inputs instead of high inputs, it can be checked by the methods for checking ordinary side-channel non-interference by reversing the roles of high inputs and low inputs [1,3,6,9,20].

Secondly, we note that the leaky login program from Example 1 does not satisfy LISCNI. This is because the program's side channel is not non-interferent with respect to low inputs. Indeed, given any secret $s \in \mathcal{S}_n$, one can vary the running times by choosing low inputs $v, v' \in \mathcal{I}_n$ with differing lengths of matching prefixes, that is, $(\mathrm{argmax}_i\, s\restriction_i = v\restriction_i) \neq (\mathrm{argmax}_i\, s\restriction_i = v'\restriction_i)$. Nevertheless, as we have shown in Examples 2 and 3, the program becomes secure once bucketing is applied. In fact, it becomes one that satisfies SRSCR as shown in Example 3. Ideally, we would like to find a relatively simple condition (on systems before bucketing is applied) that covers many systems that would become secure by applying bucketing. However, finding such a condition that covers a system like the leaky login program may be non-trivial. Indeed, predicting that the leaky login program become secure after applying bucketing appears to require more subtle analysis of interaction between low inputs and high inputs. (In fact, it can be shown that arbitrarily partitioning the side-channel outputs to a small number of buckets does not ensure security for this program.) Extending the technique to cover such scenarios is left for future work.

3.3 Combining Bucketing and Constant-Time Implementation Compositionally

We show that the LISCNI condition may be applied compositionally with the constant-time implementation technique (technically, we will only apply the condition (2) of LISCNI compositionally). As we shall show next, the combined approach is able to ensure security of some non-constant-time systems that cannot

[7] The latter holds because (f, ϵ)-security is asymptotic and the probability that any regular-channel adversary of the computation class may correctly guess the secret for this system is negligible (under the computational hardness assumption). Therefore, a similar analysis can be done for any sub-polynomial number of buckets.

be made sure by applying bucketing globally to the whole system. We remark that, in contrast to those of the previous sections of the paper, the results of this section are more specialized to the case of timing channels. First, we formalize the notion of constant-time implementation.

```
while (sec > 0) {
  sec = sec - 1;
}
while (inp > 0) {
  inp = inp - 1;
}
return true;
```

Fig. 3. A non-constant-time program that cannot be made secure by globally applying bucketing.

Definition 6 (Constant-Time). Let $f : \mathbb{N} \to \mathbb{N}$ and $\epsilon : \mathbb{N} \to (0, 1]$. We say that a system C satisfies the *constant-time* condition (or, *timing-channel non-interference*) with f and ϵ, written $\mathsf{CT}(f, \epsilon)$, if the following is satisfied:

(1) C is regular-channel (f, ϵ)-secure; and
(2) For all $n \in \mathbb{N}$, $v \in \mathcal{I}_n$, and $s_1, s_2 \in \mathcal{S}_n$, $\mathsf{sc}_n(s_1, v) = \mathsf{sc}_n(s_2, v)$.

Note that CT requires that the side channel is non-interferent (with respect to secrets). The following theorem is immediate from the definition, and states that CT is a sufficient condition for security.

Theorem 3 (CT Soundness). *If C satisfies $\mathsf{CT}(f, \epsilon)$, then C is (f, ϵ)-secure.*

To motivate the combined application of CT and LISCNI, let us consider the following example which is neither constant-time nor can be made secure by (globally) applying bucketing.

Example 5. Figure 3 shows a simple, albeit contrived, program that we will use to motivate the combined approach. Here, `sec` is a n-bit secret and `inp` is a n-bit attacker-controlled input. Both `sec` and `inp` are interpreted as unsigned n-bit integers where $-$ and $>$ are the usual unsigned integer subtraction and comparison operations. The regular channel always outputs `true` and hence is non-interferent. Therefore, only the timing channel is of concern.

The program can be formalized as $C_{\texttt{comp}}$ where for all $n \in \mathbb{N}$,

- $\mathcal{S}_n = \mathcal{I}_n = \{0, 1\}^n$;
- $\mathcal{O}_n^{\mathsf{rc}} = \{\bullet\}$;
- $\mathcal{O}_n^{\mathsf{sc}} = \{i \in \mathbb{N} \mid i \leq 2^{n+1}\}$;
- For all $(s, v) \in \mathcal{S}_n \times \mathcal{I}_n$, $\mathsf{rc}_n(s, v) = \bullet$; and
- For all $(s, v) \in \mathcal{S}_n \times \mathcal{I}_n$, $\mathsf{sc}_n(s, v) = s + v$.

Note that the side channel outputs the sum of the high input and the low input. It is easy to see that the system is not constant-time (i.e., not $\mathsf{CT}(f, \epsilon)$ for any f and ϵ). Furthermore, the system is not secure as is, because an adversary can immediately recover the secret by querying with any input and subtracting the input from the side-channel output.

Also, it is easy to see that the system does not satisfy $\mathsf{LISCNI}(f, \epsilon)$ for any f and ϵ either, because its side-channel outputs are not independent of low inputs. In fact, we can show that arbitrarily applying bucketing (globally) to the system does not guarantee security. To see this, let us consider applying bucketing with just two buckets whereby the buckets partition the possible running times in two halves so that running times less than or equal to 2^n fall into the first bucket and those greater than 2^n fall into the other bucket. After applying bucketing, the system is C' where

- $\mathsf{rc}\langle C' \rangle$, $\mathcal{S}\langle C' \rangle$, $\mathcal{I}\langle C' \rangle$, and $\mathcal{O}^{\mathsf{rc}}\langle C' \rangle$ are same as those of $C_{\mathtt{comp}}$;
- For all $n \in \mathbb{N}$, $\mathcal{O}^{\mathsf{sc}}\langle C' \rangle_n = \{0, 1\}$; and
- For all $n \in \mathbb{N}$ and $(s, v) \in \mathcal{S}_n \times \mathcal{I}_n$, $\mathsf{sc}\langle C' \rangle_n(s, v) = 0$ if $s + v \leq 2^n$, and $\mathsf{sc}\langle C' \rangle_n(s, v) = 1$ otherwise.

We show that there exists an efficient adaptive attack against C'. Let $s \in \mathcal{S}_n$. The adversary $\mathcal{A}$ recovers s by only making linearly many queries via the following process. First, $\mathcal{A}$ queries with the input $v_1 = 2^{n-1}$. By observing the side-channel output, $\mathcal{A}$ will know whether $0 \leq s \leq 2^{n-1}$ (i.e., the side-channel output was 0) or $2^{n-1} < s \leq 2^n$ (i.e., the side-channel output was 1). In the former case, $\mathcal{A}$ picks the input $v_2 = 2^{n-1} + 2^{n-2}$ for the next query, and in the latter case, he picks $v_2 = 2^{n-2}$. Continuing the process in a binary search manner and reducing the space of possible secrets by 1/2 in each query, $\mathcal{A}$ is able to hone in on s within n many queries. Therefore, C' is not (n, ϵ)-secure for any ϵ. ▲

Next, we present the compositional bucketing approach. Roughly, our compositionality theorem (Theorem 4) states that the sequential composition of a constant-time system with a system whose side channel is non-interferent with respect to low inputs can be made secure by applying bucketing to only the non-constant-time component. As with LISCNI, the degree of security of the composed system is relative to the that of the regular channel and the granularity of buckets.

To state the compositionality theorem, we explicitly separate the conditions on side channels of CT and LISCNI from those on regular channels and introduce terminologies that only refer to the side-channel conditions. Let us fix C. We say that C satisfies $\mathsf{CT}^{\mathsf{sc}}$, if it satisfies condition (2) of CT, that is, for all $n \in \mathbb{N}$, $v \in \mathcal{I}_n$, and $s_1, s_2 \in \mathcal{S}_n$, $\mathsf{sc}_n(s_1, v) = \mathsf{sc}_n(s_2, v)$. Also, we say that C satisfies $\mathsf{LISCNI}^{\mathsf{sc}}$ if it satisfies condition (2) of LISCNI, that is, for all $n \in \mathbb{N}$, $s \in \mathcal{S}_n$, and $v_1, v_2 \in \mathcal{I}_n$, $\mathsf{sc}_n(s, v_1) = \mathsf{sc}_n(s, v_2)$. Next, we define sequential composition of systems.

Definition 7 (Sequential Composition). Let $C^\dagger$ and $C^\ddagger$ be systems such that $\mathcal{S}\langle C^\dagger \rangle = \mathcal{S}\langle C^\ddagger \rangle$, $\mathcal{I}\langle C^\dagger \rangle = \mathcal{I}\langle C^\ddagger \rangle$, and for all $n \in \mathbb{N}$, $\mathcal{O}^{\mathsf{sc}}\langle C^\ddagger \rangle_n \subseteq \mathbb{N}$ and

$\mathcal{O}^{\mathsf{sc}}\langle C^\ddagger\rangle_n \subseteq \mathbb{N}$. The *sequential composition* of $C^\dagger$ with $C^\ddagger$, written $C^\dagger; C^\ddagger$, is the system C such that

- $\mathcal{S}\langle C\rangle = \mathcal{S}(C^\dagger)$ and $\mathcal{I}\langle C\rangle = \mathcal{I}(C^\dagger)$; and
- For all $n \in \mathbb{N}$ and $(s, v) \in \mathcal{S}_n \times \mathcal{I}_n$, $\mathsf{sc}\langle C'\rangle_n(s, v) = \mathsf{sc}\langle C^\dagger\rangle_n(s, v) + \mathsf{sc}\langle C^\ddagger\rangle_n(s, v)$.

We note that the definition of sequential composition specifically targets the case when the side channel is a timing channel, and says that the side-channels outputs are numeric values and that the side-channel output of the composed system is the sum of those of the components. Also, the definition leaves the composition of regular channels open, and allows the regular channel of the composed system to be any function from $\mathcal{S}_n \times \mathcal{I}_n$. We are now ready to state the compositionality theorem.

Theorem 4 (Compositionality). *Let $C^\dagger$ be a system that satisfies* $\mathsf{LISCNI}^{\mathsf{sc}}$ *and $C^\ddagger$ be a system that satisfies* $\mathsf{CT}^{\mathsf{sc}}$. *Suppose that $Bkt_k(C^\dagger); C^\ddagger$ is regular-channel (f, ϵ)-secure where $k \cdot \epsilon \leq 1$. Then, $Bkt_k(C^\dagger); C^\ddagger$ is (f, ϵ')-secure, where $\epsilon' = 1 - 1/k + \epsilon$.*

Proof. By Theorem 1, it suffices to show that $Bkt_k(C^\dagger); C^\ddagger$ satisfies $\mathsf{SRSCR}(f, k\cdot\epsilon, 1/k)$. By an argument similar to the proof of Theorem 2, there must be an indexed family of sets of secrets S' such that, for all $n \in \mathbb{N}$, (a) $S'_n \subseteq \mathcal{S}_n$, (b) $|S'_n| \geq |\mathcal{S}_n|/k$, and (c) for all $s_1, s_2 \in S'_n$ and $v_1, v_2 \in \mathcal{I}_n$, $\mathsf{sc}\langle Bkt_k(C^\dagger)\rangle_n(s_1, v_1) = \mathsf{sc}\langle Bkt_k(C^\dagger)\rangle_n(s_2, v_2)$. We define an indexed family of sets of sets of secrets S^{res} to be such that S^{res}_n is the singleton set $\{S'_n\}$ for each n.

We show that $C = Bkt_k(C^\dagger); C^\ddagger$ satisfies conditions (1), (2), and (3) of $\mathsf{SRSCR}(f, k\cdot\epsilon, 1/k)$ with the restricted secret subsets S^{res} defined above. Firstly, (1) is satisfied because $|S'_n| \geq |\mathcal{S}_n|/k$. Also, because $Bkt_k(C^\dagger); C^\ddagger$ is regular-channel (f, ϵ)-secure, we can show that (2) is satisfied by an argument similar to the one in the proof of Theorem 2.

It remains to show that (3) is satisfied. It suffices to show that for all $n \in \mathbb{N}$, $v \in \mathcal{I}_n$, and $s_1, s_2 \in S'_n$, $\mathsf{sc}\langle C\rangle_n(s_1, v) = \mathsf{sc}\langle C\rangle_n(s_2, v)$. That is, the side channel of the composed system is non-interferent (with respect to high inputs) for the subset S'. By the definition of the sequential composition, for all $v \in \mathcal{I}_n$ and $s \in \mathcal{S}_n$, $\mathsf{sc}\langle C\rangle_n(s, v) = \mathsf{sc}\langle Bkt_k(C^\dagger)\rangle_n(s, v) + \mathsf{sc}\langle C^\ddagger\rangle_n(s, v)$. Therefore, for all $v \in \mathcal{I}_n$ and $s_1, s_2 \in S'_n$,

$$\begin{aligned}
\mathsf{sc}\langle C\rangle_n(s_1, v) &= \mathsf{sc}\langle Bkt_k(C^\dagger)\rangle_n(s_1, v) + \mathsf{sc}\langle C^\ddagger\rangle_n(s_1, v) \\
&= \mathsf{sc}\langle Bkt_k(C^\dagger)\rangle_n(s_2, v) + \mathsf{sc}(C^\ddagger)_n(s_2, v) \\
&= \mathsf{sc}\langle C\rangle_n(s_2, v)
\end{aligned}$$

because $\mathsf{sc}\langle C^\ddagger\rangle_n(s_1, v) = \mathsf{sc}\langle C^\ddagger\rangle_n(s_2, v)$ by $\mathsf{CT}^{\mathsf{sc}}$ of $C^\ddagger$, and $\mathsf{sc}\langle Bkt_k(C^\dagger)\rangle_n(s_1, v)$ $= \mathsf{sc}\langle Bkt_k(C^\dagger)\rangle_n(s_2, v)$ by (c) above. □

We note that the notion of sequential composition is symmetric. Therefore, Theorem 4 implies that the composing the components in the reverse order, that is, $C^\ddagger; Bkt_k(C^\dagger)$, is also secure provided that its regular channel is secure.

The compositionality theorem suggests the following compositional approach to ensuring security. Given a system C that is a sequential composition of a component whose side channel outputs are independent of high inputs (i.e., satisfies $\mathsf{CT}^{\mathsf{sc}}$) and a component whose side channel outputs are independent of low inputs (i.e., satisfies $\mathsf{LISCNI}^{\mathsf{sc}}$), we can ensure the security of C by proving its regular-channel security and applying bucketing only to the non-constant-time component.

Example 6. Let us apply compositional bucketing to the system $C_{\mathtt{comp}}$ from Example 5. Recall that the system is neither constant-time nor applying bucketing to the whole system ensures its security. The system can be seen as the sequential composition $C_{\mathtt{comp}} = C^{\dagger}; C^{\ddagger}$ where $C^{\dagger}$ and $C^{\ddagger}$ satisfy the following:

- $\mathcal{S}$ and $\mathcal{I}$ are as in $C_{\mathtt{comp}}$;
- For all $n \in \mathbb{N}$, $\mathcal{O}^{\mathsf{sc}}\langle C^{\dagger}\rangle_n = \mathcal{O}^{\mathsf{sc}}\langle C^{\ddagger}\rangle_n = \{i \in \mathbb{N} \mid i \leq 2^n\}$; and
- For all $n \in \mathbb{N}$ and $(s, v) \in \mathcal{S}_n \times \mathcal{I}_n$, $\mathsf{sc}\langle C^{\dagger}\rangle_n(s, v) = s$ and $\mathsf{sc}\langle C^{\ddagger}\rangle_n(s, v) = v$.

Note that $C^{\ddagger}$ satisfies $\mathsf{CT}^{\mathsf{sc}}$ as its side-channel outputs are high-input independent, and, $C^{\dagger}$ satisfies $\mathsf{LISCNI}^{\mathsf{sc}}$ as its side-channel outputs are low-input independent. By applying bucketing only to the component $C^{\dagger}$, we obtain the system $Bkt_k(C^{\dagger}); C^{\ddagger}$. The regular-channel of $Bkt_k(C^{\dagger}); C^{\ddagger}$ (i.e., that of $C_{\mathtt{comp}}$) is (f, ϵ)-secure for any f and negligible ϵ because it is non-interferent (with respect to high inputs) and the probability that an adversary may recover a secret for such a system is at most $1/|\mathcal{S}_n|$.[8] Therefore, by Theorem 4, $Bkt_k(C^{\dagger}); C^{\ddagger}$ is (f, ϵ)-secure for any f and negligible ϵ. ▲

The above example shows that compositional bucketing can be used to ensure security of non-constant-time systems that cannot be made secure by a whole-system bucketing. It is interesting to observe that the constant-time condition, $\mathsf{CT}^{\mathsf{sc}}$, requires the side-channel outputs to be independent of high inputs but allows dependency on low inputs, while $\mathsf{LISCNI}^{\mathsf{sc}}$ is the dual and says that the side-channel outputs are independent of low inputs but may depend on high inputs. Our compositionality theorem (Theorem 4) states that a system consisting of such parts can be made secure by applying bucketing only to the part that satisfies the latter condition.

It is easy to see that sequentially composing components that satisfy $\mathsf{CT}^{\mathsf{sc}}$ results in a system that satisfies $\mathsf{CT}^{\mathsf{sc}}$, and likewise, sequentially composing components that satisfy $\mathsf{LISCNI}^{\mathsf{sc}}$ results in a system that satisfies $\mathsf{LISCNI}^{\mathsf{sc}}$. Therefore, such compositions can be used freely in conjunction with the compositional bucketing technique of this section. We also conjecture that components that are made secure by compositional bucketing can themselves be sequentially composed to form a secure system (possibly with some decrease in the degree of security). We leave a more detailed investigation for future work.

---

[8] Therefore, a similar analysis can be done for any strictly sub-exponential number of buckets.

4 Related Work

As remarked in Sect. 1, much research has been done on defending against timing attacks and more generally side channel attacks. For instance, there have been experimental evaluation on the effectiveness of bucketing and other timing-channel mitigation schemes [14,18], and other works have proposed information-theoretic methods for formally analyzing the security of (deterministic and probabilistic) systems against adaptive adversaries [12,25].

However, few prior works have formally analyzed the effect of bucketing on timing channel security (or similar techniques for other side channels) against adaptive adversaries. Indeed, to our knowledge, the only prior work to do so are the series of works by Köpf et al. [26,27] who investigated the effect of bucketing applied to blinded cryptography algorithms. They show that applying bucketing to a blinded cryptography algorithm whose regular channel is IND-CCA2 secure results in an algorithm that is IND-CCA2 secure against timing-channel-observing adversaries. In addition, they show bounds on information leaked by such bucketed blinded cryptography algorithms in terms of quantitative information flow [5,28,33,39,40]. By contrast, we analyze the effect of applying bucketing to general systems, show that bucketing is in general insufficient against adaptive adversaries, and present novel conditions that guarantee security against such adversaries. (In fact, the results of [26,27] may be seen as an instance of our LISCNI condition because blinding makes the behavior of cryptographic algorithms effectively independent of attacker-controlled inputs.) Also, our results are given in the form of (f, ϵ)-security, which can provide precise bounds on the number of queries needed by adaptive adversaries to recover secrets.

Next, we compare our work with the works on constant-time implementations (i.e., timing-channel non-interference) [1,3,6,9,20,22]. The previous works have proposed methods for verifying that the given system is constant-time [3,6,9,20] or transforming it to one that is constant-time [1,22]. As we have also discussed in this paper (cf. Theorem 3), it is easy to see that the constant-time condition directly transfers the regular-channel-only security to the security for the case with timing channels. By contrast, security implied by bucketing is less straightforward. In this paper, we have shown that bucketing is in general insufficient to guarantee the security of systems even when their regular channel is perfectly secure. And, we have presented results that show that, under certain conditions, the regular-channel-only security can be transferred to the side-channel-observing case to certain degrees. Because there are advantages of bucketing such as efficiency and ease of implementation [7,14,26,27,41], we hope that our results will contribute to a better understanding of the bucketing technique and foster further research on the topic.

5 Conclusion and Future Work

In this paper, we have presented a formal analysis of the effectiveness of the bucketing technique against adaptive timing-channel-observing adversaries. We have shown that bucketing is in general insufficient against such adversaries, and presented two novel conditions, SRSCR and LISCNI, that guarantee security against such adversaries. SRSCR states that a system that satisfies it is secure, whereas LISCNI states that the a system that satisfies it becomes secure when bucketing is applied. We have shown that both conditions facilitate proving the security of systems against adaptive side-channel-observing adversaries by allowing a system designer to prove the security of the system's regular channel separately from the concerns of its side-channel behavior. By doing so, the security of the regular-channel is transferred, to certain degrees, to the full side-channel-aware security. We have also shown that the LISCNI condition can be used in conjunction with the constant-time implementation technique in a compositional manner to further increase its applicability. We have formalized our results via the notion of (f, ϵ)-security, which gives precise bounds on the number of queries needed by adaptive adversaries to recover secrets.

While we have instantiated our results to timing channel and bucketing, many of the results are actually quite general and are applicable to side channels other than timing channels. Specifically, aside from the compositional bucketing result that exploits the "additive" nature of timing channels, the results are applicable to any side channels and techniques that reduce the number of possible side-channel observations.

As future work, we would like to extend our results to probabilistic systems. Currently, our results are limited to deterministic systems, and such an extension would be needed to assess the effect of bucketing when it is used together with countermeasure techniques that involve randomization. We would also like to improve the conditions and the security bounds thereof to be able to better analyze systems such as the leaky login program shown in Examples 1, 2 and 3. Finally, we would like to extend the applicability of the compositional bucketing technique by considering more patterns of compositions, such as sequentially composing components that themselves have been made secure by compositional bucketing.

Acknowledgements. We thank the anonymous reviewers for useful comments. This work was supported by JSPS KAKENHI Grant Numbers 17H01720 and 18K19787, JSPS Core-to-Core Program, A.Advanced Research Networks, JSPS Bilateral Collaboration Research, and Office of Naval Research (ONR) award #N00014-17-1-2787.

References

1. Agat, J.: Transforming out timing leaks. In: POPL (2000)
2. Aguirre, A., Barthe, G., Gaboardi, M., Garg, D., Strub, P.: A relational logic for higher-order programs. In: PACMPL, vol. 1, issue ICFP (2017)
3. Almeida, J.B., Barbosa, M., Barthe, G., Dupressoir, F., Emmi, M.: Verifying constant-time implementations. In: USENIX Security Symposium (2016)
4. Almeida, J.B., Barbosa, M., Pinto, J.S., Vieira, B.: Formal verification of side-channel countermeasures using self-composition. Sci. Comput. Program. **78**(7), 796–812 (2013)

5. Alvim, M.S., Chatzikokolakis, K., Palamidessi, C., Smith, G.: Measuring information leakage using generalized gain functions. In: CSF (2012)
6. Antonopoulos, T., Gazzillo, P., Hicks, M., Koskinen, E., Terauchi, T., Wei, S.: Decomposition instead of self-composition for proving the absence of timing channels. In: PLDI (2017)
7. Askarov, A., Zhang, D., Myers, A.C.: Predictive black-box mitigation of timing channels. In: CCS (2010)
8. Barthe, G., D'Argenio, P.R., Rezk, T.: Secure information flow by self-composition. Math. Struct. Comput. Sci. **21**(6), 1207–1252 (2011)
9. Barthe, G., Grégoire, B., Laporte, V.: Secure compilation of side-channel countermeasures: the case of cryptographic "constant-time". In: CSF (2018)
10. Benton, N.: Simple relational correctness proofs for static analyses and program transformations. In: POPL (2004)
11. Blot, A., Yamamoto, M., Terauchi, T.: Compositional synthesis of leakage resilient programs. In: POST (2017)
12. Boreale, M., Pampaloni, F.: Quantitative information flow under generic leakage functions and adaptive adversaries. Logical Methods Comput. Sci. **11**(4:5), 1–31 (2015)
13. Clarkson, M.R., Schneider, F.B.: Hyperproperties. J. Comput. Secur. **18**(6), 1157–1210 (2010)
14. Dantas, Y.G., Gay, R., Hamann, T., Mantel, H., Schickel, J.: An evaluation of bucketing in systems with non-deterministic timing behavior. In: Janczewski, L.J., Kutyłowski, M. (eds.) SEC 2018. IAICT, vol. 529, pp. 323–338. Springer, Cham (2018). https://doi.org/10.1007/978-3-319-99828-2_23
15. Doychev, G., Köpf, B., Mauborgne, L., Reineke, J.: CacheAudit: a tool for the static analysis of cache side channels. ACM Trans. Inf. Syst. Secur. **18**(1), 4 (2015)
16. Eldib, H., Wang, C.: Synthesis of masking countermeasures against side channel attacks. In: Biere, A., Bloem, R. (eds.) CAV 2014. LNCS, vol. 8559, pp. 114–130. Springer, Cham (2014). https://doi.org/10.1007/978-3-319-08867-9_8
17. Gandolfi, K., Mourtel, C., Olivier, F.: Electromagnetic analysis: concrete results. In: Koç, Ç.K., Naccache, D., Paar, C. (eds.) CHES 2001. LNCS, vol. 2162, pp. 251–261. Springer, Heidelberg (2001). https://doi.org/10.1007/3-540-44709-1_21
18. Gay, R., Mantel, H., Sudbrock, H.: An empirical bandwidth analysis of interrupt-related covert channels. IJSSE **6**(2), 1–22 (2015)
19. Goguen, J.A., Meseguer, J.: Security policies and security models. In: IEEE Symposium on Security and Privacy (1982)
20. Hedin, D., Sands, D.: Timing aware information flow security for a JavaCard-like bytecode (2005)
21. Ishai, Y., Sahai, A., Wagner, D.: Private circuits: securing hardware against probing attacks. In: Boneh, D. (ed.) CRYPTO 2003. LNCS, vol. 2729, pp. 463–481. Springer, Heidelberg (2003). https://doi.org/10.1007/978-3-540-45146-4_27
22. Kobayashi, N., Shirane, K.: Type-based information analysis for low-level languages. In: APLAS (2002)
23. Kocher, P.C.: Timing attacks on implementations of Diffie-Hellman, RSA, DSS, and other systems. In: Koblitz, N. (ed.) CRYPTO 1996. LNCS, vol. 1109, pp. 104–113. Springer, Heidelberg (1996). https://doi.org/10.1007/3-540-68697-5_9
24. Kocher, P., Jaffe, J., Jun, B.: Differential power analysis. In: Wiener, M. (ed.) CRYPTO 1999. LNCS, vol. 1666, pp. 388–397. Springer, Heidelberg (1999). https://doi.org/10.1007/3-540-48405-1_25
25. Köpf, B., Basin, D.A.: Automatically deriving information-theoretic bounds for adaptive side-channel attacks. J. Comput. Secur. **19**(1), 1–31 (2011)

26. Köpf, B., Dürmuth, M.: A provably secure and efficient countermeasure against timing attacks. In: CSF (2009)
27. Köpf, B., Smith, G.: Vulnerability bounds and leakage resilience of blinded cryptography under timing attacks. In: CSF (2010)
28. Malacaria, P.: Assessing security threats of looping constructs. In: POPL (2007)
29. Malacaria, P.: Algebraic foundations for quantitative information flow. Math. Struct. Comput. Sci. **25**(2), 404–428 (2015)
30. Pasareanu, C.S., Phan, Q., Malacaria, P.: Multi-run side-channel analysis using symbolic execution and max-SMT. In: CSF (2016)
31. Quisquater, J.-J., Samyde, D.: ElectroMagnetic Analysis (EMA): measures and counter-measures for smart cards. In: Attali, I., Jensen, T. (eds.) E-smart 2001. LNCS, vol. 2140, pp. 200–210. Springer, Heidelberg (2001). https://doi.org/10.1007/3-540-45418-7_17
32. Reynolds, J.C.: The Craft of Programming. Prentice Hall International Series in Computer Science. Prentice Hall, London (1981)
33. Smith, G.: On the foundations of quantitative information flow. In: de Alfaro, L. (ed.) FoSSaCS 2009. LNCS, vol. 5504, pp. 288–302. Springer, Heidelberg (2009). https://doi.org/10.1007/978-3-642-00596-1_21
34. Sousa, M., Dillig, I.: Cartesian Hoare logic for verifying k-safety properties. In: PLDI (2016)
35. Terauchi, T., Aiken, A.: Secure information flow as a safety problem. In: Hankin, C., Siveroni, I. (eds.) SAS 2005. LNCS, vol. 3672, pp. 352–367. Springer, Heidelberg (2005). https://doi.org/10.1007/11547662_24
36. Tromer, E., Osvik, D.A., Shamir, A.: Efficient cache attacks on AES, and countermeasures. J. Cryptol. **23**(1), 37–71 (2010)
37. Volpano, D.M., Irvine, C.E., Smith, G.: A sound type system for secure flow analysis. J. Comput. Secur. **4**(2/3), 167–187 (1996)
38. Yasuoka, H., Terauchi, T.: Quantitative information flow - verification hardness and possibilities. In: CSF (2010)
39. Yasuoka, H., Terauchi, T.: On bounding problems of quantitative information flow. J. Comput. Secur. **19**(6), 1029–1082 (2011)
40. Yasuoka, H., Terauchi, T.: Quantitative information flow as safety and liveness hyperproperties. Theor. Comput. Sci. **538**, 167–182 (2014)
41. Zhang, D., Askarov, A., Myers, A.C.: Language-based control and mitigation of timing channels. In: PLDI (2012)

A Dependently Typed Library for Static Information-Flow Control in IDRIS

Simon Gregersen(✉), Søren Eller Thomsen, and Aslan Askarov

Aarhus University, Aarhus, Denmark
{gregersen,sethomsen,askarov}@cs.au.dk

Abstract. Safely integrating third-party code in applications while protecting the confidentiality of information is a long-standing problem. Pure functional programming languages, like Haskell, make it possible to enforce lightweight information-flow control through libraries like **MAC** by Russo. This work presents DEPSEC, a **MAC** inspired, dependently typed library for static information-flow control in IDRIS. We showcase how adding dependent types increases the expressiveness of state-of-the-art static information-flow control libraries and how DEPSEC matches a special-purpose dependent information-flow type system on a key example. Finally, we show novel and powerful means of specifying statically enforced declassification policies using dependent types.

Keywords: Information-flow control · Dependent types · Idris

1 Introduction

Modern software applications are increasingly built using libraries and code from multiple third parties. At the same time, protecting confidentiality of information manipulated by such applications is a growing, yet long-standing problem. Third-party libraries could in general have been written by anyone and they are usually run with the same privileges as the main application. While powerful, such privileges open up for abuse.

Traditionally, access control [7] and encryption have been the main means for preventing data dissemination and leakage, however, such mechanisms fall short when third-party code needs access to sensitive information to provide its functionality. The key observation is that these mechanisms only place restrictions on the access to information but not its propagation. Once information is accessed, the accessor is free to improperly transmit or leak the information in some form, either by intention or error.

Language-based Information-Flow Control [36] is a promising technique for enforcing information security. Traditional enforcement techniques analyze how information at different security levels flows within a program ensuring that information flows only to appropriate places, suppressing illegal flows. To achieve this, most information-flow control tools require the design of new languages, compilers, or interpreters (e.g. [12,17,22,23,26,29,39]). Despite a large, growing

F. Nielson and D. Sands (Eds.): POST 2019, LNCS 11426, pp. 51–75, 2019.
https://doi.org/10.1007/978-3-030-17138-4_3

body of work on language-based information-flow security, there has been little adoption of the proposed techniques. For information-flow policies to be enforced in such systems, the whole system has to be written in new languages – an inherently expensive and time-consuming process for large software systems. Moreover, in practice, it might very well be that only small parts of an application are governed by information-flow policies.

Pure functional programming languages, like Haskell, have something to offer with respect to information security as they strictly separate side-effect free and side-effectful code. This makes it possible to enforce lightweight information-flow control through libraries [11,20,34,35,42] by constructing an embedded domain-specific security sub-language. Such libraries enforce a secure-by-construction programming model as any program written against the library interface is not capable of leaking secrets. This construction forces the programmer to write security-critical code in the sub-language but otherwise allows them to freely interact and integrate with non-security critical code written in the full language. In particular, static enforcement libraries like **MAC** [34] are appealing as no run-time checks are needed and code that exhibits illegal flows is rejected by the type checker at compile-time. Naturally, the expressiveness of Haskell's type system sets the limitation on which programs can be deemed secure and which information flow policies can be guaranteed.

Dependent type theories [24,31] are implemented in many programming languages such as Coq [13], Agda [32], Idris [8], and F* [44]. Programming languages that implement such theories allow types to dependent on values. This enables programmers to give programs a very precise type and increased confidence in its correctness.

In this paper, we show that dependent types provide a direct and natural way of expressing precise data-dependent security policies. Dependent types can be used to represent rich security policies in environments like databases and data-centric web applications where, for example, new classes of users and new kinds of data are encountered at run-time and the security level depends on the manipulated data itself [23]. Such dependencies are not expressible in less expressive systems like **MAC**. Among other things, with dependent types, we can construct functions where the security level of the output depends on an argument:

```
getPassword : (u : Username) -> Labeled u String
```

Given a user name `u`, `getPassword` retrieves the corresponding password and classifies it at the security level of `u`. As such, we can express much more precise security policies that can depend on the manipulated data.

Idris is a general-purpose functional programming language with full-spectrum dependent types, that is, there is no restrictions on which values may appear in types. The language is strongly influenced by Haskell and has, among others, inherited its strict encapsulation of side-effects. Idris essentially asks the question: "What if Haskell had full dependent types?" [9]. This work, essentially, asks:

"What if **MAC** had full dependent types?"

We address this question using IDRIS because of its positioning as a general-purpose language rather than a proof assistant. All ideas should be portable to equally expressive systems with full dependent types and strict monadic encapsulation of side-effects.

In summary, the contributions of this paper are as follows.

- We present DEPSEC, a **MAC** inspired statically enforced dependently typed information-flow control library for IDRIS.
- We show how adding dependent types strictly increases the expressiveness of state-of-the-art static information-flow control libraries and how DEPSEC matches the expressiveness of a special-purpose dependent information-flow type system on a key example.
- We show how DEPSEC enables and aids the construction of policy-parameterized functions that abstract over the security policy.
- We show novel and powerful means to specify statically-ensured declassification using dependent types for a wide variety of policies.
- We show progress-insensitive noninterference [1] for the core library in a sequential setting.

Outline. The rest of the paper proceeds through a presentation of the DEPSEC library (Sect. 2); a conference manager case study (Sect. 3) and the introduction of policy-parameterized functions (Sect. 4) both showcasing the expressiveness of DEPSEC; means to specify statically-ensured declassification policies (Sect. 5); soundness of the core library (Sect. 6); and related work (Sect. 7).

All code snippets presented in the following are extracts from the source code. All source code is implemented in IDRIS 1.3.1. and available at

https://github.com/simongregersen/DepSec.

1.1 Assumptions and Threat Model

In the rest of this paper, we require that code is divided up into trusted code, written by someone we trust, and untrusted code, written by a potential attacker. The trusted computing base (TCB) has no restrictions, but untrusted code does not have access to modules providing input/output behavior, the data constructors of the domain specific language and a few specific functions related to declassification. In IDRIS, this means that we specifically do not allow access to `IO` functions and `unsafePerformIO`. In DEPSEC, constructors and functions marked with a TCB comment are inaccessible to untrusted code. Throughout the paper we will emphasize when this is the case.

We require that all definitions made by untrusted code are total, that is, defined for all possible inputs and are guaranteed to terminate. This is necessary if we want to trust proofs given by untrusted code. Otherwise, it could construct an element of the empty type from which it could prove anything:

```
empty : Void
empty = empty
```

In IDRIS, this can be checked using the `--total` compiler flag. Furthermore, we do not consider concurrency nor any internal or termination covert channels.

2 The DepSec Library

In information-flow control, labels are used to model the sensitivity of data. Such labels usually form a security lattice [14] where the induced partial ordering $\sqsubseteq$ specifies allowed flows of information and hence the security policy. For example, $\ell_1 \sqsubseteq \ell_2$ specifies that data with label ℓ_1 is allowed to flow to entities with label ℓ_2. In DepSec, labels are represented by values that form a verified join semilattice implemented as IDRIS interfaces[1]. That is, we require proofs of the lattice properties when defining an instance of `JoinSemilattice`.

```
interface JoinSemilattice a where
  join : a -> a -> a
  associative :
    (x, y, z : a) -> x `join` (y `join` z) = (x `join` y) `join` z
  commutative : (x, y : a)    -> x `join` y = y `join` x
  idempotent  : (x : a)       -> x `join` x = x
```

Dependent function types (often referred to as Π types) in IDRIS can express such requirements. If `A` is a type and `B` is a type indexed by a value of type `A` then `(x : A) -> B` is the type of functions that map arguments `x` of type `A` to values of type `B x`.

A lattice induces a partial ordering, which gives a direct way to express flow constraints. We introduce a verified partial ordering together with an implementation of this for `JoinSemilattice`. That is, to define an instance of the `Poset` interface we require a concrete instance of an associated data type `leq` as well as proofs of necessary algebraic properties of `leq`.

```
interface Poset a where
  leq : a -> a -> Type
  reflexive     : (x : a) -> x `leq` x
  antisymmetric : (x, y : a) -> x `leq` y -> y `leq` x -> x = y
  transitive    : (x, y, z : a) -> x `leq` y -> y `leq` z -> x `leq` z

implementation JoinSemilattice a => Poset a where
  leq x y = (x `join` y = y)
  ...
```

This definition allows for generic functions to impose as few restrictions as possible on the user while being able to exploit the algebraic structure in proofs, as will become evident in Sects. 3 and 4. For the sake of the following case studies, we also have a definition of a `BoundedJoinSemilattice` requiring a least element `Bottom` of an instance of `JoinSemilattice` and a proof of the element being the unit.

[1] Interfaces in IDRIS are similar to type classes in Haskell.

```
data Labeled : label -> Type -> Type where
  MkLabeled : valueType -> Labeled label valueType -- TCB

data DIO : l -> Type -> Type where
  MkDIO : IO valueType -> DIO l valueType -- TCB

Monad (DIO l) where
  ...

label : Poset label => {l : label} -> a -> Labeled l a

unlabel : Poset label => {l, l' : label}
       -> {auto flow : l `leq` l'}
       -> Labeled l a
       -> DIO l' a

plug : Poset label => {l, l' : label}
    -> DIO l' a
    -> {auto flow : l `leq` l'}
    -> DIO l (Labeled l' a)

run : DIO l a -> IO a -- TCB

lift : IO a -> DIO l a -- TCB
```

Fig. 1. Type signature of the core DEPSEC API.

The Core API. Figure 1 presents the type signature of DEPSEC's core API. Notice that names beginning with a lower case letter that appear as a parameter or index in a type declaration will be automatically bound as an implicit argument in IDRIS, and the `auto` annotation on implicit arguments means that IDRIS will attempt to fill in the implicit argument by searching the calling context for an appropriate value.

Abstract data type `Labeled` ℓ a denotes a value of type a with sensitivity level ℓ. We say that `Labeled` ℓ a is *indexed* by ℓ and *parameterized* by a. Abstract data type `DIO` ℓ a denotes a secure computation that handles values with sensitivity level ℓ and results in a value of type a. It is internally represented as a wrapper around the regular `IO` monad that, similar to the one in Haskell, can be thought of as a state monad where the state is the entire world. Notice that both data constructors `MkLabeled` and `MkDIO` are not available to untrusted code as this would allow pattern matching and uncontrolled unwrapping of protected entities. As a consequence, we introduce functions `label` and `unlabel` for labeling and unlabeling values. Like Rajani and Garg [33], but unlike **MAC**, the type signature of `label` imposes no lattice constraints on the computation context. This does not leak information as, if $l \sqsubseteq l'$ and a computation c has type `DIO` l' (`Labeled` l V) for any type V, then there is no way for the labeled return value of c to escape the computation context with label l'.

As in **MAC**, the API contains a function `plug` that safely integrates sensitive computations into less sensitive ones. This avoids the need for nested computations and *label creep*, that is, the raising of the current label to a point where the computation can no longer perform useful tasks [34,47]. Finally, we also have functions `run` and `lift` that are only available to trusted code for unwrapping of the `DIO` ℓ monad and lifting of the `IO` monad into the `DIO` ℓ monad.

Labeled Resources. Data type `Labeled` ℓ a is used to denote a labeled IDRIS value with type a. This is an example of a *labeled resource* [34]. By itself, the core library does not allow untrusted code to perform any side effects but we can safely incorporate, for example, file access and mutable references as other labeled resources. Figure 2 presents type signatures for files indexed by security levels used for secure file handling while mutable references are available in the accompanying source code. Abstract data type `SecFile` ℓ denotes a secure file with sensitivity level ℓ. As for `Labeled` ℓ a, the data constructor `MkSecFile` is not available to untrusted code.

The function `readFile` takes as input a secure file `SecFile l'` and returns a computation with sensitivity level `l` that returns a labeled value with sensitivity level `l'`. Notice that the `l` $\sqsubseteq$ `l'` flow constraint is required to enforce the *no read-up* policy [7]. That is, the result of the computation returned by `readFile` only involves data with sensitivity at most `l`. The function `writeFile` takes as input a secure file `SecFile l''` and a labeled value of sensitivity level `l'`, and it returns a computation with sensitivity level `l` that returns a labeled value with sensitivity level `l''`. Notice that both the `l` $\sqsubseteq$ `l'` and `l'` $\sqsubseteq$ `l''` flow constraints are required, essentially enforcing the *no write-down* policy [7], that is, the file never receives data more sensitive than its sensitivity level.

Finally, notice that the standard library functions for reading and writing files in IDRIS used to implement the functions in Fig. 2 do not raise exceptions. Rather, both functions return an instance of the sum type `Either`. We stay consistent with IDRIS' choice for this instead of adding exception handling as done in **MAC**.

```
data SecFile : {label : Type} -> (l : label) -> Type where
  MkSecFile : (path : String) -> SecFile l -- TCB

readFile : Poset label => {l,l' : label}
        -> {auto flow : l `leq` l'}
        -> SecFile l'
        -> DIO l (Labeled l' (Either FileError String))

writeFile : Poset label => {l,l',l'' : label}
         -> {auto flow : l `leq` l'} -> {auto flow' : l' `leq` l''}
         -> SecFile l''
         -> Labeled l' String
         -> DIO l (Labeled l'' (Either FileError ()))
```

Fig. 2. Type signatures for secure file handling.

3 Case Study: Conference Manager System

This case study showcases the expressiveness of DEPSEC by reimplementing a conference manager system with a fine-grained data-dependent security policy introduced by Lourenço and Caires [23]. Lourenço and Caires base their development on a minimal λ-calculus with references and collections and they show how secure operations on relevant scenarios can be modelled and analysed using *dependent information flow types*. Our reimplementation demonstrates how DEPSEC matches the expressiveness of such a special-purpose built dependent type system on a key example.

In this scenario, a user is either a regular user, an author user, or a program committee (PC) member. The conference manager contains information about the users, their submissions, and submission reviews. This data is stored in lists of references to records, and the goal is to statically ensure, by typing, the confidentiality of the data stored in the conference manager system. As such, the security policy is:

- A registered user's information is not observable by other users.
- The content of a paper can be seen by its authors as well as its reviewers.
- Comments to the PC of a submission's review can only be seen by other members that are also reviewers of that submission.
- The only authors that are allowed to see the grade and the review of the submission are those that authored that submission.

To achieve this security policy, Lourenço and Caires make use of indexed security labels [22]. The security level U is partitioned into a number of security compartments such that $U(uid)$ represents the compartment of the registered user with id uid. Similarly, the security level A is indexed such that $A(uid, sid)$ stands for the compartment of data belonging to author uid and their submission sid, and PC is indexed such that $PC(uid, sid)$ stands for data belonging to the PC member with user id uid assigned to review the submission with id sid. Furthermore, levels $\top$ and $\bot$ are introduced such that, for example, $U(\bot) \sqsubseteq U(uid) \sqsubseteq U(\top)$. Now, the security lattice is defined using two equations:

$$\forall uid, sid.\ U(uid) \sqsubseteq A(uid, sid) \tag{1}$$

$$\forall uid1, uid2, sid.\ A(uid1, sid) \sqsubseteq PC(uid2, sid) \tag{2}$$

Lourenço and Caires are able to type a list of submissions with a dependent sum type that assigns the content of the paper the security level $A(uid, sid)$, where uid and sid are fields of the record. For example, if a concrete submission with identifier 2 was made by the user with identifier 1, the content of the paper gets classified at security level $A(1, 2)$. In consequence, $A(1, 2) \sqsubseteq PC(n, 2)$ for any uid n and the content of the paper is only observable by its assigned reviewers. Similar types are given for the list of user information and the list of submission reviews, enforcing the security policy described in the above.

To express this policy in DEPSEC, we introduce abstract data types `Id` and `Compartment` (cf. Fig. 3) followed by an implementation of the `BoundedJoinSemilattice` interface that satisfies Eqs. (1) and (2).

```
data Id : Type where          data Compartment : Type where
  Top : Id                      U  : Id -> Compartment
  Nat : Nat -> Id               A  : Id -> Id -> Compartment
  Bot : Id                      PC : Id -> Id -> Compartment
```

Fig. 3. Abstract data types for the conference manager sample security lattice.

```
record User where
  constructor MkUser
  uid   : Id
  name  : Labeled (U uid) String
  univ  : Labeled (U uid) String
  email : Labeled (U uid) String

record Submission where
  constructor MkSubmission
  uid   : Id
  sid   : Id
  title : Labeled (A uid sid) String
  abs   : Labeled (A uid sid) String
  paper : Labeled (A uid sid) String

record Review where
  constructor MkReview
  uid     : Id
  sid     : Id
  PC_only : Labeled (PC uid sid) String
  review  : Labeled (A Top sid) String
  grade   : Labeled (A Top sid) Integer
```

Fig. 4. Conference manager types encoded with DepSec.

Using the above, the required dependent sum types can easily be encoded with DepSec in Idris as presented in Fig. 4. With these typings in place, implementing the examples from Lourenço and Caires [23] is straightforward. For example, the function `viewAuthorPapers` takes as input a list of submissions and a user identifier `uid1` from which it returns a computation that returns a list of submissions authored by the user with identifier `uid1`. Notice that `uid` denotes the automatically generated record projection function that retrieves the field `uid` of the record, and that `(x: A ** B)` is notation for a dependent pair (often referred to as a Σ type) where `A` and `B` are types and `B` may depend on `x`.

```
viewAuthorPapers : Submissions
                -> (uid1 : Id)
                -> DIO Bottom (List (sub : Submission ** uid1 = (uid sub)))
```

The `addCommentSubmission` operation is used by the PC members to add comments to the submissions. The function takes as input a list of reviews, a user identifier of a PC member, a submission identifier, and a comment with label `A uid1 sid1`. It returns a computation that updates the `PC_only` field in the review of the paper with identifier `sid1`.

```
addCommentSubmission : Reviews -> (uid1 : Id) -> (sid1 : Id)
                    -> Labeled (A uid1 sid1) String
                    -> DIO Bottom ()
```

Notice that to implement this specific type signature, up-classification is necessary to assign the comment with type `Labeled (A uid1 sid1) String` to a field with type `Labeled (PC uid sid1) String`. This can be achieved soundly with the `relabel` primitive introduced by Vassena et al. [47] as `A uid1 sid1` $\sqsubseteq$ `PC uid sid1`. We include this primitive in the accompanying source code together with several other examples. The entire case study amounts to about 300 lines of code where half of the lines implement and verify the lattice.

4 Policy-Parameterized Functions

A consequence of using a dependently typed language, and the design of DEPSEC, is that functions can be defined such that they abstract over the security policy while retaining precise security levels. This makes it possible to reuse code across different applications and write other libraries on top of DEPSEC. We can exploit the existence of a lattice `join`, the induced poset, and their verified algebraic properties to write such functions.

```
readTwoFiles : BoundedJoinSemilattice label
            => {l, l' : label}
            -> SecFile l
            -> SecFile l'
            -> DIO Bottom (Labeled (join l l') (Either FileError String))
readTwoFiles file1 file2 {l} {l'} =
  do file1' <- readFile {flow = leq_bot_x l} file1
     file2' <- readFile {flow = leq_bot_x l'} file2
     let dio : DIO (join l l') (Either FileError String)
       = do c1 <- unlabel {flow = join_x_xy l l'} file1'
            c2 <- unlabel {flow = join_y_xy l l'} file2'
            pure $ case (c1, c2) of
                        (Right c1', Right c2') => Right $ c1' ++ c2'
                        (Left e1, _) => Left e1
                        (_, Left e2) => Left e2
     plug {flow = leq_bot_x (join l l')} dio
```

Fig. 5. Reading two files to a string labeled with the join of the labels of the files.

Figure 5 presents the function `readTwoFiles` that is parameterized by a bounded join semilattice. It takes two secure files with labels `l` and `l'` as input and returns a computation that concatenates the contents of the two files labeled with the join of `l` and `l'`. To implement this, we make use of the `unlabel` and `readFile` primitives from Figs. 1 and 2, respectively. This computation unlabels the contents of the files and returns the concatenation of the contents if no file error occurred. Notice that `pure` is the IDRIS function for monadic return, corresponding to the `return` function in Haskell. Finally, this computation is plugged into the surrounding computation. Notice how the usage of `readFile` and `unlabel` introduces several proof obligations, namely $\bot \sqsubseteq$ `l`, `l'`, `l` $\sqcup$ `l'` and `l`, `l'` $\sqsubseteq$ `l` $\sqcup$ `l'`. When working on a concrete lattice these obligations are usually fulfilled by IDRIS' automatic proof search but, currently, such proofs need to be given manually in the general case. All obligations follow immediately from the algebraic properties of the bounded semilattice and are given in three auxiliary lemmas `leq_bot_x`, `join_x_xy`, and `join_y_xy` available in the accompanying source code (amounting to 10 lines of code).

Writing functions operating on a fixed number of resources is limiting. However, the function in Fig. 5 can easily be generalized to a function working on an arbitrary data structure containing files with different labels from an arbitrary lattice. Similar to the approach taken by Buiras et al. [11] that hide the label of a labeled value using a data type definition, we hide the label of a secure file with a dependent pair

```
GenFile : Type -> Type
GenFile label = (l : label ** SecFile l)
```

that abstracts away the concrete sensitivity level of the file. Moreover, we introduce a specialized join function

```
joinOfFiles : BoundedJoinSemilattice label
           => List (GenFile label)
           -> label
```

that folds the `join` function over a list of file sensitivity labels. Now, it is possible to implement a function that takes as input a list of files, reads the files, and returns a computation that concatenates all their contents (if no file error occurred) where the return value is labeled with the join of all their sensitivity labels.

```
readFiles : BoundedJoinSemilattice a
         => (files: (List (GenFile a)))
         -> DIO Bottom (Labeled (joinOfFiles files)
                                (Either (List FileError) String))
```

When implementing this, one has to satisfy non-trivial proof obligations as, for example, that $l \sqsubseteq$ `joinOfFiles(files)` for all secure files $f \in$ `files` where the label of f is l. While provable (in 40 lines of code in our development), if equality is decidable for elements of the concrete lattice we can postpone such proof obligations to a point in time where it can be solved by reflexivity of equality. By defining a decidable lattice order

```
decLeq : JoinSemilattice a => DecEq a => (x, y : a) -> Dec (x `leq` y)
decLeq x y = decEq (x `join` y) y
```

we can get such a proof "for free" by inserting a dynamic check of whether the flow is allowed. With this, a `readFiles'` function with the exact same functionality as the original `readFiles` function can be implemented with minimum effort. In the below, `prf` is the proof that the label `l` of `file` may flow to `joinOfFiles files`.

```
readFiles' : BoundedJoinSemilattice a => DecEq a
          => (files: (List (GenFile a)))
          -> DIO Bottom (Labeled (joinOfFiles files)
                         (Either (List FileError) String))
readFiles' files =
  ...
  case decLeq l (joinOfFiles files) of
    Yes prf => ...
    No _ => ...
```

The downside of this is the introduction of a negative case, the `No`-case, that needs handling even though it will never occur if `joinOfFiles` is implemented correctly.

In combination with `GenFile`, `decLeq` can be used to implement several other interesting examples. For instance, a function that reads all files with a sensitivity label below a certain label to a string labeled with that label. The accompanying source code showcases multiple such examples that exploit decidable equality.

5 Declassification

Realistic applications often release some secret information as part of their intended behavior; this action is known as *declassification.*

In DEPSEC, trusted code may declassify secret information without adhering to any security policy as trusted code has access to both the `DIO` ℓ a and `Labeled` ℓ a data constructors. However, only giving trusted code the power of declassification is limiting as we want to allow the use of third-party code as much as possible. The main challenge we address is how to grant untrusted code the right amount of power such that declassification is only possible in the intended way.

Sabelfeld and Sands [38] identify four dimensions of declassification: *what*, *who*, *where*, and *when*. In this section, we present novel and powerful means for static declassification with respect to three of the four dimensions and illustrate these with several examples. To statically enforce different declassification policies we take the approach of Sabelfeld and Myers [37] and use escape hatches, a special kind of functions. In particular, we introduce the notion of a *hatch builder*; a function that creates an escape hatch for a particular resource and which can only be used when a certain condition is met. Such an escape hatch can therefore be used freely by untrusted code.

5.1 The *what* Dimension

Declassification policies related to the *what* dimension place restrictions on exactly "what" and "how much" information is released. It is in general difficult to statically predict how data to be declassified is manipulated or changed by programs [35] but exploiting dependent types can get us one step closer.

To control what information is released, we introduce the notion of a *predicate hatch builder* only available to trusted code for producing hatches for untrusted code.

```
predicateHatchBuilder : Poset lt => {l, l' : lt} -> {D, E : Type}
                     -> (d : D)
                     -> (P : D -> E -> Type)
                     -> (d : D ** Labeled l (e : E ** P d e)
                                -> Labeled l' E) -- TCB
```

Intuitively, the hatch builder takes as input a data structure `d` of type `D` followed by a predicate `P` upon `d` and something of type `E`. It returns a dependent pair of the initial data structure and a declassification function from sensitivity level `l` to `l'`. To actually declassify a labeled value `e` of type `E` one has to provide a proof that `P d e` holds. Notice that this proof may be constructed in the context of the sensitivity level `l` that we are declassifying from.

The reason for parameterizing the predicate `P` by a data structure of type `D` is to allow declassification to be restricted to a specific context or data structure. This is used in the following example of an auction system, in which only the highest bid of a specific list of bids can be declassified.

Example. Consider a two point lattice where $\mathtt{L} \sqsubseteq \mathtt{H}$, $\mathtt{H} \not\sqsubseteq \mathtt{L}$ and an auction system where participants place bids secretly. All bids are labeled `H` and are put into a data structure `BidLog`. In the end, we want only the winning bid to be released and hence declassified to label `L`. To achieve this, we define a declassification predicate `HighestBid`.

```
HighestBid : BidLog -> Bid -> Type
HighestBid = \log, b => (Elem (label b) log, MaxBid b log)
```

Informally, given a log `log` of labeled bids and a bid `b`, the predicate states that the bid is in the log, `Elem (label b) log`, and that it is the maximum bid, `MaxBid b log`. We apply `predicateHatchBuilder` to a log of bids and the `HighestBid` predicate to obtain a specialized escape hatch of type `BidHatch` that enforces the declassification policy defined by the predicate.

```
BidHatch : Type
BidHatch = (log : BidLog ** Labeled H (b : Bid ** HighestBid log b)
                             -> Labeled L Bid)
```

This hatch can be used freely by untrusted code when implementing the auction system. By constructing a function

```
getMaxBid : (r : BidLog) -> DIO H (b : Bid ** HighestBid r b)
```

untrusted code can plug the resulting computation into an `L` context and declassify the result value using the argument `hatch` function.

```
auction : BidHatch -> DIO L (Labeled L Bid)
auction ([] ** _) = pure $ label ("no bids", 0)
auction (r :: rs ** hatch) =
  do max <- plug (getMaxBid (r :: rs))
     let max' : Labeled L Bid = hatch max
     ...
```

To show the HighestBid predicate (which in our implementation comprises 40 lines of code), untrusted code will need a generalized unlabel function that establishes the relationship between label and the output of unlabel. The only difference is its return type: a computation that returns a value and a proof that when labeling this value we will get back the initial input. This definition poses no risk to soundness as the proof is protected by the computation sensitivity level.

```
unlabel' : Poset lt => {l,l': lt}
        -> {auto flow: l `leq` l'}
        -> (labeled: Labeled l a)
        -> DIO l' (c : a ** label c = labeled)
```

Limiting Hatch Usage. Notice how escape hatches, generally, can be used an indefinite number of times. The `Control.ST` library [10] provides facilities for creating, reading, writing, and destroying state in the type of IDRIS functions and, especially, allows tracking of state change in a function type. This allows us to limit the number of times a hatch can be used. Based on a concept of resources, a dependent type STrans tracks how resources change when a function is invoked. Specifically, a value of type `STrans m returnType in_res out_res` represents a sequence of actions that manipulate state where `m` is an underlying computation context in which the actions will be executed, `returnType` is the return type of the sequence, `in_res` is the required list of resources available before executing the sequence, and `out_res` is the list of resources available after executing the sequence.

To represent state transitions more directly, ST is a type level function that computes an appropriate STrans type given a underlying computation context, a result type, and a list of *actions*, which describe transitions on resources. Actions can take multiple forms but the one we will make use of is of the form `lbl ::: ty_in :-> ty_out` that expresses that the resource `lbl` begins in state `ty_in` and ends in state `ty_out`. By instantiating ST with `DIO l` as the underlying computation context:

```
DIO' : l -> (ty : Type) -> List (Action ty) -> Type
DIO' l = ST (DIO l)
```

and use it together with a resource Attempts, we can create a function limit that applies its first argument `f` to its second argument `arg` with `Attempts (S n)` as its initial required state and `Attempts n` as the output state.

```
limit : (f : a -> b) -> (arg : a)
     -> DIO' l b [attempts ::: Attempts (S n) :-> Attempts n]
```

That is, we encode that the function consumes "an attempt." With the limit function it is possible to create functions where users are forced, by typing, to specify how many times it is used.

As an example, consider a variant of an example by Russo et al. [35] where we construct a specialized hatch passwordHatch that declassifies the boolean comparison of a secret number with an arbitrary number.

```
passwordHatch : (labeled : Labeled H Int)
              -> (guess : Int)
              -> DIO' l Bool [attempts ::: Attempts (S n) :-> Attempts n]
passwordHatch (MkLabeled v) = limit (\g => g == v)
```

To use this hatch, untrusted code is forced to specify how many times it is used.

```
pwCheck : Labeled H Int
       -> DIO' L () [attempts ::: Attempts (3 + n) :-> Attempts n]
pwCheck pw =
  do x1 <- passwordHatch pw 1
     x2 <- passwordHatch pw 2
     x3 <- passwordHatch pw 3
     x4 <- passwordHatch pw 4 -- type error!
     ...
```

5.2 The *who* and *when* Dimensions

To handle declassification policies related to *who* may declassify information and *when* declassification may happen we introduce the notion of a *token hatch builder* only available to trusted code for producing hatches for untrusted code to use.

```
tokenHatchBuilder : Poset labelType => {l, l' : labelType} -> {E, S : Type}
                 -> (Q : S -> Type)
                 -> (s : S ** Q s) -> Labeled l E -> Labeled l' E -- TCB
```

The hatch builder takes as input a predicate `Q` on something of type `S` and returns a declassification function from sensitivity level `l` to `l'` given that the user can prove the existence of some `s` such that `Q s` holds. As such, by limiting when and how untrusted can obtain a value that satisfy predicate `Q`, we can construct several interesting declassification policies.

The rest of this section discusses how predicate hatches can be used for time-based and authority-based control of declassification; the use of the latter is demonstrated on a case study.

Time-Based Hatches. To illustrate the idea of token hatches for the *when* dimension of declassification, consider the following example. Let `Time` be an abstract data type with a data constructor only available to trusted code and `tick : DIO l Time` a function that returns the current system time wrapped in the `Time` data type such that this is the only way for untrusted code to construct anything of type `Time`. Notice that this does not expose an unrestricted timer API as untrusted code can not inspect the actual value.

Now, we instantiate the token hatch builder with a predicate that demands the existence of a `Time` token that is greater than some specific value.

```
TimeHatch : Time -> Type
TimeHatch t = (t' ** t <= t' = True) -> Labeled H Nat -> Labeled L Nat
```

As such, `TimeHatch t` can only be used after a specific point in time `t` has passed as only then untrusted code will be able to satisfy the predicate.

```
timer : Labeled H Nat -> TimeHatch t -> DIO L ()
timer secret {t} timeHatch =
  do time <- tick
     case decEq (t <= time) True of
       Yes prf =>
         let declassified : Labeled L Nat = timeHatch (time ** prf) secret
         ...
       No _ => ...
```

Authority-Based Hatches. The *Decentralized Labeling Model* (DLM) [27] marks data with a set of principals who owns the information. While executing a program, the program is given *authority*, that is, it is authorized to act on behalf of some set of principals. Declassification simply makes a copy of the released data and marks it with the same set of principals but excludes the authorities.

Similarly to Russo et al. [35], we adapt this idea such that it works on a security lattice of `Principal`s, assign authorities with security levels from the lattice, and let authorities declassify information at that security level.

To model this, we define the abstract data type `Authority` with a data constructor available only to trusted code so that having an instance of `Authority s` corresponds to having the authority of the principal `s`. Notice how assignment of authorities to pieces of code consequently is a part of the trusted code. Now, we instantiate the token hatch builder with a predicate that demands the authority of `s` to declassify information at that level.

```
authHatch : { l, l' : Principal }
         -> (s ** (l = s, Authority s))
         -> Labeled l a -> Labeled l' a
authHatch {l} = tokenHatchBuilder (\s => (l = s, Authority s))
```

That is, `authHatch` makes it possible to declassify information at level `l` to `l'` given an instance of the `Authority l` data type.

Example. Consider the scenario of an online dating service that has the distinguishing feature of allowing its users to specify the visibility of their profiles at a fine-grained level. To achieve this, the service allows users to provide a *discovery agent* that controls their visibility. Consider a user, Bob, whose implementation of the discovery agent takes as input his own profile and the profile of another user, say Alice. The agent returns a possibly side-effectful computation that returns an option type indicating whether Bob wants to be discovered by Alice. If that is the case, a profile is returned by the computation with the information about Bob that he wants Alice to be able to see. When Alice searches for candidate matches, her profile is run against the discovery agents of all candidates and the result is added to her browsing queue.

To implement this dating service, we define the record type `ProfileInfo A` that contains personal information related to principal `A`.

```
record ProfileInfo (A : Principal) where
  constructor MkProfileInfo
  name      : Labeled A String
  gender    : Labeled A String
  birthdate : Labeled A String
  ...
```

The interesting part of the dating service is the implementation of discovery agents. Figure 6 presents a sample discovery agent that matches all profiles with the opposite gender and only releases information about the name and gender. The discovery agent demands the authority of `A` and takes as input two profiles `a : ProfileInfo A` and `b : ProfileInfo B`. The resulting computation security level is `B` so to incorporate information from `a` into the result, declassification is needed. This is achieved by providing `authHatch` with the authority proof of `A`. The discovery agent `sampleDiscoverer` in Fig. 6 unlabels `B`'s gender, declassifies and unlabels `A`'s gender and name, and compares the two genders. If the genders match, a profile with type `ProfileInfo B` only containing the name and gender of `A` is returned. Otherwise, `Nothing` is returned indicating that `A` does not want to be discovered. Notice that `Refl` is the constructor for the built-in equality type in IDRIS and it is used to construct the proof of equality between principals required by the hatch.

```
sampleDiscoverer : {A, B : Principal}
                 -> Authority A
                 -> (a : ProfileInfo A)
                 -> (b : ProfileInfo B)
                 -> DIO B (Maybe (ProfileInfo B))
sampleDiscoverer {A} {B} auth a b =
  do bGender <- unlabel $ gender b
     aGender <- unlabel $ authHatch (A ** (Refl, auth)) (gender a)
     aName <- unlabel $ authHatch (A ** (Refl, auth)) (name a)
     case decEq bGender aGender of
       Yes _ => pure Nothing
       No _  => pure (Just (MkProfileInfo aName aGender "" "" ""))
```

Fig. 6. A discovery agent that matches with all profiles of the opposite gender and only releases the name and gender.

6 Soundness

Recent works [46,47] present a mechanically-verified model of **MAC** and show progress-insensitive noninterference (PINI) for a sequential calculus. We use this work as a starting point and discuss necessary modification in the following. Notice that this work does not consider any declassification mechanisms and neither do we; we leave this as future work.

The proof relies on the *two-steps erasure* technique, an extension of the *term erasure* [21] technique that ensures that the same public output is produced if secrets are erased before or after program execution. The technique relies on a type-driven erasure function ε_{ℓ_A} on terms and configurations where ℓ_A denotes the attacker security level. A configuration consists of an ℓ-indexed compartmentalized store Σ and a term t. A configuration $\langle \Sigma, t \rangle$ is erased by erasing t and by erasing Σ pointwise, i.e. $\varepsilon_{\ell_A}(\Sigma) = \lambda \ell . \varepsilon_{\ell_A}(\Sigma(\ell))$. On terms, the function essentially rewrites data and computations above ℓ_A to a special $\bullet$ value. The full definition of the erasure function is available in the full version of this paper [15]. From this definition, the definition of low-equivalence of configurations follows.

Definition 1. *Let c_1 and c_2 be configurations. c_1 and c_2 are said to be ℓ_A-equivalent, written $c_1 \approx_{\ell_A} c_2$, if and only if $\varepsilon_{\ell_A}(c_1) \equiv \varepsilon_{\ell_A}(c_2)$.*

After defining the erasure function, the noninterference theorem follows from showing a *single-step simulation* relationship between the erasure function and a small-step reduction relation: erasing sensitive data from a configuration and then taking a step is the same as first taking a step and then erasing sensitive data. This is the content of the following proposition.

Proposition 1. *If $c_1 \approx_{\ell_A} c_2$, $c_1 \to c_1'$, and $c_2 \to c_2'$ then $c_1' \approx_{\ell_A} c_2'$.*

The main theorem follows by repeated applications of Proposition 1.

Theorem 1 (PINI). *If $c_1 \approx_{\ell_A} c_2$, $c_1 \Downarrow c_1'$, and $c_2 \Downarrow c_2'$ then $c_1' \approx_{\ell_A} c_2'$.*

Both the statement and the proof of noninterference for DepSec are mostly similar to the ones for **MAC** and available in the full version of this paper [15]. Nevertheless, one has to be aware of a few subtleties.

First, one has to realize that even though dependent types in a language like Idris may depend on data, the data itself is not a part of a value of a dependent type. Recall the type `Vect n Nat` of vectors of length `n` with components of type `Nat` and consider the following program.

```
length : Vect n a -> Nat
length {n = n} xs = n
```

This example may lead one to believe that it is possible to extract data from a dependent type. This is *not* the case. Both `n` and `a` are implicit arguments to the `length` function that the compiler is able to infer. The actual type is

```
length : {n : Nat} -> {a : Type} -> Vect n a -> Nat
```

As a high-level dependently typed functional programming language, Idris is elaborated to a low-level core language based on dependent type theory [9]. In the elaboration process, such implicit arguments are made explicit when functions are defined and inferred when functions are invoked. This means that in the underlying core language, only explicit arguments are given. Our modeling given in the full version of this paper reflects this fact soundly.

Second, to model the extended expressiveness of DepSec, we extend both the semantics and the type system with compile-time pure-term reduction and higher-order dependent types. These definitions are standard (defined for IDRIS by Brady [9]) and available in the full version of our paper. Moreover, as types now become first-class terms, the definition of ε_{ℓ_A} has to be extended to cover the new kinds of terms. As before, primitive types are unaffected by the erasure function, but dependent and indexed types, such as the type `DIO`, have to be erased homomorphically, e.g., ε_{ℓ_A} (`DIO` ℓ τ : `Type`) $\triangleq$ `DIO` $\varepsilon_{\ell_A}(\ell)$ $\varepsilon_{\ell_A}(\tau)$. The intuition of why this is sensible comes from the observation that indexed dependent types considered as terms may contain values that will have to be erased. This is purely a technicality of the proof. If defined otherwise, the erasure function would not commute with capture-avoiding substitution on terms, $\varepsilon_{\ell_A}(t[v/x]) = \varepsilon_{\ell_A}(t)[\varepsilon_{\ell_A}(v)/x]$, which is vital for the remaining proof.

7 Related Work

Security Libraries. The pioneering and formative work by Li and Zdancewic [20] shows how *arrows* [18], a generalization of monads, can provide information-flow control without runtime checks as a library in Haskell. Tsai et al. [45] further extend this work to handle side-effects, concurrency, and heterogeneous labels. Russo et al. [35] eliminate the need for arrows and implement the security library **SecLib** in Haskell based solely on monads. Rather than labeled values, this work introduces a monad which statically label side-effect free values. Furthermore, it presents combinators to dynamically specify and enforce declassification policies that bear a resemblance to the policies that DEPSEC are able to enforce statically.

The security library **LIO** [41,42] dynamically enforces information-flow control in both sequential and concurrent settings. Stefan et al. [40] extend the security guarantees of this work to also cover exceptions. Similar to this work, Stefan et al. [42] present a simple API for implementing secure conference reviewing systems in **LIO** with support for data-dependent security policies.

Inspired by the design of **SecLib** and **LIO**, Russo [34] introduces the security library **MAC**. The library statically enforces information-flow control in the presence of advanced features like exceptions, concurrency, and mutable data structures by exploiting Haskell's type system to impose flow constraints. Vassena and Russo [46], Vassena et al. [47] show progress-insensitive noninterference for **MAC** in a sequential setting and progress-sensitive noninterference in a concurrent setting, both using the two-steps erasure technique.

The flow constraints enforcing confidentiality of read and write operations in DEPSEC are identical to those of **MAC**. This means that the examples from **MAC** that do not involve concurrency can be ported directly to DEPSEC. To the best of our knowledge, data-dependent security policies like the one presented in Sect. 3 cannot be expressed and enforced in **MAC**, unlike **LIO** that allows such policies to be enforced dynamically. DEPSEC allows for such security policies to be enforced statically. Moreover, Russo [34] does not consider declassification. To address the static limitations of **MAC**, **HLIO** [11] takes a hybrid approach by exploiting advanced features in Haskell's type-system like singleton types and constraint polymorphism. Buiras et al. [11] are able to statically enforce information-flow control while allowing selected security checks to be deferred until run-time.

Dependent Types for Security. Several works have considered the use of dependent types to capture the nature of data-dependent security policies. Zheng and Myers [51,52] proposed the first dependent security type system for dealing with dynamic changes to runtime security labels in the context of Jif [29], a full-fledged IFC-aware compiler for Java programs, where similar to our work, operations on labels are modeled at the level of types. Zhang et al. [50] use dependent types in a similar fashion for the design of a hardware description language for timing-sensitive information-flow security.

A number of functional languages have been developed with dependent type systems and used to encode value-dependent information flow properties, e.g. Fine [43]. These approaches require the adoption of entirely new languages and compilers where DEPSEC is embedded in an already existing language. Morgenstern and Licata [25] encode an authorization and IFC-aware programming language in Agda. However, their encoding does not consider side-effects. Nanevski et al. [30] use dependent types to verify information flow and access control policies in an interactive manner.

Lourenço and Caires [23] introduce the notion of *dependent information-flow types* and propose a *fine-grained* type system; every value and function have an associated security level. Their approach is different to the *coarse-grained* approach taken in our work where only some computations and values have associated security labels. Rajani and Garg [33] show that both approaches are equally expressive for static IFC techniques and Vassena et al. [48] show the same for dynamic IFC techniques.

Principles for Information Flow. Bastys et al. [6] put forward a set of informal principles for information flow security definitions and enforcement mechanisms: *attacker-driven security, trust-aware enforcement, separation of policy annotations and code, language-independence, justified abstraction, and permissiveness.*

DEPSEC follows the principle of trust-aware enforcement, as we make clear the boundary between the trusted and untrusted components in the program. Additionally, the design of our declassification mechanism follows the principle of separation of policy annotations and code. The use of dependent types increases the permissiveness of our enforcement as we discuss throughout the paper. While our approach is not fully language-independent, we posit that the approach may be ported to other programming languages with general-purpose dependent types.

Declassification Enforcement. Our hatch builders are reminiscent of downgrading policies of Li and Zdancewic [19]. For example, similar to them, DEPSEC's declassification policies naturally express the idea of *delimited release* [36] that provides explicit characterization of the declassifying computation. Here, DEPSEC's policies can express a broad range of policies that can be expressed through predicates, an improvement over simple expression-based enforcement mechanisms for delimited release [4,5,36].

An interesting point in the design of declassification policies is *robust declassification* [49] that demands that untrusted components must not affect information release. *Qualified robustness* [2,28] generalizes this notion by giving untrusted code a limited ability to affect information release through the introduction of an explicit endorsement operation. Our approach is orthogonal to both notions of robustness as the intent is to let the untrusted components declassify information but only under very controlled circumstances while adhering to the security policy.

8 Conclusion and Future Work

In this paper, we have presented DepSec – a library for statically enforced information-flow control in Idris. Through several case studies, we have showcased how the DepSec primitives increase the expressiveness of state-of-the-art information-flow control libraries and how DepSec matches the expressiveness of a special-purpose dependent information-flow type system on a key example. Moreover, the library allows programmers to implement policy-parameterized functions that abstract over the security policy while retaining precise security levels.

By taking ideas from the literature and by exploiting dependent types, we have shown powerful means of specifying statically enforced declassification policies related to *what*, *who*, and *when* information is released. Specifically, we have introduced the notion of predicate hatch builders and token hatch builders that rely on the fulfillment of predicates and possession of tokens for declassification. We have also shown how the `ST` monad [10] can be used to limit hatch usage statically.

Finally, we have discussed the necessary means to show progress-insensitive noninterference in a sequential setting for a dependently typed information-flow control library like DepSec.

Future Work. There are several avenues for further work. Integrity is vital in many security policies and is not considered in **MAC** nor DepSec. It will be interesting to take integrity and the presence of concurrency into the dependently typed setting and consider internal and termination covert channels as well. It also remains to prove our declassification mechanisms sound. Here, attacker-centric epistemic security conditions [3,16] that intuitively express many declassification policies may be a good starting point.

Acknowledgements. Thanks are due to Mathias Vorreiter Pedersen, Bas Spitters, Alejandro Russo, and Marco Vassena for their valuable insights and the anonymous reviewers for their comments on this paper. This work is partially supported by DFF project 6108-00363 from The Danish Council for Independent Research for the Natural Sciences (FNU), Aarhus University Research Foundation, and the Concordium Blockchain Research Center, Aarhus University, Denmark.

References

1. Askarov, A., Hunt, S., Sabelfeld, A., Sands, D.: Termination-insensitive noninterference leaks more than just a bit. In: Jajodia, S., Lopez, J. (eds.) ESORICS 2008. LNCS, vol. 5283, pp. 333–348. Springer, Heidelberg (2008). https://doi.org/10.1007/978-3-540-88313-5_22
2. Askarov, A., Myers, A.C.: Attacker control and impact for confidentiality and integrity. Log. Methods Comput. Sci. **7**(3) (2011). https://doi.org/10.2168/LMCS-7(3:17)2011
3. Askarov, A., Sabelfeld, A.: Gradual release: unifying declassification, encryption and key release policies. In: 2007 IEEE Symposium on Security and Privacy (S&P 2007), Oakland, California, USA, 20–23 May 2007, pp. 207–221. IEEE Computer Society (2007). https://doi.org/10.1109/SP.2007.22
4. Askarov, A., Sabelfeld, A.: Localized delimited release: combining the what and where dimensions of information release. In: Hicks, M.W. (ed.) Proceedings of the 2007 Workshop on Programming Languages and Analysis for Security, PLAS 2007, San Diego, California, USA, 14 June 2007, pp. 53–60. ACM (2007). https://doi.org/10.1145/1255329.1255339
5. Askarov, A., Sabelfeld, A.: Tight enforcement of information-release policies for dynamic languages. In: Proceedings of the 22nd IEEE Computer Security Foundations Symposium, CSF 2009, Port Jefferson, New York, USA, 8–10 July 2009, pp. 43–59. IEEE Computer Society (2009). https://doi.org/10.1109/CSF.2009.22
6. Bastys, I., Piessens, F., Sabelfeld, A.: Prudent design principles for information flow control. In: Proceedings of the 13th Workshop on Programming Languages and Analysis for Security, pp. 17–23. ACM (2018)
7. Bell, D.E., La Padula, L.J.: Secure computer system: unified exposition and multics interpretation. Technical report. MITRE Corp., Bedford, MA (1976)
8. Brady, E.: IDRIS—systems programming meets full dependent types. In: Jhala, R., Swierstra, W. (eds.) Proceedings of the 5th ACM Workshop Programming Languages meets Program Verification, PLPV 2011, Austin, TX, USA, 29 January 2011, pp. 43–54. ACM (2011). https://doi.org/10.1145/1929529.1929536
9. Brady, E.: Idris, a general-purpose dependently typed programming language: design and implementation. J. Funct. Program. **23**(5), 552–593 (2013). https://doi.org/10.1017/S095679681300018X
10. Brady, E.: State machines all the way down, January 2016. http://idris-lang.org/drafts/sms.pdf
11. Buiras, P., Vytiniotis, D., Russo, A.: HLIO: mixing static and dynamic typing for information-flow control in Haskell. In: Fisher, K., Reppy, J.H. (eds.) Proceedings of the 20th ACM SIGPLAN International Conference on Functional Programming, ICFP 2015, Vancouver, BC, Canada, 1–3 September 2015, pp. 289–301. ACM (2015). https://doi.org/10.1145/2784731.2784758
12. Chapman, R., Hilton, A.: Enforcing security and safety models with an information flow analysis tool. In: McCormick, J.W., Sward, R.E. (eds.) Proceedings of the 2004 Annual ACM SIGAda International Conference on Ada: The Engineering of Correct and Reliable Software for Real-Time & Distributed Systems Using Ada and Related Technologies 2004, Atlanta, GA, USA, 14 November 2004, pp. 39–46. ACM (2004). https://doi.org/10.1145/1032297.1032305
13. Coquand, T., Huet, G.P.: The calculus of constructions. Inf. Comput. **76**(2/3), 95–120 (1988). https://doi.org/10.1016/0890-5401(88)90005-3

14. Denning, D.E., Denning, P.J.: Certification of programs for secure information flow. Commun. ACM **20**(7), 504–513 (1977). https://doi.org/10.1145/359636.359712
15. Gregersen, S., Thomsen, S.E., Askarov, A.: A dependently typed library for static information-flow control in Idris (2019). arXiv:1902.06590
16. Halpern, J.Y., O'Neill, K.R.: Secrecy in multiagent systems. ACM Trans. Inf. Syst. Secur. **12**(1), 5:1–5:47 (2008). https://doi.org/10.1145/1410234.1410239
17. Hedin, D., Birgisson, A., Bello, L., Sabelfeld, A.: JSFlow: tracking information flow in Javascript and its APIs. In: Cho, Y., Shin, S.Y., Kim, S., Hung, C., Hong, J. (eds.) Symposium on Applied Computing, SAC 2014, Gyeongju, Republic of Korea, 24–28 March 2014, pp. 1663–1671. ACM (2014). https://doi.org/10.1145/2554850.2554909
18. Hughes, J.: Generalising monads to arrows. Sci. Comput. Program. **37**(1–3), 67–111 (2000). https://doi.org/10.1016/S0167-6423(99)00023-4
19. Li, P., Zdancewic, S.: Downgrading policies and relaxed noninterference. In: Palsberg, J., Abadi, M. (eds.) Proceedings of the 32nd ACM SIGPLAN-SIGACT Symposium on Principles of Programming Languages, POPL 2005, Long Beach, California, USA, 12–14 January 2005, pp. 158–170. ACM (2005). https://doi.org/10.1145/1040305.1040319
20. Li, P., Zdancewic, S.: Encoding information flow in Haskell. In: 19th IEEE Computer Security Foundations Workshop (CSFW-19 2006), Venice, Italy, 5–7 July 2006, p. 16. IEEE Computer Society (2006). https://doi.org/10.1109/CSFW.2006.13
21. Li, P., Zdancewic, S.: Arrows for secure information flow. Theor. Comput. Sci. **411**(19), 1974–1994 (2010). https://doi.org/10.1016/j.tcs.2010.01.025
22. Liu, J., George, M.D., Vikram, K., Qi, X., Waye, L., Myers, A.C.: Fabric: a platform for secure distributed computation and storage. In: Matthews, J.N., Anderson, T.E. (eds.) Proceedings of the 22nd ACM Symposium on Operating Systems Principles 2009, SOSP 2009, Big Sky, Montana, USA, 11–14 October 2009, pp. 321–334. ACM (2009). https://doi.org/10.1145/1629575.1629606
23. Lourenço, L., Caires, L.: Dependent information flow types. In: Rajamani, S.K., Walker, D. (eds.) Proceedings of the 42nd Annual ACM SIGPLAN-SIGACT Symposium on Principles of Programming Languages, POPL 2015, Mumbai, India, 15–17 January 2015, pp. 317–328. ACM (2015). https://doi.org/10.1145/2676726.2676994
24. Martin-Löf, P., Sambin, G.: Intuitionistic Type Theory, vol. 9. Bibliopolis, Naples (1984)
25. Morgenstern, J., Licata, D.R.: Security-typed programming within dependently typed programming. In: Hudak, P., Weirich, S. (eds.) Proceeding of the 15th ACM SIGPLAN International Conference on Functional Programming, ICFP 2010, Baltimore, Maryland, USA, 27–29 September 2010, pp. 169–180. ACM (2010). https://doi.org/10.1145/1863543.1863569
26. Myers, A.C.: JFlow: practical mostly-static information flow control. In: Appel, A.W., Aiken, A. (eds.) Proceedings of the 26th ACM SIGPLAN-SIGACT Symposium on Principles of Programming Languages, POPL 1999, San Antonio, TX, USA, 20–22 January 1999, pp. 228–241. ACM (1999). https://doi.org/10.1145/292540.292561
27. Myers, A.C., Liskov, B.: Protecting privacy using the decentralized label model. ACM Trans. Softw. Eng. Methodol. **9**(4), 410–442 (2000). https://doi.org/10.1145/363516.363526

28. Myers, A.C., Sabelfeld, A., Zdancewic, S.: Enforcing robust declassification. In: 17th IEEE Computer Security Foundations Workshop (CSFW-17 2004), Pacific Grove, CA, USA, 28–30 June 2004, pp. 172–186. IEEE Computer Society (2004). https://doi.org/10.1109/CSFW.2004.9
29. Myers, A.C., Zheng, L., Zdancewic, S., Chong, S., Nystrom, N.: Jif 3.0: Java information flow, July 2006
30. Nanevski, A., Banerjee, A., Garg, D.: Verification of information flow and access control policies with dependent types. In: 32nd IEEE Symposium on Security and Privacy, S&P 2011, Berkeley, California, USA, 22–25 May 2011, pp. 165–179. IEEE Computer Society (2011). https://doi.org/10.1109/SP.2011.12
31. Nordström, B., Petersson, K., Smith, J.M.: Programming in Martin-Löf's Type Theory: An Introduction. Clarendon Press, New York (1990)
32. Norell, U.: Towards a Practical Programming Language Based on Dependent Type Theory, vol. 32. Citeseer (2007)
33. Rajani, V., Garg, D.: Types for information flow control: labeling granularity and semantic models. In: 31st IEEE Computer Security Foundations Symposium, CSF 2018, Oxford, United Kingdom, 9–12 July 2018, pp. 233–246. IEEE Computer Society (2018). https://doi.org/10.1109/CSF.2018.00024
34. Russo, A.: Functional pearl: two can keep a secret, if one of them uses Haskell. In: Proceedings of the 20th ACM SIGPLAN International Conference on Functional Programming, ICFP 2015, Vancouver, BC, Canada, 1–3 September 2015, pp. 280–288 (2015). https://doi.org/10.1145/2784731.2784756
35. Russo, A., Claessen, K., Hughes, J.: A library for light-weight information-flow security in Haskell. In: Gill, A. (ed.) Proceedings of the 1st ACM SIGPLAN Symposium on Haskell, Haskell 2008, Victoria, BC, Canada, 25 September 2008, pp. 13–24. ACM (2008). https://doi.org/10.1145/1411286.1411289
36. Sabelfeld, A., Myers, A.C.: Language-based information-flow security. IEEE J. Sel. Areas Commun. **21**(1), 5–19 (2003). https://doi.org/10.1109/JSAC.2002.806121
37. Sabelfeld, A., Myers, A.C.: A model for delimited information release. In: Futatsugi, K., Mizoguchi, F., Yonezaki, N. (eds.) ISSS 2003. LNCS, vol. 3233, pp. 174–191. Springer, Heidelberg (2004). https://doi.org/10.1007/978-3-540-37621-7_9
38. Sabelfeld, A., Sands, D.: Dimensions and principles of declassification. In: 18th IEEE Computer Security Foundations Workshop (CSFW-18 2005), Aix-en-Provence, France, 20–22 June 2005, pp. 255–269. IEEE Computer Society (2005). https://doi.org/10.1109/CSFW.2005.15
39. Simonet, V.: Flow Caml in a nutshell. In: Hutton, G. (ed.) Proceedings of the first APPSEM-II Workshop, Nottingham, United Kingdom, March 2003
40. Stefan, D., Mazières, D., Mitchell, J.C., Russo, A.: Flexible dynamic information flow control in the presence of exceptions. J. Funct. Program. **27**, e5 (2017). https://doi.org/10.1017/S0956796816000241
41. Stefan, D., Russo, A., Buiras, P., Levy, A., Mitchell, J.C., Mazières, D.: Addressing covert termination and timing channels in concurrent information flow systems. In: Thiemann, P., Findler, R.B. (eds.) ACM SIGPLAN International Conference on Functional Programming, ICFP 2012, Copenhagen, Denmark, 9–15 September 2012, pp. 201–214. ACM (2012). https://doi.org/10.1145/2364527.2364557
42. Stefan, D., Russo, A., Mitchell, J.C., Mazières, D.: Flexible dynamic information flow control in Haskell. In: Claessen, K. (ed.) Proceedings of the 4th ACM SIGPLAN Symposium on Haskell, Haskell 2011, Tokyo, Japan, 22 September 2011, pp. 95–106. ACM (2011). https://doi.org/10.1145/2034675.2034688

43. Swamy, N., Chen, J., Chugh, R.: Enforcing stateful authorization and information flow policies in Fine. In: Gordon, A.D. (ed.) ESOP 2010. LNCS, vol. 6012, pp. 529–549. Springer, Heidelberg (2010). https://doi.org/10.1007/978-3-642-11957-6_28
44. Swamy, N., Chen, J., Fournet, C., Strub, P., Bhargavan, K., Yang, J.: Secure distributed programming with value-dependent types. In: Chakravarty, M.M.T., Hu, Z., Danvy, O. (eds.) Proceeding of the 16th ACM SIGPLAN International Conference on Functional Programming, ICFP 2011, Tokyo, Japan, 19–21 September 2011, pp. 266–278. ACM (2011). https://doi.org/10.1145/2034773.2034811
45. Tsai, T., Russo, A., Hughes, J.: A library for secure multi-threaded information flow in Haskell. In: 20th IEEE Computer Security Foundations Symposium, CSF 2007, Venice, Italy, 6–8 July 2007, pp. 187–202. IEEE Computer Society (2007). https://doi.org/10.1109/CSF.2007.6
46. Vassena, M., Russo, A.: On formalizing information-flow control libraries. In: Proceedings of the 2016 ACM Workshop on Programming Languages and Analysis for Security, PLAS@CCS 2016, Vienna, Austria, 24 October 2016, pp. 15–28 (2016). https://doi.org/10.1145/2993600.2993608
47. Vassena, M., Russo, A., Buiras, P., Waye, L.: MAC a verified static information-flow control library. J. Log. Algebr. Methods Program. **95**, 148–180 (2018). http://www.sciencedirect.com/science/article/pii/S235222081730069X
48. Vassena, M., Russo, A., Garg, D., Rajani, V., Stefan, D.: From fine- to coarse-grained dynamic information flow control and back. PACMPL **3**(POPL), 76:1–76:31 (2019). https://doi.org/10.1145/2694344.2694372
49. Zdancewic, S., Myers, A.C.: Robust declassification. In: 14th IEEE Computer Security Foundations Workshop (CSFW-14 2001), Cape Breton, Nova Scotia, Canada, 11–13 June 2001, pp. 15–23. IEEE Computer Society (2001). https://doi.org/10.1109/CSFW.2001.930133
50. Zhang, D., Wang, Y., Suh, G.E., Myers, A.C.: A hardware design language for timing-sensitive information-flow security. In: Özturk, Ö., Ebcioglu, K., Dwarkadas, S. (eds.) Proceedings of the Twentieth International Conference on Architectural Support for Programming Languages and Operating Systems, ASPLOS 2015, Istanbul, Turkey, 14–18 March 2015, pp. 503–516. ACM (2015). https://doi.org/10.1145/2694344.2694372
51. Zheng, L., Myers, A.C.: Dynamic security labels and noninterference (extended abstract). In: Dimitrakos, T., Martinelli, F. (eds.) Formal Aspects in Security and Trust. IFIP, vol. 173, pp. 27–40. Springer, Boston (2005). https://doi.org/10.1007/0-387-24098-5_3
52. Zheng, L., Myers, A.C.: Dynamic security labels and static information flow control. Int. J. Inf. Secur. **6**(2–3), 67–84 (2007). https://doi.org/10.1007/s10207-007-0019-9

Achieving Safety Incrementally with Checked C

Andrew Ruef[1](✉), Leonidas Lampropoulos[1,2], Ian Sweet[1], David Tarditi[3], and Michael Hicks[1]

[1] University of Maryland, College Park, USA
{awruef,llampro,ins,mwh}@cs.umd.edu
[2] University of Pennsylvania, Philadelphia, USA
[3] Microsoft Research, Kirkland, USA
dtarditi@microsoft.com

Abstract. Checked C is a new effort working toward a memory-safe C. Its design is distinguished from that of prior efforts by truly being an *extension* of C: Every C program is also a Checked C program. Thus, one may make incremental safety improvements to existing codebases while retaining backward compatibility. This paper makes two contributions. First, to help developers convert existing C code to use so-called *checked* (i.e., safe) pointers, we have developed a preliminary, automated porting tool. Notably, this tool takes advantage of the flexibility of Checked C's design: The tool need not perfectly classify every pointer, as required of prior all-or-nothing efforts. Rather, it can make a best effort to convert more pointers accurately, without letting inaccuracies inhibit compilation. However, such partial conversion raises the question: If safety violations can still occur, what sort of advantage does using Checked C provide? We draw inspiration from research on migratory typing to make our second contribution: We prove a *blame* property that renders so-called *checked regions* blameless of any run-time failure. We formalize this property for a core calculus and mechanize the proof in Coq.

1 Introduction

Vulnerabilities that compromise *memory safety* are at the heart of many attacks. *Spatial safety*, one aspect of memory safety, is ensured when any pointer dereference is always within the memory allocated to that pointer. *Buffer overruns* violate spatial safety, and still constitute a common cause of vulnerability. During 2012–2018, buffer overruns were the source of 9.7% to 18.4% of CVEs reported in the NIST vulnerability database [27], constituting the leading single cause of CVEs.

The source of memory unsafety starts with the language definitions of C and C++, which render out-of-bounds pointer dereferences "undefined." Traditional compilers assume they never happen. Many efforts over the last 20 years have aimed for greater assurance by proving that accesses are in bounds, and/or preventing out-of-bounds accesses from happening via inserted dynamic checks [1–10,12,15,16,18,22,25,26,29]. This paper focuses on *Checked C*, a new, freely

F. Nielson and D. Sands (Eds.): POST 2019, LNCS 11426, pp. 76–98, 2019.
https://doi.org/10.1007/978-3-030-17138-4_4

available[1] language design for a memory-safe C [11], currently focused on spatial safety. Checked C draws substantial inspiration from prior safe-C efforts but differs in two key ways, both of which focus on backward compatibility with, and incremental improvement of, regular C code.

Mixing Checked and Legacy Pointers. First, as outlined in Sect. 2, Checked C permits intermixing checked (safe) pointers and legacy pointers. The former come in three varieties: pointers to single objects `_Ptr<τ>`; pointers to arrays `_Array_ptr<τ>`, and NUL-terminated arrays `_Nt_array_ptr<τ>`. The latter two have an associated clause that describes their known length in terms of constants and other program variables. The specified length is used to either prove pointer dereferences are safe or, barring that, serves as the basis of dynamic checks inserted by the compiler.

Importantly, checked pointers are represented as in normal C—no changes to pointer structure (e.g., by "fattening" a pointer to include its bounds) are imposed. As such, interoperation with legacy C is eased. Moreover, the fact that checked and legacy pointers can be intermixed in the same module eases the porting process, including porting via automated tools. For example, CCured [26] works by automatically classifying existing pointers and compiling them for safety. This classification is necessarily conservative. For example, if a function `f(p)` is mostly called with safe pointers, but once with an unsafe one (e.g., a "wild" pointer in CCured parlance, perhaps constructed from an `int`), then the classification of `p` as unsafe will propagate backwards, poisoning the classification of the safe pointers, too. The programmer will be forced to change the code and/or pay a higher cost for added (but unnecessary) run-time checks.

On the other hand, in the Checked C setting, if a function uses a pointer safely then its parameter can be typed that way. It is then up to a caller whose pointer arguments cannot also be made safe to insert a local cast. Section 5 presents a preliminary, whole-program analysis called *checked-c-convert* that utilizes the extra flexibility afforded by mixing pointers to partially convert a C program to a Checked C program. On a benchmark suite of five programs totaling more than 200K LoC, we find that thousands of pointer locations are made more precise than would have been if using a more conservative algorithm like that of CCured. The *checked-c-convert* tool is distributed with the publicly available Checked C codebase.

Avoiding Blame with Checked Regions. An important question is what "safety" means in a program with a mix of checked and unchecked pointers. In such a program, safety violations are still possible. How, then, does one assess that a program is safer due to checking some, but not all, of its pointers? Providing a formal answer to this question constitutes the core contribution of this paper.

Unlike past safe-C efforts, Checked C specifically distinguishes parts of the program that are and may not be fully "safe." So-called *checked regions* differ from unchecked ones in that they can *only* use checked pointers—dereference

[1] https://github.com/Microsoft/checkedc.

or creation of unchecked pointers, unsafe casts, and other potentially dangerous constructs are disallowed. Using a core calculus for Checked C programs called CoreChkC, defined in Sect. 3, we prove in Sect. 4 these restrictions are sufficient to ensure that *checked code cannot be blamed.* That is, checked code is internally safe, and any run-time failure can be attributed to unchecked code, even if that failure occurs in a checked region. This proof has been fully mechanized in the Coq proof assistant.[2] Our theorem fills a gap in the literature on *migratory typing* for languages that, like Checked C, use an *erasure* semantics, meaning that no extra dynamic checks are inserted at checked/unchecked code boundaries [14]. Moreover, our approach is lighter weight than the more sophisticated techniques used by the RustBelt project [17], and constitutes a simpler first step toward a safe, mixed-language design. We say more in Sect. 6.

2 Overview of Checked C

We begin by describing the approach to using Checked C and presenting a brief overview of the language extensions, using the example in Fig. 1. For more about the language see Elliott et al. [11]. The approach works as follows:

1. Programmers start with an existing unsafe C program and annotated header files for existing C libraries. The annotations describe the expected behavior of functions with respect to bounds.
2. The programmers run a porting tool that modifies the unsafe C program to use the Checked C extensions. The tool identifies simple cases where _Ptr can be used. This lets the programmers focus on pointers that need bounds declarations or that are used unsafely.
3. The programmers add bounds declarations and checked regions to the remaining code. The programmers work incrementally, which lets the program be compiled and tested as it gradually becomes safer.
4. The programmers use a C compiler extended to handle the Checked C extension to compile the program. The compiler inserts runtime null and bounds checks and optimizes them out if it can.
5. At runtime, if a null check or bounds check fails, a runtime error is signaled and the process is terminated.

The programmers repeat steps 3–5 until as much code as possible (ideally, the entire program) has been made safe.

Checked Pointers. As mentioned in the introduction, Checked C supports three varieties of *checked* (safe) pointers: pointers to single objects _Ptr$<\tau>$; pointers to arrays _Array_ptr$<\tau>$, and NUL-terminated arrays _Nt_array_ptr $<\tau>$. The dat field of **struct** buf, defined in Fig. 1(b), is an _Array_ptr<**char**>; its length is specified by sz field in the same **struct**, as indicated by the count annotation. _Nt_array_ptr $<\tau>$ types are similar. The q argument of the alloc_buf

[2] https://github.com/plum-umd/checkedc/tree/master/coq.

```
void copy(
  char* dst : byte_count(n),
  const char* src : byte_count(n),
   size_t n);
```

(a) copy prototype

```
struct buf
{
   _Array_ptr<char> dat
     : count(sz−1);
  unsigned int len;/* len≤ sz */
  unsigned int sz;
};
```

(b) Type definition

```
static char region[MAX]; // unchecked
static unsigned int idx = 0;

_Checked void alloc_buf(
  _Ptr<struct buf> q,
  _Array_ptr<const char> src : count(len),
  unsigned int len)
{
  if (len > q→sz) {
    if (idx < MAX && len ≤MAX − idx) {
      _Unchecked {
        q→dat = &region[idx];
        q→sz = len;
      }
      idx += len;
    } else {
      bug("out of region memory");
    }
  }
  copy(q→buf, src, len);
  q→len = len;
}
```

(c) Code with checked and unchecked pointers

Fig. 1. Example Checked C code (slightly simplified for readability)

function in Fig. 1(c) is _Ptr<**struct** buf>. This function overwrites the contents of q with those in the second argument src, an array whose length is specified by the third argument, len. Variables with checked pointer types or containing checked pointers must be initialized when they are declared.

Checked Arrays. Checked C also supports a checked array type, which is designated by prefixing the dimension of an array declaration with the keyword **_Checked**. For example, **int** arr **_Checked**[5] declares a 5-element integer array where accesses are always bounds checked. A checked array of τ implicitly converts to an _Array_ptr<τ> when accessing it. In our example, the array region has an unchecked array type because the **_Checked** keyword is omitted.

Checked and Unchecked Regions. Returning to alloc_buf: If q→dat is too small (len > q→sz) to hold the contents of src, the function allocates a block from the static region array, whose free area starts at index idx. Designating a checked _Array_ptr<**char**> from a pointer into the middle of the (unchecked) region array is not allowed in checked code, so it must be done within the designated **_Unchecked** block. Within such blocks the programmer has the full freedom of C, along with the ability to create and use checked pointers. Checked code, as designated by the **_Checked** annotation (e.g., as on the alloc_buf function or on a block nested within unchecked code) may not use unchecked pointers or arrays. It also may not define or call functions without prototypes and variable argument functions.

Interface Types. Once alloc_buf has allocated q→dat it calls copy to transfer the data into it, from src. Checked C permits normal C functions, such as those in an existing library, to be given an *interface type.* This is the type that Checked C code should use in a checked region. In an unchecked region, either the original type *or* the interface type may be used. This allows the function to be called with unchecked types or checked types. For copy, this type is shown in Fig. 1(a).

Interface types can also be attached to definitions within a Checked C file, not just prototypes declared for external libraries. Doing so permits the same function to be called from an unchecked region (with either checked or unchecked types) or a checked region (there it will always have the checked type). For example, if we wanted alloc_buf to be callable from unchecked code with unchecked pointers, we could define its prototype as

```
void alloc_buf(
  struct buf *q : itype(_Ptr<struct buf>),
  const char *src : itype(_Array_ptr<const char>) count(len),
  unsigned int len);
```

Implementation Details. Checked C is implemented as an extension to the Clang/ LLVM compiler.[3] The clang front-end inserts run-time checks for the evaluation of lvalue expressions whose results are derived from checked pointers and that will be used to access memory. Accessing a _Ptr<τ> requires a null check, while accessing an _Array_ptr<τ> requires both null and bounds checks. The code for these checks is handed to the LLVM backend, which will remove checks if it can prove they will always pass. In general, such checks are the only source of Checked C run-time overhead. Preliminary experiments on some small, pointer-intensive benchmarks show running time overhead to be around 8.6%, on average [11].

3 Formalism: CoreChkC

This section presents a formal language CoreChkC that models the essence of Checked C. The language is designed to be simple but nevertheless highlight Checked C's key features: checked and unchecked pointers, and checked and unchecked code blocks. We prove our key theoretical result—*checked code cannot be blamed* for a spatial safety violation—in the next section.

3.1 Syntax

The syntax of CoreChkC is presented in Fig. 2. Types τ classify word-sized objects while types ω also include multi-word objects. The type $\texttt{ptr}^m\omega$ types a pointer, where m identifies its *mode*: mode c identifies a Checked C safe pointer, while mode u represents an unchecked pointer. In other words $\texttt{ptr}^c\tau$ is a checked pointer type _Ptr<τ> while $\texttt{ptr}^u\tau$ is an unchecked pointer type $\tau *$.

[3] https://github.com/Microsoft/checkedc-clang.

$$
\begin{array}{llll}
\text{Mode} & m & ::= & c \mid u \\
\text{Word types} & \tau & ::= & \texttt{int} \mid \texttt{ptr}^m \omega \\
\text{Types} & \omega & ::= & \tau \mid \texttt{struct}\ T \mid \texttt{array}\ n\ \tau \\
\text{Expressions} & e & ::= & n^\tau \mid x \mid \texttt{let}\ x\ =\ e_1\ \texttt{in}\ e_2 \mid \texttt{malloc@}\omega \mid (\tau)e \\
 & & \mid & e_1 + e_2 \mid \&e{\rightarrow}f \mid *e \mid *e_1 = e_2 \mid \texttt{unchecked}\ e \\
\text{Structdefs} & D & \in & T \rightharpoonup fs \\
\text{Fields} & fs & ::= & \tau\ \texttt{f} \mid \tau\ \texttt{f}; fs
\end{array}
$$

Fig. 2. CoreChkC Syntax

Multiword types ω include `struct` records, and arrays of type τ having size n, i.e., $\texttt{ptr}^c\texttt{array}\ n\ \tau$ represents a checked array pointer type _Array_ptr<τ> with bounds n. We assume `structs` are defined separately in a map D from struct names to their constituent field definitions.

Programs are represented as expressions e; we have no separate class of program statements, for simplicity. Expressions include (unsigned) integers n^τ and local variables x. Constant integers n are annotated with type τ to indicate their intended type. As in an actual implementation, pointers in our formalism are represented as integers. Annotations help formalize type checking and the safety property it provides; they have no effect on the semantics except when τ is a checked pointer, in which case they facilitate null and bounds checks. Variables x, introduced by let-bindings $\texttt{let}\ x\ =\ e_1\ \texttt{in}\ e_2$, can only hold word-sized objects, so all `structs` can only be accessed by pointers.

Checked pointers are constructed using $\texttt{malloc@}\omega$, where ω is the type (and size) of the allocated memory. Thus, `malloc@int` produces a pointer of type $\texttt{ptr}^c\texttt{int}$ while `malloc@(array 10 int)` produces one of type $\texttt{ptr}^c(\texttt{array}\ 10\ \texttt{int})$. Unchecked pointers can only be produced by the cast operator, $(\tau)e$, e.g., by doing $(\texttt{ptr}^u\texttt{int})\texttt{malloc@int}$. Casts can also be used to coerce between integer and pointer types and between different multi-word types.

Pointers are read via the $*$ operator, and assigned to via the $=$ operator. To read or write `struct` fields, a program can take the address of that field and read or write that address, e.g., $x{\rightarrow}f$ is equivalent to $*(\&x{\rightarrow}f)$. To read or write an array, the programmer can use pointer arithmetic to access the desired element, e.g., $x[i]$ is equivalent to $*(x + i)$.

By default, CoreChkC expressions are assumed to be checked. Expression e in $\texttt{unchecked}\ e$ is unchecked, giving it additional freedom: Checked pointers may be created via casts, and unchecked pointers may be read or written.

Design Notes. CoreChkC leaves out many interesting C language features. We do not include an operation for freeing memory, since this paper is concerned about spatial safety, not temporal safety. CoreChkC models statically sized arrays but supports dynamic indexes; supporting dynamic sizes is interesting but not meaningful enough to justify the complexity it would add to the formalism. Making `ints` unsigned simplifies handling pointer arithmetic. We do not model

$$\begin{array}{lll} \text{Heap} & H & \in \mathbb{Z} \rightharpoonup \mathbb{Z} \times \tau \\ \text{Result} & r & ::= e \mid \texttt{Null} \mid \texttt{Bounds} \\ \text{Contexts} & E & ::= \_ \mid \texttt{let}\ x = E\ \texttt{in}\ e \mid E + e \mid n + E \\ & & \mid\ \&E \rightarrow f \mid (\tau)E \mid *E \mid *E = e \mid *n = E \mid \texttt{unchecked}\ E \end{array}$$

Fig. 3. Semantics definitions

control operators or function calls, whose addition would be straightforward.[4] CoreChkC does not have a `checked` e expression for nesting within `unchecked` expressions, but supporting it would be easy.

3.2 Semantics

Figure 4 defines the small-step operational semantics for CoreChkC expressions in the form of judgment $H; e \longrightarrow^m H; r$. Here, H is a *heap*, which is a partial map from integers (representing pointer addresses) to type-annotated integers n^τ. Annotation m is the *mode* of evaluation, which is either c for checked mode or u for unchecked mode. Finally, r is a *result*, which is either an expression e, `Null` (indicating a null pointer dereference), or `Bounds` (indicating an out-of-bounds array access). An unsafe program execution occurs when the expression reaches a *stuck* state—the program is not an integer n^τ, and yet no rule applies. Notably, this could happen if trying to dereference a pointer n that is actually invalid, i.e., $H(n)$ is undefined.

The semantics is defined in the standard manner using *evaluation contexts* E. We write $E[e_0]$ to mean the expression that results from substituting e_0 into the "hole" ($\_$) of context E. Rule C-Exp defines normal evaluation. It decomposes an expression e into a context E and expression e_0 and then evaluates the latter via $H; e_0 \rightsquigarrow H'; e_0'$, discussed below. The evaluation mode m is constrained by the $mode(E)$ function, also given in Fig. 4. The rule and this function ensure that when evaluation occurs within e in some expression `unchecked` e, then it does so in unchecked mode u; otherwise it may be in checked mode c. Rule C-Halt halts evaluation due to a failed null or bounds check.

The rules prefixed with E- are those of the computation semantics $H; e_0 \rightsquigarrow H'; e_0'$. The semantics is implicitly parameterized by struct map D. The rest of this section provides additional details for each rule, followed by a discussion of CoreChkC's type system.

Rule E-Binop produces an integer n_3 that is the sum of arguments n_1 and n_2. As mentioned earlier, the annotations τ on literals n^τ indicate the type the program has ascribed to n. When a type annotation is not a checked pointer, the semantics ignores it. In the particular case of E-Binop for example, addition

[4] Function calls $f(e')$ can be modeled by `let` $x = e_1$ `in` e_2, where we can view x as function f's parameter, e_2 as its body, and e_1 as its actual argument. Calls to unchecked functions from checked code can thus be simulated by having an `unchecked` e expression for e_2.

Rule	Reduction	Condition
E-BINOP	$H; n_1^{\tau_1} + n_2^{\tau_2} \rightsquigarrow H; n_3^{\tau_3}$	where $n_3 = n_1 + n_2$ $\tau_1 = \mathtt{ptr}^c(\mathtt{array}\ l\ \tau) \land n_1 \neq 0 \Rightarrow$ $\tau_3 = \mathtt{ptr}^c(\mathtt{array}\ (l - n_2)\ \tau)$ $\tau_1 \neq \mathtt{ptr}^c(\mathtt{array}\ l\ \tau) \Rightarrow \tau_3 = \tau_1$
E-CAST	$H; (\tau)n^{\tau'} \rightsquigarrow H; n^{\tau}$	
E-DEREF	$H; *n^{\tau} \rightsquigarrow H; n_1^{\tau_1}$	where $n_1^{\tau_1} = H(n)$ $\forall\ l\ \tau'.\ \tau = \mathtt{ptr}^c(\mathtt{array}\ l\ \tau') \Rightarrow l > 0$
E-ASSIGN	$H; *n^{\tau} = n_1^{\tau_1} \rightsquigarrow H'; n_1^{\tau_1}$	where $H(n)$ defined $\forall\ l\ \tau'.\ \tau = \mathtt{ptr}^c(\mathtt{array}\ l\ \tau') \Rightarrow l > 0$ $H' = H[n \mapsto n_1^{\tau_1}]$
E-AMPER	$H; \&n^{\tau} \rightarrow f_i \rightsquigarrow H; n_0^{\tau_0}$	where $\tau = \mathtt{ptr}^{m'}\ \mathtt{struct}\ T$ $D(T) = \tau_1 f_1; ...; \tau_k f_k$ for $1 \leq i \leq k$ $m' \neq c \lor n \neq 0 \Rightarrow$ $n_0 = n + i \land \tau_0 = \mathtt{ptr}^{m'}\ \tau_i$
E-MALLOC	$H; \mathtt{malloc@}\omega \rightsquigarrow H', n_1^{\mathtt{ptr}^c \omega}$	where $\text{sizeof}(\omega) = k$ and $k > 0$ $n_1 ... n_k$ consecutive $n_1 \neq 0$ and $H(n_1)...H(n_k)$ undefined $\tau_1, ..., \tau_k = \text{types}(D, \omega)$ $H' = H[n_1 \mapsto 0^{\tau_1}]...[n_k \mapsto 0^{\tau_k}]$
E-LET	$H; \mathtt{let}\ x = n^{\tau}\ \mathtt{in}\ e \rightsquigarrow H; e[x \mapsto n^{\tau}]$	
E-UNCHECKED	$H; \mathtt{unchecked}\ n^{\tau} \rightsquigarrow H; n^{\tau}$	
X-DEREFOOB	$H; *n^{\tau} \rightsquigarrow H; \mathtt{Bounds}$	where $\tau = \mathtt{ptr}^c(\mathtt{array}\ 0\ \tau_1)$
X-ASSIGNOOB	$H; *n^{\tau} = n_1^{\tau_1} \rightsquigarrow H; \mathtt{Bounds}$	where $\tau = \mathtt{ptr}^c(\mathtt{array}\ 0\ \tau_1)$
X-DEREFNULL	$H; *0^{\tau} \rightsquigarrow H; \mathtt{Null}$	where $\tau = \mathtt{ptr}^c \omega$
X-ASSIGNNULL	$H; *0^{\tau} = n_1^{\tau'} \rightsquigarrow H; \mathtt{Null}$	where $\tau = \mathtt{ptr}^c(\mathtt{array}\ l\ \tau_1)$
X-AMPERNULL	$H; \&0^{\tau} \rightarrow f_i \rightsquigarrow H; \mathtt{Null}$	where $\tau = \mathtt{ptr}^c \mathtt{struct}\ T$
X-BINOPNULL	$H; 0^{\tau} + n^{\tau'} \rightsquigarrow H; \mathtt{Null}$	where $\tau = \mathtt{ptr}^c(\mathtt{array}\ l\ \tau_1)$

C-EXP

$$\frac{e = E[e_0] \quad m = mode(E) \lor m = u \qquad H; e_0 \rightsquigarrow H'; e_0' \quad e' = E[e_0']}{H; e \longrightarrow^m H'; e'}$$

C-HALT

$$\frac{e = E[e_0] \quad m = mode(E) \lor m = u \qquad H; e_0 \rightsquigarrow H'; r \text{ where } r = \mathtt{Null} \text{ or } r = \mathtt{Bounds}}{H; e \longrightarrow^m H'; r}$$

$$\begin{array}{ll}
mode(_) & = c \\
mode(\mathtt{unchecked}\ E) & = u \\
mode(\mathtt{let}\ x = E\ \mathtt{in}\ e) & = \\
\quad mode(E + e) & = \\
\quad mode(n + E) & = \\
\quad mode(\&E \rightarrow f) & = \\
\quad mode((\tau)E) & = \\
\quad mode(*E) & = \\
\quad mode(*E = e) & = \\
\quad mode(*n = E) & = mode(E)
\end{array}$$

Fig. 4. Operational semantics

$n_1^{\tau_1} + n_2^{\tau_2}$ ignores τ_1 and τ_2 when τ_1 is not a checked pointer, and simply annotates the result with it. However, when τ is a checked pointer, the rules use it to model bounds checks; in particular, dereferencing n^{τ} where τ is $\mathtt{ptr}^c(\mathtt{array}\ l\ \tau_0)$ produces `Bounds` when $l = 0$ (more below). As such, when n_1 is a non-zero, checked pointer to an array and n_2 is an `int`, result n_3 is annotated as a pointer to an array with its bounds suitably updated.[5] Checked pointer arithmetic on 0 is disallowed; see below.

Rules E-Deref and E-Assign confirm the bounds of checked array pointers: the length l must be positive for the dereference to be legal. The rule permits the program to proceed for non-checked or non-array pointers (but the type system will forbid them).

Rule E-Amper takes the address of a `struct` field, according to the type annotation on the pointer, as long the pointer is not zero or not checked.

Rule E-Malloc allocates a checked pointer by finding a string of free heap locations and initializing each to 0, annotated to the appropriate type. Here, types(D, ω) returns k types, where these are the types of the corresponding memory words; e.g., if ω is a `struct` then these are the types of its fields (looked up in D), while if ω is an array of length k containing values of type τ, then we will get back k τ's. We require $k \neq 0$ or the program is stuck (a situation precluded by the type system).

Rule E-Let uses a substitution semantics for local variables; notation $e[x \mapsto n^{\tau}]$ means that all occurrences of x in e should be replaced with n^{τ}.

Rule E-Unchecked returns the result of an unchecked block.

Rules with prefix X- describe failures due to bounds checks and null checks on checked pointers. These are analogues to the E-Assign, E-Deref, E-Binop, and E-Amper cases. The first two rules indicate a bounds violation for size-zero array pointers. The next two indicate an attempt to dereference a null pointer. The last two indicate an attempt to construct a checked pointer from a null pointer via field access or pointer arithmetic.

3.3 Typing

The typing judgment $\Gamma; \sigma \vdash_m e : \tau$ says that expression e has type τ under environment Γ and scope σ when in mode m. A scope σ is an additional environment consisting of a set of literals; it is used to type cyclic structures (in Rule T-PtrC, below) that may arise during program evaluation. The heap H and struct map D are implicit parameters of the judgment; they do not appear because they are invariant in derivations. `unchecked` expressions are typed in mode u; otherwise we may use either mode.

Γ maps variables x to types τ, and is used in rules T-Var and T-Let as usual. Rule T-Base ascribes type τ to literal n^{τ}. This is safe when τ is `int` (always). If τ is an unchecked pointer type, a dereference is only allowed by the type system to be in unchecked code (see below), and as such any sort of failure (including a stuck program) is not a safety violation. When n is 0 then τ can be anything, including a checked pointer type, because dereferencing n would (safely) produce `Null`. Finally, if τ is $\texttt{ptr}^c(\texttt{array}\ 0\ \tau')$ then dereferencing n would (safely) produce `Bounds`.

[5] Here, $l - n_2$ is natural number arithmetic: if $n_2 > l$ then $l - n_2 = 0$. This would have to be adjusted if the language contained subtraction, or else bounds information would be unsound.

$$\textsc{T-Var}\quad \frac{x : \tau \in \Gamma}{\Gamma; \sigma \vdash_m x : \tau} \qquad \textsc{T-VConst}\quad \frac{n^\tau \in \sigma}{\Gamma; \sigma \vdash_m n^\tau : \tau} \qquad \textsc{T-Let}\quad \frac{\Gamma; \sigma \vdash_m e_1 : \tau_1 \qquad \Gamma, x : \tau_1; \sigma \vdash_m e_2 : \tau}{\Gamma; \sigma \vdash_m \texttt{let}\ x = e_1\ \texttt{in}\ e_2 : \tau}$$

$$\textsc{T-Base}\quad \frac{\begin{array}{c}\tau = \texttt{int} \vee \tau = \texttt{ptr}^u\omega \ \vee n = 0 \ \vee \\ \tau = \texttt{ptr}^c(\texttt{array}\ 0\ \tau')\end{array}}{\Gamma; \sigma \vdash_m n^\tau : \tau} \qquad \textsc{T-PtrC}\quad \frac{\begin{array}{c}\tau = \texttt{ptr}^c\omega \qquad \tau_0, ..., \tau_{j-1} = \text{types}(D, \omega) \\ \Gamma; \sigma, n^\tau \vdash_m H(n+k) : \tau_k \quad 0 \leq k < j\end{array}}{\Gamma; \sigma \vdash_m n^\tau : \tau}$$

$$\textsc{T-Amper}\quad \frac{\begin{array}{c}\Gamma; \sigma \vdash_m e : \texttt{ptr}^m\texttt{struct}\ T \\ D(T) = ...; \tau_f\ f; ...\end{array}}{\Gamma; \sigma \vdash_m \&e \rightarrow f : \texttt{ptr}^m\tau_f} \qquad \textsc{T-BinopInt}\quad \frac{\begin{array}{c}\Gamma; \sigma \vdash_m e_1 : \texttt{int} \\ \Gamma; \sigma \vdash_m e_2 : \texttt{int}\end{array}}{\Gamma; \sigma \vdash_m e_1 + e_2 : \texttt{int}}$$

$$\textsc{T-Malloc}\quad \frac{\text{sizeof}(\omega) > 0}{\Gamma; \sigma \vdash_m \texttt{malloc@}\omega : \texttt{ptr}^c\omega}$$

$$\textsc{T-Unchecked}\quad \frac{\Gamma; \sigma \vdash_u e : \tau}{\Gamma; \sigma \vdash_m \texttt{unchecked}\ e : \tau} \qquad \textsc{T-Cast}\quad \frac{m = c \Rightarrow \tau \neq \texttt{ptr}^c\omega\ (\text{for any}\ \omega) \qquad \Gamma; \sigma \vdash_m e : \tau'}{\Gamma; \sigma \vdash_m (\tau)e : \tau}$$

$$\textsc{T-Deref}\quad \frac{\begin{array}{c}\Gamma; \sigma \vdash_m e : \texttt{ptr}^{m'}\omega \\ \omega = \tau \vee \omega = \texttt{array}\ n\ \tau \\ m' = u \Rightarrow m = u\end{array}}{\Gamma; \sigma \vdash_m *e : \tau} \qquad \textsc{T-Index}\quad \frac{\begin{array}{c}\Gamma; \sigma \vdash_m e_1 : \texttt{ptr}^{m'}(\texttt{array}\ n\ \tau) \\ \Gamma; \sigma \vdash_m e_2 : \texttt{int} \\ m' = u \Rightarrow m = u\end{array}}{\Gamma; \sigma \vdash_m *(e_1 + e_2) : \tau}$$

$$\textsc{T-Assign}\quad \frac{\begin{array}{c}\Gamma; \sigma \vdash_m e_1 : \texttt{ptr}^{m'}\omega \qquad \Gamma; \sigma \vdash_m e_2 : \tau \\ \omega = \tau \vee \omega = \texttt{array}\ n\ \tau \\ m' = u \Rightarrow m = u\end{array}}{\Gamma; \sigma \vdash_m *e_1 = e_2 : \tau} \qquad \textsc{T-IndAssign}\quad \frac{\begin{array}{c}\Gamma; \sigma \vdash_m e_1 : \texttt{ptr}^{m'}(\texttt{array}\ n\ \tau) \\ \Gamma; \sigma \vdash_m e_2 : \texttt{int} \qquad \Gamma; \sigma \vdash_m e_3 : \tau \\ m' = u \Rightarrow m = u\end{array}}{\Gamma; \sigma \vdash_m *(e_1 + e_2) = e_3 : \tau}$$

Fig. 5. Typing

Rule T-PtrC is perhaps the most interesting rule of CoreChkC. It ensures checked pointers of type $\texttt{ptr}^c\omega$ are consistent with the heap, by confirming the pointed-to heap memory has types consistent with ω, recursively. When doing this, we extend σ with n^τ to properly handle cyclic heap structures; σ is used by RuleT-VConst.

To make things more concrete, consider the following program that constructs a cyclic cons cell, using a standard single-linked list representation:

$$D(node) = \texttt{int}\ val;\ \texttt{ptr}^c\ \texttt{struct}\ node$$

$$\texttt{let}\ p = \texttt{malloc@struct}\ node\ \texttt{in}\ *(\&p \rightarrow next) = p$$

After executing the program above, the heap would look something like the following, where n is the integer value of p. That is, the n-th location of the heap contains 0 (the default value for field *val* picked by `malloc`), while the $(n+1)$-th location, which corresponds to field *next*, contains the literal n.

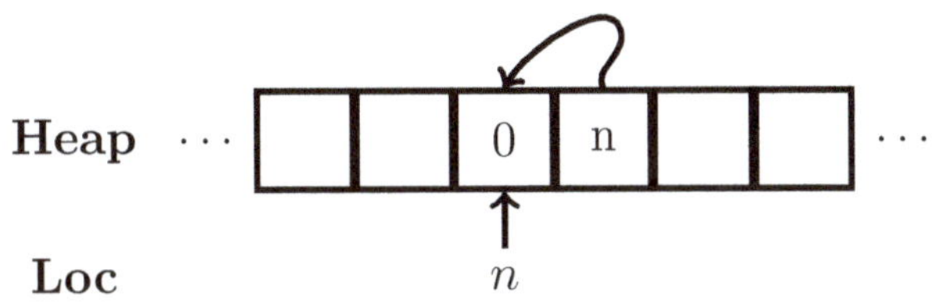

How can we type the pointer $n^{\texttt{ptr}^c\texttt{struct}\ node}$ in this heap without getting an infinite typing judgment?

$$\Gamma; \sigma \vdash_c n^{\texttt{ptr}^c\texttt{struct}\ node} : \texttt{ptr}^c\texttt{struct}\ node$$

That's where the scope comes in, to break the recursion. In particular, using Rule T-PtrC and `struct` *node*'s definition, we would need to prove two things:

$$\Gamma; \sigma, n^{\texttt{ptr}^c\texttt{struct}\ node} \vdash_c H(n+0) : \texttt{int}$$

and

$$\Gamma; \sigma, n^{\texttt{ptr}^c\texttt{struct}\ node} \vdash_c H(n+1) : \texttt{ptr}^c\texttt{struct}\ node$$

Since $H(n+0) = 0$, as `malloc` zeroes out its memory, we can trivially prove the first goal using Rule T-Base. However, the second goal is almost exactly what we set out to prove in the first place! If not for the presence of the scope σ, the proof the n is typeable would be infinite! However, by adding $n^{\texttt{ptr}^c\texttt{struct}\ node}$ to the scope, we are essentially assuming it is well-typed to type its contents, and the desired result follows by Rule T-VConst.[6]

A key feature of T-PtrC is that it effectively confirms that all pointers reachable from the given one are consistent; it says nothing about other parts of the heap. So, if a set of checked pointers is only reachable via unchecked pointers then we are not concerned whether they are consistent, since they cannot be directly dereferenced by checked code.

Back to the remaining rules, T-Amper and T-BinopInt are unsurprising. Rule T-Malloc produces checked pointers so long as the pointed-to type ω is not zero-sized, i.e., is not `array` $0\ \tau$. Rule T-Unchecked introduces unchecked mode, relaxing access rules. Rule T-Cast enforces that checked pointers cannot be cast targets in checked mode.

Rules T-Deref and T-Assign type pointer accesses. These rules require unchecked pointers only be dereferenced in unchecked mode. Rule T-Index permits

[6] For readers familiar with coinduction [28], this proof technique is similar: to prove a coinductive property P one would assume P but need to use it *productively* in a subterm; similarly here, we can assume a pointer is well-typed when we attempt to type heap locations that are reachable from it.

reading a computed pointer to an array, and rule T-IndAssign permits writing to one. These rules are not strong enough to permit updating a pointer to an array after performing arithmetic on it. In general, Checked C's design permits overcoming such limitations through selective use of casts in unchecked code. (That said, our implementation is more flexible in this particular case.)

4 Checked Code Cannot Be Blamed

Our main formal result is that well-typed programs will never fail with a spatial safety violation that is due to a checked region of code, i.e., *checked code cannot be blamed.* This section presents the main result and outlines its proof. We have mechanized the full proof using the Coq proof assistant. The development is roughly 3500 lines long, including comments. It is freely available at https://github.com/plum-umd/checkedc/tree/master/coq.

4.1 Progress and Preservation

The blame theorem is proved using the two standard syntactic type-safety notions of Progress and Preservation, adapted for CoreChkC. Progress indicates that a (closed) well-typed program either is a value, can take a step (in either mode), or else is stuck in unchecked code. A program is in unchecked mode if its expression e only type checks in mode u, or its (unique) context E has mode u.

Theorem 1 (Progress). *If* $\cdot \vdash_m e : \tau$ *(under heap* H*) then one of the following holds:*

- e *is an integer* n^τ
- *There exists* H', m', *and* r *such that* $H; e \longrightarrow^{m'} H'; r$ *where* r *is either some* e', `Null`, *or* `Bounds`.
- $m = u$ *or* $e = E[e'']$ *and* $mode(E) = u$ *for some* E, e''.

Preservation indicates that if a well-typed program in checked mode takes a checked step then the resulting program is also well-typed in checked mode.

Theorem 2 (Preservation). *If* $\Gamma; \cdot \vdash_c e : \tau$ *(under a heap* H*) and* $H; e \longrightarrow^c H'; r$ *(for some* H', r*), then and* $r = e'$ *implies* $H \rhd H'$ *and* $\Gamma; \cdot \vdash_c e' : \tau$ *(under heap* H'*).*

We write $H \rhd H'$ to mean that for all n^τ if $\cdot \vdash_c n^\tau : \tau$ under H then $\cdot \vdash_c n^\tau : \tau$ under H' as well.

The proofs of both theorems are by induction on the typing derivation. The Preservation proof is the most delicate, particularly ensuring $H \rhd H'$ despite the creation or modification of cyclic data structures. Crucial to the proof were two lemmas dealing with the scope, *weakening* and *strengthening*.

The first lemma, scope weakening, allows us to arbitrarily extend a scope with any literal $n_0^{\tau_0}$.

Lemma 1 (Weakening). *If* $\Gamma; \sigma \vdash_m n^\tau : \tau$ *then* $\Gamma; \sigma, n_0^{\tau_0} \vdash_m n^\tau : \tau$*, for all* $n_0^{\tau_0}$*.*

Intuitively, this lemma holds because if a proof of $\Gamma; \sigma \vdash_m n^\tau : \tau$ relies on the rule T-VCONST, then that $n_1^{\tau_1} \in \sigma$ for some $n_1^{\tau_1}$. But then $n_1^{\tau_1} \in (\sigma, n_0^{\tau_0})$ as well. Importantly, the scope σ is a *set* of n^τ and not a map from n to τ. As such, if $n'^{\tau'}$ is already present in σ, adding $n'^{\tau'_0}$ will not clobber it. Allowing the same literal to have multiple types is of practical importance. For example a pointer n to a struct could be annotated with the type of the struct, or the type of the first field of the struct, or `int`; all may safely appear in the environment.

Consider the proof that $n^{\texttt{ptr}^c\texttt{struct}\ node}$ is well typed for the heap given in Sect. 3.3. After applying Rule T-PTRC, we used the fact that $n^{\texttt{ptr}^c\texttt{struct}\ node} \in \sigma, n^{\texttt{ptr}^c\texttt{struct}\ node}$ to prove that the *next* field of the struct is well typed. If we were to replace σ with another scope $\sigma, n_0^{\tau_0}$ for some typed literal $n_0^{\tau_0}$ (and as a result any scope that is a superset of σ), the inclusion $n^{\texttt{ptr}^c\texttt{struct}\ node} \in \sigma, n_0^{\tau_0}, n^{\texttt{ptr}^c\texttt{struct}\ node}$ still holds and our pointer is still well-typed.

Conversely, the second lemma, scope strengthening, allows us to remove a literal from a scope, if that literal is well typed in an empty context.

Lemma 2 (Strengthening). *If* $\Gamma; \sigma \vdash_m n_1^{\tau_1} : \tau_1$ *and* $\Gamma; \cdot \vdash_m n_2^{\tau_2} : \tau_2$*, then* $\Gamma; \sigma \backslash \{n_2^{\tau_2}\} \vdash_m n_1^{\tau_1} : \tau_1$*.*

Informally, if the fact that $n_2^{\tau_2}$ is in the scope is used in the proof of well-typedness of $n_1^{\tau_1}$ to prove that $n_2^{\tau_2}$ is well-typed for some scope σ, then we can just use the proof that it is well-typed in an empty scope, along with weakening, to reach the same conclusion.

Looking back again at the proof of the previous section, we know that

$$\Gamma; \cdot \vdash_c n : \texttt{ptr}^c\texttt{struct}\ node$$
and
$$\Gamma; \sigma, n^{\texttt{ptr}^c\texttt{struct}\ node} \vdash_c \&n \rightarrow next : \texttt{ptr}^c\texttt{struct}\ node$$

While the proof of the latter fact relies on $n^{\texttt{ptr}^c\texttt{struct}\ node}$ being in scope, that would not be necessary if we knew (independently) that it was well-typed. That would essentially amount to unrolling the proof by one step.

4.2 Blame

With progress and preservation we can prove a *blame theorem*: Only unchecked code can be blamed as the ultimate reason for a stuck program.

Theorem 3 (Checked code cannot be blamed). *Suppose* $\cdot \vdash_c e : \tau$ *(under heap* H*) and there exists* H_i*,* m_i*, and* e_i *for* $1 \leq i \leq k$ *such that* $H; e \longrightarrow^{m_1} H_1; e_1 \longrightarrow^{m_2} \ldots \longrightarrow^{m_k} H_k; e_k$*. If* $H_k; e_k$ *is stuck then the source of the issue is unchecked code.*

Proof. Suppose $\cdot \vdash_c e_k : \tau$ (under heap H_k). By Progress, the only way the $H_k; e_k$ can be stuck is if $e_k = E[e'']$ and $mode(E) = u$; i.e., the term's redex is in unchecked code. Otherwise $H_k; e_k$ is not well typed, i.e., $\cdot \nvdash_c e_k : \tau$ (under heap H_k). As such, one of the steps of the evaluation was in unchecked code, i.e., there must exist some i where $1 \leq i \leq k$ and $m_i = u$. This is because, by Preservation, a well-typed program in checked mode that takes a checked step always leads to a well-typed program in checked mode.

This theorem means that a code reviewer can focus on unchecked code regions, trusting that checked ones are safe.

5 Porting Assistance

Porting legacy code to use Checked C's features can be tedious and time consuming. To assist the process, we developed a source-to-source translator called *checked-c-convert* that discovers some safely-used pointers and rewrites them to be checked. This algorithm is based on one used by CCured [26], but exploits Checked C's allowance of mixing checked and unchecked pointers to make less conservative decisions.

The *checked-c-convert* translator works by (1) traversing a program's abstract syntax tree (AST) to generate constraints based on pointer variable declaration and use; (2) solving those constraints; and (3) rewriting the program. These rewrites consist of promoting some declared pointer types to be *checked*, some parameter types to be *bounds-safe interfaces*, and inserting some casts. *checked-c-convert* aims to produce a well-formed Checked C program whose changes from the original are minimal and unsurprising. A particular challenge is to preserve syntactic structure of the program. A rewritten program should be recognizable by the author and it should be usable as a starting point for both the development of new features and additional porting. The *checked-c-convert* tool is implemented as a clang `libtooling` application and is freely available.

5.1 Constraint Logic and Solving

The basic approach is to infer a *qualifier* q_i for each defined pointer variable i. Inspired by CCured's approach [26], qualifiers can be either PTR, ARR and UNK, ordered as a lattice $PTR < ARR < UNK$. Those variables with inferred qualifier PTR can be rewritten into `_Ptr<τ>` types, while those with UNK are left as is. Those with the ARR qualifier are eligible to have `_Array_ptr<τ>` type. For the moment we only signal this fact in a comment and do not rewrite because we cannot always infer proper bounds expressions.

Qualifiers are introduced at each pointer variable declaration, i.e., parameter, variable, field, etc. Constraints are introduced as a pointer is used, and take one of the following forms:

$$\begin{array}{ll} q_i = PTR & q_i \neq PTR \\ q_i = ARR & q_i \neq ARR \\ q_i = UNK & q_i \neq UNK \\ q_i = q_j & q_i = ARR \Rightarrow q_j = ARR \\ & q_i = UNK \Rightarrow q_j = UNK \end{array}$$

An expression that performs arithmetic on a pointer with qualifier q_i, either via `+` or `[]`, introduces a constraint $q_i = ARR$. Assignments between pointers introduce aliasing constraints of the form $q_i = q_j$. Casts introduce implication constraints based on the relationship between the sizes of the two types. If the sizes are not comparable, then both constraint variables in an assignment-based cast are constrained to *UNK* via an equality constraint. One difference from CCured is the use of negation constraints, which are used to fix a constraint variable to a particular Checked C type (e.g., due to an existing `_Ptr`$<\tau>$ annotation). These would cause problems for CCured, as they might introduce unresolvable conflicts. But Checked C's allowance of checked and unchecked code can resolve them using explicit casts and bounds-safe interfaces, as discussed below.

One problem with unification-based analysis is that a single unsafe use might "pollute" the constraint system by introducing an equality constraint to *UNK* that transitively constrains unified qualifiers to *UNK* as well. For example, casting a **struct** pointer to a **unsigned char** buffer to write to the network would cause all transitive uses of that pointer to be unchecked. The tool takes advantage of Checked C's ability to mix checked and unchecked pointers to solve this problem. In particular, constraints for each function are solved locally, using separate qualifier variables for each external function's declared parameters.

5.2 Algorithm

Our modular algorithm runs as follows:

1. The AST for every compilation unit is traversed and constraints are generated based on the uses of pointer variables. Each pointer variable `x` that appears at a physical location in the program is given a unique constraint variable q_i at the point of declaration. Uses of `x` are identified with the constraint variable created at the point of declaration. A distinction is made for parameter and return variables depending on if the associated function definition is a *declaration* or a *definition*:
   - *Declaration*: There may be multiple declarations. The constraint variables for the parameters and return values in the declarations are all constrained to be equal to each other. At call sites, the constraint variables used for a function's parameters and return values come from those in the declaration, not the definition (unless there is no declaration).

   - *Definition*: There will only be one definition. These constraint variables are not constrained to be equal to the variables in the declarations. This enables modular (per function) reasoning.
2. After the AST is traversed, the constraints are solved using a fast, unification-focused algorithm [26]. The result is a set of satisfying assignments for constraint variables q_i.
3. Then, the AST is re-traversed. At each physical location associated with a constraint variable, a re-write decision is made based on the value of the constraint variable. These physical locations are variable declaration statements, either as members of a **struct**, function variable declarations, or parameter variable declarations. There is a special case, which is any constraint variable appearing at a parameter position, either at a function declaration/definition, or, a call site. That case is discussed in more detail next.
4. All of the re-write decisions are then applied to the source code.

5.3 Resolving Conflicts

Defining distinct constraint variables for function declarations, used at call-sites, and function definitions, used within that function, can result in conflicting solutions. If there is a conflict, then the declaration's solution is safer than the definition, or the definition's is safer than the declaration's. Which case we are in can be determined by considering the relationship between the variables' valuations in the qualifier lattice. There are three cases:

- *No imbalance*: In this case, the re-write is made based on the value of the constraint variable in the solution to the unification.
- *Declaration (caller) is safer than definition (callee)*: In this case, there is nothing to do for the function, since the function does unknown things with the pointer. This case will be dealt with at the call site by inserting a cast.
- *Decalaration (caller) is less safe than definition (callee)*: In this case, there are call sites that are unsafe, but the function itself is fine. We can re-write the function declaration and definition with a bounds-safe interface.

Example: caller is safer than callee: Consider a function that makes unsafe use of the parameter within the body of the function, but a callee of the function passes an argument that is only ever used safely.

```
void f(int *a) {
  *(int **)a = a;
}

void caller (void) {
  int q = 0;
  int *p = &q;
  f(p);
}
```

Here, we cannot make a safe since its use is outside Checked C's type system. Relying on a unification-only approach, this fact would poison all arguments passed to f too, i.e., p in caller. This is unfortunate, since p is used safely inside of caller. Our algorithm remedies this situation by doing the conversion and inserting a cast:

```

void caller (void) {
  int q = 0;
  _Ptr<int> p = &q;
  f((int*)p);
}
```

The presence of the cast indicates to the programmer that perhaps there is something in f that should be investigated.

Example: caller less safe than callee: Now consider a function that makes safe use of the parameter within the body of the function, but a caller of the function might perform casts or other unsafe operations on an argument it passes.

```
void f(int *a) {
  *a = 0;
}

void caller (void) {
  int q = 0;
  f1(&q);
  f1 (((int*) 0x8f8000));
}
```

If considered in isolation, the function f is safe and the parameter could be rewritten to _Ptr<int>. However, it is used from an unsafe context. In an approach with pure unification, like CCured, this unsafe use at the call-site would pollute the classification at the definition. Our algorithm considers solutions and call sites and definitions independently. Here, the uses of f in caller are less safe than those in the f's definition so the rewriter would insert a bounds-safe interface for f:

```
void f(int *a : itype(_Ptr<int>)) {
  *a = 0;
}
```

The `itype` syntax indicates that a can be supplied by the caller as either an int∗ or a _Ptr<τ>, but the function body will treat a as a _Ptr<τ>. (See Sect. 2 for more on interface types.)

This approach has advantages and disadvantages. It favors making the fewest number of modifications across a project. An alternative to using interface types would be to change the parameter type to a _Ptr<τ> directly, and then insert casts at each call site. This would tell the programmer where potentially bogus pointer values were, but would also increase the number of changes made. Our approach does not immediately tell the programmer where the pointer changes need to be made. However, the Checked C compiler will do that if the programmer takes a bounds-safe interface and manually converts it into a non-interface _Ptr<*T*> type. Every location that would require a cast will fail to type check, signaling to the programmer to have a closer look.

Table 1. Number of pointer declarations converted through automated porting

Program	# of *	% _Ptr	Arr.	Unk.	Casts(Calls)	Ifcs(Funcs)	LOC
zlib 1.2.8	4514	46%	5%	49%	8 (300)	464 (1188)	17388
sqlite 3.18.1	34230	38%	3%	59%	2096 (29462)	9132 (23305)	106806
parson	1132	35%	1%	64%	3 (378)	340 (454)	2320
lua 5.3.4	15114	23%	1%	76%	175 (1443)	784 (2708)	13577
libtiff 4.0.6	34518	26%	1%	73%	495 (1986)	1916 (5812)	62439

5.4 Experimental Evaluation

We carried out a preliminary experimental evaluation of the efficacy of *checked-c-convert*. To do so, we ran it on five targets—programs and libraries—and recorded how many pointer types the rewriter converted and how many casts were inserted. We chose these targets as they constitute legacy code used in commodity systems, and in security-sensitive contexts.

Running *checked-c-convert* took no more than 30 min to run, for each target. Table 1 contains the results. The first and last column indicate the target, its version, and the lines of code it contains (per `cloc`). The second column (**# of** *) counts the number of pointer definitions or declarations in the program, i.e., places that might get rewritten when porting. The next three columns (**% _Ptr**, **Arr.**, **Unk.**) indicate the percentages of these that were determined to be *PTR*, *ARR*, or *UNK*, respectively, where only those in **% _Ptr** induce a rewriting action. The results show that a fair number of variables can be automatically rewritten as safe, single pointers (_Ptr<*T*>). After investigation, there are usually two reasons that a pointer cannot be replaced with a _Ptr<*T*>: either some arithmetic is performed on the pointer, or it is passed as a parameter to a library function for which a bounds-safe interface does not exist.

The next two columns (**Casts(Calls)**, **Ifcs(Funcs)**) examine how our rewriting algorithm takes advantage of Checked C's support for incremental conversion. In particular, column 6 (**Casts(Calls)**) counts how many times we cast a safe pointer at the call site of a function deemed to use that pointer unsafely; in parentheses we indicate the total number of call sites in the program. Column 7 (**Ifcs(Funcs)**) counts how often a function definition or declaration has its type rewritten to use an interface type, where the total declaration/definition count is in parentheses. This rewriting occurs when the function itself uses at least one of its parameters safely, but at least one caller provides an argument that is deemed unsafe. Both columns together represent an improvement in precision, compared to unification-only, due to Checked C's focus on backward compatibility.

This experiment represents the first step a developer would take to adopting Checked C into their project. The values converted into _Ptr<τ> by the re-writer need never be considered again during the rest of the conversion or by subsequent software assurance/bug finding efforts.

6 Related Work

There has been substantial prior work that aims to address the vulnerability presented by C's lack of memory safety. A detailed discussion of how this work compares to Checked C can be found in Elliott et al. [11]. Here we discuss approaches for automating C safety, as that is most related to work on our rewriting algorithm. We also discuss prior work generally on *migratory typing*, which aims to support backward compatible migration of an untyped/less-typed program to a statically typed one.

Security Mitigations. The lack of memory safety in C and C++ has serious practical consequences, especially for security, so there has been extensive research toward addressing it automatically. One approach is to attempt to detect memory corruption after it has happened or prevent an attacker from exploiting a memory vulnerability. Approaches deployed in practice include stack canaries [31], address space layout randomization (ASLR) [34], data-execution prevention (DEP), and control-flow integrity (CFI) [1]. These defenses have led to an escalating series of measures and counter-measures by attackers and defenders [32]. These approaches do not prevent data modification or data disclosure attacks, and they can be defeated by determined attackers who use those attacks. By contrast, enforcing memory safety avoids these issues.

Memory-Safe C. Another important line of prior work aims to enforce memory safety for C; here we focus on projects that aim to do so (mostly) automatically in a way related to our rewriting algorithm. CCured [26] is a source-to-source rewriter that transforms C programs to be safe automatically. CCured's goal is end-to-end soundness for the entire program. It uses a whole-program analysis that divides pointers into fat pointers (which allow pointer arithmetic and unsafe casts) and thin pointers (which do not). The use of fat pointers causes problems interoperating with existing libraries and systems, making the CCured approach impractical when that is necessary. Other systems attempt to overcome the limitations of fat pointers by storing the bounds information in a separate metadata space [24,25] or within unused bits in 64-bit pointers [19] (though this approach is unsound [13]). These approaches can add substantial overhead; e.g., Softbound's overhead for spatial safety checking is 67%. Deputy [38] uses backward-compatible pointer representations with types similar to those in Checked C. It supports inference local to a function, but resorts to manual annotations at function and module boundaries. None of these systems permit intermixing safe and unsafe pointers within a module, as Checked C does, which means that some code simply needs to be rewritten rather than included but clearly marked within _Unchecked blocks.

Migratory Typing. Checked C is closely related to work supporting migratory typing [35] (aka gradual typing [30]). In that setting, portions of a program written in a dynamically typed language can be annotated with static types. For Checked C, legacy C plays the role of the dynamically typed language and checked regions play the role of statically typed portions. In migratory typing, one typically proves that a fully annotated program is statically type-safe. What about mixed programs? They can be given a semantics that checks static types at boundary crossings [21]. For example, calling a statically typed function from dynamically typed code would induce a dynamic check that the passed-in argument has the specified type. When a function is passed as an argument, this check must be deferred until the function is called. The delay prompted research on proving *blame*: Even if a failure were to occur within static code, it could be blamed on bogus values provided by dynamic code [36]. This semantics is, however, slow [33], so many languages opt for what Greenman and Felleisen [14] term the *erasure semantics*: No checks are added and no notion of blame is proved, i.e., failures in statically typed code are not formally connected to errors in dynamic code. Checked C also has erasure semantics, but Theorem 3 is able to lay blame with the unchecked code.

Rust. Rust [20] is a programming language, like C, that supports zero-cost abstractions, but like Checked C, aims to be safe. Rust programs may have designated unsafe blocks in which certain rules are relaxed, potentially allowing run-time failures. As with Checked C, the question is how to reason about the safety of a program that contains any amount of unsafe code. The RustBelt project [17] proposes to use a semantic [23], rather than syntactic [37], account of soundness, in which (1) types are given meaning according to what terms inhabit them; (2) type rules are sound when interpreted semantically; and (3) semantic well typing implies safe execution. With this approach, unsafe code can be (manually) proved to inhabit the semantic interpretation of its type, in which case its use by type-checked code will be safe.

We view our approach as complementary to that of RustBelt, perhaps constituting the first step in mixed-language safety assurance. In particular, we employ a simple, syntactic proof that checked code is safe and unchecked code can always be blamed for a failure—no proof about any particular unsafe code is required. Stronger assurance that programs are safe despite using mixed code could employ the (more involved and labor-intensive) RustBelt approach.

7 Conclusions and Future Work

This paper has presented CoreChkC, a core formalism for Checked C, an extension to C aiming to provide spatial safety. CoreChkC models Checked C's safe (checked) and unsafe (legacy) pointers; while these pointers can be intermixed, use of legacy pointers is severely restricted in *checked regions* of code. We prove that these restrictions are efficacious: *checked code cannot be blamed* in the sense that any spatial safety violation must be directly or indirectly due to an unsafe operation outside a checked region. Our formalization and proof are mechanized in the Coq proof assistant; this mechanization is available at https://github.com/plum-umd/checkedc/tree/master/coq.

The freedom to intermix safe and legacy pointers in Checked C programs affords flexibility when porting legacy code. We show this is true for *automated porting* as well. A whole-program rewriting algorithm we built is able to make more pointers safe than it would if pointer types were all-or-nothing; we do this by taking advantage of Checked C's allowed casts and interface types. The tool implementing this algorithm, *checked-c-convert*, is distributed with Checked C at https://github.com/Microsoft/checkedc-clang.

As future work, we are interested in formalizing other aspects of Checked C, notably its *subsumption algorithm* and support for *flow-sensitive* typing (to handle pointer arithmetic), to prove that these aspects of the implementation are correct. We are also interested in expanding support for the rewriting algorithm, by using more advanced static analysis techniques to infer numeric bounds suitable for re-writing array types. Finally, we hope to automatically infer regions of code that could be enclosed within checked regions.

Acknowledgments. We would like to thank the anonymous reviewers for helpful comments on drafts of this paper, and Sam Elliott for contributions to the portions of the design and implementation of Checked C presented in this paper. This research was funded in part by the U.S. National Science Foundation under grants CNS-1801545 and EDU-1319147.

References

1. Abadi, M., Budiu, M., Erlingsson, Ú., Ligatti, J.: Control-flow integrity. In: ACM Conference on Computer and Communications Security (2005)
2. Akritidis, P., Costa, M., Castro, M., Hand, S.: Baggy bounds checking: an efficient and backwards-compatible defense against out-of-bounds errors. In: Proceedings of the 18th Conference on USENIX Security Symposium (2009)
3. Austin, T.M., Breach, S.E., Sohi, G.S.: Efficient detection of all pointer and array access errors. In: SIGPLAN Not., vol. 29, no. 6, June 1994
4. Baratloo, A., Singh, N., Tsai, T.: Transparent run-time defense against stack smashing attacks. In: Proceedings of the Annual Conference on USENIX Annual Technical Conference (2000)
5. Bhatkar, S., DuVarney, D.C., Sekar, R.: Address obfuscation: an efficient approach to combat a broad range of memory error exploits. In: Proceedings of the 12th Conference on USENIX Security Symposium, vol. 12 (2003)
6. Condit, J., Hackett, B., Lahiri, S.K., Qadeer, S.: Unifying type checking and property checking for low-level code. In: POPL 2009: Proceedings of the 36th Annual ACM SIGPLAN-SIGACT Symposium on Principles of Programming Languages. Association for Computing Machinery, New York (2009)

7. Condit, J., Harren, M., Anderson, Z., Gay, D., Necula, G.C.: Dependent types for low-level programming. In: Proceedings of European Symposium on Programming (ESOP 2007) (2007)
8. Cowan, C., et al.: Stackguard: automatic adaptive detection and prevention of buffer-overflow attacks. In: Proceedings of the 7th Conference on USENIX Security Symposium, vol. 7 (1998)
9. Dhurjati, D., Adve, V.: Backwards-compatible array bounds checking for C with very low overhead. In: Proceedings of the 28th International Conference on Software Engineering (2006)
10. Duck, G.J., Yap, R.H.C.: Heap bounds protection with low fat pointers. In: Proceedings of the 25th International Conference on Compiler Construction (2016)
11. Elliott, A.S., Ruef, A., Hicks, M., Tarditi, D.: Checked C: Making C safe by extension. In: Proceedings of the IEEE Conference on Secure Development (SecDev), September 2018
12. Frantzen, M., Shuey, M.: StackGhost: hardware facilitated stack protection. In: Proceedings of the 10th Conference on USENIX Security Symposium, vol. 10 (2001)
13. Gil, R., Okhravi, H., Shrobe, H.: There's a hole in the bottom of the C: on the effectiveness of allocation protection. In: Proceedings of the IEEE Conference on Secure Development (SecDev), September 2018
14. Greenman, B., Felleisen, M.: A spectrum of type soundness and performance. Proc. ACM Program. Lang. **2**(ICFP) (2018)
15. Grossman, D., Hicks, M., Jim, T., Morrisett, G.: Cyclone: a type-safe dialect of C. C/C++ Users J. **23**(1), 112–139 (2005)
16. Jones, R.W.M., Kelly, P.H.J.: Backwards-compatible bounds checking for arrays and pointers in C programs. In: Kamkar, M., Byers, D. (eds.) Third International Workshop on Automated Debugging. Linkoping Electronic Conference Proceedings, Linkoping University Electronic Press, May 1997. http://www.ep.liu.se/ea/cis/1997/009/
17. Jung, R., Jourdan, J.H., Krebbers, R., Dreyer, D.: RustBelt: securing the foundations of the rust programming language. Proc. ACM Program. Lang. **2**(POPL), 66 (2017)
18. Kiriansky, V., Bruening, D., Amarasinghe, S.P.: Secure execution via program shepherding. In: Proceedings of the 11th USENIX Security Symposium, pp. 191–206. USENIX Association, Berkeley (2002). http://dl.acm.org/citation.cfm?id=647253.720293
19. Kwon, A., Dhawan, U., Smith, J.M., Knight Jr., T.F., DeHon, A.: Low-fat pointers: compact encoding and efficient gate-level implementation of fat pointers for spatial safety and capability-based security. In: Proceedings of the 2013 ACM SIGSAC Conference on Computer & #38; Communications Security, CCS 2013, pp. 721–732. ACM, New York (2013). https://doi.org/10.1145/2508859.2516713, http://doi.acm.org/10.1145/2508859.2516713
20. Matsakis, N.D., Klock II, F.S.: The rust language. In: ACM SIGAda Annual Conference on High Integrity Language Technology (2014)
21. Matthews, J., Findler, R.B.: Operational semantics for multi-language programs. In: POPL (2007)
22. Microsoft Corporation: Control flow guard (2016). https://msdn.microsoft.com/en-us/library/windows/desktop/mt637065(v=vs.85).aspx. Accessed April 27 2016
23. Milner, R.: A theory of type polymorphism in programming. J. Comput. Syst. Sci. **17**(3), 348–375 (1978)

24. Intel memory protection extensions (MPX) (2018). https://software.intel.com/en-us/isa-extensions/intel-mpx
25. Nagarakatte, S., Zhao, J., Martin, M.M., Zdancewic, S.: SoftBound: highly compatible and complete spatial memory safety for C. In: Proceedings of the 30th ACM SIGPLAN Conference on Programming Language Design and Implementation (2009)
26. Necula, G.C., Condit, J., Harren, M., McPeak, S., Weimer, W.: CCured: type-safe retrofitting of legacy software. ACM Trans. Program. Lang. Syst. (TOPLAS) **27**(3), 477–526 (2005)
27. NIST vulnerability database. https://nvd.nist.gov. Accessed 17 May 2017
28. Sangiorgi, D., Rutten, J.: Advanced Topics in Bisimulation and Coinduction, vol. 52. Cambridge University Press, Cambridge (2011)
29. Serebryany, K., Bruening, D., Potapenko, A., Vyukov, D.: AddressSanitizer: a fast address sanity checker. In: Proceedings of the 2012 USENIX Conference on Annual Technical Conference (2012)
30. Siek, J.G., Taha, W.: Gradual typing for functional languages. In: Workshop on Scheme and Functional Programming (2006)
31. Steffen, J.L.: Adding run-time checking to the Portable C Compiler. Softw. Pract. Exper. **22**(4), 305–316 (1992)
32. Szekeres, L., Payer, M., Wei, T., Song, D.: SoK: eternal war in memory. In: Proceedings of the 2013 IEEE Symposium on Security and Privacy (2013)
33. Takikawa, A., Feltey, D., Greenman, B., New, M.S., Vitek, J., Felleisen, M.: Is sound gradual typing dead? In: POPL (2016)
34. PaX Team: http://pax.grsecurity.net/docs/aslr.txt (2001)
35. Tobin-Hochstadt, S., et al.: Migratory typing: ten years later. In: 2nd Summit on Advances in Programming Languages (SNAPL 2017), vol. 71, pp. 17:1–17:17 (2017)
36. Wadler, P., Findler, R.B.: Well-typed programs can't be blamed. In: Castagna, G. (ed.) ESOP 2009. LNCS, vol. 5502, pp. 1–16. Springer, Heidelberg (2009). https://doi.org/10.1007/978-3-642-00590-9_1
37. Wright, A.K., Felleisen, M.: A syntactic approach to type soundness. Inf. Comput. **115**(1), 38–94 (1994)
38. Zhou, F., et al.: SafeDrive: safe and recoverable extensions using language-based techniques. In: 7th Symposium on Operating System Design and Implementation (OSDI 2006). USENIX Association, Seattle (2006)

Wys*: A DSL for Verified Secure Multi-party Computations

Aseem Rastogi[1(✉)], Nikhil Swamy[2], and Michael Hicks[3]

[1] Microsoft Research, Bangalore, India
aseemr@microsoft.com
[2] Microsoft Research, Redmond, USA
nswamy@microsoft.com
[3] University of Maryland, College Park, USA
mwh@cs.umd.edu

Abstract. Secure multi-party computation (MPC) enables a set of mutually distrusting parties to cooperatively compute, using a cryptographic protocol, a function over their private data. This paper presents Wys*, a new domain-specific language (DSL) for writing *mixed-mode* MPCs. Wys* is an embedded DSL hosted in F*, a verification-oriented, effectful programming language. Wys* source programs are essentially F* programs written in a custom MPC effect, meaning that the programmers can use F*'s logic to verify the correctness and security properties of their programs. To reason about the distributed runtime semantics of these programs, we formalize a deep embedding of Wys*, also in F*. We mechanize the necessary metatheory to prove that the properties verified for the Wys* source programs carry over to the distributed, multi-party semantics. Finally, we use F*'s extraction to extract an interpreter that we have proved matches this semantics, yielding a partially verified implementation. Wys* is the first DSL to enable formal verification of MPC programs. We have implemented several MPC protocols in Wys*, including private set intersection, joint median, and an MPC-based card dealing application, and have verified their correctness and security.

1 Introduction

Secure multi-party computation (MPC) enables two or more parties to compute a function f over their private inputs x_i so that parties don't see each others' inputs, but rather only see the output $f(x_1, ..., x_n)$. Using a trusted third party to compute f would achieve this goal, but in fact we can achieve it using one of a variety of cryptographic protocols carried out only among the participants [12,26,58,65]. One example use of MPC is private set intersection (PSI): the x_i could be individuals' personal interests, and the function f computes their intersection, revealing which interests the group has in common, but not any interests that they don't. MPC has also been used for auctions [18], detecting tax fraud [16], managing supply chains [33], privacy preserving statistical analysis [31], and more recently for machine learning tasks [19,21,30,38,44].

F. Nielson and D. Sands (Eds.): POST 2019, LNCS 11426, pp. 99–122, 2019.
https://doi.org/10.1007/978-3-030-17138-4_5

Typically, cryptographic protocols expect f to be specified as a boolean or arithmetic circuit. Programming directly with circuits and cryptography is painful, so starting with the Fairplay project [40] many researchers have designed higher-level domain-specific languages (DSLs) for programming MPCs [6,14,17, 19,23,27,29,34,37,39,45,48,49,52,56,61]. These DSLs compile source code to circuits which are then given to the underlying cryptographic protocol. While doing this undoubtedly makes it easier to program MPCs, these languages still have several drawbacks regarding both security and usability.

This paper presents WYS*, a new MPC DSL that addresses several problems in prior DSLs. Unlike most previous MPC DSLs, WYS* is not a standalone language, but is rather an embedded DSL hosted in F* [59], a full-featured, verification-oriented, effectful programming language. WYS* has the following two distinguishing elements:

1. A program logic for MPC (Sects. 2 and 3). In their most general form, MPC applications are *mixed-mode*: they consist of parties performing (potentially different) local, in-clear computations (e.g. I/O, preprocessing inputs) interleaved with joint, secure computations. WYS* is the first MPC DSL to provide a program logic to formally reason about the *correctness and security* of such applications, e.g., to prove that the outputs will not reveal too much information about a party's inputs [41].[1]

To avoid reasoning about separate programs for each party, WYS* builds on the basic programming model of the Wysteria MPC DSL [52] that allows applications to be written as a single specification. WYS* presents a *shallow embedding* of the Wysteria programming model in F*. When writing WYS* source programs, programmers essentially write F* programs in a new Wys effect, against a library of MPC combinators. The pre- and postcondition specifications on the combinators encode a program logic for MPC. The logic provides *observable traces*—a novel addition to the Wysteria semantics—which programmers can use to specify security properties such as delimited release [55]. Since WYS* programs are F* programs, F* computes verification conditions (VCs) for them which are discharged using Z3 [2] as usual.

We prove the soundness of the program logic—that the properties proven about the WYS* source programs carry over when these programs are run by multiple parties in a distributed manner—also in F*. The proof connects the pre- and postconditions of the WYS* combinators to their distributed semantics in two steps. First, we implement the combinators in F*, proving the validity of their pre- and postconditions against their implementation. Next, we reason about this implementation and the distributed runtime semantics through a deep embedding of WYS* in F*. Essentially, we deep-embed the WYS* combinator abstract syntax trees (ASTs) as an F* datatype and formalize two operational semantics for them: a conceptual single-threaded semantics that models their

[1] Our attacker model is the "honest-but-curious" model where the attackers are the participants themselves, who play their roles in the protocol faithfully, but are motivated to infer as much as they can about the other participants' secrets by observing the protocol. Section 2.3 makes the security model of WYS* more precise.

F* implementation, and the actual distributed semantics that models the multi-party runs of the programs. We prove, in F*, that the single-threaded semantics is sound with respect to the distributed semantics (Sect. 3). While we use F*, the program logic is general and it should be possible to embed it in other verification frameworks (e.g., in Coq, in the style of Hoare Type Theory [46]).

2. A full-featured, partially verified implementation (Sect. 3). WYS*'s implementation is, in part, formally verified. The hope is that formal verification will reduce the occurrence of security threatening bugs, as it has in prior work [15,36,50,63,64].

We define an interpreter in F* that operates over the WYS* ASTs produced by a custom F* extraction for the Wys effect. While the local computations are executed locally by the interpreter, the interpreter compiles secure-computation ASTs to circuits, on the fly, and executes them using the Goldreich, Micali and Wigderson (GMW) multi-party computation protocol [26]. The WYS* AST (and hence the interpreter) does not "bake in" standard F* constructs like numbers and lists. Rather, inherited language features appear abstractly in the AST, and their semantics is handled by a foreign function interface (FFI). This permits WYS* programs to take advantage of existing code and libraries available in F*.

To prove the interpreter behaves correctly, we prove, in F*, that it correctly implements the formalized distributed semantics. The circuit library and the GMW implementation are not verified—while it is possible to verify the circuit library [4], verifying a GMW implementation is an open research question. But the stage is set for verified versions to be plugged into the WYS* codebase. We characterize the Trusted Computing Base (TCB) of the WYS* toolchain in Sect. 3.5.

Using WYS* we have implemented several programs, including PSI, joint median, and a card dealing application (Sect. 4). For PSI and joint median we implement two versions: a straightforward one and an optimized one that improves performance but increases the number of adversary-observable events. We formally prove that the optimized and unoptimized versions are equivalent, both functionally and w.r.t. privacy of parties' inputs. Our card dealing application relies on WYS*'s support for secret shares [57]. We formally prove that the card dealing algorithm always deals a fresh card.

In sum, WYS* constitutes the first DSL that supports proving security and correctness properties about MPC programs, which are executed by a partially verified implementation of a full-featured language. No prior DSL provides these benefits (Sect. 5). The WYS* implementation, example programs, and proofs are publicly available on Github at https://github.com/FStarLang/FStar/tree/stratified_last/examples/wysteria.[2]

2 Verifying and Deploying WYS* Programs

We illustrate the main concepts of WYS* by showing, in several stages, how to program, optimize, and verify the two-party joint median example [32,53].

[2] This development was done on an older F* version, but the core ideas of what we present here apply to the present version as well.

In this example, two parties, Alice and Bob, each have a set of n distinct, locally sorted integers, and they want to compute the median of the union of their sets without revealing anything else; our running example fixes $n = 2$, for simplicity.

2.1 Secure Computations with as_sec

In Wys*, as in its predecessor Wysteria [52], an MPC is written as a single specification that executes in one of the two *computation modes*. The primary mode is called sec mode. In it, a computation is carried out using an MPC protocol among multiple principals. Here is the joint median in Wys*:

```
1 let median a b in_a in_b =
2   as_sec {a, b} (fun () → let cmp = fst (reveal in_a) > fst (reveal in_b) in
3                           let x3 = if cmp then fst (reveal in_a) else snd (reveal in_a) in
4                           let y3 = if cmp then snd (reveal in_b) else fst (reveal in_b) in
5                           if x3 > y3 then y3 else x3)
```

The four arguments to median are, respectively, principal identifiers for Alice and Bob, and Alice and Bob's secret inputs expressed as tuples. In Wys*, values specific to each principal are *sealed* with the principal's name (which appears in the sealed container's type). As such, the types of in_a and in_b are, respectively, sealed {a} (int ∗ int) and sealed {b} (int ∗ int). The as_sec ps f construct indicates that thunk f should be run in sec mode among principals in the set ps. In this mode, the code has access to the secrets of the principals ps, which it can reveal using the reveal coercion. As we will see later, the type of reveal ensures that parties cannot reveal each others' inputs outside sec mode.[3] Also note that the code freely uses standard F* library functions like fst and snd. The example extends naturally to $n > 2$ [3].

To run this program, both Alice and Bob would start a Wys* interpreter at their host and direct it to run the median function Upon reaching the as_sec thunk, the interpreters coordinate with each other to compute the result using the underlying MPC protocol. Section 2.5 provides more details.

2.2 Optimizing median with as_par

Although median gets the job done, it can be inefficient for large n. However, it turns out if we reveal the result of comparison on line 2 to both the parties, then the computation on line 3 (resp. line 4) can be performed locally by Alice (resp. Bob) without the need of cryptography. Doing so can massively improve performance: previous work [32] has observed a 30× speedup for $n = 64$.

This optimized variant is a *mixed-mode* computation, where participants perform some local computations interleaved with small, jointly evaluated secure computations. Wys*'s second computation mode, par mode, supports such mixed-mode computations. The construct as_par ps f states that each principal in ps should locally execute the thunk f, simultaneously; any principal not in

[3] The runtime representation of sealed a v at b's host is an opaque constant • (Sect. 2.5).

the set ps simply skips the computation. Within f, while running in par mode, principals may engage in secure computations via as_sec.

Here is an optimized version of median using as_par:

```
1 let median_opt a b in_a in_b =
2   let cmp = as_sec {a, b} (fun () → fst (reveal in_a) > fst (reveal in_b)) in
3   let x3 = as_par {a} (fun () → if cmp then fst (reveal in_a) else snd (reveal (in_a))) in
4   let y3 = as_par {b} (fun () → if cmp then snd (reveal in_b) else fst (reveal (in_b))) in
5   as_sec {a, b} (fun () → if reveal x3 > reveal y3 then reveal y3 else reveal x3)
```

The secure computation on line 2 *only* computes cmp and returns the result to both the parties. Line 3 is then a par mode computation involving only Alice in which she discards one of her inputs based on cmp. Similarly, on line 4, Bob discards one of his inputs. Finally, line 5 compares the remaining inputs using as_sec and returns the result as the final median.

One might wonder whether the par mode is necessary. Could we program the local parts of a mixed-mode program in normal F*, and use a special compiler to convert the sec mode parts to circuits and pass them to a GMW MPC service? We could, but it would complicate both writing MPCs and formally reasoning that the whole computation is correct and secure. In particular, programmers would need to write one program for each party that performs a different local computation (as in median_opt). The potential interleaving among local computations and their synchronization behavior when securely computing together would be a source of possible error and thus must be considered in any proof. For example, Alice's code might have a bug in it that prevents it from reaching a synchronization point with Bob, to do a GMW-based MPC. For WYS*, the situation is much simpler. Programmers may write and maintain a single program. This program can be formally reasoned about directly using a SIMD-style, "single-threaded" semantics, per the soundness result from Sect. 3.4. This semantics permits reasoning about the coordinated behavior of multiple principals, without worry about the effects of interleavings or wrong synchronizations. Thanks to par mode, invariants about coordinated local computations are directly evident since we can soundly assume the lockstep behavior (e.g., loop iterations in the PSI example in Sect. 4).

2.3 Embedding a Type System for WYS* in F*

Designing high-level, multi-party computations is relatively easy using Wysteria's abstractions. Before trying to run such a computation, we might wonder:

1. Is it *realizable*? For example, does a computation that is claimed to be executed only by some principals ps (e.g., using an as_par ps or an as_sec ps) only ever access data belonging to ps?
2. Is it *correct?* For example, does median_opt correctly compute the median of Alice and Bob's inputs?
3. Is it *secure*? For example, do the optimizations in median_opt, which produce more visible outputs, potentially leak more about the inputs?

By embedding Wys* in F* and leveraging its extensible, monadic, dependent type-and-effect system, we address each of these three questions. We define a new indexed monad called Wys for computations that use MPC combinators as_sec and as_par. Using Wys along with the sealed type, we can ensure that protocols are realizable. Using F*'s capabilities for formal verification, we can reason about a computation's correctness. By characterizing observable events as part of Wys, we can define trace properties of MPC programs to reason about their security.

To elaborate on the last: we are interested in *application-level* security properties, assuming that the underlying cryptographic MPC protocol (GMW [26] in our implementation) is secure. In particular, the Wys monad models the *ideal* behavior of sec mode—a secure computation reveals only the final output and nothing else. Thus the programmer could reason, for example, that optimized MPC programs reveal no more than their unoptimized versions. To relate the proofs over ideal functionality to the actual implementation, as is standard, we rely on the security of the cryptographic protocol and the composition theorem [20] to postulate that the implementation securely realizes the ideal specification.

The Wys monad. The Wys monad provides several features. First, all DSL code is typed in this monad, encapsulating it from the rest of F*. Within the monad, computations and their specifications can make use of two kinds of *ghost state*: *modes* and *traces*. The mode of a computation indicates whether the computation is running in an as_par or in an as_sec context. The trace of a computation records the sequence and nesting structure of outputs of the jointly executed as_sec expressions—the result of a computation and its trace constitute its observable behavior. The Wys monad is, in essence, the product of a reader monad on modes and a writer monad on traces [43,62].

Formally, we define the following F* types for modes and traces. A mode Mode m ps is a pair of a mode tag (either Par or Sec) and a set of principals ps. A trace is a forest of trace element (telt) trees. The leaves of the trees record messages TMsg x that are received as the result of executing an as_sec thunk. The tree structure represented by the TScope ps t nodes record the set of principals that are able to observe the messages in the trace t.

```
type mtag = Par | Sec
type mode = Mode: m:mtag → ps:prins → mode
type telt = TMsg : x:α → telt | TScope: ps:prins → t:list telt → telt
type trace = list telt
```

Every Wys* computation e has a monadic computation type Wys t pre post. The type indicates that e is in the Wys monad (so it may perform multi-party computations); t is its result type; pre is a precondition on the mode in which e may be executed; and post is a postcondition relating the computation's mode, its result value, and its trace of observable events. When run in a context with mode m satisfying the precondition predicate pre m, e may produce the trace tr, and if and when it returns, the result is a t-typed value v validating post m v tr. The style of indexing a monad with a computation's pre- and postcondition is a standard technique [7,47,59]—we defer the definition of the monad's bind and return to the actual implementation and focus instead on specifications of WYS* specific combinators. We describe as_sec, reveal, and as_par, and how we give them types in F*, leaving the rest to the online technical report [54]. By convention, any free variables in the type signatures are universally prenex quantified.

Defining as_sec *in* WYS*

```
1 val as_sec: ps:prins → f:(unit → Wys a pre post) → Wys a
2   (requires (fun m → m=Mode Par ps ∧ pre (Mode Sec ps)))
3   (ensures (fun m r tr → tr=[TMsg r] ∧ ∃t. post (Mode Sec ps) r t)))
```

The type of as_sec is *dependent* on the first parameter, ps. Its second argument f is the thunk to be evaluated in sec mode. The result's computation type has the form Wys a (requires ϕ) (ensures ψ), for some precondition and postcondition predicates ϕ and ψ, respectively. We use the requires and ensures keywords for readability—they are not semantically significant.

The precondition of as_sec is a predicate on the mode m of the computation in whose context as_sec ps f is called. For all the ps to jointly execute f, we require all of them to transition to perform the as_sec ps f call simultaneously, i.e., the current mode must be Mode Par ps. We also require the precondition pre of f to be valid once the mode has transitioned to Mode Sec ps—line 2 says just this.

The postcondition of as_sec is a predicate relating the initial mode m, the result r:a, and the trace tr of the computation. Line 3 states that the trace of a secure computation as_sec ps f is just a singleton [TMsg r], reflecting that its execution reveals only result r. Additionally, it ensures that the result r is related to the mode in which f is run (Mode Sec ps) and some trace t according to post, the postcondition of f. The API models the "ideal functionality" of secure computation protocols (such as GMW) where the participants only observe the final result.

Defining reveal *in* WYS*. As discussed earlier, a value v of type sealed ps t encapsulates a t value that can be accessed by calling reveal v. This call should only succeed under certain circumstances. For example, in par mode, Bob should not be able to reveal a value of type sealed {Alice} int. The type of reveal makes the access control rules clear:

```
val unseal: sealed ps α → Ghost α

val reveal: x:sealed ps α → Wys α
  (requires (fun m → m.mode=Par ⟹ m.ps ⊆ ps ∧ m.mode=Sec ⟹ m.ps ∩ ps ≠ ∅))
  (ensures (fun m r tr → r=unseal x ∧ tr=[]))
```

The unseal function is a Ghost function, meaning that it can only be used in specifications for reasoning purposes. On the other hand, reveal can be called in the concrete WYS* programs. Its precondition says that when executing in Mode Par ps', *all* current participants must be listed in the seal, i.e., ps' $\subseteq$ ps. However, when executing in Mode Sec ps', only a subset of current participants is required: ps' $\cap$ ps $\neq \emptyset$. This is because the secure computation is executed jointly by all of ps', so it can access any of their individual data. The postcondition of reveal relates the result r to the argument x using the unseal function.

Defining as_par *in* Wys*

```
val as_par: ps:prins → (unit → Wys a pre post) → Wys (sealed ps a)
  (requires (fun m → m.mode=Par ∧ ps ⊆ m.ps ∧ can_seal ps a ∧ pre (Mode Par ps)))
  (ensures (fun m r tr → ∃t. tr=[TScope ps t] ∧ post (Mode Par ps) (unseal r) t)))
```

The type of as_par enforces the current mode to be Par, and ps to be a subset of current principals. Importantly, the API scopes the trace t of f to model the fact that any observables of f are only visible to the principals in ps. Note that as_sec did not require such scoping, as there ps and the set of current principals in m are the same. The can_seal predicate enforces that a is a zero-order type (i.e. closures cannot be sealed), and that in case a is already a sealed type, its set of principals is a subset of ps.

2.4 Correctness and Security Verification

Using the Wys monad and the sealed type, we can write down precise types for our median and median_opt programs, proving various useful properties. We discuss the statements of the main lemmas and the overall proof structure. By programming the protocols as a single specification using the high-level abstractions provided by Wys*, our proofs are relatively straightforward—in all the proofs of this section, F* required no additional hints. In particular, we rely heavily on the view that both parties execute (different fragments of) the same code, thus avoiding the unwieldy task of reasoning about low-level message passing.

Correctness and Security of median. We first define a pure specification of median of two int tuples:

```
let median_of (x1, x2) (y1, y2) = let (_, m, _, _) = sort x1 x2 y1 y2 in m
```

Further, we capture the preconditions using the following predicate:

```
let median_pre (x1, x2) (y1, y2) = x1 < x2 ∧ y1 < y2 ∧ distinct x1 x2 y1 y2
```

Using these, we prove the following top-level specification for median:

```
val median: in_a:sealed {a} (int ∗ int) → in_b:sealed {b} (int ∗ int) → Wys int
  (requires (fun m → m = Mode Par {a, b})) (∗ should be called in the Par mode ∗)
  (ensures (fun m r tr → let in_a, in_b = unseal in_a, unseal in_b in
     (median_pre in_a in_b ⟹ r = median_of in_a in_b) ∧
(∗ functional correctness ∗)
     tr = [TMsg r])) (∗ trace is just the final value ∗)
```

This signature establishes that when Alice and Bob simultaneously execute median (in Par mode), with secrets in_a and in_b, then, if and when the protocol terminates, (a) if their inputs satisfy the precondition median_pre, then the result is the joint median of their inputs and (b) the observable trace consists only of the final result, as there is but a single as_sec thunk in median, i.e., it is *secure*.

Correctness and Security of median_opt. The security proof of median_opt is particularly interesting, because the program intentionally reveals more than just the final result, i.e., the output of the first comparison. We would like to verify that this additional information does not compromise the privacy of the parties' inputs. To do this, we take the following approach.

First, we characterize the observable trace of median_opt as a pure, specification-only function. Then, using relational reasoning, we prove a *noninteference with delimited release* property [55] on these traces. Essentially we prove that, for two runs of median_opt where Bob's inputs and the output median are the same, the observable traces are also the same irrespective of Alice's inputs. Thus, from Alice's perspective, the observable trace does not reveal more to Bob than what the output already does. We prove this property symmetrically for Bob.

We start by defining a trace function for median_opt:

```
let opt_trace a b (x1, _) (y1, _) r = [
  TMsg (x1 > y1); (* observable from the first as_sec *)
  TScope {a} []; TScope {b} []; (* observables from two local as_par *)
  TMsg r ] (* observable from the final as_sec *)
```

A trace will have four elements: output of the first as_sec computation, two empty scoped traces for the two local as_par computations, and the final output.

Using this function, we prove correctness of median_opt, thus:

```
val median_opt: in_a:sealed {a} (int * int) → in_b:sealed {b} (int * int) → Wys int
  (requires (fun m → m = Mode Par {a, b})) (* should be called in the Par mode *)
  (ensures (fun m r tr → let in_a = unseal in_a in let in_b = unseal in_b in
    (median_pre in_a in_b ⟹ r = median_of in_a in_b) ∧
(* functional correctness *)
   tr = opt_trace a b in_a in_b r
(* opt_trace precisely describes the observable trace *)
```

The delimited release property is then captured by the following lemma:

```
val median_opt_is_secure_for_alice: a:prin → b:prin
  → in_a1:(int * int) → in_a2:(int * int) → in_b:(int * int) (* possibly diff a1, a2 *)
  → Lemma (requires (median_pre in_a1 in_b ∧ median_pre in_a2 in_b ∧
                     median_of in_a1 in_b = median_of in_a2 in_b)) (* but same median *)
          (ensures (opt_trace a b in_a1 in_b (median_of in_a1 in_b) = (* ensures .. *)
                     opt_trace a b in_a2 in_b (median_of in_a2 in_b))) (* .. same trace *)
```

The lemma proves that for two runs of median_opt where Bob's input and the final output remain same, but Alice's inputs vary arbitrarily, the observable traces are the same. As such, no more information about information leaks about Alice's inputs via the traces than what is already revealed by the output. We also prove a symmetrical lemma median_opt_is_secure_for_bob.

In short, because the Wys monad provides programmers with the observable traces in the logic, they can then be used to prove properties, relational or otherwise, in the pure fragment of F* outside the Wys monad. We present more examples and their verification details in Sect. 4.

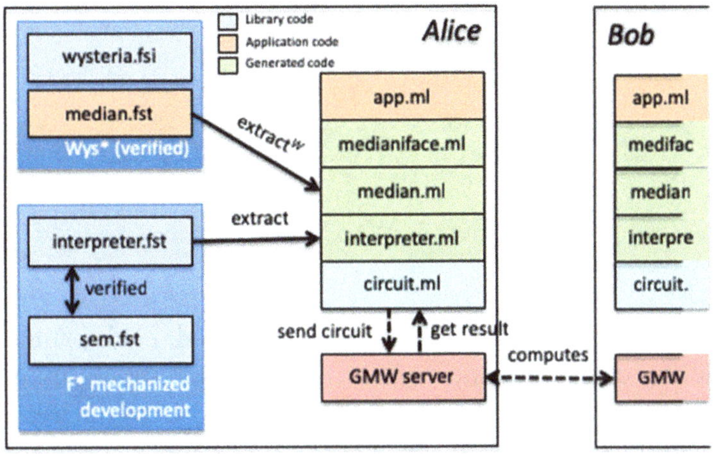

Fig. 1. Architecture of an Wys* deployment

2.5 Deploying Wys* Programs

Having defined a proved-secure MPC program in Wys*, how do we run it? Doing so requires the following steps (Fig. 1). First, we run the F* compiler in a special mode that *extracts* the Wys* code (say psi.fst), into the Wys* AST as a data structure (in psi.ml). Except for the Wys* specific nodes (as_sec, as_par, etc.), the rest of the program is extracted into *FFI nodes* that indicate the use of, or calls into, functionality provided by F* itself.

The next step is for each party to run the extracted AST using the Wys* interpreter. This interpreter is written in F* and we have proved (see Sect. 3.5) that it implements a deep embedding of the Wys* semantics, also specified in F* (Figs. 5 and 6, Sect. 3). The interpreter is extracted to OCaml by the usual F* extraction. Each party's interpreter executes the AST locally until it reaches an as_sec ps f node, where the interpreter's back-end compiles f, on-the-fly, for particular values of the secrets in f's environment, to a boolean circuit. First-order, loop-free code can be compiled to a circuit; Wys* provides specialized support for several common combinators (e.g., fst, snd, list combinators such as List.intersect, List.mem, List.nth etc.).

The circuit is handed to a library by Choi et al. [22] that implements the GMW [26] MPC protocol. Running the GMW protocol involves the parties in ps generating and communicating (XOR-based) secret shares [57] for their secret inputs, and then cooperatively evaluating the boolean circuit for f over them. While our implementation currently uses the GMW protocol, it should be possible to plugin other MPC protocols as well.

One obvious question is how both parties are able to get this process off the ground, given that they don't know some of the inputs (e.g., other parties' secrets). The sealed abstraction helps here. Recall that for median, the types of the inputs are of the form sealed {a} (int ∗ int) and sealed {b} (int ∗ int). When the program is run on Alice's host, the former will be a pair of Alice's values, whereas the latter will be an opaque constant (which we denote as •). The reverse will

$$
\begin{array}{rl}
\text{Principal } p \quad & \text{Principal set } s \quad \text{FFI const } \mathsf{c}, \mathsf{f} \\
\text{Constant } c ::= & p \mid s \mid () \mid \top \mid \bot \mid \mathsf{c} \\
\text{Expression } e ::= & \mathsf{as\_par}\ e_1\ e_2 \mid \mathsf{as\_sec}\ e_1\ e_2 \mid \mathsf{seal}\ e_1\ e_2 \mid \mathsf{reveal}\ e \mid \mathsf{ffi}\ \mathsf{f}\ \bar{e} \\
\mid & \mathsf{mkmap}\ e_1\ e_2 \mid \mathsf{project}\ e_1\ e_2 \mid \mathsf{concat}\ e_1\ e_2 \\
\mid & c \mid x \mid \mathsf{let}\ x = e_1\ \mathsf{in}\ e_2 \mid \lambda x.e \mid e_1\ e_2 \mid \mathsf{fix}\ f.\lambda x.e \mid \mathsf{if}\ e_1\ \mathsf{then}\ e_2\ \mathsf{else}\ e_3
\end{array}
$$

Fig. 2. Wys⋆ syntax

be true on Bob's host. When the circuit is constructed, each principal links their non-opaque inputs to the relevant input wires of the circuit. Similarly, the output map component of each party is derived from their output wires in the circuit, and thus, each party only gets to see their own output.

3 Formalizing and Implementing Wys⋆

In the previous section, we presented examples of verifying properties about Wys⋆ programs using F⋆'s logic. However, these programs are not executed using the F⋆ (single-threaded) semantics; they have a distributed semantics involving multiple parties. So, how do the properties that we verify using F⋆ carry over?

In this section, we present the metatheory that answers this question. First, we formalize the Wys⋆ single-threaded (ST) semantics, that faithfully models the F⋆ semantics of the Wys⋆ API presented in Sect. 2. Next, we formalize the distributed (DS) semantics that multiple parties use to run Wys⋆ programs. Then we prove the former is *sound* with respect to the latter, so that properties proved of programs under ST apply when run under DS. We have mechanized the proof of this theorem in F⋆.

3.1 Syntax

Figure 2 shows the complete syntax of Wys⋆. Principals and principal sets are first-class values, and are denoted by p and s respectively. Constants in the language also include () (unit), booleans ($\top$ and $\bot$), and FFI constants c. Expressions e include the regular forms for functions, applications, let bindings, etc. and the Wys⋆-specific constructs. Among the ones that we have not seen in Sect. 2, expression mkmap e_1 e_2 creates a map from principals in e_1 (which is a principal set) to the value computed by e_2. project e_1 e_2 projects the value of principal e_1 from the map e_2, and concat e_1 e_2 concatenates the two maps. The maps are used if an as_sec computation returns different outputs to the parties.

Host language (i.e., F⋆) constructs are also part of the syntax of Wys⋆, including constants c for strings, integers, lists, tuples, etc. Likewise, host language functions/primitives can be called from Wys⋆—ffi f $\bar{e}$ is the invocation of a host-language function f with arguments $\bar{e}$. The FFI confers two benefits. First, it simplifies the core language while still allowing full consideration of security relevant properties. Second, it helps the language scale by incorporating many of the standard features, libraries, etc. from the host language.

$$
\begin{array}{rl}
\text{Map } m & ::= \cdot \mid m[p \mapsto v] \\
\text{Value } v & ::= p \mid s \mid () \mid \top \mid \bot \mid m \mid \mathsf{v} \mid (L, \lambda x.e) \mid (L, \mathsf{fix}\ f.\lambda x.e) \mid \mathsf{sealed}\ s\ v \mid \bullet \\
\text{Mode } M & ::= \mathsf{Par}\ s \mid \mathsf{Sec}\ s \\
\text{Context } E & ::= \langle\rangle \mid \mathsf{as\_par}\ \langle\rangle\ e \mid \mathsf{as\_par}\ v\ \langle\rangle \mid \mathsf{as\_sec}\ \langle\rangle\ e \mid \mathsf{as\_sec}\ v\ \langle\rangle \mid \ldots \\
\text{Frame } F & ::= (M, L, E, T) \\
\text{Stack } X & ::= \cdot \mid F, X \\
\text{Environment } L & ::= \cdot \mid L[x \mapsto v] \\
\text{Trace element } t & ::= \mathsf{TMsg}\ v \mid \mathsf{TScope}\ s\ T \\
\text{Trace } T & ::= \cdot \mid t, T \\
\text{Configuration } C & ::= M; X; L; T; e \\
\\
\text{Par component } P & ::= \cdot \mid P[p \mapsto C] \\
\text{Sec component } S & ::= \cdot \mid S[s \mapsto C] \\
\text{Protocol } \pi & ::= P; S
\end{array}
$$

Fig. 3. Runtime configuration syntax

S-ASPAR
$$
\frac{e_1 = \mathsf{as\_par}\ s\ (L_1, \lambda x.e) \quad M = \mathsf{Par}\ s_1 \qquad s \subseteq s_1 \quad X_1 = (M; L; \mathsf{seal}\ s\ \langle\rangle; T), X}{M; X; L; T; e_1 \rightarrow \mathsf{Par}\ s; X_1; L_1[x \mapsto ()]; \cdot; e}
$$

S-PARRET
$$
\frac{X = (M_1; L_1; \mathsf{seal}\ s\ \langle\rangle; T_1), X_1 \qquad \mathsf{can\_seal}\ s\ v \quad T_2 = \mathsf{append}\ T_1\ [\mathsf{TScope}\ s\ T]}{M; X; L; T; v \rightarrow M_1; X_1; L_1; T_2; \mathsf{sealed}\ s\ v}
$$

S-ASSEC
$$
\frac{e_1 = \mathsf{as\_sec}\ s\ (L_1, \lambda x.e) \quad M = \mathsf{Par}\ s \qquad X_1 = (M; L; \langle\rangle\ T), X}{M; X; L; T; e_1 \rightarrow \mathsf{Sec}\ s; X_1; L_1[x \mapsto ()]; \cdot; e}
$$

S-SECRET
$$
\frac{M = \mathsf{Sec}\ \_ \quad X = (M_1; L_1; \langle\rangle; T), X_1 \qquad T_1 = \mathsf{append}\ T\ [\mathsf{TMsg}\ v]}{M; X; L; \cdot; v \rightarrow M_1; X_1; L_1; T_1; v}
$$

Fig. 4. WYS* ST semantics (selected rules)

3.2 Single-Threaded Semantics

We formalize the semantics in the style of Hieb and Felleisen [24], where the redex is chosen by (standard, not shown) *evaluation contexts* E, which prescribe left-to-right, call-by-value evaluation order. The ST semantics, a model of the F* semantics and the WYS* API, defines a judgment $C \rightarrow C'$ that represents a single step of an abstract machine (Fig. 4). Here, C is a *configuration* $M; X; L; T; e$. This five-tuple consists of a mode M, a stack X, a local environment L, a trace T, and an expression e. The syntax for these elements is given in Fig. 3. The value form v represents the host language (FFI) values. The stack and environment are standard; trace T and mode M were discussed in the previous section.

For space reasons, we focus on the two main WYS* constructs as_par and as_sec. Our technical report [54] shows other WYS* specific constructs.

Rules S-ASPAR and S-PARRET (Fig. 4) reduce an as_par expression once its arguments are fully evaluated—its first argument s is a principal set, while the second argument $(L_1, \lambda x.e)$ is a closure where L_1 captures the free variables of thunk $\lambda x.e$. S-ASPAR first checks that the current mode M is Par and contains all the principals from the set s. It then pushes a seal s $\langle\rangle$ frame on the stack, and

P-PAR
$$\frac{C \rightsquigarrow C'}{P[p \mapsto C]; S \longrightarrow P[p \mapsto C']; S}$$

P-ENTER
$$\frac{\forall p \in s.\ P[p].e = \mathsf{as\_sec}\ s\ (L_p, \lambda x.e) \quad s \notin \mathsf{dom}(S) \quad L = \mathsf{combine}\ \bar{L}_p}{P; S \longrightarrow P; S[s \mapsto \mathsf{Sec}\ s; \cdot; L[x \mapsto ()]; \cdot; e]}$$

P-SEC
$$\frac{C \rightarrow C'}{P; S[s \mapsto C] \longrightarrow P; S[s \mapsto C']}$$

P-EXIT
$$\frac{S[s] = \mathsf{Sec}\ s; \cdot; L; T; v \quad P' = \forall p \in s.\ P[p \mapsto P[p] \triangleleft (\mathsf{slice\_v}\ p\ v)] \quad S' = S \setminus s}{P; S \longrightarrow P'; S'}$$

Fig. 5. Distributed semantics, multi-party rules

L-ASPAR1
$$\frac{e_1 = \mathsf{as\_par}\ s\ (L_1, \lambda x.e) \quad p \in s \quad X_1 = (M; L; \mathsf{seal}\ s\ \langle\rangle; T), X}{\mathsf{Par}\ p; X; L; T; e_1 \rightsquigarrow \mathsf{Par}\ p; X_1; L_1[x \mapsto ()]; \cdot; e}$$

L-PARRET
$$\frac{X = (M; L_1; \mathsf{seal}\ s\ \langle\rangle; T_1), X_1 \quad T_2 = \mathsf{append}\ T_1\ T \quad v_1 = \mathsf{sealed}\ s\ v}{\mathsf{Par}\ p; X; L; T; v \rightsquigarrow \mathsf{Par}\ p; X_1; L_1; T_2; v_1}$$

L-ASPAR2
$$\frac{p \notin s}{\mathsf{Par}\ p; X; L; T; \mathsf{as\_par}\ s\ (L_1, \lambda x.e) \rightsquigarrow \mathsf{Par}\ p; X; L; T; \mathsf{sealed}\ s\ \bullet}$$

Fig. 6. Distributed semantics, selected local rules (the mode M is always $\mathsf{Par}\ p$)

starts evaluating e under the environment $L_1[x \mapsto ()]$. The rule S-ASPARRET pops the frame and seals the result, so that it is accessible only to the principals in s. The rule also creates a trace element $\mathsf{TScope}\ s\ T$, essentially making observations during the reduction of e (i.e., T) visible only to principals in s.

Turning to as_sec, the rule S-ASSEC checks the precondition of the API, and the rule S-ASSECRET generates a trace observation $\mathsf{TMsg}\ v$, as per the postcondition of the API. As mentioned before, as_sec semantics models the ideal, trusted third-party semantics of secure computations where the participants only observe the final output. We can confirm that the rules implement the types of as_par and as_sec shown in Sect. 2.

3.3 Distributed Semantics

In the DS semantics, principals evaluate the same program locally and asynchronously until they reach a secure computation, at which point they synchronize to jointly perform the computation. The semantics consists of two parts: (a) a judgment of the form $\pi \longrightarrow \pi'$ (Fig. 5), where a protocol π is a tuple $(P; S)$ such that P maps each principal to its local configuration and S maps a set of principals to the configuration of an ongoing, secure computation; and (b) a local evaluation judgment $C \rightsquigarrow C'$ (Fig. 6) to model how a single principal behaves while in par mode.

Rule P-PAR in Fig. 5 models a single party taking a step, per the local evaluation rules. Figure 6 shows these rules for as_par. (See technical report [54] for more local evaluation rules.) A principal either participates in the as_par computation, or skips it. Rules L-ASPAR1 and L-PARRET handle the case when $p \in s$, and so, the principal p participates in the computation. The rules closely mirror the corresponding ST semantics rules in Fig. 4. One difference in the rule L-ASPARRET is that the trace T is not scoped. In the DS semantics, traces only contain TMsg elements; i.e., a trace is the (flat) list of secure computation outputs observed by that active principal. If $p \notin s$, then the principal skips the computation with the result being a sealed value containing the opaque constant $\bullet$ (rule L-ASPAR2). The contents of the sealed value do not matter, since the principal will not be allowed to unseal the value anyway.

As should be the case, there are no local rules for as_sec—to perform a secure computation parties need to combine their data and jointly do the computation. Rule P-ENTER in Fig. 5 handles the case when principals enter a secure computation. It requires that all the principals $p \in s$ must have the expression form as_sec s $(L_p, \lambda x.e)$, where L_p is their local environment associated with the closure. Each party's local environment contains its secret values (in addition to some public values). Conceptually, a secure computation *combines* these environments, thereby producing a joint view, and evaluates e under the combination. We define an auxiliary combine function for this purpose:

```
combine_v (•, v) = v
combine_v (v, •) = v
combine_v (sealed s v1, sealed s v2) = sealed s (combine_v v1 v2)
...
```

The rule P-ENTER combines the principals' environments, and creates a new entry in the S map. The principals are now waiting for the secure computation to finish. Rule P-SEC models a stepping rule inside the sec mode.

The rule P-EXIT applies when a secure computation has completed and returns results to the waiting principals. If the secure computation terminates with value v, each principal p gets the value slice_v p v. The slice_v function is analogous to combine, but in the opposite direction—it strips off the parts of v that are not accessible to p:

```
slice_v p (sealed s v) = sealed s •, if p ∉ s
slice_v p (sealed s v) = sealed s (slice_v p v), if p ∈ s
...
```

In the rule P-EXIT, the $\triangleleft$ notation is defined as:

$M; X; L; T; \_ \ \triangleleft\ v = M; X; L; \mathsf{append}\ T\ [\mathsf{TMsg}\ v]; v$

That is, the returned value is also added to the principal's trace to note their observation of the value.

3.4 Metatheory

Our goal is to show that the ST semantics faithfully represents the semantics of Wys* programs as they are executed by multiple parties, i.e., according to the DS semantics. We do this by proving *simulation* of the ST semantics by the DS semantics, and by proving *confluence* of the DS semantics. Our F* development mechanizes all the metatheory presented in this section.

Simulation. We define a slice s C function that returns the corresponding protocol π_C for an ST configuration C. In the P component of π_C, each principal $p \in s$ is mapped to their *slice* of the protocol. For slicing values, we use the same slice_v function as before. Traces are sliced as follows:

```
slice_tr p (TMsg v) = [TMsg (slice_v p v)]
slice_tr p (TScope s T) = slice_tr p T, if p ∈ s
slice_tr p (TScope s T) = [], if p ∉ s
```

The slice of an expression (e.g., the source program) is itself. For all other components of C, slice functions are defined analogously.

We say that C is *terminal* if it is in Par mode and is fully reduced to a value (i.e. when $C = \_; X; \_; \_; e$, e is a value and X is empty). Similarly, a protocol $\pi = (P, S)$ is terminal if S is empty and all the local configurations in P are terminal. The simulation theorem is then the following:

Theorem 1 (Simulation of ST by DS). *Let s be the set of all principals. If $C_1 \to^* C_2$, and C_2 is terminal, then there exists some derivation* (slice s C_1) $\longrightarrow^*$ (slice s C_2) *such that* (slice s C_2) *is terminal.*

To state *confluence*, we first define the notion of *strong termination.*

Definition 1 (Strong termination). *If all possible runs of protocol π terminate at π_t, we say π* strongly terminates in *π_t, written $\pi \Downarrow \pi_t$.*

Our confluence result then says:

Theorem 2 (Confluence of DS). *If $\pi \longrightarrow^* \pi_t$ and π_t is terminal, then $\pi \Downarrow \pi_t$.*

Combining the two theorems, we get a corollary that establishes the soundness of the ST semantics w.r.t. the DS semantics:

Corollary 1 (Soundness of ST semantics). *Let s be the set of all principals. If $C_1 \to^* C_2$, and C_2 is terminal, then* (slice s C_1) $\Downarrow$ (slice s C_2).

Now suppose that for a Wys* source program, we prove in F* a postcondition that the result is sealed alice n, for some $n > 0$. By the soundness of the ST semantics, we can conclude that when the program is run in the DS semantics, it may diverge, but if it terminates, alice's output will also be sealed alice n, and for all other principals their outputs will be sealed alice $\bullet$. Aside from the correspondence on results, our semantics also covers correspondence on traces. Thus the correctness and security properties that we prove about a Wys* program using F*'s logic, hold for the program that actually runs.

3.5 Implementation

The formal semantics presented in the prior section is mechanized as an inductive type in F*. This style is useful for proving properties, but does not directly translate to an implementation. Therefore, we implement an interpretation function step in F* and prove that it corresponds to the rules; i.e., that for all input configurations C, step$(C) = C'$ implies that $C \rightarrow C'$ according to the semantics. Then, the core of each principal's implementation is an F* stub function tstep that repeatedly invokes step on the AST of the source program (produced by the F* extractor run in a custom mode), unless the AST is an as_sec node. Functions step and tstep are extracted to OCaml by the standard F* extraction process.

Local evaluation is not defined for the as_sec node, so the stub implements what amounts to P-ENTER and P-EXIT from Fig. 5. When the stub notices the program has reached an as_sec expression, it calls into a circuit library we have written that converts the AST of the second argument of as_sec to a boolean circuit. This circuit and the encoded inputs are communicated to a co-hosted server that implements the GMW MPC protocol [22]. The server evaluates the circuit, coordinating with the GMW servers of the other principals, and sends back the result. The circuit library decodes the result and returns it to the stub. The stub then carries on with the local evaluation. Our FFI interface currently provides a form of monomorphic, first-order interoperability between the (dynamically typed) interpreter and the host language.

Our F* formalization of the Wys* semantics, including the AST specification, is 1900 lines of code. This formalization is used both by the metatheory as well as by the (executable) interpreter. The metatheory that connects the ST and DS semantics (Sect. 3) is 3000 lines. The interpreter and its correctness proof are another 290 lines of F* code. The interpreter step function is essentially a big switch-case on the current expression, that calls into the functions from the semantics specification. The tstep stub is another 15 lines. The size of the circuit library, not including the GMW implementation, is 836 lines. The stub, the implementation of GMW, the circuit library, and F* toolchain (including the custom Wys* extraction mode) are part of our Trusted Computing Base (TCB).

4 Applications

In addition to joint median, presented in Sect. 2, we have implemented and proved properties of two other MPC applications, *dealing for online card games* and *private set intersection* (PSI).

Card Dealing. We have implemented an MPC-based card dealing application in Wys*. Such an application can play the role of the dealer in a game of online poker, thereby eliminating the need to trust the game portal for card dealing. The application relies on Wys*'s support for *secret shares* [57]. Using secret shares, the participating parties can share a value in a way that none of the parties can observe the actual value individually (each party's share consists of some random-looking bytes), but they can recover the value by combining their shares in sec mode.

In the application, the parties maintain a list of secret shares of already dealt cards (the number of already dealt cards is public information). To deal a new card, each party first generates a random number locally. The parties then perform a secure computation to compute the sum of their random numbers modulo 52, let's call it n. The output of the secure computation is secret shares of n. Before declaring n as the newly dealt card, the parties needs to ensure that the card n has not already been dealt. To do so, they iterate over the list of secret shares of already dealt cards, and for each element of the list, check that it is different from n. The check is performed in a secure computation that simply combines the shares of n, combines the shares of the list element, and checks the equality of the two values. If n is different from all the previously dealt cards, it is declared to be the new card, else the parties repeat the protocol by again generating a fresh random number each.

Wys* provides the following API for secret shares:

```
type Sh: Type → Type
type can_sh: Type → Type
assume Cansh_int: can_sh int

val v_of_sh: sh:Sh α → Ghost α
val ps_of_sh: sh:Sh α → Ghost prins

val mk_sh: x:α → Wys (Sh α)
    (requires (fun m → m.mode = Sec ∧ can_sh α))
    (ensures (fun m r tr → v_of_sh r = x ∧ ps_of_sh r = m.ps ∧ tr = []))
val comb_sh: x:Sh α → Wys α (requires (fun m → m.mode = Sec ∧ ps_of_sh x = m.ps))
                            (ensures (fun m r tr → v_of_sh x = r ∧ tr = []))
```

Type Sh α types the shares of values of type α. Our implementation currently supports shares of int values only; the can_sh predicate enforces this restriction on the source programs. Extending secret shares support to other types (such as pairs) should be straightforward (as in [52]). Functions v_of_sh and ps_of_sh are marked Ghost, meaning that they can only be used in specifications for reasoning purposes. In the concrete code, shares are created and combined using the mk_sh and comb_sh functions. Together, the specifications of these functions enforce that the shares are created and combined by the same set of parties (through ps_of_sh), and that comb_sh recovers the original value (through v_of_sh). The Wys* interpreter transparently handles the low-level details of extracting shares from the GMW implementation of Choi et al. (mk_sh), and reconstituting the shares back (comb_sh).

In addition to implementing the card dealing application in Wys*, we have formally verified that the returned card is fresh. The signature of the function that checks for freshness of the newly dealt card is as follows (abc is the set of three parties in the computation):

```
val check_fresh: l:list (Sh int){∀ s'. mem s' l ⟹ ps_of_sh s' = abc}
  → s:Sh int{ps_of_sh s = abc}
  → Wys bool (requires (fun m → m = Mode Par abc))
    (ensures (fun _ r _ → r ⟺ (∀ s'. mem s' l ⟹ not (v_of_sh s' = v_of_sh s))))
```

The specification says that the function takes two arguments: l is the list of secret shares of already dealt cards, and s is the secret shares of the newly dealt card. The function returns a boolean r that is true iff the concrete value (v_of_sh) of s is different from the concrete values of all the elements of the list l. Using F*, we verify that the implementation of check_fresh meets this specification.

PSI. Consider a dating application that enables its users to compute their common interests without revealing all of them. This is an instance of the more general private set intersection (PSI) problem [28].

We implement a straightforward version of PSI in WYS*:

```
let psi a b (input_a:sealed {a} (list int)) (input_b:sealed {b} (list int)) (l_a:int) (l_b:int) =
  as_sec {a,b} (fun () → List.intersect (reveal input_a) (reveal input_b) l_a l_b)
```

where the input sets are expressed as lists with public lengths.

Huang et al. [28] provide an optimized PSI algorithm that performs much better when the density of common elements in the two sets is high. We implement their algorithm in WYS*. The optimized version consists of two nested loops – an outer loop for Alice's set and an inner loop for Bob's – where an iteration of the inner loop compares the current element of Alice's set with the current element of Bob's. The nested loops are written using as_par so that both Alice and Bob execute the loops in lockstep (note that the set sizes are public), while the comparison in the inner loop happens using as_sec. Instead of naive l_a ∗ l_b comparisons, Huang et al. [28] observe that once an element of Alice's set ax matches an element of Bob's set bx, the inner loop can return immediately, skipping the comparisons of ax with the rest of Bob's set. Furthermore, bx can be removed from Bob's set, excluding it from any further comparisons with other elements in Alice's set. Since there are no repeats in the input sets, all the excluded comparisons are guaranteed to be false. We show the full code and its performance comparison with psi in the technical report [54].

As with the median example from Sect. 2, the optimized PSI intentionally reveals more for performance gains. As such, we would like to verify that the optimizations do not reveal more about parties' inputs. We take the following stepwise refinement approach. First, we characterize the trace of the optimized implementation as a pure function trace_psi_opt la lb (omitted for space reasons), and show that the trace of psi_opt is precisely trace_psi_opt la lb.

Then, we define an intermediate PSI implementation that has the same nested loop structure, but performs l_a ∗ l_b comparisons without any optimizations. We characterize the trace of this intermediate implementation as the pure function trace_psi, and show that it precisely captures the trace.

To show that trace_psi does not reveal more than the intersection of the input sets, we prove the following lemma.

```
Ψ la₀ la₁ lb₀ lb₁ ≝ (* possibly diff input sets, but with *)
  la₀ ∩ lb₀ = la₁ ∩ lb₁ ∧ (* intersections the same *)
  length la₀ = length la₁ ∧ length lb₀ = length lb₁ (* lengths the same *)

val psi__interim_is_secure: la₀:_ → lb₀:_ → la₁:_ → lb₁:_ → Lemma
  (requires (Ψ la₀ la₁ lb₀ lb₁))
  (ensures (permutation (trace_psi la₀ lb₀) (trace_psi la₁ lb₁)))
```

The lemma essentially says that for two runs on same length inputs, if the output is the same, then the resulting traces are permutation of each other.[4] We can reason about the traces of psi_interim up to permutation because Alice has no prior knowledge of the choice of representation of Bob's set (Bob can shuffle his list), so cannot learn anything from a permutation of the trace.[5] This establishes the security of psi_interim.

Finally, we can connect psi_interim to psi_opt by showing that there exists a function f, such that for any trace tr=trace_psi la lb, the trace of psi_opt, trace_psi_opt la lb, can be computed by f (length la) (length lb) tr. In other words, the trace produced by the optimized implementation can be computed using a function of information already available to Alice (or Bob) when she (or he) observes a run of the secure, unoptimized version psi_interim la lb. As such, the optimizations do not reveal further information.

5 Related Work

Source MPC Verification. While the verification of the underlying crypto protocols has received some attention [4,5], verification of the correctness and security properties of MPC source programs has remained largely unexplored, surprisingly so given that the goal of MPC is to preserve the privacy of secret inputs. The only previous work that we know of is Backes et al. [9] who devise an applied pi-calculus based abstraction for MPC, and use it for formal verification. For an auction protocol that computes the min function, their abstraction comprises about 1400 lines of code. Wys*, on the other hand, enables direct verification of the higher-level MPC source programs, and not their models, and in addition provides a partially verified toolchain.

Wysteria. Wys*'s computational model is based on the programming abstractions of a previous MPC DSL, Wysteria [52]. Wys*'s realization as an embedded DSL in F* makes important advances. In particular, Wys* (a) enhances the Wysteria semantics to include a notion of observable traces, and provides the novel capability to prove security and correctness properties about mixed-mode MPC source programs, (b) expands the programming constructs available by drawing on features and libraries of F*, and (c) adds assurance via a (partially) proved-correct interpreter.

Verified MPC Toolchain. Almeida et al. [4] build a verified toolchain consisting of (a) a verified circuit compiler from (a subset of) C to boolean circuits, and (b) a verified implementation of Yao's [65] garbled circuits protocol for 2-party MPC. They use CompCert [36] for the former, and EasyCrypt [11] for the latter. These are significant advances, but there are several distinctions from our work. The MPC programs in their toolchain are not *mixed-mode*, and thus it cannot express

[4] Holding Bob's (resp. Alice's) inputs fixed and varying Alice's (resp. Bob's) inputs, as done for median in Sect. 2.4, is covered by this more general property.

[5] We could formalize this observation using a probabilistic, relational variant of F* [10].

examples like median_opt and the optimized PSI. Their framework does not enable formal verification of source programs like Wys* does. It may be possible to use other frameworks for verifying C programs (e.g. Frama-C [1]), but it is inconvenient as one has to work in the subset of C that falls in the intersection of these tools. Wys* is also more general as it supports general n-party MPC; e.g., the card dealing application in Sect. 4 has 3 parties. Nevertheless, Wys* may use their verified Yao implementation for the special case of 2 parties.

MPC DSLs and DSL Extensions. In addition to Wysteria several other MPC DSLs have been proposed in the literature [14,17,27,29,34,37,39,48,49,52,56,61]. Most of these languages have standalone implementations, and the (usability/scalability) drawbacks that come with them. Like Wys*, a few are implemented as language extensions. Launchbury et al. [35] describe a Haskell-embedded DSL for writing low-level "share protocols" on a multi-server "SMC machine". OblivC [66] is an extension to C for two-party MPC that annotates variables and conditionals with an obliv qualifier to identify private inputs; these programs are compiled by source-to-source translation. The former is essentially a shallow embedding, and the latter is compiler-based; Wys* is unique in that it combines a shallow embedding to support source program verification and a deep embedding to support a non-standard target semantics. Recent work [19,21] compiles to cryptographic protocols that include both arithmetic and boolean circuits; the compiler decides which fragments of the program fall into which category. It would be interesting work to integrate such a backend in Wys*.

Mechanized Metatheory. Our verification results are different from a typical verification result that might either mechanize metatheory for an idealized language [8], or might prove an interpreter or compiler correct w.r.t. a formal semantics [36]—we do both. We mechanize the metatheory of Wys* establishing the soundness of the conceptual ST semantics w.r.t. the actual DS semantics, and mechanize the proof that the interpreter implements the correct DS semantics.

General DSL Implementation Strategies. DSLs (for MPC or other purposes) are implemented in various ways, such as by developing a standalone compiler/interpreter, or by shallow or deep embedding in a host language. Our approach bears relation to the approach taken in LINQ [42], which embeds a query language in normal C# programs, and implements these programs by extracting the query syntax tree and passing it to a *provider* to implement for a particular backend. Other researchers have embedded DSLs in verification-oriented host languages (e.g., Bedrock [13] in Coq [60]) to permit formal proofs of DSL programs. Low* [51] is a shallow embedding of a small, sequential, well-behaved subset of C in F* that extracts to C using a F*-to-C compiler. Low* has been used to verify and implement several cryptographic constructions. Fromherz et al. [25] present a deep embedding of a subset of x64 assembly in F* that allows efficient verification of assembly and its interoperation with C code generated from Low*. They design (and verify) a custom VC generator for the deeply embedded DSL, that allows for the proofs of assembly crypto routines to scale.

6 Conclusions

This paper has presented WYS*, the first DSL to enable formal verification of efficient source MPC programs as written in a full-featured host programming language, F*. The paper presented examples such as joint median, card dealing, and PSI, and showed how the DSL enables their correctness and security proofs. WYS* implementation, examples, and proofs are publicly available on Github.

Acknowledgments. We would like to thank the anonymous reviewers, Catalin Hriţcu, and Matthew Hammer for helpful comments on drafts of this paper. This research was funded in part by the U.S. National Science Foundation under grants CNS-1563722, CNS-1314857, and CNS-1111599.

References

1. Frama-c. https://frama-c.com/
2. Z3 theorem prover. z3.codeplex.com
3. Aggarwal, G., Mishra, N., Pinkas, B.: Secure computation of the kth-ranked element. In: Cachin, C., Camenisch, J.L. (eds.) EUROCRYPT 2004. LNCS, vol. 3027, pp. 40–55. Springer, Heidelberg (2004). https://doi.org/10.1007/978-3-540-24676-3_3
4. Almeida, J.B., et al.: A fast and verified software stack for secure function evaluation. In: Proceedings of the 2017 ACM SIGSAC Conference on Computer and Communications Security, CCS 2017 (2017)
5. Almeida, J.B., et al.: Verified implementations for secure and verifiable computation (2014)
6. Araki, T., et al.: Generalizing the SPDZ compiler for other protocols. In: Proceedings of the 2018 ACM SIGSAC Conference on Computer and Communications Security, CCS 2018 (2018)
7. Atkey, R.: Parameterised notions of computation. J. Funct. Program. **19**, 335–376 (2009). https://doi.org/10.1017/S095679680900728X. http://journals.cambridge.org/article_S095679680900728X
8. Aydemir, B.E., et al.: Mechanized metatheory for the masses: the POPLMARK challenge. In: Hurd, J., Melham, T. (eds.) TPHOLs 2005. LNCS, vol. 3603, pp. 50–65. Springer, Heidelberg (2005). https://doi.org/10.1007/11541868_4
9. Backes, M., Maffei, M., Mohammadi, E.: Computationally sound abstraction and verification of secure multi-party computations. In: IARCS Annual Conference on Foundations of Software Technology and Theoretical Computer Science (FSTTCS 2010) (2010)
10. Barthe, G., Fournet, C., Grégoire, B., Strub, P., Swamy, N., Béguelin, S.Z.: Probabilistic relational verification for cryptographic implementations. In: The 41st Annual ACM SIGPLAN-SIGACT Symposium on Principles of Programming Languages, POPL 2014, San Diego, CA, USA, 20–21 January 2014, pp. 193–206 (2014). https://doi.org/10.1145/2535838.2535847
11. Barthe, G., Grégoire, B., Heraud, S., Béguelin, S.Z.: Computer-aided security proofs for the working cryptographer. In: Rogaway, P. (ed.) CRYPTO 2011. LNCS, vol. 6841, pp. 71–90. Springer, Heidelberg (2011). https://doi.org/10.1007/978-3-642-22792-9_5

12. Beaver, D., Micali, S., Rogaway, P.: The round complexity of secure protocols. In: STOC (1990)
13. Bedrock, a coq library for verified low-level programming. http://plv.csail.mit.edu/bedrock/
14. Ben-David, A., Nisan, N., Pinkas, B.: FairplayMP: a system for secure multi-party computation. In: CCS (2008)
15. Bhargavan, K., Fournet, C., Kohlweiss, M., Pironti, A., Strub, P.Y.: Implementing TLS with verified cryptographic security. In: IEEE Symposium on Security & Privacy, Oakland, pp. 445–462 (2013). http://www.ieee-security.org/TC/SP2013/papers/4977a445.pdf
16. Bogdanov, D., Jõemets, M., Siim, S., Vaht, M.: How the Estonian Tax and Customs Board Evaluated a tax fraud detection system based on secure multi-party computation. In: Böhme, R., Okamoto, T. (eds.) FC 2015. LNCS, vol. 8975, pp. 227–234. Springer, Heidelberg (2015). https://doi.org/10.1007/978-3-662-47854-7_14
17. Bogdanov, D., Laur, S., Willemson, J.: Sharemind: a framework for fast privacy-preserving computations. In: Jajodia, S., Lopez, J. (eds.) ESORICS 2008. LNCS, vol. 5283, pp. 192–206. Springer, Heidelberg (2008). https://doi.org/10.1007/978-3-540-88313-5_13
18. Bogetoft, P., et al.: Secure multiparty computation goes live. In: Dingledine, R., Golle, P. (eds.) FC 2009. LNCS, vol. 5628, pp. 325–343. Springer, Heidelberg (2009). https://doi.org/10.1007/978-3-642-03549-4_20
19. Büscher, N., Demmler, D., Katzenbeisser, S., Kretzmer, D., Schneider, T.: HyCC: compilation of hybrid protocols for practical secure computation. In: Proceedings of the 2018 ACM SIGSAC Conference on Computer and Communications Security, CCS 2018 (2018)
20. Canetti, R.: Security and composition of multiparty cryptographic protocols. J. Cryptol. **13**(1), 143–202 (2000). https://doi.org/10.1007/s001459910006
21. Chandran, N., Gupta, D., Rastogi, A., Sharma, R., Tripathi, S.: EzPC: programmable, efficient, and scalable secure two-party computation for machine learning. Cryptology ePrint Archive, Report 2017/1109 (2017). https://eprint.iacr.org/2017/1109
22. Choi, S.G., Hwang, K.W., Katz, J., Malkin, T., Rubenstein, D.: Secure multi-party computation of Boolean circuits with applications to privacy in on-line marketplaces (2011). http://eprint.iacr.org/
23. Crockett, E., Peikert, C., Sharp, C.: Alchemy: a language and compiler for homomorphic encryption made easy. In: Proceedings of the 2018 ACM SIGSAC Conference on Computer and Communications Security, CCS 2018 (2018)
24. Felleisen, M., Hieb, R.: The revised report on the syntactic theories of sequential control and state. Theoret. Comput. Sci. **103**(2), 235–271 (1992)
25. Fromherz, A., Giannarakis, N., Hawblitzel, C., Parno, B., Rastogi, A., Swamy, N.: A verified, efficient embedding of a verifiable assembly language. In: 46th ACM SIGPLAN Symposium on Principles of Programming Languages, POPL 2019 (2019)
26. Goldreich, O., Micali, S., Wigderson, A.: How to play ANY mental game. In: STOC (1987)
27. Holzer, A., Franz, M., Katzenbeisser, S., Veith, H.: Secure two-party computations in ANSI C. In: CCS (2012)
28. Huang, Y., Evans, D., Katz, J.: Private set intersection: are garbled circuits better than custom protocols? In: NDSS (2012)
29. Huang, Y., Evans, D., Katz, J., Malka, L.: Faster secure two-party computation using garbled circuits. In: USENIX (2011)

30. Juvekar, C., Vaikuntanathan, V., Chandrakasani, A.: GAZELLE: a low latency framework for secure neural network inference. In: USENIX Security 2018 (2018)
31. Kamm, L.: Privacy-preserving statistical analysis using secure multi-party computation. Ph.D. thesis, University of Tartu (2015)
32. Kerschbaum, F.: Automatically optimizing secure computation. In: CCS (2011)
33. Kerschbaum, F., et al.: Secure collaborative supply-chain management. Computer **44**(9), 38–43 (2011)
34. Laud, P., Randmets, J.: A domain-specific language for low-level secure multiparty computation protocols. In: Proceedings of the 22nd ACM SIGSAC Conference on Computer and Communications Security, CCS 2015 (2015)
35. Launchbury, J., Diatchki, I.S., DuBuisson, T., Adams-Moran, A.: Efficient lookup-table protocol in secure multiparty computation. In: ICFP (2012)
36. Leroy, X.: Formal verification of a realistic compiler. Commun. ACM **52**(7), 107–115 (2009)
37. Liu, C., Huang, Y., Shi, E., Katz, J., Hicks, M.: Automating efficient RAM-model secure computation. In: IEEE Symposium on Security and Privacy, Oakland (2014)
38. Liu, J., Juuti, M., Lu, Y., Asokan, N.: Oblivious neural network predictions via MiniONN transformations. In: Proceedings of the 2017 ACM SIGSAC Conference on Computer and Communications Security, CCS 2017 (2017)
39. Malka, L.: VMCrypt: modular software architecture for scalable secure computation. In: CCS (2011)
40. Malkhi, D., Nisan, N., Pinkas, B., Sella, Y.: Fairplay: a secure two-party computation system. In: USENIX Security (2004)
41. Mardziel, P., Hicks, M., Katz, J., Hammer, M., Rastogi, A., Srivatsa, M.: Knowledge inference for optimizing and enforcing secure computations. In: Proceedings of the Annual Meeting of the US/UK International Technology Alliance (2013)
42. Meijer, E., Beckman, B., Bierman, G.: LINQ: reconciling object, relations and xml in the .net framework. In: Proceedings of the 2006 ACM SIGMOD International Conference on Management of Data, SIGMOD 2006, p. 706. ACM, New York (2006). https://doi.org/10.1145/1142473.1142552
43. Moggi, E.: Notions of computation and monads. Inf. Comput. **93**(1), 55–92 (1991). https://doi.org/10.1016/0890-5401(91)90052-4
44. Mohassel, P., Zhang, Y.: SecureML: a system for scalable privacy-preserving machine learning. In: IEEE S&P (2017)
45. Mood, B., Gupta, D., Carter, H., Butler, K.R.B., Traynor, P.: Frigate: a validated, extensible, and efficient compiler and interpreter for secure computation. In: IEEE EuroS&P (2016)
46. Nanevski, A., Morrisett, G., Shinnar, A., Govereau, P., Birkedal, L.: Ynot: dependent types for imperative programs. In: Proceedings of the 13th ACM SIGPLAN International Conference on Functional Programming, ICFP (2008)
47. Nanevski, A., Morrisett, J.G., Birkedal, L.: Hoare type theory, polymorphism and separation. J. Funct. Program. **18**(5–6), 865–911 (2008). http://ynot.cs.harvard.edu/papers/jfpsep07.pdf
48. Nielsen, J.D.: Languages for secure multiparty computation and towards strongly typed macros. Ph.D. thesis (2009)
49. Nielsen, J.D., Schwartzbach, M.I.: A domain-specific programming language for secure multiparty computation. In: PLAS (2007)
50. PolarSSL verification kit (2015). http://trust-in-soft.com/polarssl-verification-kit/
51. Protzenko, J., et al.: Verified low-level programming embedded in F* (ICFP) (2017)

52. Rastogi, A., Hammer, M.A., Hicks, M.: Wysteria: a programming language for generic, mixed-mode multiparty computations. In: Proceedings of the 2014 IEEE Symposium on Security and Privacy (2014)
53. Rastogi, A., Mardziel, P., Hammer, M., Hicks, M.: Knowledge inference for optimizing secure multi-party computation. In: PLAS (2013)
54. Rastogi, A., Swamy, N., Hicks, M.: WYS*: a DSL for verified secure multi-party computations (2019). https://arxiv.org/abs/1711.06467
55. Sabelfeld, A., Myers, A.C.: A model for delimited information release. In: Futatsugi, K., Mizoguchi, F., Yonezaki, N. (eds.) ISSS 2003. LNCS, vol. 3233, pp. 174–191. Springer, Heidelberg (2004). https://doi.org/10.1007/978-3-540-37621-7_9
56. Schropfer, A., Kerschbaum, F., Muller, G.: L1 - an intermediate language for mixed-protocol secure computation. In: COMPSAC (2011)
57. Shamir, A.: How to share a secret. Commun. ACM **22**(11), 612–613 (1979)
58. Shamir, A., Rivest, R.L., Adleman, L.M.: Mental poker. In: Klarner, D.A. (ed.) The Mathematical Gardner, pp. 37–43. Springer, Boston (1981). https://doi.org/10.1007/978-1-4684-6686-7_5
59. Swamy, N., et al.: Dependent types and multi-monadic effects in F*. In: POPL (2016)
60. The Coq Development Team: The Coq proof assistant. http://coq.inria.fr
61. VIFF, the virtual ideal functionality framework. http://viff.dk/
62. Wadler, P.: Monads for functional programming. In: Jeuring, J., Meijer, E. (eds.) AFP 1995. LNCS, vol. 925, pp. 24–52. Springer, Heidelberg (1995). https://doi.org/10.1007/3-540-59451-5_2. http://dl.acm.org/citation.cfm?id=647698.734146
63. Yang, J., Hawblitzel, C.: Safe to the last instruction: automated verification of a type-safe operating system. In: Proceedings of the 31st ACM SIGPLAN Conference on Programming Language Design and Implementation, PLDI 2010 (2010)
64. Yang, X., Chen, Y., Eide, E., Regehr, J.: Finding and understanding bugs in C compilers. In: Proceedings of ACM SIGPLAN 2011 Conference on Programming Language Design and Implementation (2011)
65. Yao, A.C.C.: How to generate and exchange secrets. In: FOCS (1986)
66. Zahur, S., Evans, D.: Obliv-C: a language for extensible data-oblivious computation. Unpublished (2015). http://oblivc.org/downloads/oblivc.pdf

Generalised Differential Privacy for Text Document Processing

Natasha Fernandes[1,2(✉)], Mark Dras[1], and Annabelle McIver[1]

[1] Macquarie University, Sydney, Australia
natasha.fernandes@hdr.mq.edu.au
[2] Inria, Paris-Saclay and École Polytechnique, Palaiseau, France

Abstract. We address the problem of how to "obfuscate" texts by removing stylistic clues which can identify authorship, whilst preserving (as much as possible) the content of the text. In this paper we combine ideas from "generalised differential privacy" and machine learning techniques for text processing to model privacy for text documents. We define a privacy mechanism that operates at the level of text documents represented as "bags-of-words"—these representations are typical in machine learning and contain sufficient information to carry out many kinds of classification tasks including *topic identification* and *authorship attribution* (of the original documents). We show that our mechanism satisfies privacy with respect to a metric for semantic similarity, thereby providing a balance between utility, defined by the semantic content of texts, with the obfuscation of stylistic clues. We demonstrate our implementation on a "fan fiction" dataset, confirming that it is indeed possible to disguise writing style effectively whilst preserving enough information and variation for accurate content classification tasks. We refer the reader to our complete paper [15] which contains full proofs and further experimentation details.

Keywords: Generalised differential privacy · Earth Mover's metric · Natural language processing · Author obfuscation

1 Introduction

Partial public release of formerly classified data incurs the risk that more information is disclosed than intended. This is particularly true of data in the form of text such as government documents or patient health records. Nevertheless there are sometimes compelling reasons for declassifying data in some kind of "sanitised" form—for example government documents are frequently released as redacted reports when the law demands it, and health records are often shared to facilitate medical research. Sanitisation is most commonly carried out by hand but, aside from the cost incurred in time and money, this approach provides no guarantee that the original privacy or security concerns are met.

We acknowledge the support of the Australian Research Council Grant DP140101119.

F. Nielson and D. Sands (Eds.): POST 2019, LNCS 11426, pp. 123–148, 2019.
https://doi.org/10.1007/978-3-030-17138-4_6

To encourage researchers to focus on privacy issues related to text documents the digital forensics community PAN@Clef ([41], for example) proposed a number of challenges that are typically tackled using *machine learning.* In this paper our aim is to demonstrate how to use ideas from *differential privacy* to address some aspects of the PAN@Clef challenges by showing how to provide strong a priori privacy guarantees in document disclosures.

We focus on the problem of *author obfuscation*, namely to automate the process of changing a given document so that as much as possible of its original substance remains, but that the author of the document can no longer be identified. Author obfuscation is very difficult to achieve because it is not clear exactly what to change that would sufficiently mask the author's identity. In fact author properties can be determined by "writing style" with a high degree of accuracy: this can include author identity [28] or other undisclosed personal attributes such as native language [33,51], gender or age [16,27]. These techniques have been deployed in real world scenarios: native language identification was used as part of the effort to identify the anonymous perpetrators of the 2014 Sony hack [17], and it is believed that the US NSA used author attribution techniques to uncover the identity of the real humans behind the fictitious persona of Bitcoin "creator" Satoshi Nakamoto.[1]

Our contribution concentrates on the perspective of the "machine learner" as an adversary that works with the standard "bag-of-words" representation of documents often used in text processing tasks. A *bag-of-words* representation retains only the original document's words and their frequency (thus forgetting the order in which the words occur). Remarkably this representation still contains sufficient information to enable the original authors to be identified (by a stylistic analysis) *as well as* the document's topic to be classified, both with a significant degree of accuracy.[2] Within this context we reframe the PAN@Clef author obfuscation challenge as follows:

> Given an input bag-of-words representation of a text document, provide a mechanism which changes the input without disturbing its topic classification, but that the author can no longer be identified.

In the rest of the paper we use ideas inspired by *$d_{\mathcal{X}}$-privacy* [9], a metric-based extension of differential privacy, to implement an automated privacy mechanism which, unlike current ad hoc approaches to author obfuscation, gives access to both solid privacy and utility guarantees.[3]

1 https://medium.com/cryptomuse/how-the-nsa-caught-satoshi-nakamoto-868affcef595.

2 This includes, for example, the character n-gram representation used for author identification in [29].

3 Our notion of utility here is similar to other work aiming at text privacy, such as [32,53].

We implement a mechanism K which takes b, b' bag-of-words inputs and produces "noisy" bag-of-words outputs determined by $K(b), K(b')$ with the following properties:

Privacy: If b, b' are classified to be "similar in topic" then, depending on a privacy parameter ϵ the *outputs* determined by $K(b)$ and $K(b')$ are also "similar to each other", irrespective of authorship.

Utility: Possible outputs determined by $K(b)$ are distributed according to a Laplace probability density function scored according to a semantic similarity metric.

In what follows we define *semantic similarity* in terms of the classic *Earth Mover's distance* used in machine learning for topic classification in text document processing.[4] We explain how to combine this with $d_{\mathcal{X}}$-privacy which extends privacy for databases to other unstructured domains (such as texts).

In Sect. 2 we set out the details of the bag-of-words representation of documents and define the Earth Mover's metric for topic classification. In Sect. 3 we define a generic mechanism which satisfies "$E_{d_{\mathcal{X}}}$-privacy" relative to the Earth Mover's metric $E_{d_{\mathcal{X}}}$ and show how to use it for our obfuscation problem. We note that our generic mechanism is of independent interest for other domains where the Earth Mover's metric applies. In Sect. 4 we describe how to implement the mechanism for data represented as real-valued vectors and prove its privacy/utility properties with respect to the Earth Mover's metric; in Sect. 5 we show how this applies to bags-of-words. Finally in Sect. 6 we provide an experimental evaluation of our obfuscation mechanism, and discuss the implications.

Throughout we assume standard definitions of probability spaces [18]. For a set $\mathcal{A}$ we write $\mathbb{D}\mathcal{A}$ for the set of (possibly continuous) probability distributions over $\mathcal{A}$. For $\eta \in \mathbb{D}\mathcal{A}$, and $A \subseteq \mathcal{A}$ a (measurable) subset we write $\eta(A)$ for the probability that (wrt. η) a randomly selected a is contained in A. In the special case of singleton sets, we write $\eta\{a\}$. If mechanism $K: \alpha \to \mathbb{D}\alpha$, we write $K(a)(A)$ for the probability that if the input is a, then the output will be contained in A.

2 Documents, Topic Classification and Earth Moving

In this section we summarise the elements from machine learning and text processing needed for this paper. Our first definition sets out the representation for documents we shall use throughout. It is a typical representation of text documents used in a variety of classification tasks.

Definition 1. *Let $\mathcal{S}$ be the set of all words (drawn from a finite alphabet). A* document *is defined to be a finite bag over $\mathcal{S}$, also called a* bag-of-words*. We denote the set of documents as $\mathbb{B}\mathcal{S}$, i.e. the set of (finite) bags over $\mathcal{S}$.*

---

[4] In NLP, this distance measure is known as the Word Mover's distance. We use the classic Earth Mover's here for generality.

Once a text is represented as a bag-of-words, depending on the processing task, further representations of the words within the bag are usually required. We shall focus on two important representations: the first is when the task is semantic analysis for eg. topic classification, and the second is when the task is author identification. We describe the representation for topic classification in this section, and leave the representation for author identification for Sects. 5 and 6.

2.1 Word Embeddings

Machine learners can be trained to classify the topic of a document, such as "health", "sport", "entertainment"; this notion of topic means that the words within documents will have particular semantic relationships to each other. There are many ways to do this classification, and in this paper we use a technique that has as a key component "word embeddings", which we summarise briefly here.

A *word embedding* is a real-valued vector representation of words where the precise representation has been experimentally determined by a neural network sensitive to the way words are used in sentences [38]. Such embeddings have some interesting properties, but here we only rely on the fact that when the embeddings are compared using a distance determined by a pseudometric[5] on $\mathbb{R}^n$, words with similar meanings are found to be close together as word embeddings, and words which are significantly different in meaning are far apart as word embeddings.

Definition 2. *An n-dimensional word embedding is a mapping $Vec : \mathcal{S} \to \mathbb{R}^n$. Given a pseudometric dist on $\mathbb{R}^n$ we define a distance on words $dist_{Vec} : \mathcal{S}\times\mathcal{S}\to\mathbb{R}_{\geq}$ as follows:*

$$dist_{Vec}(w_1, w_2) \ := \ dist(Vec(w_1), Vec(w_2)) \ .$$

Observe that the property of a pseudometric on $\mathbb{R}^n$ carries over to $\mathcal{S}$.

Lemma 1. *If dist is a pseudometric on $\mathbb{R}^n$ then $dist_{Vec}$ is also a pseudometric on $\mathcal{S}$.*

Proof. Immediate from the definition of a pseudometric: i.e. the triangle equality and the symmetry of $dist_{Vec}$ are inherited from dist.

Word embeddings are particularly suited to language analysis tasks, including topic classification, due to their useful semantic properties. Their effectiveness depends on the quality of the embedding *Vec*, which can vary depending on the size and quality of the training data. We provide more details of the particular

[5] Recall that a pseudometric satisfies both the triangle inequality and symmetry; but different words could be mapped to the same vector and so $dist_{Vec}(w_1, w_2) = 0$ no longer implies that $w_1 = w_2$.

embeddings in Sect. 6. Topic classifiers can also differ on the choice of underlying metric *dist*, and we discuss variations in Sect. 3.2.

In addition, once the word embedding *Vec* has been determined, and the distance *dist* has been selected for comparing "word meanings", there are a variety of semantic similarity measures that can be used to compare documents, for us bags-of-words. In this work we use the "Word Mover's Distance", which was shown to perform well across multiple text classification tasks [31].

The *Word Mover's Distance* is based on the classic *Earth Mover's Distance* [43] used in transportation problems with a given distance measure. We shall use the more general Earth Mover's definition with *dist*[6] as the underlying distance measure between words. We note that our results can be applied to problems outside of the text processing domain.

Let $X, Y \in \mathbb{B}\mathcal{S}$; we denote by X the tuple $\langle x_1^{a_1}, x_2^{a_2}, \ldots, x_k^{a_k}\rangle$, where a_i is the number of times that x_i occurs in X. Similarly we write $Y = \langle y_1^{b_1}, y_2^{b_2}, \ldots, y_l^{b_l}\rangle$; we have $\sum_i a_i = |X|$ and $\sum_j b_j = |Y|$, the sizes of X and Y respectively. We define a *flow matrix* $F \in \mathbb{R}_{\geq 0}^{k \times l}$ where F_{ij} represents the (non-negative) amount of flow from $x_i \in X$ to $y_j \in Y$.

Definition 3 *(Earth Mover's Distance). Let $d_\mathcal{S}$ be a (pseudo)metric over $\mathcal{S}$. The Earth Mover's Distance with respect to $d_\mathcal{S}$, denoted by $E_{d_\mathcal{S}}$, is the solution to the following linear optimisation:*

$$E_{d_\mathcal{S}}(X,Y) \quad := \quad \min \sum_{x_i \in X} \sum_{y_j \in Y} d_\mathcal{S}(x_i, y_j) F_{ij} \ , \quad \textit{subject to:} \tag{1}$$

$$\sum_{i=1}^{k} F_{ij} = \frac{b_j}{|Y|} \quad \textit{and} \quad \sum_{j=1}^{l} F_{ij} = \frac{a_i}{|X|}\ , \quad F_{ij} \geq 0, \quad 1 \leq i \leq k, 1 \leq j \leq l \tag{2}$$

where the minimum in (1) is over all possible flow matrices F subject to the constraints (2). In the special case that $|X| = |Y|$, the solution is known to satisfy the conditions of a (pseudo)metric [43] which we call the Earth Mover's Metric.

In this paper we are interested in the special case $|X| = |Y|$, hence we use the term *Earth Mover's metric* to refer to $E_{d_\mathcal{S}}$.

We end this section by describing how texts are prepared for machine learning tasks, and how Definition 3 is used to distinguish documents. Consider the text snippet "The President greets the press in Chicago". The first thing is to remove all "stopwords" – these are words which do not contribute to semantics, and include things like prepositions, pronouns and articles. The words remaining are those that contain a great deal of semantic and stylistic traits.[7]

---

[6] In our experiments we take *dist* to be defined by the Euclidean distance.

[7] In fact the way that stopwords are used in texts turn out to be characteristic features of authorship. Here we follow standard practice in natural language processing to remove them for efficiency purposes and study the privacy of what remains. All of our results apply equally well had we left stopwords in place.

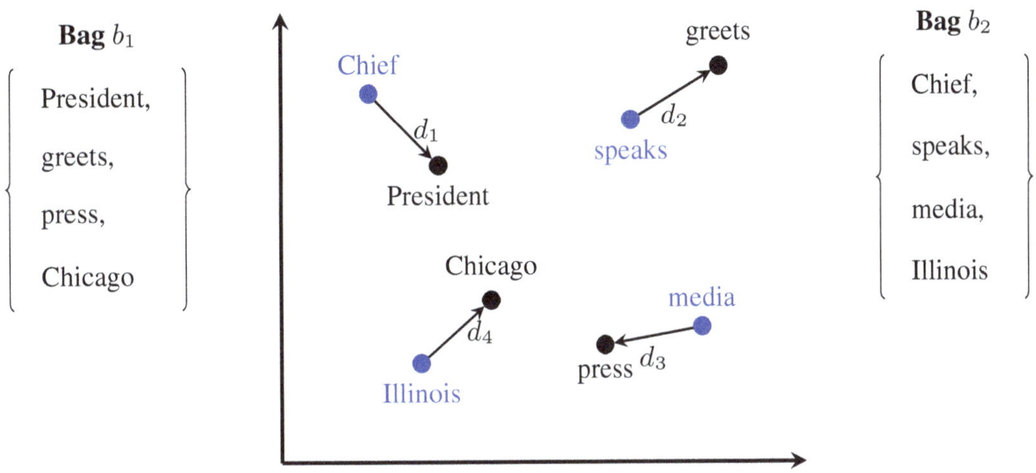

Fig. 1. Earth Mover's metric between sample documents.

In this case we obtain the bag:

$$b_1 \quad := \quad \langle \text{President}^1,\ \text{greets}^1,\ \text{press}^1,\ \text{Chicago}^1 \rangle \ .$$

Consider a second bag: $b_2 := \langle \text{Chief}^1, \text{speaks}^1, \text{media}^1, \text{Illinois}^1 \rangle$, corresponding to a different text. Figure 1 illustrates the optimal flow matrix which solves the optimisation problem in Definition 3 relative to $d_{\mathcal{S}}$. Here each word is mapped completely to another word, so that $F_{i,j} = 1/4$ when $i = j$ and 0 otherwise. We show later that this is always the case between bags of the same size. With these choices we can compute the distance between b_1, b_2:

$$\begin{aligned} E_{d_{\mathcal{S}}}(b_1, b_2) &= \frac{1}{4}(d_{\mathcal{S}}(\text{President}, \text{Chief}) + d_{\mathcal{S}}(\text{greets}, \text{speaks}) + \\ &\qquad d_{\mathcal{S}}(\text{press}, \text{media}) + d_{\mathcal{S}}(\text{Chicago}, \text{Illinois})) \\ &= 2.816\ . \end{aligned} \tag{3}$$

For comparison, consider the distance between b_1 and b_2 to a third document, $b_3 := \langle \text{Chef}^1, \text{breaks}^1, \text{cooking}^1, \text{record}^1 \rangle$. Using the same word embedding metric,[8] we find that $E_{d_{\mathcal{S}}}(b_1, b_3) = 4.121$ and $E_{d_{\mathcal{S}}}(b_2, b_3) = 3.941$. Thus b_1, b_2 would be classified as semantically "closer" to each other than to b_3, in line with our own (linguistic) interpretation of the original texts.

3 Differential Privacy and the Earth Mover's Metric

Differential Privacy was originally defined with the protection of individuals' data in mind. The intuition is that privacy is achieved through "plausible deniability", i.e. whatever output is obtained from a query, it could have just as

[8] We use the same word2vec-based metric as per our experiments; this is described in Sect. 6.

easily have arisen from a database that does not contain an individual's details, as from one that does. In particular, there should be no easy way to distinguish between the two possibilities. Privacy in text processing means something a little different. A "query" corresponds to releasing the topic-related contents of the document (in our case the bag-of-words)—this relates to the utility because we would like to reveal the semantic content. The privacy relates to investing *individual documents* with plausible deniability, rather than *individual authors* directly. What this means for privacy is the following. Suppose we are given two documents b_1, b_2 written by two distinct authors A_1, A_2, and suppose further that b_1, b_2 are changed through a privacy mechanism so that it is difficult or impossible to distinguish between them (by any means). Then it is also difficult or impossible to determine whether the authors of the original documents are A_1 or A_2, or some other author entirely. This is our aim for obfuscating authorship whilst preserving semantic content.

Our approach to obfuscating documents replaces words with other words, governed by probability distributions over possible replacements. Thus the type of our mechanism is $\mathbb{B}\mathcal{S} \to \mathbb{D}(\mathbb{B}\mathcal{S})$, where (recall) $\mathbb{D}(\mathbb{B}\mathcal{S})$ is the set of probability distributions over the set of (finite) bags of $\mathcal{S}$. Since we are aiming to find a careful trade-off between utility and privacy, our objective is to ensure that there is a high probability of outputting a document with a similar topic as the input document. As explained in Sect. 2, topic similarity of documents is determined by the Earth Mover's distance relative to a given (pseudo)metric on word embeddings, and so our privacy definition must also be relative to the Earth Mover's distance.

Definition 4 *(Earth Mover's Privacy). Let $\mathcal{X}$ be a set, and $d_\mathcal{X}$ be a (pseudo)metric on $\mathcal{X}$ and let $E_{d_\mathcal{X}}$ be the Earth Mover's metric on $\mathbb{B}\mathcal{X}$ relative to $d_\mathcal{X}$. Given $\epsilon \geq 0$, a mechanism $K : \mathbb{B}\mathcal{X} \to \mathbb{D}(\mathbb{B}\mathcal{X})$ satisfies $\epsilon E_{d_\mathcal{X}}$-privacy iff for any $b, b' \in \mathbb{B}\mathcal{X}$ and $Z \subseteq \mathbb{B}\mathcal{X}$:*

$$K(b)(Z) \quad \leq \quad e^{\epsilon E_{d_\mathcal{X}}(b,b')} K(b')(Z) \; . \tag{4}$$

Definition 4 tells us that when two documents are measured to be very close, so that $\epsilon E_{d_\mathcal{X}}(b, b')$ is close to 0, then the multiplier $e^{\epsilon E_{d_\mathcal{X}}(b,b')}$ is approximately 1 and the outputs $K(b)$ and $K(b')$ are almost identical. On the other hand the more that the input bags can be distinguished by $E_{d_\mathcal{X}}$, the more their outputs are likely to differ. This flexibility is what allows us to strike a balance between utility and privacy; we discuss this issue further in Sect. 5 below.

Our next task is to show how to implement a mechanism that can be proved to satisfy Definition 4. We follow the basic construction of Dwork et al. [12] for lifting a differentially private mechanism $K: \mathcal{X} \to \mathbb{D}\mathcal{X}$ to a differentially private mechanism $\underline{K}^\star: \mathcal{X}^N \to \mathbb{D}\mathcal{X}^N$ on *vectors* in $\mathcal{X}^N$. (Note that, unlike a bag, a vector imposes a fixed order on its components.) Here the idea is to apply K independently to each component of a vector $v \in \mathcal{X}^N$ to produce a random output vector, also in $\mathcal{X}^N$. In particular the probability of outputting some vector v' is the product:

$$\underline{K}^{\star}(v)\{v'\} \quad = \quad \prod_{1\leq i\leq N} K(v_i)\{v_i'\} \; . \tag{5}$$

Thanks to the compositional properties of differential privacy when the underlying metric on $\mathcal{X}$ satisfies the triangle inequality, it's possible to show that the resulting mechanism $\underline{K}^{\star}$ satisfies the following privacy mechanism [13]:

$$\underline{K}^{\star}(v)(Z) \quad \leq \quad e^{M_{d_{\mathcal{X}}}(v,v')}\underline{K}^{\star}(v')(Z) \; , \tag{6}$$

where $M_{d_{\mathcal{X}}}(v,v') := \sum_{1\leq i\leq N} d_{\mathcal{X}}(v_i, v_i')$, the Manhattan metric relative to $d_{\mathcal{X}}$.

However Definition 4 does not follow from (6), since Definition 4 operates on bags of size N, and the Manhattan distance between any vector representation of bags is *greater* than $N \times E_{d_{\mathcal{X}}}$. Remarkably however, it turns out that $K^{\star}$ –the mechanism that applies K independently to each item in a given bag– in fact satisfies the much stronger Definition 4, as the following theorem shows, provided the input bags have the same size as each other.

Theorem 1. *Let $d_{\mathcal{X}}$ be a pseudo-metric on $\mathcal{X}$ and let $K : \mathcal{X} \to \mathbb{D}\mathcal{X}$ be a mechanism satisfying $\epsilon d_{\mathcal{X}}$-privacy, i.e.*

$$K(x)(Z) \quad \leq \quad e^{\epsilon d_{\mathcal{X}}(x,x')}K(x')(Z) \; , \; \textit{for all } x, x' \in \mathcal{X}, \;\; Z \subseteq \mathcal{X}. \tag{7}$$

Let $K^{\star} : \mathbb{B}\mathcal{X} \to \mathbb{D}(\mathbb{B}\mathcal{X})$ be the mechanism obtained by applying K independently to each element of X for any $X \in \mathbb{B}\mathcal{X}$. Denote by $K^{\star}\!\downarrow\! N$ the restriction of $K^{\star}$ to bags of fixed size N. Then $K^{\star}\!\downarrow\! N$ satisfies $\epsilon N E_{d_{\mathcal{X}}}$-privacy.

Proof (Sketch). The full proof is given in our complete paper [15]; here we sketch the main ideas.

Let b, b' be input bags, both of size N, and let c a possible output bag (of $K^{\star}$). Observe that both output bags determined by $K^{\star}(b_1), K^{\star}(b_2)$ and c also have size N. We shall show that (4) is satisfied for the set containing the singleton element c and multiplier ϵN, from which it follows that (4) is satisfied for all sets Z.

By Birkhoff-von Neumann's theorem [26], in the case where all bags have the same size, the minimisation problem in Definition 3 is optimised for transportation matrix F where all values F_{ij} are either 0 or $1/N$. This implies that the optimal transportation for $E_{d_{\mathcal{X}}}(b,c)$ is achieved by moving each word in the bag b to a (single) word in bag c. The same is true for $E_{d_{\mathcal{X}}}(b',c)$ and $E_{d_{\mathcal{X}}}(b,b')$. Next we use a vector representation of bags as follows. For bag b, we write $\underline{b}$ for a vector in $\mathcal{X}^N$ such that each element in b appears at some $\underline{b}_i$.

Next we fix $\underline{b}$ and $\underline{b'}$ to be vector representations of respectively b, b' in $\mathcal{X}^N$ such that the optimal transportation for $E_{d_{\mathcal{X}}}(b,b')$ is

$$E_{d_{\mathcal{X}}}(b,b') \quad = \quad 1/N\times \sum_{1\leq i\leq N} d_{\mathcal{X}}(\underline{b}_i, \underline{b}_i') \quad = \quad M_{d_{\mathcal{X}}}(\underline{b}, \underline{b'})/N \; . \tag{8}$$

The final fact we need is to note that there is a relationship between $K^{\star}$ acting on bags of size N and $\underline{K}^{\star}$ which acts on vectors in $\mathcal{X}^N$ by applying K

independently to each component of a vector: it is characterised in the following way. Let b, c be bags and let $\underline{b}, \underline{c}$ be any vector representations. For permutation $\sigma \in \{1 \dots N\} \to \{1 \dots N\}$ write $\underline{c}^\sigma$ to be the vector with components permuted by σ, so that $\underline{c}_i^\sigma = \underline{c}_{\sigma(i)}$. With these definitions, the following equality between probabilities holds:

$$K^\star(b)\{c\} \quad = \quad \sum_\sigma \underline{K}^\star(\underline{b})\{\underline{c}^\sigma\} \;, \tag{9}$$

where the summation is over all permutations that give distinct vector representations of c. We now compute directly:

$$\begin{array}{lll} & K^\star(b)\{c\} & \\ = & \sum_\sigma \underline{K}^\star(\underline{b})\{\underline{c}^\sigma\} & \text{"(9) for } b, c\text{"} \\ \leq & \sum_\sigma e^{\epsilon M_d(\underline{b}, \underline{b}')} \underline{K}^\star(\underline{b}')\{\underline{c}^\sigma\} & \text{"(6) for } \underline{b}, \underline{b}', \underline{c}\text{"} \\ = & e^{\epsilon N E_d(\underline{b}, \underline{b}')} \sum_\sigma \underline{K}^\star(\underline{b}')\{\underline{c}^\sigma\} & \text{"Arithmetic and (8)"} \\ = & e^{\epsilon N E_d(\underline{b}, \underline{b}')} K^\star(b')\{c\} \;, & \text{"(9) for } b', c\text{"} \end{array}$$

as required.

3.1 Application to Text Documents

Recall the bag-of-words

$$b_2 \quad := \quad \langle \text{Chief}^1, \text{speaks}^1, \text{media}^1, \text{Illinois}^1 \rangle \;,$$

and assume we are provided with a mechanism K satisfying the standard $\epsilon d_{\mathcal{X}}$-privacy property (7) for individual words. As in Theorem 1 we can create a mechanism K^* by applying K independently to each word in the bag, so that, for example the probability of outputting $b_3 = \langle \text{Chief}^1, \text{breaks}^1, \text{cooking}^1, \text{record}^1 \rangle$ is determined by (9):

$$K^\star(b_2)(\{b_3\}) \quad = \quad \sum_\sigma \prod_{1 \leq i \leq 4} K(b_{2i})\{\underline{b_3}_i{}^\sigma\} \;.$$

By Theorem 1, $K^\star$ satisfies $4\epsilon E_{d_S}$-privacy. Recalling (3) that $E_{d_S}(b_1, b_2) = 2.816$, we deduce that if $\epsilon \sim 1/16$ then the output distributions $K^\star(b_1)$ and $K^\star(b_2)$ would differ by the multiplier $e^{2.816 \times 4/16} \sim 2.02$; but if $\epsilon \sim 1/32$ those distributions differ by only 1.42. In the latter case it means that the outputs of $K^\star$ on b_1 and b_2 are almost indistinguishable.

The parameter ϵ depends on the randomness implemented in the basic mechanism K; we investigate that further in Sect. 4.

3.2 Properties of Earth Mover's Privacy

In machine learning a number of "distance measures" are used in classification or clustering tasks, and in this section we explore some properties of privacy when we vary the underlying metrics of an Earth Mover's metric used to classify complex objects.

Let $v, v' \in \mathbb{R}^n$ be real-valued n-dimensional vectors. We use the following (well-known) metrics. Recall in our applications we have looked at bags-of-words, where the words themselves are represented as n-dimensional vectors.[9]

1. Euclidean: $\|v-v'\| \;:=\; \sqrt{\sum_{1\le i\le n}(v_i - v'_i)^2}$
2. Manhattan: $\lfloor v-v' \rfloor \;:=\; \sum_{1\le i\le n}|v_i - v'_i|$

Note that the Euclidean and Manhattan distances determine pseudometrics on words as defined at Definition 2 and proved at Lemma 1.

Lemma 2. *If $d_{\mathcal{X}} \le d_{\mathcal{X}'}$ (point-wise), then $E_{d_{\mathcal{X}}} \le E_{d_{\mathcal{X}'}}$ (point-wise).*

Proof. Trivial, by contradiction. If $d_{\mathcal{X}} \le d_{\mathcal{X}'}$ and $F_{ij}, F^\star_{ij}$ are the minimal flow matrices for $E_{d_{\mathcal{X}}}, E_{d_{\mathcal{X}'}}$ respectively, then $F^\star_{ij}$ is a (strictly smaller) minimal solution for $E_{d_{\mathcal{X}}}$ which contradicts the minimality of F_{ij}.

Corollary 1. *If $d_{\mathcal{X}} \le d_{\mathcal{X}'}$ (point-wise), then $E_{d_{\mathcal{X}}}$-privacy implies $E_{d_{\mathcal{X}'}}$-privacy.*

This shows that, for example, $E_{\|\cdot\|}$-privacy implies $E_{\lfloor\cdot\rfloor}$-privacy, and indeed any distance measure d which exceeds the Euclidean distance then $E_{\|\cdot\|}$-privacy implies E_d-privacy.

We end this section by noting that Definition 4 satisfies *post-processing*; i.e. that privacy does not decrease under post processing. We write $K;K'$ for the composition of mechanisms $K, K' : \mathbb{B}\mathcal{X} \to \mathbb{D}(\mathbb{B}\mathcal{X})$, defined:

$$(K;K')(b)(Z) \;:=\; \sum_{b':\mathbb{B}\mathcal{X}} K(b)(\{b'\}) \times K'(b')(Z)\;. \tag{10}$$

Lemma 3 *[Post processing]. If $K, K' : \mathbb{B}\mathcal{X} \to \mathbb{D}(\mathbb{B}\mathcal{X})$ and K is $\epsilon E_{d_{\mathcal{X}}}$-private for (pseudo)metric d on $\mathcal{X}$ then $K;K'$ is $\epsilon E_{d_{\mathcal{X}}}$-private.*

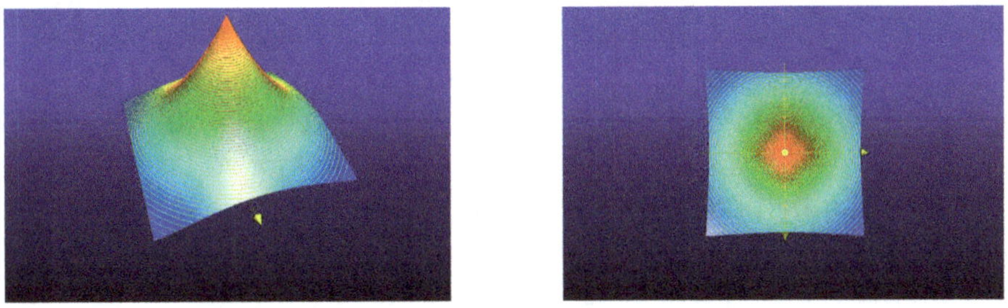

3D plot   Contour diagram

Fig. 2. Laplace density function Lap^2_ϵ in $\mathbb{R}^2$

[9] As we shall see, in the machine learning analysis *documents* are represented as bags of n-dimensional vectors (word embeddings), where each bag contains N such vectors.

4 Earth Mover's Privacy for Bags of Vectors in $\mathbb{R}^n$

In Theorem 1 we have shown how to promote a privacy mechanism on components to $E_{d_\mathcal{X}}$-privacy on a bag of those components. In this section we show how to implement a privacy mechanism satisfying (7), when the components are represented by high dimensional vectors in $\mathbb{R}^n$ and the underlying metric is taken Euclidean on $\mathbb{R}^n$, which we denote by $\|\cdot\|$.

We begin by summarising the basic probabilistic tools we need. A *probability density function* (PDF) over some domain $\mathcal{D}$ is a function $\phi : \mathcal{D} \to [0, 1]$ whose value $\phi(z)$ gives the "relative likelihood" of z. The probability density function is used to compute the probability of an outcome "$z \in A$", for some region $A \subseteq \mathcal{D}$ as follows:

$$\int_A \phi(x)\ dx\ . \tag{11}$$

In differential privacy, a popular density function used for implementing mechanisms is the *Laplacian*, defined next.

Definition 5. *Let $n \geq 0$ be an integer $\epsilon > 0$ be a real, and $v \in \mathbb{R}^n$. We define the Laplacian probability density function in n-dimensions:*

$$Lap^n_\epsilon(v) \quad := \quad c^\epsilon_n \times e^{-\epsilon\|v\|}\ ,$$

where $\|v\| = \sqrt{(v_1^2 + \cdots + v_n^2)}$, and c^ϵ_n is a real-valued constant satisfying the integral equation $1 = \int \ldots \int_{\mathbb{R}^n} Lap^n_\epsilon(v) dv_1 \ldots dv_n$.

When $n = 1$, we can compute $c^\epsilon_1 = \epsilon/2$, and when $n = 2$, we have that $c^\epsilon_2 = \epsilon^2/2\pi$.

In privacy mechanisms, probability density functions are used to produce a "noisy" version of the released data. The benefit of the Laplace distribution is that, besides creating randomness, the likelihood that the released value is different from the true value decreases exponentially. This implies that the utility of the data release is high, whilst at the same time masking its actual value. In Fig. 2 the probability density function $Lap^2_\epsilon(v)$ depicts this situation, where we see that the highest relative likelihood of a randomly selected point on the plane being close to the origin, with the chance of choosing more distant points diminishing rapidly. Once we are able to select a vector v' in $\mathbb{R}^n$ according to Lap^n_ϵ, we can "add noise" to any given vector v as $v{+}v'$, so that the true value v is highly likely to be perturbed only a small amount.

In order to use the Laplacian in Definition 5, we need to implement it. Andrés et al. [4] exhibited a mechanism for $Lap^2_\epsilon(v)$, and here we show how to extend that idea to the general case. The main idea of the construction for $Lap^2_\epsilon(v)$ uses the fact that any vector on the plane can be represented by spherical coordinates (r, θ), so that the probability of selecting a vector distance no more than r from the origin can be achieved by selecting r and θ independently. In order to obtain a distribution which overall is equivalent to $Lap^2_\epsilon(v)$, Andrés et al. computed that r must be selected according to a well-known distribution called the "Lambert W" function, and θ is selected uniformly over the unit circle. In our generalisation to $Lap^n_\epsilon(v)$, we observe that the same idea is valid [6]. Observe first that every vector in $\mathbb{R}^n$ can be expressed as a pair (r, p), where r is the distance from the origin, and p is a point in B^n, the unit *hypersphere* in $\mathbb{R}^n$. Now selecting vectors according to $Lap^n_\epsilon(v)$ can be achieved by independently selecting r and p, but this time r must be selected according to the *Gamma distribution*, and p must be selected uniformly over B^n. We set out the details next.

Definition 6. *The* Gamma distribution *of (integer) shape n and scale $\delta > 0$ is determined by the probability density function:*

$$Gam^n_\delta(r) \quad := \quad \frac{r^{n-1}e^{-r/\delta}}{\delta^n(n-1!)} \ . \tag{12}$$

Definition 7. *The uniform distribution over the surface of the unit hypersphere B^n is determined by the probability density function:*

$$Uniform^n(v) \quad := \quad \frac{\Gamma(\frac{n}{2})}{n\pi^{n/2}} \ \text{if} \ \ v \in B^n \ \ \text{else} \ \ 0 \ , \tag{13}$$

where $B^n := \{v \in \mathbb{R}^n \mid \|v\| = 1\}$, and $\Gamma(\alpha) := \int_0^\infty x^{\alpha-1}e^{-x}\,dx$ is the "Gamma function".

With Definitions 6 and 7 we are able to provide an implementation of a mechanism which produces noisy vectors around a given vector in $\mathbb{R}^n$ according to the Laplacian distribution in Definition 5. The first task is to show that our decomposition of Lap^n_ϵ is correct.

Lemma 4. *The n-dimensional Laplacian $Lap^n_\epsilon(v)$ can be realised by selecting vectors represented as (r, p), where r is selected according to $Gam^n_{1/\epsilon}(r)$ and p is selected independently according to $Uniform^n(p)$.*

Proof (Sketch). The proof follows by changing variables to spherical coordinates and then showing that $\int_A Lap^n_\epsilon(v)\,dv$ can be expressed as the product of independent selections of r and p.

We use a spherical-coordinate representation of v as:

$r := \|v\|$, *and*
$v_1 := r\cos\theta_1$, $v_2 := r\sin\theta_1\cos\theta_2$, $\ldots$ $v_n := r\sin\theta_1\sin\theta_2\ldots$, $\sin\theta_{n-2}\sin\theta_{n-1}$.

Next we assume for simplicity that A is a hypersphere of radius R; with that we can reason:

$$\int_A Lap^n_\epsilon(v)\,dv$$

$=$ "Definition 5; A is a hypersphere"

$$\int_{\|v\|\leq R} c^\epsilon_n \times e^{-\epsilon|v|}\,dv$$

$=$ "$\|v\| = \sqrt{v_1^2 + \cdots + v_n^2}$"

$$\int_{\|v\|\leq R} c^\epsilon_n \times e^{-\epsilon\sqrt{v_1^2+\cdots+v_n^2}}\,dv$$

$=$ "Change of variables to spherical coordinates; see below (14)"

$$\int_{r\leq R}\int_{A_\theta} c^\epsilon_n \times e^{-\epsilon r}\,\frac{\partial(z_1,z_2,\ldots,z_n)}{\partial(r,\theta_1,\ldots,\theta_{n-1})}\,dr d\theta_1\ldots d\theta_{n-1}$$

$=$ "See below (14)"

$$\int_{r\leq R}\int_{A_\theta} c^\epsilon_n \times e^{-\epsilon r} r^{n-1}\sin^{n-2}\theta_1\sin^{n-3}\theta_2\ldots\sin^2\theta_{n-3}\sin\theta_{n-2}\,dr d\theta_1\ldots d\theta_{n-1} \ .$$

Now rearranging we can see that this becomes a product of two integrals. The first $\int_{r\leq R} e^{-\epsilon r} r^{n-1}$ is over the radius, and is proportional to the integral of the Gamma distribution Definition 6; and the second is an integral over the angular coordinates and is proportional to the surface of the unit hypersphere, and corresponds to the PDF at (7). Finally, for the "see below's" we are using the "Jacobian":

$$\frac{\partial(z_1, z_2, \ldots, z_n)}{\partial(r, \theta_1, \ldots, \theta_{n-1})} = r^{n-1} \sin^{n-2}\theta_1 \sin^{n-3}\theta_2 \ldots \tag{14}$$

(For full details, see our complete paper [15].)

We can now assemble the facts to demonstrate the n-Dimensional Laplacian.

Theorem 2 (n-Dimensional Laplacian). *Given $\epsilon > 0$ and $n \in \mathbb{Z}^+$, let $K : \mathbb{R}^n \to \mathbb{D}\mathbb{R}^n$ be a mechanism that, given a vector $x \in \mathbb{R}^n$ outputs a noisy value as follows:*

$$x \stackrel{K}{\longmapsto} x + x'$$

where x' is represented as (r, p) with $r \geq 0$, distributed according to $Gam^n_{1/\epsilon}(r)$ and $p \in B^n$ distributed according to $Uniform^n(p)$. Then K satisfies (7) from Theorem 1, i.e. K satisfies $\epsilon\|\cdot\|$-privacy where $\|\cdot\|$ is the Euclidean metric on $\mathbb{R}^n$.

Proof (Sketch). Let $z, y \in \mathbb{R}^n$. We need to show that for any (measurable) set $A \subseteq \mathbb{R}^n$ that:

$$K(z)(A)/K(y)(A) \quad \leq \quad e^{\epsilon\|z-y\|} \; . \tag{15}$$

However (15) follows provided that the probability densities of respectively $K(z)$ and $K(y)$ satisfy it. By Lemma 4 the probability density of $K(z)$, as a function of x is distributed as $Lap^n_\epsilon(z{-}x)$; and similarly for the probability density of $K(y)$. Hence we reason:

$$\begin{array}{lll} & Lap^n_\epsilon(z{-}x)/Lap^n_\epsilon(y{-}x) & \\ = & c^\epsilon_n {\times} e^{-\epsilon\|z-x\|}/c^\epsilon_n {\times} e^{-\epsilon\|y-x\|} & \text{"Definition 5"} \\ = & e^{-\epsilon\|z-x\|} \times e^{\epsilon\|y-x\|} & \text{"Arithmetic"} \\ \leq & e^{\epsilon\|z-y\|} \; , & \text{"Triangle inequality; } s \mapsto e^s \text{ is monotone"} \end{array}$$

as required.

Theorem 2 reduces the problem of adding Laplace noise to vectors in $\mathbb{R}^n$ to selecting a real value according to the Gamma distribution and an independent uniform selection of a unit vector. Several methods have been proposed for generating random variables according to the Gamma distribution [30] as well as for the uniform selection of vectors on the unit n-sphere [35]. The uniform selection of a unit vector has also been described in [35]; it avoids the transformation to spherical coordinates by selecting n random variables from the standard normal distribution to produce vector $v \in \mathbb{R}^n$, and then normalising to output $\frac{v}{|v|}$.

4.1 Earth Mover's Privacy in $\mathbb{BR}^n$

Using the n-dimensional Laplacian, we can now implement an algorithm for $\epsilon NE_{\|\cdot\|}$-privacy. Algorithm 1 takes a bag of n-dimensional vectors as input and applies the n-dimensional Laplacian mechanism described in Theorem 2 to each vector in the bag, producing a noisy bag of n-dimensional vectors as output. Corollary 2 summarises the privacy guarantee.

Algorithm 1. Earth Mover's Privacy Mechanism

```
Require: vector v, dimension n, epsilon ε
procedure GenerateNoisyVector(v, n, ε)
    r ← Gamma(n, 1/ε)
    u ← U(n)
    return v + ru
end procedure
Require: bag X, dimension n, epsilon ε
procedure GeneratePrivateBag(X, n, ε)
    Z ← ()
    for all x ∈ X do
        z ← GenerateNoisyVector(x, n, ε)
        add z to Z
    end for
    return Z
end procedure
```

Corollary 2. *Algorithm 1 satisfies $\epsilon NE_{\|\cdot\|}$-privacy, relative to any two bags in $\mathbb{BR}^n$ of size N.*

Proof. Follows from Theorems 1 and 2.

4.2 Utility Bounds

We prove a lower bound on the utility for this algorithm, which applies for high dimensional data representations. Given an output element x, we define Z to be the set of outputs within distance $\Delta > 0$ from x. Recall that the distance function is a measure of utility, therefore $Z = \{z \mid E_{\|\cdot\|}(x, z) \leq \Delta\}$ represents the set of vectors within utility Δ of x. Then we have the following:

Theorem 3. *Given an input bag b consisting of N n-dimensional vectors, the mechanism defined by Algorithm 1 outputs an element from $Z = \{z \mid E_{\|\cdot\|}(b, z) \leq \Delta\}$ with probability at least*

$$1 - e^{-\epsilon N\Delta} e_{n-1}(\epsilon N\Delta) ,$$

whenever $\epsilon N\Delta \leq n/e$. (Recall that $e_k(\alpha) = \sum_{0\leq i\leq k} \frac{\alpha^i}{i!}$, the sum of the first $k+1$ terms in the series for e^α.)

Proof (Sketch). Let $\underline{b} \in (\mathbb{R}^n)^N$ *be a (fixed) vector representation of the bag* b. *For* $v \in (\mathbb{R}^n)^N$, *let* $v^\circ \in \mathbb{B}\mathbb{R}^n$ *be the bag comprising the* N *components if* v. *Observe that* $NE_{\|\cdot\|}(b, v^\circ) \le M_{\|\cdot\|}(\underline{b}, v)$, *and so*

$$Z_M = \{v \mid M_{\|\cdot\|}(\underline{b}, v) \le N\Delta\} \quad \subseteq \quad \{v \mid E_{\|\cdot\|}(b, v^\circ) \le \Delta\} = Z_E \ . \tag{16}$$

Thus the probability of outputting an element of Z *is the same as the probability of outputting* Z_E, *and by (16) that is at least the probability of outputting an element from* Z_M *by applying a standard* n*-dimensional Laplace mechanism to each of the components of* $\underline{b}$. *We can now compute:*

Probability of outputting an element in Z_E

$\geq$ *"(16)"*

$$\int \cdots \int_{v \in Z_M} \prod_{1 \le i \le N} Lap^n_\epsilon(\underline{b}_i - v_i) dv_1 \ldots dv_N$$

$=$ *"Lemma 4"*

$$\int \cdots \int_{v \in Z_M} \prod_{1 \le i \le N} c^\epsilon_n e^{-\epsilon \|\underline{b}_i - v_i\|} dv_1 \ldots dv_N \ .$$

The result follows by completing the multiple integrals and applying some approximations, whilst observing that the variables in the integration are n*-dimensional vector valued. (The details appear in our complete paper [15].)*

We note that in our application word embeddings are typically mapped to vectors in $\mathbb{R}^{300}$, thus we would use $n \sim 300$ in Theorem 3.

5 Text Document Privacy

In this section we bring everything together, and present a privacy mechanism for text documents; we explore how it contributes to the author obfuscation task described above. Algorithm 2 describes the complete procedure for taking a document as a bag-of-words, and outputting a "noisy" bag-of-words. Depending on the setting of parameter ϵ, the output bag will be likely to be classified to be on a similar topic as the input.

Algorithm 2 uses a function *Vec* to turn the input document into a bag of word embeddings; next Algorithm 1 produces a noisy bag of word embeddings, and, in a final step the inverse Vec^{-1} is used to reconstruct an actual bag-of-words as output. In our implementation of Algorithm 2, described below, we compute $Vec^{-1}(x)$ to be the word w that minimises the Euclidean distance $\|z - Vec(w)\|$. The next result summarises the privacy guarantee for Algorithm 2.

Theorem 4. *Algorithm 2 satisfies* $\epsilon N E_{d_S}$*-privacy, where* $d_S = dist_{Vec}$. *That is to say: given input documents (bags)* b, b' *both of size* N, *and* c *a possible output bag, define the following quantities as follows:* $k := E_{\|\cdot\|}(Vec^\star(b), Vec^\star(b'))$, $pr(b, c)$ *and* $pr(b', c)$ *are the respective probabilities that* c *is output given the input was* b *or* b'. *Then:*

$$pr(b, c) \quad \le \quad e^{\epsilon N k} \times pr(b', c) \ .$$

Algorithm 2. Document privacy mechanism

Require: Bag-of-words b, dimension n, epsilon ϵ, Word embedding $Vec : \mathcal{S} \rightarrow \mathbb{R}^n$

```
1: procedure GenerateNoisyBagOfWords(b, n, ε, Vec)
2:     X ← Vec*(b)
3:     Z ← GeneratePrivateBag(X, n, ε)
4:     return (Vec^{-1})*(Z)
5: end procedure
```

Note that $Vec^\star : \mathbb{B}\mathcal{S} \rightarrow \mathbb{B}\mathbb{R}^n$ applies Vec to each word in a bag b, and $(Vec^{-1})^\star : \mathbb{B}\mathbb{R}^n \rightarrow \mathbb{B}\mathcal{S}$ reverses this procedure as a post-processing step; this involves determining the word w that minimises the Euclidean distance $\|z - Vec(w)\|$ for each z in Z.

Proof. The result follows by appeal to Theorem 2 for privacy on the word embeddings; the step to apply Vec^{-1} to each vector is a post-processing step which by Lemma 3 preserves the privacy guarantee.

Although Theorem 4 utilises ideas from differential privacy, an interesting question to ask is how it contributes to the PAN@Clef author obfuscation task, which recall asked for mechanisms that preserve content but mask features that distinguish authorship. Algorithm 2 does indeed attempt to preserve content (to the extent that the topic can still be determined) but it does not directly "remove stylistic features".[10] So has it, in fact, disguised the author's characteristic style? To answer that question, we review Theorem 4 and interpret what it tells us in relation to author obfuscation.

The theorem implies that it is indeed possible to make the (probabilistic) output from two distinct documents b, b' almost indistinguishable by choosing ϵ to be extremely small in comparison with $N \times E_{\|\cdot\|}(Vec^\star(b), Vec^\star(b'))$. However, if $E_{\|\cdot\|}(Vec^\star(b), Vec^\star(b'))$ is very large – meaning that b and b' are on entirely different topics, then ϵ would need to be so tiny that the noisy output document would be highly unlikely to be on a topic remotely close to either b or b' (recall Lemma 3).

This observation is actually highlighting the fact that, in some circumstances, the topic itself is actually a feature that characterises author identity. (First-hand accounts of breaking the world record for highest and longest free fall jump would immediately narrow the field down to the title holder.) This means that *any* obfuscating mechanism would, as for Algorithm 2, only be able to obfuscate documents so as to disguise the author's identity if there are several authors who write on similar topics. And it is in that spirit, that we have made the first step towards a satisfactory obfuscating mechanism: provided that documents are similar in topic (i.e. are close when their embeddings are measured by $E_{\|\cdot\|}$) they can be obfuscated so that it is unlikely that the content is disturbed, but that the contributing authors cannot be determined easily.

[10] Although, as others have noted [53], the bag-of-words representation already removes many stylistic features. We note that our privacy guarantee does not depend on this side-effect.

We can see the importance of the "indistinguishability" property wrt. the PAN obfuscation task. In stylometry analysis the representation of words for eg. author classification is completely different to the word embeddings which have used for topic classification. State-of-the-art author attribution algorithms represent words as "character n-grams" [28] which have been found to capture stylistic clues such as systematic spelling errors. A *character 3-gram* for example represents a given word as the complete list of substrings of length 3. For example character 3-gram representations of "color" and "colour" are:

- "color" $\mapsto$ ⟦ "col", "olo", "lor" ⟧
- "colour" $\mapsto$ ⟦ "col", "olo", "lou", "our" ⟧

For author identification, any output from Algorithm 2 would then need to be further transformed to a bag of character n-grams, as a post processing step; by Lemma 3 this additional transformation preserves the privacy properties of Algorithm 2. We explore this experimentally in the next section.

6 Experimental Results

Document Set. The PAN@Clef tasks and other similar work have used a variety of types of text for author identification and author obfuscation. Our desiderata are that we have multiple authors writing on one topic (so as to minimise the ability of an author identification system to use topic-related cues) and to have more than one topic (so that we can evaluate utility in terms of accuracy of topic classification). Further, we would like to use data from a domain where there are potentially large quantities of text available, and where it is already annotated with author and topic.

Given these considerations, we chose "fan fiction" as our domain. Wikipedia defines *fan fiction* as follows: "Fan fiction ... is fiction about characters or settings from an original work of fiction, created by fans of that work rather than by its creator." This is also the domain that was used in the PAN@Clef 2018 author attribution challenge,[11] although for this work we scraped our own dataset. We chose one of the largest fan fiction sites and the two largest "fandoms" there;[12] these fandoms are our topics. We scraped the stories from these fandoms, the largest proportion of which are for use in training our topic classification model. We held out two subsets of size 20 and 50, evenly split between fandoms/topics, for the evaluation of our privacy mechanism.[13] We follow the evaluation framework of [28]: for each author we construct an known-author TEXT and an unknown-author SNIPPET that we have to match to an author on

[11] https://pan.webis.de/clef18/pan18-web/author-identification.html.

[12] https://www.fanfiction.net/book/, with the two largest fandoms being Harry Potter (797,000 stories) and Twilight (220,000 stories).

[13] Our Algorithm 2 is computationally quite expensive, because each word $w = Vec^{-1}(x)$ requires the calculation of Euclidean distance with respect to the whole vocabulary. We thus use relatively small evaluation sets, as we apply the algorithm to them for multiple values of ϵ.

the basis of the known-author texts. (See Appendix in our complete paper [15] for more detail.)

Word Embeddings. There are sets of word embeddings trained on large datasets that have been made publicly available. Most of these, however, are already normalised, which makes them unsuitable for our method. We therefore use the Google News word2vec embeddings as the only large-scale unnormalised embeddings available. (See Appendix in our complete paper [15] for more detail.)

Inference Mechanisms. We have two sorts of machine learning inference mechanisms: our adversary mechanism for author identification, and our utility-related mechanism for topic classification. For each of these, we can define inference mechanisms both within the same representational space or in a different representational space. As we noted above, in practice both author identification adversary and topic classification will use different representations, but examining same-representation inference mechanisms can give an insight into what is happening within that space.

Different-Representation Author Identification. For this we use the algorithm by [28]. This algorithm is widely used: it underpins two of the winners of PAN shared tasks [25,47]; is a common benchmark or starting point for other methods [19,39,44,46]; and is a standard inference attacker for the PAN shared task on authorship obfuscation.[14] It works by representing each text as a vector of space-separated character n-gram counts, and comparing repeatedly sampled subvectors of known-author texts and snippets using cosine similarity. We use as a starting point the code from a reproducibility study [40], but have modified it to improve efficiency. (See Appendix in our complete paper [15] for more details.)

Different-Representation Topic Classification. Here we choose fastText [7,22], a high-performing supervised machine learning classification system. It also works with word embeddings; these differ from word2vec in that they are derived from embeddings over character n-grams, learnt using the same skipgram model as word2vec. This means it is able to compute representations for words that do not appear in the training data, which is helpful when training with relatively small amounts of data; also useful when training with small amounts of data is the ability to start from pretrained embeddings trained on out-of-domain data that are then adapted to the in-domain (here, fan fiction) data. After training, the accuracy on a validation set we construct from the data is 93.7% (see [15] for details).

Same-Representation Author Identification. In the space of our word2vec embeddings, we can define an inference mechanism that for an unknown-author snippet chooses the closest known-author text by Euclidean distance.

---

[14] http://pan.webis.de/clef17/pan17-web/author-obfuscation.html.

Same-Representation Topic Classification. Similarly, we can define an inference mechanism that considers the topic classes of neighbours and predicts a class for the snippet based on that. This is essentially the standard k "Nearest Neighbours" technique (k-NN) [21], a non-parametric method that assigns the majority class of the k nearest neighbours. 1-NN corresponds to classification based on a Voronoi tesselation of the space, has low bias and high variance, and asymptotically has an error rate that is never more than twice the Bayes rate; higher values of k have a smoothing effect. Because of the nature of word embeddings, we would not expect this classification to be as accurate as the fastText classification above: in high-dimensional Euclidean space (as here), almost all points are approximately equidistant. Nevertheless, it can give an idea about how a snippet with varying levels of noise added is being shifted in Euclidean space with respect to other texts in the same topic. Here, we use $k = 5$. Same-representation author identification can then be viewed as 1-NN with author as class.

Table 1. Number of correct predictions of author/topic in the 20-author set (left) and 50-author set (right), using 1-NN for same-representation author identification (SRauth), 5-NN for same-representation topic classification (SRtopic), the Koppel algorithm for different-representation author identification (DRauth) and fastText for different-representation topic classification (DRtopic).

	20-author set			
ϵ	SRauth	SRtopic	DRauth	DRtopic
none	12	16	15	18
30	8	18	16	18
25	8	18	14	17
20	5	11	11	16
15	2	11	12	17
10	0	15	11	19

	50-author set			
ϵ	SRauth	SRtopic	DRauth	DRtopic
none	19	36	27	43
30	19	37	29	43
25	17	34	24	41
20	12	28	19	42
15	9	22	13	42
10	1	24	10	43

Results: Table 1 contains the results for both document sets, for the unmodified snippets ("none") or with the privacy mechanism of Algorithm 2 applied with various levels of ϵ: we give results for ϵ between 10 and 30, as at $\epsilon = 40$ the text does not change, while at $\epsilon = 1$ the text is unrecognisable. For the 20-author set, a random guess baseline would give 1 correct author prediction, and 10 correct topic predictions; for the 50-author set, these values are 1 and 25 respectively.

Performance on the unmodified snippets using different-representation inference mechanisms is quite good: author identification gets 15/20 correct for the 20-author set and 27/50 for the 50-author set; and topic classification 18/20 and 43/50 (comparable to the validation set accuracy, although slightly lower, which is to be expected given that the texts are much shorter). For various levels of ϵ, with our different-representation inference mechanisms we see broadly the behaviour we expected: the performance of author identification drops, while topic classification holds roughly constant. Author identification here does not drop to chance levels: we speculate that this is because (in spite of our choice of dataset for this purpose) there are still some topic clues that the algorithm of [28] takes advantage of: one author of Harry Potter fan fiction might prefer to write about a particular character (e.g. Severus Snape), and as these character names are not in our word2vec vocabulary, they are not replaced by the privacy mechanism.

In our same-representation author identification, though, we do find performance starting relatively high (although not as high as the different-representation algorithm) and then dropping to (worse than) chance, which is the level we would expect for our privacy mechanism. The k-NN topic classification, however, shows some instability, which is probably an artefact of the problems it faces with high-dimensional Euclidean spaces. (Refer to our complete arXiv paper [15] for a sample of texts and nearest neighbours.)

7 Related Work

Author Obfuscation. The most similar work to ours is by Weggenmann and Kerschbaum [53] who also consider the author obfuscation problem but apply standard differential privacy using a Hamming distance of 1 between all documents. As with our approach, they consider the simplified utility requirement of topic preservation and use word embeddings to represent documents. Our approach differs in our use of the Earth Mover's metric to provide a strong utility measure for document similarity.

An early work in this area by Kacmarcik et al. [23] applies obfuscation by modifying the most important stylometric features of the text to reduce the effectiveness of author attribution. This approach was used in Anonymouth [36], a semi-automated tool that provides feedback to authors on which features to modify to effectively anonymise their texts. A similar approach was also followed by Karadhov et al. [24] as part of the PAN@Clef 2017 task.

Other approaches to author obfuscation, motivated by the PAN@Clef task, have focussed on the stronger utility requirement of semantic sensibility [5,8,34]. Privacy guarantees are therefore ad hoc and are designed to increase misclassification rates by the author attribution software used to test the mechanism.

Most recently there has been interest in training neural networks models which can protect author identity whilst preserving the semantics of the original document [14,48]. Other related deep learning methods aim to obscure other author attributes such as gender or age [10,32]. While these methods produce strong empirical results, they provide no formal privacy guarantees. Importantly, their goal also differs from the goal of our paper: they aim to obscure properties of authors in the *training set* (with the intention of the author-obscured learned representations being made available), while we assume that an adversary may have access to raw training data to construct an inference mechanism with full knowledge of author properties, and in this context aim to hide the properties of some other text external to the training set.

Machine Learning and Differential Privacy. Outside of author attribution, there is quite a body of work on introducing differential privacy to machine learning: [13] gives an overview of a classical machine learning setting; more recent deep learning approaches include [1,49]. However, these are generally applied in other domains such as image processing: text introduces additional complexity because of its discrete nature, in contrast to the continuous nature of neural networks. A recent exception is [37], which constructs a differentially private language model using a recurrent neural network; the goal here, as for instances above, is to hide properties of data items in the training set.

Generalised Differential Privacy. Also known as $d_{\mathcal{X}}$-privacy [9], this definition was originally motivated by the problem of geo-location privacy [4]. Despite its generality, $d_{\mathcal{X}}$-privacy has yet to find significant applications outside this domain; in particular, there have been no applications to text privacy.

Text Document Privacy. This typically refers to the sanitisation or redaction of documents either to protect the identity of individuals or to protect the confidentiality of their sensitive attributes. For example, a medical document may be modified to hide specifics in the medical history of a named patient. Similarly, a classified document may be redacted to protect the identity of an individual referred to in the text.

Most approaches to sanitisation or redaction rely on first identifying sensitive terms in the text, and then modifying (or deleting) only these terms to produce a sanitised document. Abril et al. [2] proposed this two-step approach, focussing on identification of terms using NLP techniques. Cumby and Ghani [11] proposed *k-confusability*, inspired by *k-anonymity* [50], to perturb sensitive terms in a document so that its (utility) class is confusable with at least k other classes. Their approach requires a complete dataset of similar documents for computing (mis)classification probabilities. Anandan et al. [3] proposed *t-plausibility* which generalises sensitive terms such that any document could have been generated from at least t other documents. Sánchez and Batet [45] proposed *C-sanitisation*, a model for both detection and protection of sensitive terms (C) using information theoretic guarantees. In particular, a *C-sanitised* document should contain no collection of terms which can be used to infer any of the sensitive terms.

Finally, there has been some work on noise-addition techniques in this area. Rodriguez-Garcia et al. [42] propose semantic noise, which perturbs sensitive terms in a document using a distance measure over the directed graph representing a predefined ontology.

Whilst these approaches have strong utility, our primary point of difference is our insistence on a differential privacy-based guarantee. This ensures that every output document could have been produced from any input document with some probability, giving the strongest possible notion of plausible-deniability.

8 Conclusions

We have shown how to combine representations of text documents with generalised differential privacy in order to implement a privacy mechanism for text documents. Unlike most other techniques for privacy in text processing, ours provides a guarantee in the style of differential privacy. Moreover we have demonstrated experimentally the trade off between utility and privacy.

This represents an important step towards the implementation of privacy mechanisms that could produce readable summaries of documents with a privacy guarantee. One way to achieve this goal would be to reconstruct readable documents from the bag-of-words output that our mechanism currently provides. A range of promising techniques for reconstructing readable texts from bag-of-words have already produced some good experimental results [20,52,54]. In future work we aim to explore how techniques such as these could be applied as a final post processing step for our mechanism.

References

1. Abadi, M., et al.: Deep learning with differential privacy. In: Proceedings of the 2016 ACM SIGSAC Conference on Computer and Communications Security, CCS 2016, pp. 308–318. ACM, New York (2016). https://doi.org/10.1145/2976749.2978318
2. Abril, D., Navarro-Arribas, G., Torra, V.: On the declassification of confidential documents. In: Torra, V., Narakawa, Y., Yin, J., Long, J. (eds.) MDAI 2011. LNCS (LNAI), vol. 6820, pp. 235–246. Springer, Heidelberg (2011). https://doi.org/10.1007/978-3-642-22589-5_22
3. Anandan, B., Clifton, C., Jiang, W., Murugesan, M., Pastrana-Camacho, P., Si, L.: t-Plausibility: generalizing words to desensitize text. Trans. Data Priv. **5**(3), 505–534 (2012)
4. Andrés, M.E., Bordenabe, N.E., Chatzikokolakis, K., Palamidessi, C.: Geo-indistinguishability: differential privacy for location-based systems. In: Proceedings of the 2013 ACM SIGSAC Conference on Computer & Communications Security, pp. 901–914. ACM (2013)
5. Bakhteev, O., Khazov, A.: Author masking using sequence-to-sequence models—notebook for PAN at CLEF 2017. In: Cappellato, L., Ferro, N., Goeuriot, L., Mandl, T. (eds.) CLEF 2017 Evaluation Labs and Workshop – Working Notes Papers, Dublin, Ireland, 11–14 September. CEUR-WS.org, September 2017. http://ceur-ws.org/Vol-1866/
6. Boisbunon, A.: The class of multivariate spherically symmetric distributions. Université de Rouen, Technical report 5, 2012 (2012)
7. Bojanowski, P., Grave, E., Joulin, A., Mikolov, T.: Enriching word vectors with subword information (2016). arXiv preprint: arXiv:1607.04606
8. Castro, D., Ortega, R., Muñoz, R.: Author masking by sentence transformation—notebook for PAN at CLEF 2017. In: Cappellato, L., Ferro, N., Goeuriot, L., Mandl, T. (eds.) CLEF 2017 Evaluation Labs and Workshop – Working Notes Papers, Dublin, Ireland, 11–14 September. CEUR-WS.org, September 2017. http://ceur-ws.org/Vol-1866/

9. Chatzikokolakis, K., Andrés, M.E., Bordenabe, N.E., Palamidessi, C.: Broadening the scope of differential privacy using metrics. In: De Cristofaro, E., Wright, M. (eds.) PETS 2013. LNCS, vol. 7981, pp. 82–102. Springer, Heidelberg (2013). https://doi.org/10.1007/978-3-642-39077-7_5
10. Coavoux, M., Narayan, S., Cohen, S.B.: Privacy-preserving neural representations of text. In: Proceedings of the 2018 Conference on Empirical Methods in Natural Language Processing, Brussels, Belgium, pp. 1–10. Association for Computational Linguistics, October–November 2018. http://www.aclweb.org/anthology/D18-1001
11. Cumby, C., Ghani, R.: A machine learning based system for semi-automatically redacting documents. In: Proceedings of the Twenty-Third Conference on Innovative Applications of Artificial Intelligence (IAAI) (2011)
12. Dwork, C., McSherry, F., Nissim, K., Smith, A.: Calibrating noise to sensitivity in private data analysis. In: Halevi, S., Rabin, T. (eds.) TCC 2006. LNCS, vol. 3876, pp. 265–284. Springer, Heidelberg (2006). https://doi.org/10.1007/11681878_14
13. Dwork, C., Roth, A., et al.: The algorithmic foundations of differential privacy. Found. Trends® Theor. Comput. Sci. **9**(3–4), 211–407 (2014)
14. Emmery, C., Manjavacas, E., Chrupała, G.: Style obfuscation by invariance (2018). arXiv preprint: arXiv:1805.07143
15. Fernandes, N., Dras, M., McIver, A.: Generalised differential privacy for text document processing. CoRR abs/1811.10256 (2018). http://arxiv.org/abs/1811.10256
16. Manuel, F., Pardo, R., Rosso, P., Potthast, M., Stein, B.: Overview of the 5th author profiling task at PAN 2017: gender and language variety identification in Twitter. In: Cappellato, L., Ferro, N., Goeuriot, L., Mandl, T. (eds.) Working Notes Papers of the CLEF 2017 Evaluation Labs. CEUR Workshop Proceedings, vol. 1866. CLEF and CEUR-WS.org, September 2017. http://ceur-ws.org/Vol-1866/
17. Global, T.: Native Language Identification (NLI) Establishes Nationality of Sony's Hackers as Russian. Technical report, Taia Global, Inc. (2014)
18. Grimmett, G., Stirzaker, D.: Probability and Random Processes, 2nd edn. Oxford Science Publications, Oxford (1992)
19. Halvani, O., Winter, C., Graner, L.: Authorship Verification based on Compression-Models. CoRR abs/1706.00516 (2017). http://arxiv.org/abs/1706.00516
20. Hasler, E., Stahlberg, F., Tomalin, M., de Gispert, A., Byrne, B.: A comparison of neural models for word ordering. In: Proceedings of the 10th International Conference on Natural Language Generation, pp. 208–212. Association for Computational Linguistics (2017). https://doi.org/10.18653/v1/W17-3531. http://aclweb.org/anthology/W17-3531
21. Hastie, T., Tibshirani, R., Friedman, J.: The Elements of Statistical Learning: Data Mining, Inference, and Prediction. SSS, 2nd edn. Springer, New York (2009). https://doi.org/10.1007/978-0-387-84858-7
22. Joulin, A., Grave, E., Bojanowski, P., Mikolov, T.: Bag of tricks for efficient text classification (2016). arXiv preprint: arXiv:1607.01759
23. Kacmarcik, G., Gamon, M.: Obfuscating document stylometry to preserve author anonymity. In: ACL, pp. 444–451 (2006)
24. Karadzhov, G., Mihaylova, T., Kiprov, Y., Georgiev, G., Koychev, I., Nakov, P.: The case for being average: a mediocrity approach to style masking and author obfuscation. In: Jones, G.J.F., et al. (eds.) CLEF 2017. LNCS, vol. 10456, pp. 173–185. Springer, Cham (2017). https://doi.org/10.1007/978-3-319-65813-1_18

25. Khonji, M., Iraqi, Y.: A slightly-modified GI-based author-verifier with lots of features (ASGALF). In: Working Notes for CLEF 2014 Conference (2014). http://ceur-ws.org/Vol-1180/CLEF2014wn-Pan-KonijEt2014.pdf
26. König, D.: Theorie der endlichen und unendlichen Graphen. Akademische Verlags Gesellschaft, Leipzig (1936)
27. Koppel, M., Argamon, S., Shimoni, A.R.: Automatically categorizing written texts by author gender. Lit. Linguist. Comput. **17**(4), 401–412 (2002). https://doi.org/10.1093/llc/17.4.401
28. Koppel, M., Schler, J., Argamon, S.: Authorship attribution in the wild. Lang. Resour. Eval. **45**(1), 83–94 (2011)
29. Koppel, M., Winter, Y.: Determining if two documents are written by the same author. JASIST **65**(1), 178–187 (2014). https://doi.org/10.1002/asi.22954
30. Kroese, D.P., Taimre, T., Botev, Z.I.: Handbook of Monte Carlo Methods, vol. 706. Wiley, New York (2013)
31. Kusner, M.J., Sun, Y., Kolkin, N.I., Weinberger, K.Q.: From word embeddings to document distances. In: Proceedings of the 32nd International Conference on Machine Learning, pp. 957–966 (2015)
32. Li, Y., Baldwin, T., Cohn, T.: Towards robust and privacy-preserving text representations. In: Proceedings of the 56th Annual Meeting of the Association for Computational Linguistics. Short Papers, vol. 2, pp. 25–30. Association for Computational Linguistics (2018). http://aclweb.org/anthology/P18-2005
33. Malmasi, S., Dras, M.: Native language identification with classifier stacking and ensembles. Comput. Linguist. **44**(3), 403–446 (2018). https://doi.org/10.1162/coli_a_00323
34. Mansoorizadeh, M., Rahgooy, T., Aminiyan, M., Eskandari, M.: Author Obfuscation using WordNet and language models—notebook for PAN at CLEF 2016. In: Balog, K., Cappellato, L., Ferro, N., Macdonald, C. (eds.) CLEF 2016 Evaluation Labs and Workshop – Working Notes Papers, Évora, Portugal, 5–8 September. CEUR-WS.org, September 2016. http://ceur-ws.org/Vol-1609/
35. Marsaglia, G., et al.: Choosing a point from the surface of a sphere. Ann. Math. Stat. **43**(2), 645–646 (1972)
36. McDonald, A.W.E., Afroz, S., Caliskan, A., Stolerman, A., Greenstadt, R.: Use fewer instances of the letter "i": toward writing style anonymization. In: Fischer-Hübner, S., Wright, M. (eds.) PETS 2012. LNCS, vol. 7384, pp. 299–318. Springer, Heidelberg (2012). https://doi.org/10.1007/978-3-642-31680-7_16
37. McMahan, H.B., Ramage, D., Talwar, K., Zhang, L.: Learning differentially private recurrent language models. In: International Conference on Learning Representations (2018). https://openreview.net/forum?id=BJ0hF1Z0b
38. Mikolov, T., Chen, K., Corrado, G., Dean, J.: Efficient estimation of word representations in vector space. CoRR abs/1301.3781 (2013). http://arxiv.org/abs/1301.3781
39. Potha, N., Stamatatos, E.: An improved *Impostors* method for authorship verification. In: Jones, G.J.F., Lawless, S., Gonzalo, J., Kelly, L., Goeuriot, L., Mandl, T., Cappellato, L., Ferro, N. (eds.) CLEF 2017. LNCS, vol. 10456, pp. 138–144. Springer, Cham (2017). https://doi.org/10.1007/978-3-319-65813-1_14
40. Potthast, M., et al.: Who wrote the web? Revisiting influential author identification research applicable to information retrieval. In: Ferro, N., et al. (eds.) ECIR 2016. LNCS, vol. 9626, pp. 393–407. Springer, Cham (2016). https://doi.org/10.1007/978-3-319-30671-1_29

41. Potthast, M., Rangel, F., Tschuggnall, M., Stamatatos, E., Rosso, P., Stein, B.: Overview of PAN'17: author identification, author profiling, and author obfuscation. In: Jones, G.J.F., et al. (eds.) CLEF 2017. LNCS, vol. 10456, pp. 275–290. Springer, Cham (2017). https://doi.org/10.1007/978-3-319-65813-1_25
42. Rodriguez-Garcia, M., Batet, M., Sánchez, D.: Semantic noise: privacy-protection of nominal microdata through uncorrelated noise addition. In: 2015 IEEE 27th International Conference on Tools with Artificial Intelligence (ICTAI), pp. 1106–1113. IEEE (2015)
43. Rubner, Y., Tomasi, C., Guibas, L.J.: The earth mover's distance as a metric for image retrieval. Int. J. Comput. Vis. **40**(2), 99–121 (2000)
44. Ruder, S., Ghaffari, P., Breslin, J.G.: Character-level and Multi-channel Convolutional Neural Networks for Large-scale Authorship Attribution. CoRR abs/1609.06686 (2016). http://arxiv.org/abs/1609.06686
45. Sánchez, D., Batet, M.: C-sanitized: a privacy model for document redaction and sanitization. J. Assoc. Inf. Sci. Technol. **67**(1), 148–163 (2016)
46. Sapkota, U., Bethard, S., Montes, M., Solorio, T.: Not all character N-grams are created equal: a study in authorship attribution. In: Proceedings of the 2015 Conference of the North American Chapter of the Association for Computational Linguistics: Human Language Technologies, Denver, Colorado, pp. 93–102. Association for Computational Linguistics, May–June 2015. http://www.aclweb.org/anthology/N15-1010
47. Seidman, S.: Authorship verification using the imposters method. In: Working Notes for CLEF 2013 Conference (2013). http://ceur-ws.org/Vol-1179/CLEF2013wn-PAN-Seidman2013.pdf
48. Shetty, R., Schiele, B., Fritz, M.: A4NT: author attribute anonymity by adversarial training of neural machine translation. In: 27th USENIX Security Symposium, pp. 1633–1650. USENIX Association (2018)
49. Shokri, R., Shmatikov, V.: Privacy-preserving deep learning. In: Proceedings of the 22nd ACM SIGSAC Conference on Computer and Communications Security, CCS 2015, pp. 1310–1321. ACM, New York (2015). https://doi.org/10.1145/2810103.2813687
50. Sweeney, L.: k-anonymity: a model for protecting privacy. Int. J. Uncertain. Fuzziness Knowl. Based Syst. **10**(5), 557–570 (2002)
51. Tetreault, J., Blanchard, D., Cahill, A.: A report on the first native language identification shared task. In: Proceedings of the Eighth Workshop on Innovative Use of NLP for Building Educational Applications, Atlanta, Georgia, pp. 48–57. Association for Computational Linguistics, June 2013. http://www.aclweb.org/anthology/W13-1706
52. Wan, S., Dras, M., Dale, R., Paris, C.: Improving grammaticality in statistical sentence generation: introducing a dependency spanning tree algorithm with an argument satisfaction model. In: Proceedings of the 12th Conference of the European Chapter of the ACL (EACL 2009), pp. 852–860. Association for Computational Linguistics (2009). http://aclweb.org/anthology/E09-1097
53. Weggenmann, B., Kerschbaum, F.: SynTF: synthetic and differentially private term frequency vectors for privacy-preserving text mining (2018). arXiv preprint: arXiv:1805.00904
54. Zhang, Y., Clark, S.: Discriminative syntax-based word ordering for text generation. Comput. Linguist. **41**(3), 503–538 (2015). https://doi.org/10.1162/COLI_a_00229

Symbolic Verification of Distance Bounding Protocols

Alexandre Debant(✉) and Stéphanie Delaune

Univ Rennes, CNRS, IRISA, Rennes, France
{alexandre.debant,stephanie.delaune}@irisa.fr

Abstract. With the proliferation of contactless applications, obtaining reliable information about distance is becoming an important security goal, and specific protocols have been designed for that purpose. These protocols typically measure the round trip time of messages and use this information to infer a distance. Formal methods have proved their usefulness when analysing standard security protocols such as confidentiality or authentication protocols. However, due to their abstract communication model, existing results and tools do not apply to distance bounding protocols.

In this paper, we consider a symbolic model suitable to analyse distance bounding protocols, and we propose a new procedure for analysing (a bounded number of sessions of) protocols in this model. The procedure has been integrated in the Akiss tool and tested on various distance bounding and payment protocols (e.g. MasterCard, NXP).

1 Introduction

In recent years, contactless communications have become ubiquitous. They are used in various applications such as access control cards, keyless car entry systems, payments, and many other applications which often require some form of authentication, and rely for this on security protocols. In addition, contactless systems aims to prevent against *relay attacks* in which an adversary mount an attack by simply forwarding messages he receives: ensuring physical proximity is a new security concern for all these applications.

Formal modelling and analysis techniques are well-adapted for verifying security protocols, and nowadays several verification tools exist, e.g. ProVerif [8], Tamarin [28]. They aim at discovering logical attacks, and therefore consider a symbolic model in which cryptographic primitives are abstracted by function symbols. Since its beginning in 80s, a lot of progress has been done in this area, and it is now a common good practice to formally analyse protocols using symbolic techniques in order to spot flaws possibly before their deployment, as it was recently done e.g. in TLS 1.3 [7,17], or for an avionic protocol [9].

This work has been partially supported by the European Research Council (ERC) under the European Union's Horizon 2020 research and innovation program (grant agreement No 714955-POPSTAR).

F. Nielson and D. Sands (Eds.): POST 2019, LNCS 11426, pp. 149–174, 2019.
https://doi.org/10.1007/978-3-030-17138-4_7

These symbolic techniques are based on the so-called Dolev Yao model [20]. In such a model, the attacker is supposed to control the entire network. He can send any message he is able to build using his current knowledge, and this message will reach its final destination instantaneously. This model is accurate enough to analyse many security protocols, e.g. authentication protocols, e-voting protocols, ... However, to analyse protocols that aim to prevent against relay attacks, some features need to be modelled in a more faithful way. Among them:

- *network topology*: any pair of nodes can communicate but depending on their distance, exchanging messages take more or less time. We will simply assume that the time needed is proportional to the distance between the two agents, and that messages can not travel faster than the speed of the light.
- *timing constraints*: protocols that aim to prevent against relay attacks typically rely on a rapid phase in which time measurements are performed. Our framework will allow us to model these time measurements through the use of timestamps put on each action.

There are some implications on the attacker model. Since communications take time, it may be interesting to consider several malicious nodes. We will assume that malicious nodes collaborate but again messages can not travel (even between malicious nodes) faster than the speed of the light.

Akiss in a Nutshell. The procedure we present in this paper builds on previous work by Chadha et al. [12], and its implementation in the tool Akiss. Akiss allows automated analysis of privacy-type properties (modelling as equivalences) when restricted to a bounded number of sessions. Cryptographic primitives may be defined through arbitrary convergent equational theories that have the finite variant property. This class includes standard cryptographic primitives as well as less commonly supported primitives such as blind signatures and zero knowledge proofs. Termination of the procedure is guaranteed for subterm convergent theories, but also achieved in practice on several examples outside this class.

The procedure behind Akiss is based on an abstract modelling of symbolic traces into first-order Horn clauses: each symbolic trace is translated into a set of Horn clauses called *seed statements*, and a dedicated resolution procedure is applied on this set to construct a set of statements which have a simple form: the so-called *solved statements*. Once the saturation of the set of seed statements is done, it is possible to decide, based solely on those solved statements, whether processes under study are equivalent or not.

Even if we are considering reachability properties (here authentication with physical proximity), in order to satisfy timing constraints, we may need to consider recipes that are discarded when performing a classical reachability analysis. Typically, in a classical reachability analysis, there is no need to consider two recipes that deduce the same message. The main advantage of Akiss is the fact that, since its original goal is to deal with equivalence, it considers more (actually almost all possible) recipes when performing the security analysis. Moreover, even if the tool has been designed to deal with equivalence-based properties, the first part of the Akiss procedure consists in computing a knowledge base which is in fact a finite representation of all possible traces (including recipes) executable by the process under study. We build on this saturation procedure in this work.

Our Contributions. We design a new procedure for verifying reachability properties for protocols written in a calculus sharing many similarities with the one introduced in [19], and that gives us a way to model faithfully distance bounding protocols. Our procedure follows the general structure of the original one described in [12]. We first model protocols as traces (see Sect. 3), and then translate them into Horn clauses (see Sect. 4). A direct generalisation would consist of keeping the saturation procedure unchanged, and simply modifying the algorithm to check the satisfiability of our additional timing constraints at the end. However, as discussed in Sect. 5, such a procedure would *not* be complete for our purposes. We therefore completely redesign the update function used during the saturation procedure using a new strategy to forbid certain steps that would otherwise systematically yield to non-termination in our final algorithm. Showing these statements are indeed unnecessary requires essential changes in the proofs of completeness of the original procedure.

This new saturation procedure yields an effective method for checking reachability properties in our calculus (see Sect. 6). Although termination of saturation is not guaranteed in theory, we have implemented our procedure and we have demonstrated its effectiveness on various examples. We report on our implementation and the various case studies we have performed in Sect. 7.

As we were unable to formally establish completeness of the procedure as implemented in the original Akiss tool (due to some mismatches between the procedure described in [12] and its implementation), we decided to bring the theory closer to the practice, and this explains several differences between our seed statements and those described originally in [12].

A full version of this paper including proofs is available at [18].

2 Background

We start by providing some background regarding distance bounding protocols. For illustrative purposes, we present a slightly simplified version of the TREAD protocol [2] together with the attack discovered by [26] (relying on the Tamarin prover). This protocol will be used along the paper as a running example.

2.1 Distance Bounding Protocols

Distance bounding protocols are cryptographic protocols that enable a verifier V to establish an upper bound on the physical distance to a prover P. They are typically based on timing the delay between sending out a challenge and receiving back the corresponding response. The first distance bounding protocol was proposed by Brands and Chaum [10], and since then various protocols have been proposed. In general, distance bounding protocols are made of two or three phases, the second one being a rapid phase during which the time measurement is performed. To improve accuracy, this challenge/response exchange during which

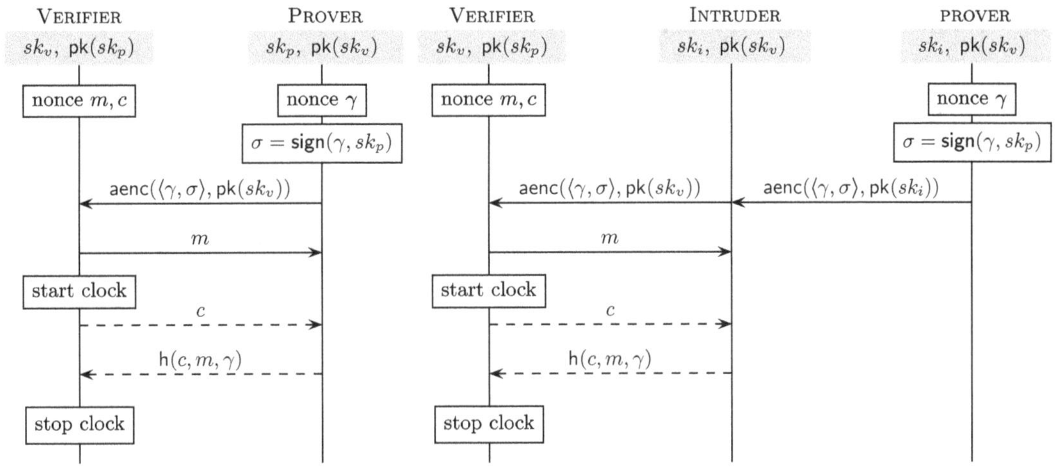

Fig. 1. TREAD protocol (left) and a mafia fraud attack (right)

the measurement is performed is repeated several times, and often performed at the bit level. Symbolic analysis does not allow us to reason at this level, and thus the rapid phase will be abstracted by a single challenge/response exchange, and operations done at bit level will be abstracted too.

For illustration purposes, we consider the TREAD protocol. As explained before, we ignore several details that are irrelevant to our symbolic security analysis, and we obtain the protocol described in Fig. 1. First, the prover generates a nonce γ, and computes the signature σ with his own key. This signature is sent to V encrypted with the public key of V. Upon reception, the verifier decrypts the message and checks the signature. Then, the verifier sends a nonce m, and starts the rapid phase during which he sends a challenge c to the prover. The protocol ends successfully if the answer given by the prover is correct and arrived before a predefined threshold.

2.2 Attacks on Distance Bounding Protocols

Typically, an attack occurs when a verifier is deceived into believing it is co-located with a given prover whereas it is not. Attacker may replay, relay and build new messages, as well as predict some timed challenges. Since the introduction of distance bounding protocols, various kinds of attacks have emerged, e.g. distance fraud, mafia fraud, distance hijacking attack, ... For instance, a distance fraud only consider a dishonest prover who tries to authenticate remotely, whereas a distance hijacking scenario allows the dishonest prover to take advantage of honest agents in the neighbourhood of the verifier.

The TREAD protocol is vulnerable to a mafia fraud attack: an honest verifier v may end successfully a session with an honest prover p thinking that this prover p is in his vicinity whereas p is actually far away. The attack is described in Fig. 1. After learning γ and a signature $\sigma = \mathsf{sign}(\gamma, sk_p)$, the malicious agent i will be able to impersonate p. At the end, the verifier v will finish his session correctly thinking that he is playing with p (who is actually far away).

2.3 Symbolic Security Analysis

The first symbolic framework developed to analyse distance bounding protocols is probably the one proposed in [27]. Since then, several formal symbolic models have been proposed: *e.g.* a model based on multiset rewriting rules has been proposed in [5], another one based on strand spaces is available in [31]. However, these models do not come with a procedure allowing one to analyse distance bounding protocols in an automatic way. Recently, some attempts have been done to rely on existing automatic verification tools, e.g. ProVerif [13,19] or Tamarin [26]. Those tools typically consider an unbounded number of sessions, and some approximations are therefore performed to tackle this problem well-known to be undecidable [21].

Here, following the long line of research on symbolic verification for a bounded number of sessions which is a problem well-known to be decidable [29,32] and for which automatic verification tools have been developed (e.g. OFMC [6], Akiss [12]), we aim to extend this approach to distance bounding protocols.

3 A Security Model Dealing with Time and Location

We assume that our cryptographic protocols are modelled using a simple process calculus sharing some similarities with the applied-pi calculus [1], and strongly inspired by the calculus introduced in [19].

3.1 Term Algebra

As usual in symbolic models, we represent messages using a term algebra. We consider a set $\mathcal{N}$ of *names* split into two disjoint sets: the set $\mathcal{N}_{\mathsf{pub}}$ of *public names* which contains the set $\mathcal{A}$ of agent names, and the set $\mathcal{N}_{\mathsf{priv}}$ of *private names*. We consider the set $\mathcal{X}$ of *message variables*, denoted $x, y, \ldots$, as well as a set $\mathcal{W}$ of *handles*: $\mathcal{W} = \{\mathsf{w}_1, \mathsf{w}_2, \ldots\}$. Variables in $\mathcal{X}$ model arbitrary data expected by the protocol, while variables in $\mathcal{W}$ are used to store messages learnt by the attacker. Given a *signature* Σ, i.e. a finite set of function symbols together with their arity, and a set of atomic data $\mathcal{A}t$, we denote $\mathcal{T}(\Sigma, \mathcal{A}t)$ the set of terms built from $\mathcal{A}t$ using function symbols in Σ. Given a term u, we denote $st(u)$ the set of the subterms occurring in u, and $vars(u)$ the set of variables occurring in u. A term u is ground when $vars(u) = \emptyset$. Then, we associate an *equational theory* E to the signature Σ which consists of a finite set of equations of the form $u = v$ with $u, v \in \mathcal{T}(\Sigma, \mathcal{X})$, and induces an equivalence relation over terms denoted $=_{\mathsf{E}}$.

Example 1. $\Sigma_{\mathsf{ex}} = \{\mathsf{aenc}, \mathsf{adec}, \mathsf{pk}, \mathsf{sign}, \mathsf{getmsg}, \mathsf{check}, \mathsf{ok}, \langle\ \rangle, \mathsf{proj}_1, \mathsf{proj}_2, \mathsf{h}\}$ allows us to model the cryptographic primitives used in the TREAD protocol presented in Sect. 2. The function symbols aenc and adec of arity 2 model asymmetric encryption, whereas sign, getmsg, check, and ok are used to model signature. The term $\mathsf{pk}(sk)$ represents the public key associated to the private key sk. We have function symbols to model pairs and projections, as well as a function h of arity 3 to model hashes. The equational theory E_{ex} associated to the signature Σ_{ex} is the relation induced by:

$$\mathsf{check}(\mathsf{sign}(x,y),\mathsf{pk}(y)) = \mathsf{ok} \quad \mathsf{proj}_1(\langle x,y\rangle) = x \quad \mathsf{adec}(\mathsf{aenc}(x,\mathsf{pk}(y)),y) = x$$
$$\mathsf{getmsg}(\mathsf{sign}(x,y)) = x \quad \mathsf{proj}_2(\langle x,y\rangle) = y$$

We consider equational theories that can be represented by a *convergent rewrite system*, i.e. we assume that there is a *confluent* and *terminating* rewrite system such that:

$$u =_{\mathsf{E}} v \Leftrightarrow u\!\downarrow = v\!\downarrow \text{for any terms } u \text{ and } v$$

where $t\!\downarrow$ denotes the normal form of t. Moreover, we assume that such a rewrite system has the *finite variant property* as introduced in [16]. This means that given a sequence $t_1, \ldots, t_n$ of terms, it is possible to compute a finite set of substitutions, denoted $\mathsf{variants}(t_1, \ldots, t_n)$, such that for any substitution ω, there exist $\sigma \in \mathsf{variants}(t_1, \ldots, t_n)$ and τ such that: $t_1\omega\!\downarrow, \ldots, t_n\omega\!\downarrow = (t_1\sigma)\!\downarrow\!\tau, \ldots, (t_n\sigma)\!\downarrow\!\tau$. Many equational theories enjoy this property, e.g. symmetric/asymmetric encryptions, signatures and blind signatures, as well as zero-knowledge proofs.

Moreover, this finite variant property implies the existence of a finite and *complete set of unifiers* and gives us a way to compute it effectively. Given a set $\mathcal{U}$ of equations between terms, a *unifier* (modulo a rewrite system $\mathcal{R}$) is a substitution σ such that $s\sigma\!\downarrow = s'\sigma\!\downarrow$ for any equation $s = s'$ in $\mathcal{U}$. A set S of unifiers is said to be *complete* for $\mathcal{U}$ if for any unifier σ, there exists $\theta \in S$ and τ such that $\sigma = \tau \circ \theta$. We denote $\mathsf{csu}_{\mathcal{R}}(\mathcal{U})$ such a set. We will rely on these notions of $\mathsf{variants}$ and csu in our procedure (see Sect. 4).

Example 2. The finite variant property is satisfied by the rewrite system $\mathcal{R}_{\mathsf{ex}}$ obtained by orienting from left to right equations in E_{ex}.

Let $\mathcal{U} = \{\mathsf{check}(t_\sigma, \mathsf{pk}(sk_p)) = \mathsf{ok}\}$ with $t_\sigma = \mathsf{proj}_2(\mathsf{adec}(x, sk_v))$. We have that $\{\theta\}$ with $\theta = \{x \to \mathsf{aenc}(\langle x_1, \mathsf{sign}(x_2, sk_p)\rangle, \mathsf{pk}(sk_v))\}$ is a complete set of unifiers for $\mathcal{U}$ (modulo $\mathcal{R}_{\mathsf{ex}}$). Now, considering the variants, let $\sigma_1 = \{x \to \mathsf{aenc}(x_1, \mathsf{pk}(sk_v))\}$, $\sigma_2 = \{x \to \mathsf{aenc}(\langle x_1, x_2\rangle, \mathsf{pk}(sk_v))\}$ and id be the identity substitution, we have that $\{id, \sigma_1, \sigma_2\}$ is a finite and complete set of variants (modulo $\mathcal{R}_{\mathsf{ex}}$) for the sequence (x, t_σ).

An attacker builds her own messages by applying function symbols to terms she already knows and which are available through variables in $\mathcal{W}$. Formally, a computation done by the attacker is a *recipe*, i.e. a term in $\mathcal{T}(\Sigma, \mathcal{W} \cup \mathcal{N}_{\mathsf{pub}} \cup \mathbb{R}^+)$.

3.2 Timing Constraints

To model time, we will use non-negative real numbers $\mathbb{R}^+$, and we may allow various operations (e.g. $+$, $-$, $\times$, ...). A time expression is constructed inductively by applying arithmetic symbols to time expressions starting with the initial set $\mathbb{R}^+$ and an infinite set $\mathcal{Z}$ of *time variables*. Then, a timing constraint is typically of the form $t_1 \sim t_2$ with $\sim \in \{<, \leq, =\}$. We do not constraint the operators since our procedure is generic in this respect provided we have a way to decide whether a set of timing constraints is satisfiable or not. In practice, our tool (see Sect. 7) will only be able to consider simple linear timing constraints.

Example 3. When modelling distance bounding protocols, we will typically consider a timing constraint of the form $z_2 - z_1 < t$ with $z_1, z_2 \in \mathcal{Z}$ and $t \in \mathbb{R}^+$. This constraint expresses that the time elapsed between the emission of a challenge and the receipt of the corresponding answer is at most t.

3.3 Process Algebra

We assume that cryptographic protocols are modelled using a simple process algebra. Following [12], we only consider a minimalistic core calculus. In particular, we do not introduce the new operator and we do not explicitly model the parallel operator. Since we only consider a bounded number of sessions (i.e. a calculus with no replication), this is at no loss of expressivity. We can simply assume that fresh names are generated from the beginning and parallel composition can be added as syntactic sugar to denote the set of all interleavings.

Syntax. We model a protocol as a finite set of traces. A *trace* T is a finite sequence (possibly empty and denoted ϵ in this case) of pairs, i.e. $T = (a_1, \mathsf{a}_1).\ldots.(a_n, \mathsf{a}_n)$ where each $a_i \in \mathcal{A}$, and a_i is an action of the form:

$$\mathsf{out}^z(u) \quad \mathsf{in}^z(x) \quad [v = v'] \quad [z := v] \quad [\![t_1 \sim t_2]\!]$$

with $x \in \mathcal{X}$, $u, v, v' \in \mathcal{T}(\Sigma, \mathcal{N} \cup \mathbb{R}^+ \cup \mathcal{X})$, $z \in \mathcal{Z}$, and $t_1 \sim t_2$ a timing constraint.

As usual, we have output and input actions. An input action acts as a binding construct for both x and z, whereas an output action acts as a binding construct for z only. For sake of clarity, we will omit the time variable z when we do not care of the precise time at which the input (resp. output) action has been performed. As usual, our calculus allows one to perform some tests on received messages, and it is also possible to extract a timestamp from a received message and perform some tests on this extracted value using timing constraints. Typically, this will allow us to model an agent that will stop executing the protocol in case an answer arrives too late.

We assume the usual definitions of *free* and *bound variables* for traces, and we assume that each variable is at most bound once. Note that, in the constructs presented above, the variables z, x are bound. Given a set $\mathcal{V}$ of variables, a trace is *locally closed w.r.t.* $\mathcal{V}$ if for any agent a, the trace obtained by considering actions executed by agent a does not contain free variables among those in $\mathcal{V}$. Such an assumption, sometimes called origination [6,15], is always satisfied when considering traces obtained by interleaving actions of a protocol. Therefore, we will only consider traces that are locally closed w.r.t. both $\mathcal{X}$ and $\mathcal{Z}$.

Contrary to the calculus introduced in [19] which assumes that there is at most one timer per thread, we are more flexible. This generalisation is not mandatory to analyse our case studies but it allows us to present our result on traces and greatly simplifies the theoretical development.

Example 4. Following our syntax, the trace corresponding to the role of the verifier played by v with p is modelled as follows:

$$\begin{aligned} T_{\mathsf{ex}} = {} & (v, \mathsf{in}(x)).\ (v, [\mathsf{check}(t_\sigma, \mathsf{pk}(sk_p)) = \mathsf{ok}]).\ (v, [t_\gamma = \mathsf{getmsg}(t_\sigma)]). \\ & (v, \mathsf{out}(m)). \\ & (v, \mathsf{out}^{z_1}(c)).\ (v, \mathsf{in}^{z_2}(y)).\ (v, [y = \mathsf{h}(c, m, t_\gamma)]).\ (v, [\![z_2 - z_1 < 2 \times t_0]\!]) \end{aligned}$$

where $t_\gamma = \mathsf{proj}_1(\mathsf{adec}(x, sk_v))$, $t_\sigma = \mathsf{proj}_2(\mathsf{adec}(x, sk_v))$, $x, y \in \mathcal{X}$, $z_1, z_2 \in \mathcal{Z}$, $m, c, sk_v, sk_p \in \mathcal{N}_{\mathsf{priv}}$, and $t_0 \in \mathbb{R}^+$ is a fixed threshold.

Of course, when performing a security analysis, other traces have to be considered. Typically, we may want to consider several instances of each role, and we will have to generate traces corresponding to all the possible interleavings of the actions composing these roles.

Semantics. The semantics of a trace is given in terms of a labeled transition system over configurations of the form $(T; \Phi; t)$, and is parametrised by a topology reflecting the fact that interactions between agents depend on their location.

Definition 1. *A topology is a tuple $\mathcal{T}_0 = (\mathcal{A}_0, \mathcal{M}_0, \mathsf{Loc}_0)$ where $\mathcal{A}_0 \subseteq \mathcal{A}$ is the finite set of agents composing the system, $\mathcal{M}_0 \subseteq \mathcal{A}_0$ represents those that are malicious, and $\mathsf{Loc}_0 : \mathcal{A}_0 \to \mathbb{R}^3$ defines the position of each agent in the space.*

In our model, the distance between two agents is given by the time it takes for a message to travel from one to another. We have that:

$$\mathsf{Dist}_{\mathcal{T}_0}(a, b) = \frac{\|\mathsf{Loc}_0(a) - \mathsf{Loc}_0(b)\|}{c_0} \quad \text{for any } a, b \in \mathcal{A}_0$$

with $\|\cdot\| : \mathbb{R}^3 \to \mathbb{R}$ the Euclidean norm and c_0 the transmission speed. We suppose, from now on, that c_0 is a constant for all agents, and thus an agent a can recover, at time $t + \mathsf{Dist}_{\mathcal{T}_0}(a, b)$, any message emitted by the agent b before $t \in \mathbb{R}^+$.

Definition 2. *Given a topology $\mathcal{T}_0 = (\mathcal{A}_0, \mathcal{M}_0, \mathsf{Loc}_0)$, a* configuration *over $\mathcal{T}_0$ is a tuple $(T; \Phi; t)$ where T is a trace locally closed w.r.t. $\mathcal{X}$ and $\mathcal{Z}$ composed of actions (a, a) with $a \in \mathcal{A}_0$, $t \in \mathbb{R}^+$, and $\Phi = \{\mathsf{w}_1 \xrightarrow{a_1, t_1} u_1, \dots, \mathsf{w}_n \xrightarrow{a_n, t_n} u_n\}$ is an* extended frame, *i.e. a substitution such that $\mathsf{w}_i \in \mathcal{W}$, $u_i \in \mathcal{T}(\Sigma, \mathcal{N} \cup \mathbb{R}^+)$, $a_i \in \mathcal{A}_0$ and $t_i \in \mathbb{R}^+$ for $1 \le i \le n$.*

Intuitively, T represents the trace that still remains to be executed; Φ represents the messages that have been outputted so far; and t is the global time.

Example 5. Continuing Example 4, we consider the topology $\mathcal{T}_0 = (\mathcal{A}_0, \mathcal{M}_0, \mathsf{Loc}_0)$ depicted on the right where $\mathcal{A}_0 = \{p, v, i\}$, and $\mathcal{M}_0 = \{i\}$.

The precise location of each agent is not relevant, only the distance between them matters. Here $\mathsf{Dist}_{\mathcal{T}_0}(v,i) < t_0$ whereas $\mathsf{Dist}_{\mathcal{T}_0}(v,p) \geq t_0$.

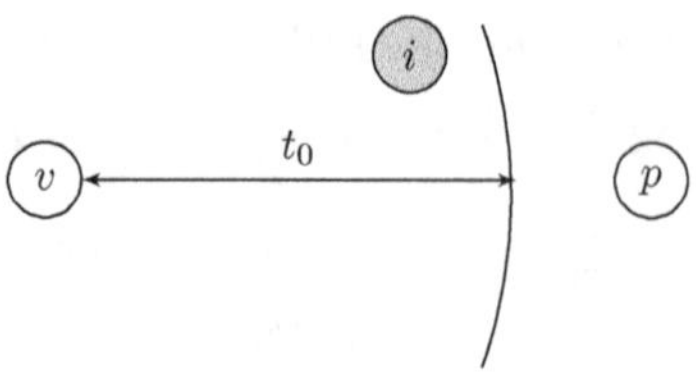

A possible configuration is $K_0 = (T_{\mathsf{ex}}; \Phi_0; 0)$ with

$$\Phi_0 = \{\mathsf{w}_1 \xrightarrow{i,0} \mathsf{pk}(sk_v),\ \mathsf{w}_2 \xrightarrow{i,0} sk_i,\ \mathsf{w}_3 \xrightarrow{p,0} \mathsf{aenc}(\langle\gamma, \mathsf{sign}(\gamma, sk_p)\rangle, \mathsf{pk}(sk_i))\}.$$

We have that v is playing the verifier's role with p (who is far away). We do not consider any prover's role but we assume that p (acting as a prover) has started a session with i and thus the corresponding encryption (here $\gamma \in \mathcal{N}_{\mathsf{priv}}$) has been added to the knowledge of the attacker (handle w_3). We also assume that $sk_i \in \mathcal{N}_{\mathsf{priv}}$, the private key of the agent $i \in \mathcal{M}_0$, is known by the attacker. A more realistic configuration would include other instances of the prover and the verifier roles and will probably give more knowledge to the attacker. This simple configuration is actually sufficient to retrieve the attack presented in Sect. 2.2. We write $\lfloor\Phi\rfloor_a^t$ for the restriction of Φ to the agent a at time t, i.e.:

$$\lfloor\Phi\rfloor_a^t = \left\{\mathsf{w}_i \xrightarrow{a_i,t_i} u_i \mid (\mathsf{w}_i \xrightarrow{a_i,t_i} u_i) \in \Phi \text{ and } a_i = a \text{ and } t_i \leq t\right\}.$$

Our labeled transition system is given in Fig. 2 and relies on labels ℓ which can be either equal to the unobservable τ action or of the form (a, a) with $a \in \mathcal{A}$, and $\mathsf{a} \in \{\mathsf{test}, \mathsf{eq}\} \cup \{\mathsf{in}(u), \mathsf{out}(u) \mid u \in \mathcal{T}(\Sigma, \mathcal{N} \cup \mathbb{R}^+)\} \cup \{\mathsf{let}(v) \mid v \in \mathbb{R}^+\}$. The TIM rule allows time to elapse and is labeled with τ (often omitted for sake of simplicity). The OUT rule allows an output action to be executed, and the outputted term will be added to the frame. Rule EQ is used to perform some tests, and those tests are evaluated modulo the equational theory. Then, the LET rule allows us to evaluate a term that is supposed to contain a real number, and could then be used in a timing constraint through the variable z. Then, we have a rule to evaluate a timing constraint. The IN rule allows an agent a to execute an input: the received message u has been sent at time t_b by an agent b who was in possession of the message at that time. In case b is a malicious agent, i.e. $b \in \mathcal{M}_0$, the message u may have been forged through a recipe R, and b has to be in possession of all the necessary information at that time. The variable z is used to store the time at which this action has been executed.

Example 6. Continuing Example 5, we may consider the following execution which aims to mimic the trace developed in Sect. 2:

$$K_0 \to_{\mathcal{T}_0} \xrightarrow{v,\mathsf{in}(t_{\mathsf{aenc}})}_{\mathcal{T}_0} \xrightarrow{v,\mathsf{eq}}_{\mathcal{T}_0} \xrightarrow{v,\mathsf{eq}}_{\mathcal{T}_0} \xrightarrow{v,\mathsf{out}(m)}_{\mathcal{T}_0} K_{\mathsf{rapid}}$$

The first arrow corresponds to an application of the rule TIM with delay $\delta_0 \geq \mathsf{Dist}_{\mathcal{T}_0}(p,i) + \mathsf{Dist}_{\mathcal{T}_0}(i,v)$. Then, the IN rule is triggered considering that the message $t_{\mathsf{aenc}} = \mathsf{aenc}(\langle\gamma, \mathsf{sign}(\gamma, sk_p)\rangle, \mathsf{pk}(sk_v))$ is sent by i at time t_i such that $\mathsf{Dist}_{\mathcal{T}_0}(p,i) \leq t_i \leq \delta_0 - \mathsf{Dist}_{\mathcal{T}_0}(i,v)$. Such a message t_{aenc} can indeed be forged by i at time t_i (using recipe $R = \mathsf{aenc}(\mathsf{adec}(\mathsf{w}_3, \mathsf{w}_2), \mathsf{w}_1)$) and thus be

TIM	$(T;\Phi;t) \xrightarrow{\tau}_{\mathcal{T}_0} (T;\Phi;t+\delta)$	with $\delta \geq 0$
OUT	$((a, \mathsf{out}^z(u)).T;\Phi;t) \xrightarrow{a,\mathsf{out}(u\downarrow)}_{\mathcal{T}_0} (T\{z \to t\};\Phi \uplus \{\mathsf{w} \xrightarrow{a,t} u\downarrow\};t)$	$\mathsf{w} \in \mathcal{W}$ fresh
EQ	$((a, [u = v]).T;\Phi;t) \xrightarrow{a,\mathsf{eq}}_{\mathcal{T}_0} (T;\Phi;t)$	if $u\downarrow = v\downarrow$
LET	$((a, [z := v].T;\Phi;t) \xrightarrow{a,\mathsf{let}(v\downarrow)}_{\mathcal{T}_0} (T\{z \to v\downarrow\};\Phi;t)$	if $v\downarrow \in \mathbb{R}^+$
TEST	$((a, [\![t_1 \sim t_2]\!]).T;\Phi;t) \xrightarrow{a,\mathsf{test}}_{\mathcal{T}_0} (T;\Phi;t)$	if $t_1 \sim t_2$ is true
IN	$((a, \mathsf{in}^z(x)).T;\Phi;t) \xrightarrow{a,\mathsf{in}(u)}_{\mathcal{T}_0} (T\{x \to u, z \to t\};\Phi;t)$	

if there exist $b \in \mathcal{A}_0$ and $t_b \in \mathbb{R}^+$ such that $t_b \leq t - \mathsf{Dist}_{\mathcal{T}_0}(b,a)$ and there exists $R \in \mathcal{T}(\Sigma, \mathcal{W} \cup \mathcal{N}_{\mathsf{pub}} \cup \mathbb{R}^+)$ such that $R\Phi\downarrow = u$. Moreover,

- if $b \in \mathcal{A}_0 \smallsetminus \mathcal{M}_0$ then $R \in dom(\lfloor\Phi\rfloor_b^{t_b}) \cup \mathcal{N}_{\mathsf{pub}} \cup \mathbb{R}^+$;
- if $b \in \mathcal{M}_0$ then for all $\mathsf{w} \in vars(R)$, there exists $c \in \mathcal{A}_0$ such that $\mathsf{w} \in dom(\lfloor\Phi\rfloor_c^{t_b - \mathsf{Dist}_{\mathcal{T}_0}(c,b)})$.

Fig. 2. Semantics of our calculus

received by v at time δ_0. Then, tests performed by v are evaluated successfully, v outputs m, and we reach the configuration $K_{\mathsf{rapid}} = (T_{\mathsf{rapid}};\Phi_{\mathsf{rapid}};\delta_0)$ where:

- $T_{\mathsf{rapid}} = (v, \mathsf{out}^{z_1}(c)).(v, \mathsf{in}^{z_2}(y)).(v, [y = \mathsf{h}(c,m,\gamma)]).(v, [\![z_2 - z_1 < 2t_0]\!])$, and
- $\Phi_{\mathsf{rapid}} = \Phi_0 \uplus \{\mathsf{w}_4 \xrightarrow{v,\delta_0} m\}$.

We can pursue this execution as follows:

$$K_{\mathsf{rapid}} \xrightarrow{v,\mathsf{out}(c)}_{\mathcal{T}_0} \rightarrow_{\mathcal{T}_0} \xrightarrow{v,\mathsf{in}(\mathsf{h}(c,m,\gamma))}_{\mathcal{T}_0} \xrightarrow{v,\mathsf{eq}}_{\mathcal{T}_0}$$
$$((v, [\![\delta_0 + 2\mathsf{Dist}_{\mathcal{T}_0}(v,i) - \delta_0 < 2t_0]\!]);\Phi_{\mathsf{rapid}} \uplus \{\mathsf{w}_5 \xrightarrow{v,\delta_0} c\};\delta_0 + 2\mathsf{Dist}_{\mathcal{T}_0}(v,i))$$

The second arrow is an application of the rule TIM with delay $2\mathsf{Dist}_{\mathcal{T}_0}(v,i)$ so that $\mathsf{h}(c,m,\gamma)$ can be received by v at time $\delta_0 + 2\mathsf{Dist}_{\mathcal{T}_0}(v,i)$. Since $\mathsf{Dist}_{\mathcal{T}_0}(v,i) < t_0$, the timing constraint is true and the last action can be executed.

The goal of this paper is to propose a new procedure for analysing a bounded number of sessions of distance bounding protocols. Once the topology is fixed, the existence of an attack can be directly encoded as a reachability property considering a finite set of traces. The following sections are thus dedicated to the study of the following problem:

Input: A trace T locally closed w.r.t. $\mathcal{X}$ and $\mathcal{Z}$, $t_0 \in \mathbb{R}^+$, and a topology $\mathcal{T}_0$.
Output: Do there exist $\ell_1, \dots, \ell_n$, Φ, and t such that $(T;\emptyset;t_0) \xrightarrow{\ell_1 \dots, \ell_n}_{\mathcal{T}_0} (\epsilon;\Phi;t)$?

4 Modelling Using Horn Clauses

Following the approach developed in Akiss [12], our procedure is based on an abstract modelling of a trace in first-order Horn clauses. Our set of seed

$$
\begin{array}{lll}
\text{OUT} & ((a, \mathsf{out}^z(u)).T;\phi) \xrightarrow{a,\mathsf{out}(u\downarrow)} (T;\phi \uplus \{\mathsf{w} \to u\}) & \text{with } \mathsf{w} \in \mathcal{W} \text{ fresh} \\
\text{EQ} & ((a, [u = v]).T;\phi) \xrightarrow{a,\mathsf{eq}} (T;\phi) & \text{if } u\downarrow = v\downarrow \\
\text{LET} & ((a, [z := v].T;\phi) \xrightarrow{a,\mathsf{let}(v\downarrow)} (T;\phi) & \\
\text{TEST} & ((a, [\![t_1 \sim t_2]\!]).T;\phi) \xrightarrow{a,\mathsf{test}} (T;\phi) & \\
\text{IN} & ((a, \mathsf{in}^z(x)).T;\phi) \xrightarrow{a,\mathsf{in}(u)} (T\{x \to u\};\phi) & \text{if } u = R\phi\downarrow \text{ for some recipe } R.
\end{array}
$$

Fig. 3. Relaxed semantics

statements is more in line with what has been implemented in Akiss for optimisation purposes rather than what is presented in [12].

4.1 Preliminaries

We consider *symbolic runs* which are finite sequences of pairs with possibly a *run variable* typically denoted y at its ends. We have that each pair (a, a) is such that $a \in \mathcal{A}$ and a is an action of the form (with $u \in \mathcal{T}(\Sigma, \mathcal{N} \cup \mathbb{R}^+ \cup \mathcal{X})$):

$$\mathsf{out}(u) \qquad \mathsf{in}(u) \qquad \mathsf{eq} \qquad \mathsf{test} \qquad \mathsf{let}(u).$$

Excluding the special variable y, a symbolic run $(a_1, \mathsf{a}_1). \ldots .(a_n, \mathsf{a}_n)$, only contains variables from the set $\mathcal{X}$. We say that it is *locally closed* if whenever a variable x occurs in an output action (resp. let action) a_j, then there exists an input action a_i occurring before (i.e. $i < j$) such that $a_i = a_j$ and $x \in vars(\mathsf{a}_i)$. Symbolic runs are often denoted $w, w', \ldots$, and we write $w \sqsubseteq w'$ when the sequence w is a prefix of w'. Given a symbolic run w_0 whose sequence of outputs is $\mathsf{out}(u_1) \cdot \ldots \cdot \mathsf{out}(u_n)$, we denote $\phi(w_0) = \{\mathsf{w}_1 \to u_1, \ldots, \mathsf{w}_n \to u_n\}$.

We also consider *symbolic recipes* which are terms in $\mathcal{T}(\Sigma, \mathcal{W} \cup \mathcal{N}_{\mathsf{pub}} \cup \mathcal{Y})$ where $\mathcal{Y}$ is a set of recipe variables disjoint from $\mathcal{X}$ and $\mathcal{W}$. We use capital letters X, Y, and Z to range over $\mathcal{Y}$.

Example 7. We consider the following symbolic run:

$$
\begin{aligned}
w_0 = {} & (v, \mathsf{in}(\mathsf{aenc}(\langle x', \mathsf{sign}(x', sk_p)\rangle, \mathsf{pk}(sk_v)))).(v, \mathsf{eq}).(v, \mathsf{eq}). \\
& (v, \mathsf{out}(m)).(v, \mathsf{out}(c)).(v, \mathsf{in}(\mathsf{h}(c, m, x'))).(v, \mathsf{eq})
\end{aligned}
$$

We have that $\phi(w_0) = \{\mathsf{w}_1 \to m, \mathsf{w}_2 \to c\}$.

Our logic is based on two predicates expressing deduction and reachability without taking into account timing constraints. More formally, given a configuration $(T; \Phi; t)$, its untimed counterpart is $(T; \phi)$ where ϕ is the untimed counterpart of Φ, i.e. a frame of the form: $\phi = \{\mathsf{w}_1 \to u_1, \ldots, \mathsf{w}_n \to u_n\}$. The relaxed semantics over untimed configurations is given in Fig. 3. Since time variables (from $\mathcal{Z}$) are not instantiated during a relaxed execution, in an untimed configuration $(T;\phi)$, the trace T is only locally closed w.r.t. $\mathcal{X}$. Our predicates are:

- a *reachability predicate*: r_w holds when the run w is executable.
- a *deduction predicate*: $\mathsf{k}_w(R,u)$ holds if the message u can be built using the recipe $R \in \mathcal{T}(\Sigma, \mathcal{N}_{\mathsf{pub}} \cup \mathbb{R}^+ \cup \mathcal{W})$ by an attacker using the outputs available after the execution of w (if this execution is possible).

Formally, we have that:

- $(T_0;\phi_0) \models \mathsf{r}_{\ell_1,\dots,\ell_n}$ if there exists $(T_n;\phi_n)$ such that $(T_0;\phi_0) \xrightarrow{\ell_1\dots\ell_n} (T_n;\phi_n)$
- $(T_0;\phi_0) \models \mathsf{k}_{\ell_1,\dots,\ell_n}(R,u)$ if for all $(T_n;\phi_n)$ such that $(T_0;\phi_0) \xrightarrow{\ell_1\dots\ell_n} (T_n;\phi_n)$ we have that $R\phi_n\!\downarrow = u$.

This semantics is extended as usual to first-order formulas built using the usual connectives (e.g. conjunction, quantification, ...)

Example 8. The frame ϕ_0 below is the untimed counterpart of Φ_0:

$$\phi_0 = \{\mathsf{w}_1 \to \mathsf{pk}(sk_v),\ \mathsf{w}_2 \to sk_i,\ \mathsf{w}_3 \to \mathsf{aenc}(\langle\gamma, \mathsf{sign}(\gamma, sk_p)\rangle, \mathsf{pk}(sk_i))\}.$$

We have that $(T_{\mathsf{ex}};\phi_0) \xrightarrow{\mathsf{tr}} (\epsilon;\phi_{\mathsf{final}})$ where ϕ_{final} is the untimed counterpart of $\Phi_{\mathsf{final}} = \Phi_{\mathsf{rapid}} \uplus \{\mathsf{w}_5 \xrightarrow{v,\delta_0} c\}$, and tr is the same sequence of labels as the one developed in Example 6, i.e.

$$(v, \mathsf{in}(t_{\mathsf{aenc}}))(v,\mathsf{eq})(v,\mathsf{eq})(v,\mathsf{out}(m))(v,\mathsf{out}(c))(v,\mathsf{in}(\mathsf{h}(c,m,\gamma)))(v,\mathsf{eq})(v,\mathsf{test}).$$

4.2 Seed Statements

We consider particular Horn clauses which we call *statements*.

Definition 3. *A* statement *is a Horn clause:* $H \Leftarrow \mathsf{k}_{w_1}(X_1,u_1),\dots,\mathsf{k}_{w_n}(X_n,u_n)$ *with* $H \in \{\mathsf{r}_{w_0}, \mathsf{k}_{w_0}(R,u)\}$ *and such that:*

- $w_0,\dots,w_n$ *are symbolic runs locally closed,* $w_i \sqsubseteq w_0$ *for any* $i \in \{1,\dots,n\}$*;*
- $u, u_1, \dots, u_n$ *are terms in* $\mathcal{T}(\Sigma, \mathcal{N} \cup \mathbb{R}^+ \cup \mathcal{X})$*;*
- $R \in \mathcal{T}(\Sigma, \mathcal{N}_{\mathsf{pub}} \cup \mathbb{R}^+ \cup \mathcal{W} \cup \{X_1,\dots,X_n\}) \smallsetminus \mathcal{Y}$*, and* $X_1,\dots,X_n$ *are distinct variables from* $\mathcal{Y}$*.*

When $H = \mathsf{k}_{w_0}(R,u)$*, we assume in addition that* $vars(u) \subseteq vars(u_1,\dots,u_n)$ *and* $R(\{X_i \to u_i\} \uplus \phi(w_0))\!\downarrow = u$*.*

In the above definition, we implicitly assume that all variables are universally quantified, i.e., all statements are ground. By abuse of language we sometimes call σ a grounding substitution for a statement $H \Leftarrow (B_1,\dots,B_n)$ when σ is grounding for each of the atomic formulas $H, B_1,\dots,B_n$. The *skeleton* of a statement f, denoted $\mathsf{skl}(f)$, is the statement where recipes are removed.

1. $\mathsf{r}_{\ell_1\sigma\tau\downarrow\cdot\ldots\cdot\ell_n\sigma\tau\downarrow} \Leftarrow \{\mathsf{k}_{\ell_1\sigma\tau\downarrow\cdot\ldots\cdot\ell_{j-1}\sigma\tau\downarrow}(X_j, x_j\sigma\tau\downarrow)\}_{j\in\mathsf{Rcv}(n)}$
for all $\sigma \in \mathsf{csu}_{\mathcal{R}}(\{v_k = v'_k\}_{k\in\mathsf{Eq}(n)})$
for all $\tau \in \mathsf{variants}_{\mathcal{R}}(\ell_1\sigma, \ldots, \ell_n\sigma)$

2. $\mathsf{k}_{\ell_1\sigma\tau\downarrow\cdot\ldots\cdot\ell_m\sigma\tau\downarrow\mathsf{y}}(\mathsf{w}_{|\mathsf{Snd}(m)|}, u_m\sigma\tau\downarrow) \Leftarrow \{\mathsf{k}_{\ell_1\sigma\tau\downarrow\cdot\ldots\cdot\ell_{j-1}\sigma\tau\downarrow}(X_j, x_j\sigma\tau\downarrow)\}_{j\in\mathsf{Rcv}(m)}$
for all $m \in \mathsf{Snd}(n)$
for all $\sigma \in \mathsf{csu}_{\mathcal{R}}(\{v_k = v'_k\}_{k\in\mathsf{Eq}(m)})$
for all $\tau \in \mathsf{variants}_{\mathcal{R}}(\ell_1\sigma, \ldots, \ell_m\sigma)$

3. $\mathsf{k}_{\mathsf{y}}(c, c) \Leftarrow$
for all $c \in \mathcal{C}$

4. $\mathsf{k}_{\mathsf{y}}(\mathsf{f}(Y_1, \ldots, Y_k), \mathsf{f}(y_1, \ldots, y_k)\tau\downarrow) \Leftarrow \{\mathsf{k}_{\mathsf{y}}(Y_j, y_j\tau\downarrow)\}_{j\in\{1,\ldots,k\}}$
for all $\mathsf{f} \in \Sigma$ of arity k
for all $\tau \in \mathsf{variants}_{\mathcal{R}}(\mathsf{f}(y_1, \ldots, y_k))$

Fig. 4. Seed statements $\mathsf{seed}(T, \mathcal{C})$

Our definition of statement is in line with the original one proposed in [12] but we state an additional invariant used to establish the completeness of our procedure.

In order to define our set of seed statements, we have to fix some naming conventions. Given a trace T of the form $(a_1, \mathsf{a}_1).(a_2, \mathsf{a}_2).\ldots.(a_n, \mathsf{a}_n)$, we assume w.l.o.g. the following naming conventions:

1. if a_i is a receive action, then $\mathsf{a}_i = \mathsf{in}^{z_i}(x_i)$, and $\ell_i = (a_i, \mathsf{in}(x_i))$;
2. if a_i is a send action, then $\mathsf{a}_i = \mathsf{out}^{z_i}(u_i)$, and $\ell_i = (a_i, \mathsf{out}(u_i))$;
3. if a_i is a test action, then $\mathsf{a}_i = [v_i = v'_i]$, and $\ell_i = (a_i, \mathsf{eq})$;
4. if a_i is a let action, then $\mathsf{a}_i = [z'_i := v_i]$, and $\ell_i = (a_i, \mathsf{let}(v_i))$.
5. if a_i is a timing constraint then $\mathsf{a}_i = [\![t_i \sim t'_i]\!]$, and $\ell_i = (a_i, \mathsf{test})$.

For each $m \in \{0, \ldots, n\}$, the sets $\mathsf{Rcv}(m)$, $\mathsf{Snd}(m)$, $\mathsf{Eq}(m)$, $\mathsf{Let}(m)$, and $\mathsf{Test}(m)$ respectively denote the set of indexes of the receive, send, equality, let, and test actions amongst $\mathsf{a}_1, \ldots, \mathsf{a}_m$. We denote by $|S|$ the cardinality of S.

Given a set $\mathcal{C} \subseteq \mathcal{N}_{\mathsf{pub}} \cup \mathbb{R}^+$, the set of *seed statements* associated to T and $\mathcal{C}$, denoted $\mathsf{seed}(T, \mathcal{C})$, is defined in Fig. 4. If $\mathcal{C} = \mathcal{N}_{\mathsf{pub}} \cup \mathbb{R}^+$, then $\mathsf{seed}(T, \mathcal{C})$ is said to be the set of seed statements associated to T and in this case we write $\mathsf{seed}(T)$ as a shortcut for $\mathsf{seed}(T, \mathcal{N}_{\mathsf{pub}} \cup \mathbb{R}^+)$. When computing seed statements, we compute complete sets of unifiers and complete sets of variants modulo $\mathcal{R}$. This allows us to get rid of the rewrite system in the remainder of our procedure and then only consider unification modulo the empty equational theory. In this case, it is well-known that (when it exists) $\mathsf{csu}_\emptyset(\mathcal{U})$ is uniquely defined up to some variable renaming, and we write $\mathsf{mgu}(u_1, u_2)$ instead of $\mathsf{csu}_\emptyset(\{u_1 = u_2\})$.

Example 9. Let $T_{\mathsf{ex}}^{+} = T_0 \cdot T_{\mathsf{ex}}$ with $T_0 = (i, \mathsf{out}(\mathsf{pk}(sk_v))).(i, \mathsf{out}(sk_i)).(p, \mathsf{out}(u))$ and $u = \mathsf{aenc}(\langle \gamma, \mathsf{sign}(\gamma, sk_p)\rangle, \mathsf{pk}(sk_i))$. The set $\mathsf{seed}(T_{\mathsf{ex}}^{+}, \emptyset)$ contains among others the statement f_1, f_2, f_3, and f_4 given below:

$\mathsf{r}_{T_0 \cdot w_0 \cdot (v,\mathsf{test})} \Leftarrow \mathsf{k}_{T_0}(X_1, \mathsf{aenc}(\langle x', \mathsf{sign}(x', sk_p)\rangle, \mathsf{pk}(sk_v))),\ \mathsf{k}_{T_0 \cdot w_0^5}(X_2, \mathsf{h}(c, m, x'))$;
$\mathsf{k}_{T_0 \cdot \mathsf{y}}(\mathsf{w}_3, u) \Leftarrow$;
$\mathsf{k}_{\mathsf{y}}(\mathsf{adec}(Y_1, Y_2), \mathsf{adec}(y_1, y_2)) \Leftarrow \mathsf{k}_{\mathsf{y}}(Y_1, y_1),\ \mathsf{k}_{\mathsf{y}}(Y_2, y_2)$; and its variant
$\mathsf{k}_{\mathsf{y}}(\mathsf{adec}(Y_1, Y_2), y_3) \Leftarrow \mathsf{k}_{\mathsf{y}}(Y_1, \mathsf{aenc}(y_3, \mathsf{pk}(y_2))),\ \mathsf{k}_{\mathsf{y}}(Y_2, y_2)$

where w_0 is given in Example 7, and w_0^5 is the prefix of w_0 of size 5.

Statement f_1 expresses that the trace is executable (in the relaxed semantics) as soon as we are able to deduce the two terms requested in input, f_2 says that the attacker knows the term u as soon as T_0 has been executed. The two remaining statements model the fact that an attacker can apply the decryption algorithm on any terms he knows (statement f_3), and this will give him access to the plaintext when the right key is used (statement f_4).

4.3 Soundness and Completeness

We now show that as far as the timing constraints are ignored, the set $\mathsf{seed}(T)$ is a sound and complete abstraction of a trace. Moreover, we have to ensure that the proof tree witnessing the existence of a given predicate in $\mathcal{H}(\mathsf{seed}(T))$ matches with the relaxed execution we have considered. This is mandatory to establish the completeness of our procedure.

Definition 4. *Given a set K of statements, $\mathcal{H}(K)$ is the smallest set of ground facts such that:*

$$\textsc{Conseq.}\ \frac{f = \left(H \Leftarrow B_1, \ldots, B_n\right) \in K \qquad B_1\sigma \in \mathcal{H}(K),\ \ldots,\ B_n\sigma \in \mathcal{H}(K) \qquad \sigma \text{ grounding for } f \qquad \mathsf{skl}(f\sigma) \text{ in normal form}}{H\sigma \in \mathcal{H}(K)}$$

Let $B_i = \mathsf{k}_{w_i}(X_i, u_i)$ for $i \in \{1, \ldots, n\}$, and w_0 the world associated to H with $v_1, \ldots, v_{k'}$ the terms occurring in input in w_0. We say that such an instance of Conseq *matches with* $\mathsf{exec} = (T; \emptyset) \overset{\ell_1, \ldots, \ell_p}{\rightsquigarrow} (S; \phi)$ *using $R_1, \ldots, R_k$ as input recipes if $w_0\sigma \sqsubseteq \ell_1, \ldots, \ell_p$, and there exist $\hat{R}_1, \ldots, \hat{R}_{k'}$ such that:*

- $\hat{R}_j(\{X_i \to u_i \mid 1 \leq i \leq n\} \uplus \phi(w_0))\downarrow = v_j$ *for $j \in \{1, \ldots, k'\}$; and*
- $\hat{R}_j\sigma = R_i$ *for $j \in \{1, \ldots, k'\}$.*

This notion of matching is extended to a proof tree π as expected, meaning that all the instances of Conseq used in π satisfy the property.

Actually, the completeness of our procedure will be established w.r.t. a subset of recipes, namely *uniform recipes*. We establish that an execution of a trace T_0 which only involves uniform recipes has a counterpart in $\mathcal{H}(\mathsf{seed}(T_0))$ which is uniform too.

Definition 5. *Given a frame* ϕ*, a recipe* R *is* uniform w.r.t. ϕ *if for any* $R_1, R_2 \in st(R)$ *such that* $R_1\phi\downarrow = R_2\phi\downarrow$*, we have that* $R_1 = R_2$*.*

Given a set K *of statements, we say that a set* $\{\pi_1, \ldots, \pi_n\}$ *of proof trees in* $\mathcal{H}(K)$ *is* uniform *if for any* $\mathsf{k}_w(R_1, t)$ *and* $\mathsf{k}_w(R_2, t)$ *that occur in* $\{\pi_1, \ldots, \pi_n\}$*, we have that* $R_1 = R_2$*.*

We are now able to state our soundness and completeness result.

Theorem 1. *Let* T_0 *be a trace locally closed w.r.t.* $\mathcal{X}$*.*

- $(T_0; \emptyset) \models g$ *for any* $g \in \mathsf{seed}(T_0) \cup \mathcal{H}(\mathsf{seed}(T_0))$*;*
- *If* $\mathsf{exec} = (T_0; \emptyset) \xrightarrow{\ell_1, \ldots, \ell_p} (S; \phi)$ *with input recipes* $R_1, \ldots, R_k$ *that are uniform w.r.t.* ϕ *then*
  1. $\mathsf{r}_{\ell_1, \ldots, \ell_p} \in \mathcal{H}(\mathsf{seed}(T_0))$*; and*
  2. *if* $R\phi\downarrow = u$ *for some recipe* R *uniform w.r.t.* ϕ *then* $\mathsf{k}_{\ell_1, \ldots, \ell_p}(R, u) \in \mathcal{H}(\mathsf{seed}(T_0))$.

  Moreover, we may assume that the proof tree witnessing these facts are uniform and match with exec *using* $R_1, \ldots, R_k$ *as input recipes.*

5 Saturation

At a high level, our procedure consists of two steps:

1. a saturation procedure which constructs a set of solved statements from the set $\mathsf{seed}(T)$; and
2. an algorithm which uses the solved statements obtained by saturation to check whether timing constraints are satisfied. This is needed to ensure that the execution obtained at step 1 is truly executable in our timed model.

5.1 Saturation Procedure

We start by describing our saturation procedure. It manipulates a set of statements called a *knowledge base.*

Definition 6. *Given a statement* $f = (H \Leftarrow B_1, \ldots, B_n)$*,*

- f *is said to be* solved *if* $B_i = \mathsf{k}_{w_i}(X_i, x_i)$ *with* $x_i \in \mathcal{X}$ *for all* $i \in \{1, \ldots, n\}$*.*
- f *is said to be* well-formed *if whenever it is solved and* $H = \mathsf{k}_w(R, u)$*, we have that* $u \notin \mathcal{X}$*.*

A set of well-formed *statements is called a* knowledge base*. If* K *is a knowledge base,* $\mathsf{solved}(K) = \{f \in K \mid f \textit{ is solved}\}$*.*

We restrict the use of the resolution rule and we only apply it on a selected atom. To formalise this, we assume a selection function sel which returns $\perp$ when applied on a solved statement, and an atom $\mathsf{k}_w(X, t)$ with $t \notin \mathcal{X}$ when applied on an unsolved statement. Resolution must be performed on this selected atom.

$$\textsc{Res}\ \frac{\begin{array}{c} f : H \Leftarrow \mathsf{k}_w(X, t), B_1, \ldots, B_n \in K \text{ such that } \mathsf{k}_w(X, t) = \mathsf{sel}(f) \\ g : \mathsf{k}_{w'}(R', t') \Leftarrow B_{n+1}, \ldots, B_m \in \mathsf{solved}(K) \quad \sigma = \mathsf{mgu}(\mathsf{k}_w(X, t), \mathsf{k}_{w'}(R', t')) \end{array}}{h\sigma \qquad \text{where } h = \Big(H \Leftarrow B_1, \ldots, B_n, B_{n+1}, \ldots, B_m\Big)}$$

Example 10. Applying resolution between f_4 and f_2 (see Example 9), we obtain:

$$\mathsf{k}_{\mathcal{T}_0\cdot\mathsf{y}}(\mathsf{adec}(\mathsf{w}_3, Y_2), \langle\gamma, \mathsf{sign}(\gamma, sk_p)\rangle) \Leftarrow \mathsf{k}_{\mathcal{T}_0\cdot\mathsf{y}}(Y_2, sk_i).$$

Then, we will derive $\mathsf{k}_{\mathcal{T}_0\cdot\mathsf{y}}(\mathsf{adec}(\mathsf{w}_3, \mathsf{w}_2), \langle\gamma, \mathsf{sign}(\gamma, sk_p)\rangle) \Leftarrow$ and this solved statement (with others) will be used to perform resolution on f_1 leading (after several resolution steps) to the statement:

$$\mathsf{r}_{\mathcal{T}_0\cdot w_0\cdot(v,\mathsf{test})} \Leftarrow \mathsf{k}_{\mathcal{T}_0}(X_1', x'),\ \mathsf{k}_{\mathcal{T}_0}(X_2', \mathsf{sign}(x', sk_p)),\ \mathsf{k}_{\mathcal{T}_0\cdot w_0^5}(X_3', x')$$

Ultimately, we will derive $\mathsf{r}_{\mathcal{T}_0\cdot w_0\sigma'\cdot(v,\mathsf{test})} \Leftarrow$ with $\sigma' = \{x' \to \gamma\}$.

During saturation, the statement obtained by resolution is given to an update function which decides whether it has to be added or not into the knowledge base (possibly after some transformations). In original Akiss, many deduction statements are discarded during the saturation procedure. This is useful to avoid non-termination issues and it is not a problem since there is no need to derive the same term (from the deduction point of view) in more than one way. Now, considering that messages need time to reach a destination, a same message emitted twice at two different locations deserves more attention.

Example 11. Let $T = (a_1, \mathsf{out}(k)).(a_2, \mathsf{out}(k)).(b, \mathsf{in}^z(x)).(b, [x = k]).(b, z < 2)$, and $\mathcal{T}_0$ be a topology such that $\mathsf{Dist}_{\mathcal{T}_0}(a_1, b) = 10$ while $\mathsf{Dist}_{\mathcal{T}_0}(a_2, b) = 1$. The configuration $(T; \emptyset; 0)$ is executable but only considering w_2 as an input recipe for x. The recipe w_1 that produces the exact same term k is not an option (even if it is outputted before w_2) since the agent a_1 who outputs it is far away from b.

Whereas the original Akiss procedure will typically discard the statement $\mathsf{k}(\mathsf{w}_2, k) \Leftarrow$ (by replacing it with an identical statement), we will keep it.

As illustrated by Example 11, we therefore need to consider more recipes (even if they deduce the same message) to accommodate timing constraints, but we have to do this in a way that does not break termination (in practice). To tackle this issue, we modified the canonicalization rule, as well as the update function to allow more deduction statements to be added in the knowledge base.

Definition 7. *The canonical form $f\Downarrow$ of a statement $f = (H \Leftarrow B_1, \ldots, B_n)$ is the statement obtained by applying the* Remove *rule given below as many times as possible.*

$$\text{Remove}\ \frac{H \Leftarrow \mathsf{k}_w(X, t),\ \mathsf{k}_w(Y, t),\ B_1, \ldots, B_n \text{ with } X \notin vars(H)}{H \Leftarrow \mathsf{k}_w(Y, t),\ B_1, \ldots, B_n}$$

The intuition is that there is no need to consider several recipes (here X and Y) to deduce the same term t when such a recipe does not occur in the head of the statement.

Then, the update of K by f denoted $K \Cup \{f\}$, is defined to be K if either $\mathsf{skl}(f\Downarrow)$ is not in normal form; or $f\Downarrow$ is solved but not well-formed. Otherwise, $K \Cup \{f\} = K \cup \{f\Downarrow\}$. To initiate our saturation procedure, we start with the initial knowledge base $K_{\mathsf{init}}(S)$ associated to a set S of statements (typically $\mathsf{seed}(T, \mathcal{C})$ for some well-chosen $\mathcal{C}$). Given a set S of statements, the initial knowledge base associated to S, denoted $K_{\mathsf{init}}(S)$, is defined to be the empty knowledge base updated by the set S, i.e. $K_{\mathsf{init}}(S) = (((\emptyset \Cup f_1) \Cup f_2) \Cup \dots f_n$ where $f_1, \dots, f_n$ is an enumeration of the statements in S. In return, the saturation procedure produces a set $\mathsf{sat}(K)$ which is actually a knowledge base.

Then, we can establish the soundness of our saturation procedure. This is relatively straightforward and follows the same lines as the original proof.

Proposition 1. *Let T_0 be a trace locally closed w.r.t. $\mathcal{X}$, $K = \mathsf{sat}(K_{\mathsf{init}}(T_0))$. We have that $(T_0; \emptyset) \models g$ for any $g \in \mathsf{solved}(K) \cup \mathcal{H}(\mathsf{solved}(K))$.*

5.2 Completeness

Completeness is more involved. Indeed, we can not expect to retrieve all the recipes associated to a given term. To ensure termination (in practice) of our procedure, we discard some statements when updating the knowledge base, and we have to justify that those statements are indeed useless. Actually, we show that considering uniform recipes is sufficient when looking for an attack trace.

However, the notion of uniform recipe does not allow one to do the proof by induction. We therefore consider a more restricted notion that we call asap recipes. The idea is to deduce a term as soon as possible but this may depend on the agent who is performing the computation. We also rely on an ordering relation which is independent of the agent who is performing the computation, and which is compatible with our notion of asap w.r.t. any agent.

Given a relaxed execution $\mathsf{exec} = (T; \emptyset) \overset{\ell_1, \dots, \ell_n}{\rightsquigarrow} (S; \phi)$ with input recipes $R_1, \dots, R_k$, we define the following relations:

- $R <^{\mathsf{in}}_{\mathsf{exec}} \mathsf{w}$ when $\ell_i = a, \mathsf{in}(u)$ with input recipe R and $\ell_j = a, \mathsf{out}(u_j)$ with output recipe w for some agent a with $i < j$;
- $R' <^{\mathsf{sub}}_{\mathsf{exec}} R$ when R' is a strict subterm of R.

Then, $<_{\mathsf{exec}}$ is the smallest transitive relation over recipes built on $dom(\phi)$ that contains $<^{\mathsf{in}}_{\mathsf{exec}}$ and $<^{\mathsf{sub}}_{\mathsf{exec}}$. As usual, we denote $\leq_{\mathsf{exec}}$ the reflexive closure of $<_{\mathsf{exec}}$.

Given a timed execution $\mathsf{exec} = (T_0; \emptyset; t_0) \xrightarrow{\ell_1, \dots, \ell_n} (S; \Phi; t)$ with $\Phi = \{\mathsf{w}_1 \xrightarrow{a_1, t_1} u_1, \dots, \mathsf{w}_n \xrightarrow{a_n, t_n} u_n\}$, we denote by $\mathsf{agent}(\mathsf{w}_i)$ (resp. $\mathsf{time}(\mathsf{w}_i)$) the agent a_i (resp. the time t_i). The relation $<^{a}_{\mathsf{exec}}$ over $dom(\Phi) \times dom(\Phi)$ with $a \in \mathcal{A}$ is defined as follows: $\mathsf{w} <^{a}_{\mathsf{exec}} \mathsf{w}'$ when:

- either $\mathsf{time}(\mathsf{w}) + \mathsf{Dist}_{\mathcal{T}}(\mathsf{agent}(\mathsf{w}), a) < \mathsf{time}(\mathsf{w}') + \mathsf{Dist}_{\mathcal{T}}(\mathsf{agent}(\mathsf{w}'), a)$;
- or $\mathsf{time}(\mathsf{w}) + \mathsf{Dist}_{\mathcal{T}}(\mathsf{agent}(\mathsf{w}), a) = \mathsf{time}(\mathsf{w}') + \mathsf{Dist}_{\mathcal{T}}(\mathsf{agent}(\mathsf{w}'), a)$, and the output w occurs before w' in the execution exec.

This order is extended on recipes as follows: $R <^a_{\mathsf{exec}} R'$ when:

1. either $\mathsf{multi}_{\mathcal{W}}(R) <^a_{\mathsf{exec}} \mathsf{multi}_{\mathcal{W}}(R')$ where $\mathsf{multi}_{\mathcal{W}}(R)$ is the multiset of variables $\mathcal{W}$ occurring in R ordered using the multiset extension of $<^a_{\mathsf{exec}}$ on variables;
2. or $\mathsf{multi}_{\mathcal{W}}(R) = \mathsf{multi}_{\mathcal{W}}(R')$ and $|R| < |R'|$ where $|R|$ is the size (number of symbols) occurring in R;
3. or $\mathsf{multi}_{\mathcal{W}}(R) = \mathsf{multi}_{\mathcal{W}}(R')$, $|R| = |R'|$, and $|st_{\mathsf{eq}}(R)| < |st_{\mathsf{eq}}(R')|$ where $st_{\mathsf{eq}}(R) = \{(S, S') \in st(R) \times st(R) \mid S \neq S' \text{ and } S\Phi\downarrow = S'\Phi\downarrow\}$ is the set of pairs of distinct syntactic subterms of R that deduce the same term.

We have that $<^a_{\mathsf{exec}}$ is a well-founded order for any $a \in \mathcal{A}$ which is compatible with $<_{\mathsf{exec}}$, i.e. $R <_{\mathsf{exec}} R'$ implies $R <^a_{\mathsf{exec}} R'$ for any agent a.

We are now able to introduce our notion of asap recipe.

Definition 8. *Let $\mathcal{T} = (\mathcal{A}, \mathcal{M}, \mathsf{Loc})$ be a topology, and* $\mathsf{exec} = (\mathcal{T}_0; \emptyset; t_0) \xrightarrow{\ell_1,\dots,\ell_n} (\mathcal{S}; \Phi; t)$ *be an execution. A recipe R is* asap w.r.t. $a \in \mathcal{A}$ *and* exec *if:*

- *either $R \in \mathcal{N}_{\mathsf{pub}} \cup \mathbb{R}^+ \cup \mathcal{W}$ and $\nexists R'$ such that $R' <_{\mathsf{exec}} R$ and $R'\Phi\downarrow = R\Phi\downarrow$;*
- *or $R = \mathsf{f}(R_1, \dots, R_k)$ with $\mathsf{f} \in \Sigma$ and $\nexists R'$ such that $R' <^a_{\mathsf{exec}} R$ and $R'\Phi\downarrow = R\Phi\downarrow$.*

We may note that our definition of being asap takes care about honest agents who are not allowed to forge messages from their knowledge using recipes not in $\mathcal{W} \cup \mathcal{N}_{\mathsf{pub}} \cup \mathbb{R}^+$. Hence, a recipe $R \in \mathcal{W}$ is not necessarily replaced by a recipe R' even if $R <^a_{\mathsf{exec}} R'$ and $R'\Phi\downarrow = R\Phi\downarrow$. Actually, such a recipe R' is not necessarily an alternative to R when $a \notin \mathcal{M}_0$.

Then, we can establish completeness of our saturation procedure w.r.t. these asap recipes.

Theorem 2. *Let K =* $\mathsf{solved}(\mathsf{sat}(K_{\mathsf{init}}(\mathcal{T}_0)))$. *Let* $\mathsf{exec} = (\mathcal{T}_0; \emptyset; t_0) \xrightarrow{\ell_1,\dots,\ell_p} (\mathcal{S}; \Phi; t)$ *be an execution with input recipes $R_1, \dots, R_k$ forged by $b_1, \dots, b_k$ and such that each R_j with $j \in \{1, \dots, k\}$ is asap w.r.t. b_j and* exec. *We have that:*

- $\mathsf{r}_{\ell_1,\dots,\ell_p} \in \mathcal{H}(K)$ *with a proof tree matching* exec *and $R_1, \dots, R_k$;*
- $\mathsf{k}_{u_0}(R, R\phi\downarrow) \in \mathcal{H}(K)$ *with a proof tree matching* exec *and $R_1, \dots, R_k$ whenever $u_0 = \ell_1, \dots, \ell_{q-1}$ for some $q \in \mathsf{Rcv}(p)$ and R is asap w.r.t. $b_{|\mathsf{Rcv}(q)|}$ and* exec.

Proof (sketch). We have that asap recipes are uniform and we can therefore apply Theorem 1. This allows us to obtain a proof tree in $\mathcal{H}(\mathsf{seed}(\mathcal{T}_0))$. Then, by induction on the proof tree, we lift it from $\mathcal{H}(\mathsf{seed}(\mathcal{T}_0))$ to $\mathcal{H}(K)$. The difficult part is when the statement obtained by resolution is not directly added in the knowledge base. It may have been modified by the rule Remove or even discarded by the update operator. In both cases, we derive a contradiction with the fact that we are considering asap recipes. ☐

Example 12. Considering the relaxed execution starting from $(T_0 \cdot T_{\mathsf{ex}}, \emptyset)$ by performing the three outputs followed by the untimed version of the execution described in Example 6, we reach (ϵ, ϕ) using recipes $R_1 = \mathsf{aenc}(\mathsf{adec}(\mathsf{w}_3, \mathsf{w}_2), \mathsf{w}_1)$ and $R_2 = \mathsf{h}(\mathsf{w}_5, \mathsf{w}_4, \mathsf{proj}_1(\mathsf{adec}(\mathsf{w}_3, \mathsf{w}_2)))$. Let K be the set of solved statements obtained by saturation, we have that $\mathsf{r}_{T_0 \cdot w_0 \sigma' \cdot (v, \mathsf{test})} \in \mathcal{H}(K)$ (see Example 10). Note that the symbolic run $T_0 \cdot w_0\sigma' \cdot (v, \mathsf{test})$ coincides with the labels used in the execution trace. Here, the proof tree is reduced to a leaf, and choosing $\hat{R}_1 = R_1$, $\hat{R}_2 = R_2$, gives us the matching we are looking for.

6 Algorithm

In this section, we first present our algorithm to verify whether a given timed configuration can be fully executed, and then discuss its correctness.

6.1 Description

Our procedure is given in Algorithm 1. We start with the set K of solved statements obtained by applying our saturation procedure on the trace T. We consider each reachability statement in K, and after instantiating the remaining variables with fresh constants using a bijection ρ, we compute for each input $(a_i, \mathsf{in}(v_i))$ occurring in $\ell'_1 \ldots, \ell'_n$ all the possible recipes that may lead to the term $v_i\rho$ and store them in the set $\overline{L_i}$. Actually, thanks to our soundness result (Proposition 1), we know that these recipes deduce the requested terms, and it only remains to check that the timing constraints are satisfied (lines 10–11).

We consider a trace T of the form $(a_1, \mathsf{a}_1).(a_2, \mathsf{a}_2).\ldots.(a_n, \mathsf{a}_n)$ locally closed w.r.t. $\mathcal{X}$ and $\mathcal{Z}$ and we assume the naming convention given in Sect. 4.2. Moreover, we denote by $\mathsf{orig}(j)$ the index of the action in the trace T that performed

Algorithm 1. Test for checking whether $(T, \emptyset, t_0)$ is executable in $\mathcal{T}_0$

1: **procedure** REACHABILITY$(K, t_0, \mathcal{T}_0)$
2:     **for all** $\mathsf{r}_{\ell'_1,\ldots,\ell'_n} \Leftarrow \mathsf{k}_{w_1}(X_1, x_1), \ldots, \mathsf{k}_{w_m}(X_n, x_m) \in K$ **do**
3:         let $c_1, \ldots, c_q$ be fresh public names such that
4:         $\rho : vars(\ell'_1, \ldots, \ell'_n) \to \{c_1, \ldots, c_k\}$ is a bijection
5:         **for all** $i \in \mathsf{Rcv}(n)$ **do**
6:             **if** $\ell'_i = (a_i, \mathsf{in}(v_i))$ **then** $\overline{L_i} = \{R \mid \mathsf{k}_{\ell'_1\rho\ldots\ell'_{i-1}\rho}(R, v_i\rho) \in \mathcal{H}(K)\}$
7:         **end for**
8:         Let $\{i_1, \ldots, i_p\} = \mathsf{Rcv}(n)$ such that $i_1 < i_2 < \ldots < i_p$
9:         **for all** $L_{i_1} \times \ldots \times L_{i_p} \in \overline{L_{i_1}} \times \ldots \times \overline{L_{i_p}}$ **do**
10:             Let $\psi = \mathsf{Timing}((T; \emptyset; t_0), L_{i_1}\rho^{-1} \ldots L_{i_p}\rho^{-1}, v_{i_1}, \ldots, v_{i_p})$.
11:             **if** ψ satisfiable **then return** true **end if**
12:         **end for**
13:     **end for**
14:     **return** false
15: **end procedure**

the jth output, i.e. $\mathsf{orig}(j)$ is the minimal k such that $|\mathsf{Snd}(k)| = j$. The function Timing takes as inputs the initial configuration, the recipes used to feed the inputs occurring in the trace, and the terms corresponding to these inputs. Note that all these terms may still contain variables from $\mathcal{Z}$. This function computes a formula that represents all the timing constraints that have to be satisfied to ensure the executability of the trace in our timed model. More formally, $\mathsf{Timing}((T;\emptyset;t_0)), R_{i_1} \dots R_{i_p}, u_{i_1} \dots u_{i_p})$ is the conjunction of the formulas:

1. $z_1 = t_0$, and $z_i \leq z_{i+1}$ for any $1 \leq i < n$;
2. $t_i \sim t'_i$ for any $i \in \mathsf{Test}(n)$ with $\mathsf{a}_i = [\![t_i \sim t'_i]\!]$;
3. $z'_i = v_i\{x_j \to u_j \mid j \in \mathsf{Rcv}(i)\}\!\downarrow$ for any $i \in \mathsf{Let}(n)$;
4. For any $i \in \mathsf{Rcv}(n)$, we consider the formula:
   - $z_{\mathsf{orig}(j)} + \mathsf{Dist}_{\mathcal{T}_0}(a_{\mathsf{orig}(j)}, a_i) \leq z_i$ if $R_i = \mathsf{w}_j$;
   - otherwise, we consider:

$$\bigvee_{b \in \mathcal{M}_0} \Big(\bigwedge_{\{j \mid \mathsf{w}_j \in vars(R_i)\}} z_{\mathsf{orig}(j)} + \mathsf{Dist}_{\mathcal{T}_0}(a_{\mathsf{orig}(j)}, b) \leq z_i - \mathsf{Dist}_{\mathcal{T}_0}(b, a_i) \Big)$$

The last step of our algorithm consists in checking whether the resulting formula ψ is satisfiable or not, i.e. whether there exists a mapping from $vars(\psi)$ to $\mathbb{R}^+$ such that the formula ψ is true. Of course, even if our procedure is generic w.r.t. to timing constraints, the procedure to check the satisfiability of ψ will depend on the constraints we consider. Actually, all the formulas encountered during our case studies are quite simple: they are expressed by equations of the form $z' - z \leq t$, and we therefore rely on the well-known Floyd-Warshall algorithm to solve them. When needed, we may rely on the simplex algorithm to solve more general linear constraints.

6.2 Termination Issues

First, we may note that to obtain an effective saturation procedure, it is important to start with a finite set of seed statements. Our set $\mathsf{seed}(T)$ is infinite but as it was proved in [12], we can restrict ourselves to perform saturation using the finite set $\mathsf{seed}(T, \mathcal{C}_T)$ where $\mathcal{C}_T$ contains the public names and the real numbers occurring in the trace T. More formally, we have that:

Lemma 1. *Let $\mathcal{C}_T$ be the finite set of public names and real numbers occurring in T, and $\mathcal{C}_{all} = \mathcal{N}_{\mathsf{pub}} \cup \mathbb{R}^+$. We have that:*

$$\mathsf{sat}(K_{\mathsf{init}}(\mathsf{seed}(T, \mathcal{C}_{all}))) = \mathsf{sat}(K_{\mathsf{init}}(\mathsf{seed}(T, \mathcal{C}_T))) \cup \{\mathsf{k_y}(c, c) \Leftarrow \ \mid \ c \in \mathcal{C}_{all}\}.$$

Nevertheless, the saturation may not terminate. We could probably avoid some non-termination issues by improving our update operator. However, ensuring termination in theory is a rather difficult problem (the proof of termination for the original Akiss procedure for subterm convergent theories is quite complex [12] – more than 20 pages). We would like to mention that we never encountered non-termination issues in practice on our case studies.

Another issue is that, when computing the set $\overline{L_i}$, we need to compute all the recipes R such that $\mathsf{k}_w(R,u) \in \mathcal{H}(K)$ for a given term u. This can be achieved using a simple backward search and will terminate since K only contains solved statements that are well-formed. The naive recursive algorithm will therefore consider terms $u_1,\ldots,u_n$ that are strict subterms of the initial term u. Note that statements that are not well-formed are discarded by our update operator: ensuring completeness of our saturation procedure when discarding statements that are not well-formed is the challenging part of our completeness proof.

6.3 Correctness of Our Algorithm

We consider a topology $\mathcal{T}_0$ and a configuration $(T;\emptyset;t_0)$ built on top of $\mathcal{T}_0$ and such that T is locally closed w.r.t. both $\mathcal{X}$ and $\mathcal{Z}$.

Theorem 3. *Let $\mathcal{C}_T \subseteq \mathcal{N}_{\mathsf{pub}} \uplus \mathbb{R}^+$ be the finite set of public names and real numbers occurring in T. Let $K = \mathsf{solved}(\mathsf{sat}(K_{\mathsf{init}}(\mathsf{seed}(T,\mathcal{C}_T))))$. We have that:*

- *if* REACHABILITY$(K,t_0,\mathcal{T}_0)$ *holds then $(T;\emptyset;t)$ is executable in $\mathcal{T}_0$;*
- *if $(T;\emptyset;t_0)$ is executable in $\mathcal{T}_0$ then* REACHABILITY$(K,t_0,\mathcal{T}_0)$ *holds.*

Soundness (item 1 above) is relatively straightforward. Item 2 is more involved. Of course, our algorithm does not consider all the possible recipes for inputs. Some recipes are discarded from our analysis. Actually, it is sufficient to focus our attention on asap recipes. To justify that this is not an issue regarding completeness, we first establish the following result.

Lemma 2. *Let $\mathsf{exec} = K_0 \xrightarrow{\ell_1,\ldots,\ell_n}_{\mathcal{T}_0} (S;\Phi;t)$ be an execution. We may assume w.l.o.g. that exec involves input recipes $R_1,\ldots,R_k$ forged by agents $b_1,\ldots,b_k$ and R_i is asap w.r.t. b_i and exec for each $i \in \{1,\ldots,k\}$.*

Then, we may apply Theorem 2 (item 1) on this "asap execution" and deduce the existence of $f = \mathsf{r}_{\ell'_1,\ldots,\ell'_n} \Leftarrow \mathsf{k}_{w_1}(X_1,x_1),\ldots,\mathsf{k}_{w_m}(X_m,x_m)$ in K and a substitution σ witnessing the fact that $\mathsf{r}_{\ell_1,\ldots,\ell_n} = \mathsf{r}_{\ell'_1\sigma,\ldots,\ell'_n\sigma} \in \mathcal{H}(K)$. Moreover, we know that f and σ match with exec and $R_1,\ldots,R_k$. Considering the symbolic recipes $\hat{R}_1,\ldots,\hat{R}_k$ witnessing this matching, and instantiating their variables with adequate fresh constants (using ρ), we can show that $\hat{R}_1\rho,\ldots,\hat{R}_k\rho$ are recipes that allow to perform the timed execution $\ell'_1\rho,\ldots,\ell'_n\rho$. Note that thanks the strong relationship we have between $R_1,\ldots,R_k$ and $\hat{R}_1,\ldots,\hat{R}_k$ (by definition of matching, $R_i = \hat{R}_i\sigma$), we know that the resulting timing constraints gathered in the formula ψ due to inputs are less restrictive, and the other ones are essentially unchanged. This allows us to ensure that the formula ψ will be satisfiable. Now, applying Lemma 2, we can assume w.l.o.g. that recipes involved in such a trace are asap, and thus according to Theorem 2 will be considered by our procedure, and put in $\overline{L_{i_1}},\ldots,\overline{L_{i_p}}$ at line 6 of Algorithm 1.

7 Implementation and Case Studies

We validate our approach by integrating our procedure in Akiss [12], and successfully used it on several case studies. All files related to the tool implementation and case studies are available at

http://people.irisa.fr/Alexandre.Debant/akiss-db.html.

7.1 Integration in Akiss

Our syntax is very close to the one presented in Sect. 3. For sake of simplicity, we sometimes omit timestamps on input/output actions. Regarding our timing constraints, our syntax only allows linear expressions of the form $z_1 - z_2 \sim z_3$ with $z_i \in \mathcal{Z} \cup \mathbb{R}^+$ and $\sim \in \{=, <, \leq\}$. These expressions are enough to model all our case studies. To ease the specification of protocols our tool support parallel composition of traces ($T_1 \mid\mid T_2$). This operator is syntactic sugar and can be translated to sets of traces in a straightforward way.

To mitigate the potential exponential blowup caused by this translation, we always favour let, equality, and test actions, as well as output actions when no timestamp occur on it. The second optimisation consists in executing input actions (without timestamps) in a raw. These optimisations will allow us to reduce the number of traces that have to be considered during our analysis, and are well-known to be sound when verifying reachability properties [4,30].

Example 13. Let $P = (a, \mathsf{in}(x_1)).(a, \mathsf{in}(x_2).(a, \mathsf{out}(u)) \mid\mid (b, \mathsf{in}(x_3)).(b, \mathsf{out}(v))$. Computing naively all the possible interleavings will give us 10 traces to analyse. The first optimisation will allow us to reduce this number to 3, and together with the second optimisation, this number falls to 2.

7.2 Case Studies

In this section we demonstrate that our tool can be effectively used to analyse distance bounding protocols and payment protocols. Our experiments have been done on a standard laptop and the results obtained confirm termination of the saturation procedure when analysing various protocols ($\times$ stands for attack, ✓ means that the protocol has been proved secure). We indicate the number of roles (running in parallel) we consider and the number of traces (due to all the possible interleaving of the roles) that have been analysed by the tool in order to conclude. Our algorithm stops as soon as an attack is found, and thus the number of possible interleavings is not relevant in this case.

We only consider two distinct topologies: one to analyse mafia fraud scenarios (2 honest agents far away with a malicious agent close to each honest agent) and one to analyse distance hijacking for which 3 agents are considered (malicious agent in the neighbourhood of the verifier on which the security property is encoded is not allowed). This may seem restrictive but it has been shown to be sufficient to capture all the possible attacks [19]. Our results are consistent with the ones obtained in [13,14,19,26].

Distance Bounding Protocols. As explained in Sect. 2 on the TREAD protocol, we ignore several details that are irrelevant to a security analysis performed in the symbolic model. Moreover, our procedure is not yet able to support the exclusive-or operator and thus it has been modelled in an abstract way when analysing the protocols BC and Swiss-Knife. When no attack was found for 2 roles, we consider more roles (and thus more traces). The fact that the performances degrade when considering additional roles is not surprising and is clearly correlated with the number of traces that have to be considered.

Payment Protocols. We have also analysed three payment protocols (and some of their variants) w.r.t. mafia fraud – the only relevant scenario for this kind of application (see [13]). It happens that these protocols are more complex to analyse than traditional distance bounding protocols. They often involve more complex messages, and a larger number of message exchanges. Moreover, in protocols MasterCard RRP and NXP, the threshold is not fixed in advance but received during the protocol execution. Due to this, these protocols fall outside the class of protocols that can be analysed by [19,26]. To our knowledge only [13] copes with this issue by proposing a security analysis in two steps: they first establish that the value of the threshold can not be manipulated by the attacker, and then analyse the protocol considering a fixed threshold. Such a protocol can be encoded in a natural way in our calculus using the let instruction $[z := v]$ that allows one to extract a timing information from a message. We analysed these protocols considering one instance of each role.

Protocol	Mafia fraud			Distance hijacking		
	roles/tr	time	status	roles/tr	time	status
TREAD-Asym [2]	2/–	1 s	×	2/–	1 s	×
SPADE [11]	2/–	2 s	×	2/–	4 s	×
TREAD-Sym [2]	4/7500	18 min	✓	2/–	1 s	×
BC [10]	4/5635	37 min	✓	2/–	1 s	×
Swiss-Knife [25]	3/1080	25 s	✓	3/7470	4 min	✓
HK [23]	3/20	1 s	✓	3/20	1 s	✓
	4/3360	58 s	✓	4/3360	47 s	✓
	5/30240	14 min	✓	5/30240	12 min	✓

8 Conclusion

We presented a novel procedure for reasoning about distance bounding protocols which has been integrated in the Akiss tool. Even though termination is not guaranteed, the tool did terminate on all practical examples that we have tested.

Protocol	# tr	time	status
NXP [24]	126	4 s	✓
MasterCard RRP [22]	35	6 min	✓
PaySafe [14]	4	308 s	✓
PaySafe-V2 [14]	–	26 s	×
PaySafe-V3 [14]	–	149 s	×

Directions for future work include improving performances of our tool and this can be achieved by parallelising our algorithm (each trace can actually be analysed independently) and/or proposing new techniques to reduce the number of interleavings. Another interesting direction would be to add the exclusive-or operator which is often used in distance bounding protocols. This will require a careful analysis of the completeness proof developed in [3] to check whether their resolution strategy is compatible with the changes done here to accommodate timing constraints.

References

1. Abadi, M., Fournet, C.: Mobile values, new names, and secure communication. In: Proceedings of the 28th Symposium on Principles of Programming Languages (POPL 2001), pp. 104–115. ACM Press (2001)
2. Avoine, G., et al.: A terrorist-fraud resistant and extractor-free anonymous distance-bounding protocol. In: Proceedings of the 12th ACM Asia Conference on Computer and Communications Security (AsiaCCS 2017), pp. 800–814. ACM (2017)
3. Baelde, D., Delaune, S., Gazeau, I., Kremer, S.: Symbolic verification of privacy-type properties for security protocols with XOR. In: 2017 IEEE 30th Computer Security Foundations Symposium (CSF), pp. 234–248. IEEE (2017)
4. Baelde, D., Delaune, S., Hirschi, L.: A reduced semantics for deciding trace equivalence. Log. Methods Comput. Sci. **13**(2), 1–48 (2017)
5. Basin, D., Capkun, S., Schaller, P., Schmidt, B.: Formal reasoning about physical properties of security protocols. ACM Trans. Inf. Syst. Secur. (TISSEC) **14**(2), 16 (2011)
6. Basin, D.A., Mödersheim, S., Viganò, L.: OFMC: a symbolic model checker for security protocols. Int. J. Inf. Secur. **4**(3), 181–208 (2005)
7. Bhargavan, K., Blanchet, B., Kobeissi, N.: Verified models and reference implementations for the TLS 1.3 standard candidate. In: Proceedings of the 38th IEEE Symposium on Security and Privacy (S&P 2017), pp. 483–502 (2017)
8. Blanchet, B.: Modeling and verifying security protocols with the applied pi calculus and ProVerif. Found. Trends Priv. Secur. **1**(1–2), 1–135 (2016)
9. Blanchet, B.: Symbolic and computational mechanized verification of the ARINC823 avionic protocols. In: Proceedings of the 30th IEEE Computer Security Foundations Symposium (CSF 2017), pp. 68–82. IEEE (2017)
10. Brands, S., Chaum, D.: Distance-bounding protocols. In: Helleseth, T. (ed.) EUROCRYPT 1993. LNCS, vol. 765, pp. 344–359. Springer, Heidelberg (1994). https://doi.org/10.1007/3-540-48285-7_30

11. Bultel, X., Gambs, S., Gerault, D., Lafourcade, P., Onete, C., Robert, J.: A prover-anonymous and terrorist-fraud resistant distance-bounding protocol. In: Proceedings of the 9th ACM Conference on Security & Privacy in Wireless and Mobile Networks, WISEC 2016, Darmstadt, Germany, 18–22 July 2016, pp. 121–133. ACM (2016)
12. Chadha, R., Cheval, V., Ciobâcă, Ş., Kremer, S.: Automated verification of equivalence properties of cryptographic protocol. ACM Trans. Comput. Logic **23**(4), 23:1–23:32 (2016)
13. Chothia, T., de Ruiter, J., Smyth, B.: Modelling and analysis of a hierarchy of distance bounding attacks. In: Proceedings of the 27th USENIX Security Symposium (USENIX 2018), pp. 1563–1580. USENIX Association (2018)
14. Chothia, T., Garcia, F.D., de Ruiter, J., van den Breekel, J., Thompson, M.: Relay cost bounding for contactless EMV payments. In: Böhme, R., Okamoto, T. (eds.) FC 2015. LNCS, vol. 8975, pp. 189–206. Springer, Heidelberg (2015). https://doi.org/10.1007/978-3-662-47854-7_11
15. Comon-Lundh, H., Cortier, V., Zălinescu, E.: Deciding security properties for cryptographic protocols. Application to key cycles. ACM Trans. Comput. Logic **11**(2), 9 (2010)
16. Comon-Lundh, H., Delaune, S.: The finite variant property: how to get rid of some algebraic properties. In: Giesl, J. (ed.) RTA 2005. LNCS, vol. 3467, pp. 294–307. Springer, Heidelberg (2005). https://doi.org/10.1007/978-3-540-32033-3_22
17. Cremers, C., Horvat, M., Hoyland, J., Scott, S., van der Merwe, T.: A comprehensive symbolic analysis of TLS 1.3. In: Proceedings of the 24th ACM Conference on Computer and Communications Security (CCS 2017), pp. 1773–1788 (2017)
18. Debant, A., Delaune, S.: Symbolic verification of distance bounding protocols. Research report, Univ Rennes, CNRS, IRISA, France, February 2019
19. Debant, A., Delaune, S., Wiedling, C.: A symbolic framework to analyse physical proximity in security protocols. In: Proceedings of the 38th IARCS Annual Conference on Foundations of Software Technology and Theoretical Computer Science (FSTTCS 2018). LIPICS (2018)
20. Dolev, D., Yao, A.: On the security of public key protocols. IEEE Trans. Inf. theory **29**(2), 198–208 (1983)
21. Durgin, N., Lincoln, P., Mitchell, J., Scedrov, A.: Undecidability of bounded security protocols. In: Proceedings of the Workshop on Formal Methods and Security Protocols (FMSP 1999), Trento, Italy (1999)
22. EMVCo: EMV contactless specifications for payment systems, version 2.6 (2016)
23. Hancke, G.P., Kuhn, M.G.: An RFID distance bounding protocol. In: Proceedings of the 1st International Conference on Security and Privacy for Emerging Areas in Communications Networks (SECURECOMM 2005), pp. 67–73. IEEE (2005)
24. Janssens, P.: Proximity check for communication devices. US Patent 9,805,228, 31 October 2017
25. Kim, C.H., Avoine, G., Koeune, F., Standaert, F.-X., Pereira, O.: The Swiss-Knife RFID distance bounding protocol. In: Lee, P.J., Cheon, J.H. (eds.) ICISC 2008. LNCS, vol. 5461, pp. 98–115. Springer, Heidelberg (2009). https://doi.org/10.1007/978-3-642-00730-9_7
26. Mauw, S., Smith, Z., Toro-Pozo, J., Trujillo-Rasua, R.: Distance-bounding protocols: verification without time and location. In: Proceedings of the 39th IEEE Symposium on Security and Privacy (S&P 2018), pp. 152–169 (2018)

27. Meadows, C., Poovendran, R., Pavlovic, D., Chang, L., Syverson, P.: Distance bounding protocols: authentication logic analysis and collusion attacks. In: Poovendran, R., Roy, S., Wang, C. (eds.) Secure Localization and Time Synchronization for Wireless Sensor and Ad Hoc Networks. ADIS, vol. 30, pp. 279–298. Springer, Boston (2007). https://doi.org/10.1007/978-0-387-46276-9_12
28. Meier, S., Schmidt, B., Cremers, C., Basin, D.: The TAMARIN prover for the symbolic analysis of security protocols. In: Sharygina, N., Veith, H. (eds.) CAV 2013. LNCS, vol. 8044, pp. 696–701. Springer, Heidelberg (2013). https://doi.org/10.1007/978-3-642-39799-8_48
29. Millen, J., Shmatikov, V.: Constraint solving for bounded-process cryptographic protocol analysis. In: Proceedings of the 8th ACM Conference on Computer and Communications Security (CCS 2001). ACM Press (2001)
30. Mödersheim, S., Viganò, L., Basin, D.A.: Constraint differentiation: search-space reduction for the constraint-based analysis of security protocols. J. Comput. Secur. **18**(4), 575–618 (2010)
31. Nigam, V., Talcott, C., Aires Urquiza, A.: Towards the automated verification of cyber-physical security protocols: bounding the number of timed intruders. In: Askoxylakis, I., Ioannidis, S., Katsikas, S., Meadows, C. (eds.) ESORICS 2016. LNCS, vol. 9879, pp. 450–470. Springer, Cham (2016). https://doi.org/10.1007/978-3-319-45741-3_23
32. Rusinowitch, M., Turuani, M.: Protocol insecurity with a finite number of sessions and composed keys is NP-complete. Theoret. Comput. Sci. **299**(1–3), 451–475 (2003)

On the Formalisation of Σ-Protocols and Commitment Schemes

David Butler[1,2(✉)], David Aspinall[1,2], and Adrià Gascón[1,3]

[1] The Alan Turing Institute, London, UK
dbutler@turing.ac.uk
[2] University of Edinburgh, Edinburgh, UK
[3] University of Warwick, Coventry, UK

Abstract. There is a fundamental relationship between Σ-protocols and commitment schemes whereby the former can be used to construct the latter. In this work we provide the first formal analysis in a proof assistant of such a relationship and in doing so formalise Σ-protocols and commitment schemes and provide proofs of security for well known instantiations of both primitives.

Every definition and every theorem presented in this paper has been checked mechanically by the Isabelle/HOL proof assistant.

Keywords: Commitment schemes · Σ-protocols · Formal verification · Isabelle/HOL

1 Introduction

In [8], Damgard elegantly showed how Σ-protocols can be used to construct commitment schemes that are perfectly hiding and computationally binding and thus showed how these two fundamental cryptographic primitives are linked. The properties of the resulting commitment scheme rely on the security of the underlying Σ-protocol. The relationship between the two is natural as Σ-protocols can be considered the building block for zero knowledge, and it is well known that commitment schemes and zero knowledge protocols are strongly related [9].

When properties of fundamental primitives are linked in such a way it is interesting to study them formally using a proof assistant to more deeply understand the nature of the relationship. In fact the proof provided of the security of the construction of commitment schemes from Σ-protocols in [8] is brief; thus to study it formally one has to consider the properties in more detail.

To achieve such a goal one must first formalise both primitives and then show the desired relations between them with respect to the individual formalisations for either primitive. To formalise and instantiate a primitive using a proof assistant one must first formalise the security definitions, then define the protocol

This work was supported by The Alan Turing Institute under the EPSRC grant EP/N510129/1.

F. Nielson and D. Sands (Eds.): POST 2019, LNCS 11426, pp. 175–196, 2019.
https://doi.org/10.1007/978-3-030-17138-4_8

that realises the primitive and then provide proofs in the proof assistant that show the defined security properties are met by the protocol.

As well as providing a deeper insight and more rigorous proof for properties in cryptography, formalisations also provide an increased confidence in cryptographic proofs. This increased level of rigour was called for by Halevi in 2005 [12], where it was proposed to approach the problem formally. One aspect of this approach is that security definitions are formally defined in an abstract way and then instantiated for different protocols that hold those security properties. The advantage of the abstract definitions is a human checker only needs to check these definitions for consistency with the literature to have confidence in the whole collection of proof. This is exactly the goal of this work.

In this paper, motivated by understanding the connection between Σ-protocols and commitment schemes we use the proof assistant Isabelle/HOL to formally reason about the two fundamental primitives and then show how a Σ-protocol can be used to construct a commitment scheme. Specifically we formally prove, with respect to our abstract definitions of commitment schemes, how the Schnorr Σ-protocol can be used to construct a perfectly hiding and computationally binding commitment scheme. In the process of achieving this we prove various Σ-protocols and commitment schemes secure in their own right.

To the best of our knowledge this is the first time the connection between Σ-protocols and commitment schemes has been considered using a proof assistant. Σ-protocols were considered in [5] and [2] and the Pedersen commitment scheme has been considered formally using EasyCrypt in [17]. We leave a discussion of the comparison of Isabelle/CryptHOL and EasyCrypt to Sect. 10.

Our formal proofs can be found at [1].

Contributions

- We provide abstract frameworks from which to reason about commitment schemes and Σ-protocols. We formalise this in Isabelle/HOL, but the structure could be used in other proof assistants.
- We instantiate this abstract framework to provide proofs of security for both primitives; the Pedersen commitment scheme, the Schnorr Σ-protocol and a second Σ-protocol based on the equality of discrete logs assumption.
- We use both the abstract frameworks to formally show how a commitment scheme can be constructed using the Schnorr Σ-protocol (following the work of [9]) and prove it secure with respect to our commitment scheme framework. In doing so we formally demonstrate the relationship between Σ-protocols and commitment schemes.
- To complete the proofs described, two other contributions were made. First, we had to define the discrete logarithm assumption in Isabelle; a notion that can be used by others in future proofs. Second, the adversary used to break this assumption, for a contradiction, outputs the division of two elements in a field. For technical reasons this is non trivial to do in Isabelle therefore we were required to develop a method to do this. This method, and its associated

proofs, can now be used by others completing cryptographic proofs inside Isabelle.
- All our protocols are shown secure in both the concrete and asymptotic cases.

Outline. In Sect. 2 we outline the structure of our formalisation and in Sect. 3 introduce the relevant theory of Isabelle/HOL and the main parts of CryptHOL [15]. In Sects. 4 and 6 we introduce our formalisation of Σ-protocols and commitment schemes receptively. Sections 5 and 7 show how we instantiate these abstract frameworks for the Schnorr and Pedersen protocols. We show how we link the two in Sect. 8 and how we construct a commitment scheme using the Schnorr Σ-protocol. Finally we conclude and discuss related work and provide a comparison with EasyCrypt in Sects. 9 and 10.

2 Formalisation Overview

In this section we first outline the structure of our formalisation and then discuss the process of instantiating the abstract frameworks to achieve formal proof in Isabelle. Then we discuss the proof method for the asymptotic security setting.

2.1 Outline of Formalisation

We begin our formalisation by abstractly defining the security properties required for both commitment schemes and Σ-protocols. This part of the formalisation is defined over abstract types, giving the flexibility for it to be instantiated for any protocol; this allows us to have confidence in the proof's integrity when considering a range of different protocols. The abstract nature of the formalisation will also allow others to use the definitions of security and structure we provide to prove security of other commitment schemes and Σ-protocols. Another benefit is we can prove some technical lemmas at the abstract level and have them at our disposal in any instantiation, thus reducing the workload for future proofs. A final advantage of the abstract definitions is that a human checker only needs to verify these definitions for consistency with the literature to have confidence in the whole collection of proof.

We instantiate the abstract frameworks to prove security of the Pedersen commitment scheme, the Schnorr Σ-protocol and a second Σ-protocol that uses a relation for the equality of discrete logarithms. Finally we use the algorithms that define the Schnorr protocol to construct a commitment scheme (as shown in [8]) and prove it secure with respect to our commitment scheme definitions using the properties obtained from the Σ-protocol proofs.

The work flow of this paper can be seen in Fig. 1 where an arrow implies the use of one theory (a formalised file in Isabelle) to achieve the next. For example we prove the 'Schnorr commitment' secure with respect to the 'Abstract Commitments' definitions and using the algorithms and properties of the 'Schnorr' protocol.

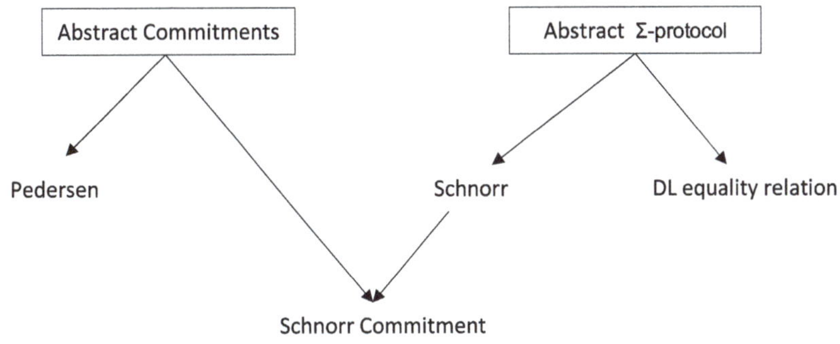

Fig. 1. The structure of the formalisation in Isabelle

2.2 Instantiating the Abstract Frameworks

At a technical level Isabelle's module system (called locales) allows the user to prove theorems abstractly, relative to given assumptions. These theorems can be reused in situations where the assumptions themselves are theorems. In our case locales allow us to define properties of security relative to fixed constants and then instantiate these definitions for explicit protocols and prove the security properties as theorems.

The overall process of instantiation can be seen as a step-by-step process given below:

1. We fix, with abstract types, the probabilistic programs (algorithms) that make up a primitive (e.g. *key_gen*, *commit*, *verify*, for commitment schemes see Fig. 6) in a locale then proceed to make the definitions of security with respect these fixed constants (e.g. define the hiding property). This can be considered as the formal specification requirements of the primitive.
2. To instantiate a protocol we must explicitly define the above fixed constants. To do this we make all types concrete and define the probabilistic programs that describe the protocol.
3. We are then able to utilise Isabelle's locale structure by importing the abstract framework using the **sublocale** command. Not only must the explicit definitions be of the correct type when importing a locale, one must also dismiss any assumptions that come with the locale. This means that our instantiation is a valid commitment scheme or Σ-protocol and allows us to refer to the security definitions made in the abstract framework and prove the properties using the explicit definitions of the instantiated protocol.

2.3 Asymptotic Security

In our formalisation we first consider security in the concrete setting. Here we assume the security parameter, n, is implicit in all algorithms that parametrise the framework. We then move to prove security in the asymptotic setting utilising Isabelle's module system. More details about this part of our formalisation are given in Sect. 8.1. We note the asymptotic setting is not considered in EasyCrypt proofs, the machinery available in Isabelle however makes it possible.

3 CryptHOL and Isabelle Background

In this section we briefly introduce the Isabelle notion we use throughout and then highlight and discuss some important aspects of CryptHOL. For more detail on CryptHOL see [6]. The full formalisation is available at [14].

3.1 Isabelle Notation

The notations we use in this paper resemble closely the syntax of Isabelle/HOL (Isabelle). For function application we write $f(x, y)$ in an uncurried form for ease of reading instead of $f\ x\ y$ as in the λ-calculus. To indicate that term t has type τ we write $t :: \tau$. Isabelle uses the symbol $\Rightarrow$ for the function type, so $a \Rightarrow b$ is the type of functions that takes an input of type a and outputs an element of type b. The type 'a denotes an abstract type. The implication arrow $\longrightarrow$ is used to separate assumptions from conclusions inside a closed HOL statement. We use $\otimes$ to denote multiplication in a group and $*$ for multiplication in a field.

3.2 CryptHOL

CryptHOL [6] is a framework for reasoning about cryptography in the computational model that is embedded inside the Isabelle/HOL theorem prover. It allows the prover to write probabilistic programs and reason about them. The computational model is based on probability theory and in particular uses probabilistic programs to define security—this can be seen for the construction of games in the game-based setting or the real and ideal views in the simulation-based setting.

To build the probabilistic programming framework CryptHOL uses the existing probability theory formalised inside Isabelle to define discrete probability distributions called sub probability mass functions (of type *spmf*). These can be thought of as probability mass functions with the property they do not have to sum to one—we can lose some probability mass. This allows us to model failure events and assertions.

Writing Probabilistic Programs. CryptHOL provides some, easy-to-read, Haskell-style do notation to write probabilistic programs where $\mathbf{do}\{x \leftarrow p;\ f(x)\}$ is the probabilistic program that samples from the distribution p and returns the *spmf* produced by f. We can also return an *spmf* using the monad operation *return*. See Fig. 2 for an example.

Proofs of security are mainly completed by manipulating the appropriate probabilistic programs. While the proofs that each manipulation is valid are not always accessible to non-experts, the effect of each manipulation can be easily seen and recognised as they are explicitly written in the do notation.

Failure Events and Assertions. We often have to reason about failure events. For example we must ensure the adversary in the hiding game (Fig. 6) outputs two valid messages for the game to proceed. Such events are handled using assertion statements

$$assert(b) = if\ b\ then\ return(\_)\ else\ \bot$$

and the *TRY p ELSE q* construct. For example *TRY* **do** $\{p\}$ *ELSE q* would distribute the probability mass not assigned by p to the distribution according to q. Picking up on our example of the hiding game; if the adversary fails to output two valid messages, the assertion fails and the *ELSE* branch is invoked resulting in the adversary not winning the hiding game.

Sampling. Sampling from sets is important in cryptography. CryptHOL gives an operation *uniform* which returns a uniform distribution over a finite set. We use two cases of this function extensively: by $sample\_uniform(q)$, where q is a natural, we denote the uniform sampling from the set $\{..< q\}$ and by *coin* we denote the uniform sampling from the set $\{True, False\}$—a coin flip.

Using sampling we are able to illustrate one difference in thought process and rigour required in a formal proof compared to a pen-and-paper proof. One time pads (OTPs) are used extensively in protocols. Often their properties are employed without thought or explanation in paper proofs as they are considered to be a simple construct. However there are some more subtle issues that sometimes need to be considered.

$$map((\lambda b.\ (x * b)\ mod\ q), (sample\_uniform(q))) = sample\_uniform(q) \tag{1}$$

Equation 1 shows the traditional OTP for multiplication in a field; a uniform sample, b, from a set of q elements, multiplied to an input, x, taken modulo q is the same as a uniform sample. However this property is only valid if x and q are coprime. This follows, in the finite field, from Fermat's Little Theorem; thus formally we have to work much harder to use such a lemma. In short, formalising a proof demonstrates many areas where a paper proof falls short in detail.

Probabilities. We must also be able to reason about the probability of events occurring. So, $\mathcal{P}[Q = x]$ denotes the subprobability mass the spmf Q assigns to the event x. We also introduce the notation $\rhd$ which denotes the binding of a sample without the need for the do notation. This can be seen in Theorem 3 where the bound variable e is sampled from *challenge* and given to $S2$.

Negligible Functions. To reason about security in the asymptotic case we must consider negligible functions. These were formalised as a part of CryptHOL. A function, $f :: (nat \Rightarrow real)$ is said to be negligible if

$$(\forall c > 0.\ f \in o(\lambda x.inverse(x^c)))$$

where o is the little o notation. We discuss the use of such functions in our proofs in Sect. 8.1.

4 Formalising Σ-Protocols

In this section we show how we formally define Σ-protocols and their security properties—it is with respect to these definitions that we prove security of the Schnorr protocol and a variant of it for equality of discrete logs in Sect. 5. For more details on the Σ-protocols see [9].

4.1 Definition of Σ-protocols

We first consider a binary relation R; for some (h, w) that satisfies R, w is a witness of h. For example, the discrete log relation is formalised as follows

$$R_{DL}(h, w) = (h = g^w \wedge w < |G|) \tag{2}$$

where g is a generator of the cyclic group G.

A Σ-protocol is a two party protocol run between a prover (P) and a verifier (V). In the protocol h is a common input to both P and V and w a private input to P such that $R(h, w)$ is true. We define the structure of a Σ-protocol as follows:

Definition 1. *A Σ-protocol has the following three part form:*

1. *Initial message: P sends message a, created with randomness r.*
2. *Challenge: V sends P a challenge, e.*
3. *Response: P responds with z to convince the verifier who either accepts or rejects.*

A conversation *can be seen as the tuple (a, e, z).*

Formally we model this as four abstract probabilistic programs whose types are given below. The inputs to relation R are h, of type *'pub_input* and w, of type *'witness*.

$$\mathit{init} :: \text{'}\mathit{pub\_input} \Rightarrow \text{'}\mathit{witness} \Rightarrow (\text{'}\mathit{rand} \times \text{'}\mathit{msg})\ \mathit{spmf} \tag{3}$$

$$\mathit{challenge} :: \text{'}\mathit{challenge}\ \mathit{spmf} \tag{4}$$

$$\mathit{response} :: \text{'}\mathit{rand} \Rightarrow \text{'}\mathit{witness} \Rightarrow \text{'}\mathit{challenge} \Rightarrow \text{'}\mathit{response}\ \mathit{spmf} \tag{5}$$

$$\mathit{check} :: \text{'}\mathit{pub\_input} \Rightarrow \text{'}\mathit{msg} \Rightarrow \text{'}\mathit{challenge} \Rightarrow \text{'}\mathit{response} \Rightarrow \mathit{bool}\ \mathit{spmf} \tag{6}$$

The challenge sent by V is defined as a random sampling (see [9]) therefore it needs no inputs here.

It is interesting to note, unlike many paper based definitions, none of our algorithms in the formalisation need take random coins as input. This is because they are already probabilistic programs and thus not deterministic by definition.

The three properties that define a Σ-protocol are completeness, special soundness and honest verifier zero-knowledge (HVZK). Special soundness ensures the prover cannot prove a false statement and HVZK says the verifier learns nothing of the witness that it cannot learn from the output of the verification and the public input.

Definition 2. *Assume the protocol run between P and V has the above form then it is said to be a Σ-protocol if the following properties hold:*

- *Completeness: if P and V follow the protocol on public input h and private input w such that $R(h, w)$ is satisfied, then V always accepts.*

$$complete(h, w) \equiv R(h, w) \longrightarrow \mathcal{P}[complete\_game(h, w) = True] = 1$$

- *Special soundness: there exists an adversary, $\mathcal{A}$ such that when given a pair of accepting conversations (on public input h) (a, e, z) and (a, e', z') where $e \neq e'$ it can compute w such that $R(h, w)$ is satisfied.*

$$s\_soundness(h, w) \equiv$$
$$\exists \mathcal{A}.\ R(h, w) \longrightarrow \mathcal{P}[s\_soundness\_game(h, w, \mathcal{A}) = True] = 1$$

- *Honest verifier Zero-Knowledge: There exists a simulator S that on input h and challenge e outputs an accepting conversation (a, e, z) with the same probability distribution as the real conversations (real_view) between P and V on input (h, w).*

$$HVZK(h, w) \equiv R(h, w) \longrightarrow (real\_view(h, w) = challenge \triangleright (\lambda e.S(h, e)))$$

In the literature the adversary for the special soundness definition and the simulator in the HVZK definition must run in polynomial time. There are challenges in formalising this notion, therefore we visually verify that the adversaries we construct for special soundness run in polynomial time and do not provide a formalisation of this property.

We define the probabilistic program *complete_game* to run the components of the protocol in an honest way. In particular we define a probabilistic program that takes as input (h, w), and then runs the four probabilistic programs of the protocol as would be done in the protocol, finally outputting the output of *check*.

The probabilistic program *s_soundness_game* is slightly more subtle. The game takes as input $(h, w, \mathcal{A})$ and must construct two accepting views to give to the adversary. The condition on these views is that the challenge in the second view must be different to that of the first. On paper this is easy to reason about as it can be considered to be intuitive but formally we must work harder. We define a new probabilistic program, $snd\_challenge(e)$, that outputs a challenge different from the original. For example, for the Schnorr protocol the challenge is a uniform sample from the field. Consequently the second challenge must uniformly sample from all elements of the field modulo the first challenge p,

$$snd\_challenge(q, p) = uniform(\{.. < q\} - \{p\}) \tag{7}$$

We must then prove all properties we required of *challenge* with respect to the new definition.

In the honest verifier zero knowledge property the real view is a probabilistic program that defines the real view (i.e., the protocol) transcript of the execution, that is (a, e, z). Intuitively if one can simulate the real view then we know there is no leakage of data, in this case the witness, during an execution of the protocol. We note that unlike previous work on the simulation based proof method [7] in MPC where the real view could only be defined in the instantiation due to different protocol structures, here we can define it solely from the algorithms used in the Σ-protocol. Both the special soundness game and the definition of the real view can be seen in Fig. 2.

Having made the above definitions we can define Σ-protocols formally as follows.

Definition 3

$$\Sigma\text{-}protocol(h, w) = complete(h, w) \wedge s\_soundness(h, w) \wedge HVZK(h, w)$$

Referring back to the diagram in Fig. 1 we can see we have completed the work for the 'Abstract Σ-protocol' box.

$$\begin{array}{l} special\_soundness\_game(h, w, \mathcal{A}) = do\ \{ \\ \quad (r, a) \leftarrow init(h, w); \\ \quad e \leftarrow challenge; \\ \quad z \leftarrow response(r, w, e); \\ \quad e' \leftarrow snd\_challenge(e); \\ \quad z' \leftarrow response(r, w, e'); \\ \quad w' \leftarrow \mathcal{A}(h, (a, e, z), (a, e', z')); \\ \quad return(w = w')\} \end{array}$$

$$\begin{array}{l} real\_view(h, w) = do\ \{ \\ \quad (r, a) \leftarrow init(h, w); \\ \quad e \leftarrow challenge; \\ \quad z \leftarrow response(r, w, e); \\ \quad return(a, e, z)\} \end{array}$$

Fig. 2. Definitions of the special soundness game and the real view for Σ-protocols.

5 Formalising the Schnorr Σ-Protocol

In this section we describe the proof of security of the Schnorr Σ-protocol. We also formalise the proof of security for a second Σ-protocol that is based on the equality of discrete logs [9]. The relation for this protocol can be seen in Eq. 8, where g' is a second generator of the cyclic group G.

$$R((h, h'), w) = \{h = g^w \wedge h' = g'^w \wedge w < |G|\} \tag{8}$$

In the interest of space here we only detail the formalisation of the Schnorr protocol. Here we provide more details of the formalisation than in other parts of the paper as well as a higher level commentary.

5.1 The Schnorr Σ-protocol

The Schnorr protocol uses a cyclic group G with generator g and considers the discrete log relation, R_{DL}, that can be seen in Eq. 2. The protocol is given in Fig. 3. The notation $\xleftarrow{\$}$ denotes uniform sampling while we use $\leftarrow$ to denote assignment.

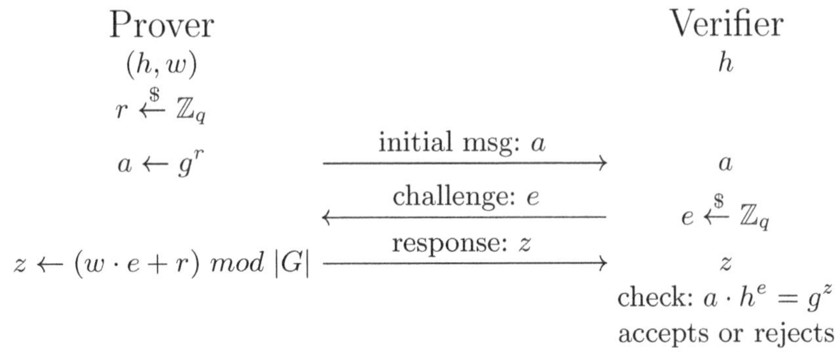

Fig. 3. The Schnorr Σ-protocol.

We consider the three properties that define a Σ-protocol in turn.

Completeness comes directly by unfolding the definitions and proving the identity $g^r \otimes (g^w)^e = g^{r+w*e}$. This is trivial, but provides Isabelle with a hint as to how to rewrite the definitions to dismiss the completeness proof.

Theorem 1. *Assume $R_{DL}(h, w)$ then*

$$\mathcal{P}[completeness\_game(h, w) = True] = 1$$

Secondly we must prove special soundness. To prove this we must construct an adversary that can extract the witness from two correct executions of the protocol. The special soundness adversary is given in Fig. 4.

$$
\begin{aligned}
&\mathcal{A}_{ss}(h, c_1, c_2) = do\ \{\\
&\quad let\ (a, e, z) = c1;\\
&\quad let\ (a', e', z') = c_2;\\
&\quad return(if\ e > e'\ then\ (z - z') * (fst(bezw((e - e'), |G|))\ mod\ |G|)\\
&\qquad\qquad\qquad else\ (z' - z) * (fst(bezw((e' - e), |G|))\ mod\ |G|))\}
\end{aligned}
$$

Fig. 4. The adversary used to prove special soundness for the Schnorr Σ-protocol. Note the output is equivalent to $\frac{z-z'}{e-e'}$. In the proof of Theorem 2 we have $a = a'$ for the messages given to the adversary.

We highlight an important contribution of our work here. The output of $\mathcal{A}_{ss}$ appears complex but actually is equivalent to $\mathcal{A}_{ss}$ outputting $\frac{z-z'}{e-e'}$ in the field. The output uses Bezout's function (*bezw*) for finding a pair of witnesses for Bezout's theorem to realise the inverse of $e - e'$. This function is given in the Isabelle number theory library.

The reason we could not define the adversary as outputting a simple division is worthy of some technical discussion. The inputs to the division are of type natural and thus any output from the division is also required to be of the same type as we are working in a field. However the output type of a division on naturals in Isabelle is a real number. Thus we must work around to output the correct value as a natural. The condition on $e > e'$ is such that the denominator is never negative as we are working with naturals. While this may look like an unnatural solution to the issue it is an effective one, and the work we provide here can be used by others when this problem arises again (it almost certainly will as division in a field is not uncommon in cryptography!). To allow us to work with an adversary defined in such a way we must prove lemmas of the form:

Lemma 1. *Assume* $a, b, w, y < |G|$, $a \neq b$ *and* $w \neq 0$ *then*

$$w = (\mathit{if}\ (a > b)\ \mathit{then}((w * a + y) - (w * b + y)) * \mathit{fst}(\mathit{bezw}((a - b), |G|) \quad (9)$$
$$\mathit{else}((w * b + y) - (w * a + y)) * \mathit{fst}(\mathit{bezw}((b - a), |G|)$$

The proof of Lemma 1 is quite involved however lemmas we require for other instances follow a similar proof method. We also prove a general lemma to compute divisions in a finite field, this is given in Lemma 2.

Lemma 2. *Assume* $gcd(a, |G|) = 1$ *then*

$$[a * \mathit{fst}(\mathit{bezw}(a, |G|)) = 1](\mathit{mod}|G|)$$

To apply statements such as Lemma 1 we often have to employ congruence rules. These allow the simplifier to use the context, in particular here on facts pertaining to the bound variables in the probabilistic programs that are required as assumptions. Using these methods we can prove special soundness.

Theorem 2. *Assume* $R(h, w)$ *then we have*

$$\mathcal{P}[\mathit{specical\_soundness\_game}(h, w, \mathcal{A}_{ss}) = \mathit{True}] = 1$$

Finally we must prove honest verifier zero knowledge. This requires us to define the real view of the protocol and show that there exists a simulator that takes as input the public input and a challenge and outputs a view that is indistinguishable from (equal as probability distributions) the real view. This technique follows the technique of simulation based proofs that was formally introduced in Isabelle in [7]. The probabilistic program defining the simulator along with the unfolded definition of the real view is given in Fig. 5.

To show HVZK we prove the two views are equal. That is,

Theorem 3. *Assume* $R_{DL}(h, w)$ *then we have*

$$\mathit{real\_view}(h, w) = (\mathit{challenge} \triangleright (\lambda e.\ S(h, e)))$$

In the definitions given in Fig. 5 the number of random samples is different in each view. We note that the extra sampling for the simulation comes from the challenge which, by definition is sampled before being given to the simulator. To prove honest verifier zero knowledge we manipulate the real view into a form where we can use Eq. 10, that describes a one time pad for addition in the field.

$$\mathit{map}(\lambda b.\ (y + b)\ \mathit{mod}\ q,\ \mathit{uniform}(q)) = \mathit{uniform}(q) \quad (10)$$

$$
\begin{array}{ll}
\mathit{real\_view}(h, w) = \mathit{do}\ \{ & S(h, e) = \mathit{do}\ \{ \\
\quad r \leftarrow \mathit{uniform}(|G|); & \quad c \leftarrow \mathit{uniform}(|G|); \\
\quad \mathit{let}(r, a) = (r, g^r); & \quad \mathit{let}\ a = g^c \otimes (h^e)^{-1}; \\
\quad c \leftarrow \mathit{uniform}(|G|); & \quad \mathit{return}\ (a, e, z)\} \\
\quad \mathit{let}\ z = (w * c + r)\ \mathit{mod}\ |G|; & \\
\quad \mathit{return}\ (a, c, z)\} &
\end{array}
$$

Fig. 5. The unfolded real view and simulator for the Schnorr protocol

To do this we must prove some basic identities about groups that provide Isabelle with hints as to rewrite the probabilistic programs. After proving the three properties we can show that the Schnorr protocol satisfies the definition of a Σ-protocol.

Theorem 4. *For the Schnorr Σ-protocol we have*

$$\Sigma\text{-}\mathit{protocol}(h, w).$$

6 Formalising Commitment Schemes

In this section we introduce our formalisation of commitment schemes and their security properties. Commitment schemes are a cryptographic primitive, run between a committer C and a verifier V, that allow the committer to commit to a chosen message, while keeping it private, and at a later time reveal the message that was committed to. For more details on commitment schemes we refer the reader to [20].

There are three phases to a commitment scheme:

1. Key generation, The key generation algorithm generates keys and sends them to both P and V respectively.
2. Commitment phase, The committer sends the verifier its committed value (or commitment), c, for the message m—the committer also computes an opening value, d, for the commitment that will be used to convince the verifier in the next stage.
3. Verification phase, The committer sends the verifier the message m and an opening value, d, with which the verifier can verify that the original committed message was m.

We formally model the three phases by fixing the types of three probabilistic programs (*key_gen*, *commit*, *verify*), seen in the locale given in Fig. 6.

The key generation algorithm outputs the keys available to the committer (ck) and the verifier (vk) respectively. If all the keys are public then we have $ck = vk$. We also fix two predicates abstractly which are needed in concrete instances later; *valid_msg* checks if a message is valid or not and $\mathcal{A}$*_cond* provides the conditions that we require from an adversary in the binding game. A paper proof can easily dismiss the adversary as failing if these conditions are not met,

```
locale abstract_com =
  fixes key_gen :: ('ck × 'vk) spmf
  and commit :: 'ck ⇒ 'plain ⇒ ('com × 'open) spmf
  and verify :: 'vk ⇒ 'plain ⇒ 'com ⇒ 'open ⇒ bool spmf
  and valid_msg :: 'plain ⇒ bool
  and 𝒜_cond :: 'com ⇒ 'plain ⇒ 'open ⇒ 'plain ⇒ 'open ⇒ bool
```

```
correct_game m = do {
  (ck, vk) ← key_gen;
  (c, d) ← commit(ck, m);
  b ← verify(vk, m, c, d);
  return b}
```

```
binding_game 𝒜 = TRY do {
  (ck, vk) ← key_gen;
  (c, m, d, m', d') ← 𝒜(ck);
  _ ← assert(𝒜_cond(c, m, d, m', d'));
  b ← verify(vk, m, c, d);
  b' ← verify(vk, m', c, d');
  return(b ∧ b')} ELSE return False
```

```
hiding_game (𝒜1, 𝒜2) = TRY do {
  (ck, vk) ← key_gen;
  ((m0, m1), σ) ← 𝒜1(vk);
  _ ← assert(valid_msg(m0) ∧ valid_msg(m1));
  b ← coin;
  (c, d) ← commit(ck, (if b then m1 else m2));
  b' ← 𝒜2(c, σ);
  return(b = b')} ELSE coin
```

Fig. 6. Abstract commitment scheme locale and definitions.

however formally we must catch this in the semantics. In fact these predicates serve another purpose too; they allow us to use the properties captured by the predicates in our reasoning at a later point in the proof. For example, for m to be a valid message we may require $m \in G$, this fact is then known to Isabelle for later use (e.g when applying Eq. 11).

6.1 Properties of Commitment Schemes

There are two main properties associated with commitment schemes: the hiding and binding properties. We note we consider a third property of correctness also, the need for this is explained at the end of the section.

Hiding. Intuitively, the hiding property is that no adversary can distinguish two committed messages. To define the hiding property we define the *hiding game* between an adversary, $\mathcal{A}$, and a benign challenger. The formal game can be seen in Fig. 6. The game asks the adversary to output two messages, one of which is committed to by the challenger and the corresponding commitment handed back to the adversary. The adversary is then asked to guess which message was committed to. The adversary wins the game if they correctly output which message was committed and handed to them.

Using the hiding game we can define the hiding advantage.

Definition 4. *The hiding advantage is the probability an adversary has of winning the hiding game.*

$$hiding\_advantage(\mathcal{A}) \equiv \mathcal{P}[hiding\_game(\mathcal{A}) = True]$$

Using this we can define perfect hiding, which holds for the Pedersen commitment scheme.

Definition 5. *For perfect hiding we require*

$$perfect\_hiding(\mathcal{A}) \equiv (hiding\_advantage(\mathcal{A}) = \frac{1}{2})$$

Binding. The binding property ensures that the committer cannot change her mind and change the message she has committed to. Again a security game is used (see Fig. 6). We challenge the adversary to bind two messages (m, m') and two opening values (d, d') to the same commitment c.

Similar to the hiding property we define the binding advantage:

Definition 6. *The binding advantage is the probability an adversary has of winning the binding game.*

$$binding\_advantage(\mathcal{A}) \equiv \mathcal{P}[binding\_game(\mathcal{A}) = True]$$

To show computational binding we must show the binding advantage is a negligible function with respect to the security parameter. This result can only be shown in the asymptotic setting as it requires an explicit security parameter. In the concrete setting we can show a reduction to a known hard problem (for the Pedersen scheme this is the discrete logarithm problem). We can then extend to the asymptotic setting. See Sect. 8.1 for more details on our proofs in the asymptotic setting.

Correctness. There is one subtlety to the binding definition meaning we must consider correctness also. If the verifier always outputs false, the binding property is met as the adversary will never win the game.

Correctness is the property that, assuming honest parties, a commitment will be verified as true by the verifier. Analogously to the hiding and binding properties we use the correctness game to define correctness.

Definition 7

$$correct(m) \equiv (\mathcal{P}[correct\_game(m) = True] = 1)$$

7 The Pedersen Commitment Scheme

In this section we discuss our formalisation of the Pedersen commitment scheme. We do not discuss the proofs in detail, but instead provide the formal results and a discussion of the interesting aspects learned from the proof.

The protocol, given in Fig. 7, is run using a cyclic group of prime order G with generator g.

Intuitively, the hiding property is observed because the message, m, is not sent explicitly, but is masked by the uniform sample, g^d (in $g^d.pk^m$). Consequently the verifier cannot distinguish between two committed messages. The property of binding is more subtle. If the adversary can bind two messages to the same committed value, then the adversary can also compute the discrete log of pk, which is in violation of the discrete log assumption which is considered hard. Correctness is immediate; the committed value, c, is $g^d.pk^m$, the verifier accepts the message if (m, d), sent by the committer is such that $g^d.pk^m = c$.

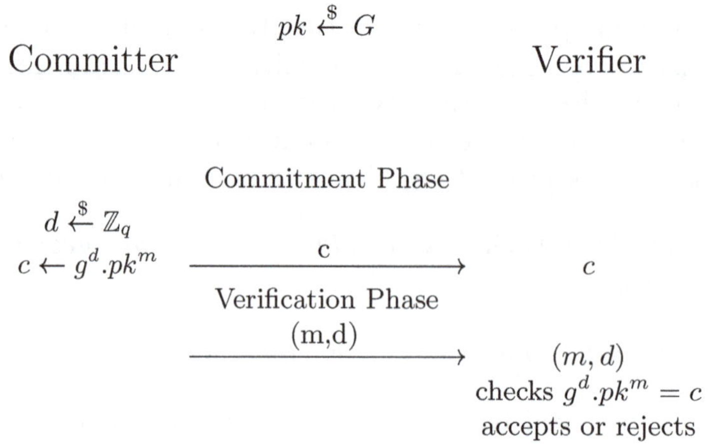

Fig. 7. The Pedersen commitment protocol.

7.1 Formal Proofs for the Pedersen Protocol

We fix a finite cyclic group, G, with generator, g, and order, $|G|$ and explicitly define the probabilistic programs that define the protocol.

Perfect Hiding. Lemma 3 shows that we have perfect hiding for the Pedersen commitment scheme.

Lemma 3. *For the Pedersen commitment scheme we have*

$$\mathcal{P}[(hiding\_game(\mathcal{A})) = True] = \frac{1}{2}$$

The security of the hiding property comes from applying the OTP lemma:

$$c \in carrier\ G \Rightarrow map((\lambda x.\ g^x \otimes c), (uniform(|G|))) = map((\lambda x.\ g^x), uniform(|G|))). \tag{11}$$

The work needed to apply the one time pad Lemma is in showing that $c \in carrier\ G$. To do this requires the use of some congruence lemmas as the property of membership of the carrier group arises from conditions on bound variables. Applying the one time pad Lemma shows the value given to the adversary is independent of m_b. Consequently the output from the adversary can be nothing more than a guess, in other words, the adversary may as well flip a coin to decide its output.

Computational Binding and Correctness. To prove the binding property we show a reduction to the discrete logarithm assumption. Hardness assumptions are a cornerstone of cryptography so we take a moment to consider how it may be formal used. One can follow a similar pattern for defining other hardness assumptions, for example see how the DDH assumption is defined in [16].

We first define the task of the adversary and then the advantage associated to the adversary. In the case of the discrete log assumption we simply provide the adversary with g^x where x is uniformly sampled and ask it to output x. We formalise such a situation as a game between the adversary and a challenger in Fig. 8.

$$
\begin{array}{l}
\mathit{dis\_log\_game}(\mathcal{A}) \ = do\ \{ \\
\quad x \leftarrow \mathit{sample\_uniform}(|G|); \\
\quad \mathit{let}\ h = g^x; \\
\quad x' \leftarrow \mathcal{A}(h); \\
\quad \mathit{return}(x = x')\}
\end{array}
$$

Fig. 8. The discrete log game.

We then define the associated advantage of the adversary when playing this game—the probability of it winning the game.

Definition 8. $\mathit{dis\_log\_advantage}(\mathcal{A}) \equiv \mathcal{P}[(\mathit{dis\_log\_game}(\mathcal{A})) = \mathit{True}]$

To prove binding we construct an adversary, $\mathit{dis\_log\_\mathcal{A}}$, using the adversary $\mathcal{A}$ that plays the binding game and show it has the same advantage against the discrete log game as $\mathcal{A}$ has against the binding game. Our adversary here takes a similar form as that used in the proof of special soundness for the Schnorr protocol. Using this we can show Lemma 4 which easily shows Theorem 5.

Lemma 4

$$\mathit{bind\_game}(\mathcal{A}) = \mathit{dis\_log\_game}(\mathit{dis\_log\_\mathcal{A}}(\mathcal{A}))$$

Theorem 5

$$\mathit{bind\_advantage}(\mathcal{A}) = \mathit{dis\_log\_advantage}(\mathcal{A})$$

Finally we prove the correctness of the Pedersen scheme. This result comes easily after proving some group identities in Isabelle.

Theorem 6. *We have*

$$\mathcal{P}[(\mathit{correct\_game}(m)) = \mathit{True}] = 1.$$

8 Using Σ-Protocols to Construct Commitment Schemes

In [8], it was shown how commitment schemes can be constructed from Σ-protocols. One can use the components of a Σ-protocol, for a relation R, to form a commitment scheme as follows:

Key Generation. The keys are generated such that the verifier receives $(h, w) \in R$ that satisfy R and the committer receives only h.

Commit. The committer runs the simulator on their key h and the message, m, they wish to commit. That is they run

$$(a, e, z) \leftarrow S(h, m)$$

and sends a to the verifier and keeps e and z as the opening values.

Verify. In the verification stage the prover sends e and z to the verifier who uses the check algorithm of the Σ-protocol to confirm that (a, e, z) is an accepting conversation, with respect to the private key w.

We recall that in the *Commit* stage we have $e = m$. The resulting commitment scheme can be shown to be perfectly hiding and computationally binding. Intuitively perfect hiding comes from the fact that the simulation is perfect (the simulated and real views are equal) and that the initial message is not dependent on the challenge. Binding holds as if a prover could output two sets of opening values, (e, z) and (e', z'), for one commitment a such that $e \neq e'$ then (a, e, z) and (a, e', z) would both be accepting conversations and by the special soundness property we could compute w, but this contradicts the hardness assumption on R. We formally prove these results in Isabelle for the commitment scheme constructed from the Schnorr Σ-protocol.

To formalise this in Isabelle we again explicitly define the constants required for commitment schemes. We define these using the constants defined for the Schnorr Σ-protocol. This requires us to import both locales (for commitment schemes and Σ-protocols) and prove all assumptions relating to them. We are then able to prove perfect hiding, computational binding and correctness of the resulting commitment scheme. In the concrete setting we show a reduction of the binding property to the discrete logarithm assumption.

Theorem 7. *For the commitment scheme constructed from the Schnorr protocol we have*

$$\mathcal{P}[correct\_game(m) = True] = 1$$

$$\mathcal{P}[hiding\_game(\mathcal{A}) = True] = \frac{1}{2}$$

$$\mathcal{P}[bind\_game(\mathcal{A}) = True] = \mathcal{P}[dis\_log(dis\_log\_\mathcal{A}(\mathcal{A})) = True]$$

This result has taken an instantiated Σ-protocol, used its components to instantiate a commitment scheme and proven this secure with respect the definitions we formalised for commitment schemes.

8.1 Asymptotic Case

So far in our formalisation the security parameter has been assumed to be implicit in all algorithms (probabilistic programs). In this section we show how we formalise proofs in the asymptotic setting using as an example the commitment scheme we have just constructed using the Schnorr Σ-protocol. In our formalisation we provide proofs in the asymptotic setting for all instantiations.

The asymptotic setting is particularly interesting in the case of commitment schemes as we can consider computational binding; a full proof will show the adversary has only negligible chance of winning the binding game.

To realise such a proof we parametrise over the family of cyclic groups, specifically we change the type from *'grp cyclic_group* to *nat* ⇒ *'grp cyclic_group*. Thus the cyclic group is parametrised by the security parameter—a natural. After importing the concrete setting parametrically for all n, all algorithms now depend explicitly on the security parameter. Moreover, due to Isabelle's module structure we are able to use results proven in the concrete setting in our newly constructed asymptotic setting. It is worth noting that results from the concrete setting can only be used once it has been proven that the import is valid, something the user is required to do when importing a module.

The properties, in the asymptotic case, for correctness and hiding can be seen in Theorem 8. Superficially, the only difference is the security parameter is an input to every statement and function. At a deeper level the proof uses the equivalent theorems from the concrete setting and the module machinery to dismiss the proof.

Theorem 8. *In the asymptotic case, for security parameter, n, we have:*

- $\mathcal{P}[correct\_game(n, msg) = True] = 1$
- $\mathcal{P}[hiding\_game(n, (\mathcal{A}(n))) = True] = \frac{1}{2}$.

The more interesting case is the proof of computational binding as we are required to show the binding advantage is negligible. In the concrete setting (Theorem 7) we showed we could construct an adversary that had the same advantage against the discrete log problem as the binding game. In the asymptotic setting we are able to assume that the discrete logarithm assumption holds; that an adversary only has a negligible chance of winning the discrete log game. Using this we can prove that the binding advantage too is negligible. This is shown in Theorem 9.

Theorem 9

$$negligible\ (\lambda n.\ bind\_advantage\ n\ (\mathcal{A}\ n)) \Longleftrightarrow \\ negligible\ (\lambda n.\ dis\_log\_advantage\ n\ (dis\_log\_\mathcal{A}\ n\ (\mathcal{A}\ n)))$$

Our formalisation provides proofs in the asymptotic case for all relevant properties presented in this paper in a similar manner as described above. We refer the reader to our formalisation for more details.

9 Conclusions

In this work we have demonstrated that commitment schemes and Σ-protocols can be formally proved secure in the computational model using a general abstract framework. Our work uses Isabelle/HOL and its modularity mechanisms, but in principle could be replicated in other interactive theorem provers.

The abstract frameworks can be used by others to formalise new commitment schemes and Σ-protocols. The advantages of reasoning back to the same general framework is that one can be sure the correct properties and definitions are being considered. This consistency is not always apparent in informal cryptographic proofs. We suggest that cryptographic advances should be monitored within a formal framework where one is required to use the exact definitions set out formally (the proof could be done on pen and paper) or provide a formal proof that the chosen definitions are equivalent. This will help alleviate the abundance of small differences in definitional approaches which undermine the field.

At the present state-of-the-art, prototyping this approach in an interactive theorem prover seems essential as it allows one to explore the reasoning and definition principles which are most effective in the domain. Eventually we may hope that bespoke foundational reasoning tools could be built which may be more usable by applied cryptographers (as is the aim of EasyCrypt, although it is not foundational).

One major advantage of our framework being implemented in Isabelle is that we can benefit from the vast infrastructure that comes with a well developed theorem prover, in contrast with custom made tools. We benefit from the interactive nature of Isabelle meaning users have flexibility but also the high level of automation and many proof engines available.

While CryptHOL and thus our framework still require a high level of specific interactive theorem proving knowledge to use, new features are being developed that make it more usable by the working cryptographer. For example recent work in Isabelle [19], monad normalisation, has made handling the commuting of samplings, a previously technical and subtle exercise, more simple. As more features like this automate the intricate details needed in proofs the barrier to entry to using CryptHOL will be significantly reduced.

Future Work. The frameworks we provide here can be used and instantiated to give formal proofs of new commitment schemes and Σ-protocols. Both of these primitives are used to provide security in the malicious model, consequently we see this work as a building block to further formal proofs here.

10 Related Work

Little work has been done on formalising the computational model, compared to the symbolic model. It is challenging as it requires mathematical reasoning about probabilities and failure events, besides logic. The CertiCrypt [3] tool built in Coq helped to capture the reasoning principles that were implemented directly in the dedicated interactive EasyCrypt tool [4]. Again in Coq, the Foundational Cryptographic Framework [18] provides a definitional language for probabilistic programs, a theory that is used to reason about programs, and a library of tactics for game-based proofs.

CryptHOL [6], formalised in Isabelle, has been used in the game-based setting [16], as well as the simulation-based paradigm [7]. Isabelle is a foundational framework that relies on a set of accepted consistent axioms [10,13] and thus provides a high guarantee of correctness in proofs.

The Pedersen commitment scheme has been proved secure in EasyCrypt in [17]. One noticeable difference between the proof effort required is in the construction of the adversary used to prove computational binding. We had to work hard in Isabelle to give the output of the adversary in the binding game as a division of two elements in the finite field. We are required to prove extra properties of the Bezout function whereas the division can be easily expressed in EasyCrypt.

10.1 Comparison with EasyCrypt

EasyCrypt is considered the state of the art in terms of proof assistants for cryptography; it was designed as a dedicated tool for the working cryptographer. It has a larger user base than CryptHOL, partially due to it having been developed a number of years before and its greater support and documentation. The barrier to entry to using EasyCrypt is lower in comparison to Isabelle. We argue however that there is room for more than one proof assistant when considering cryptographic proof; in fact we suggest that it is essential to the development of formal proof in this area. Growth in an area of research is rarely achieved by considering only one approach; different proof assistants allow for different proof styles and thus different insights into the cryptographic proofs at a fundamental level.

One such difference in approach is the ability to follow paper proofs explicitly. Isabelle's deep and extensive foundations in mathematical logic meaning there is a large amount of machinery available to the user when completing proofs. This allows one to more closely follow the proof method given in the paper proof. In EasyCrypt sometimes this is not possible. For example in [11] the authors had to prove on paper that the security definitions they formalised were equivalent to the traditional definitions in the literature. At a technical level this is because the proof technique in EasyCrypt is often to reduce proofs to showing properties about the equivalence of programs. This is not necessarily a weakness of EasyCrypt, as it allows for new insights into proof techniques but it highlights a difference between the two systems.

Finally, when using CryptHOL in Isabelle all proofs are checked with respect the same logical core. That is, the whole CryptHOL framework resides within Isabelle. However, some fundamental properties in EasyCrypt are outsourced to be proven in Coq. Thus one could consider the approach of CryptHOL and Isabelle to be more foundational.

Acknowledgements. We are grateful to Andreas Lochbihler for providing and continuing to develop CryptHOL and for his kind help given with using it.

References

1. https://github.com/alan-turing-institute/Crypto-Commit-Sigma-Isabelle
2. Bacelar Almeida, J., Barbosa, M., Bangerter, E., Barthe, G., Krenn, S., Zanella Béguelin, S.: Full proof cryptography: verifiable compilation of efficient zero-knowledge protocols. In: ACM Conference on Computer and Communications Security, pp. 488–500. ACM (2012)
3. Barthe, G., Grégoire, B., Zanella Béguelin, S.: Formal certification of code-based cryptographic proofs. In: POPL, pp. 90–101. ACM (2009)
4. Barthe, G., Grégoire, B., Heraud, S., Zanella Béguelin, S.: Computer-aided security proofs for the working cryptographer. In: Rogaway, P. (ed.) CRYPTO 2011. LNCS, vol. 6841, pp. 71–90. Springer, Heidelberg (2011). https://doi.org/10.1007/978-3-642-22792-9_5
5. Barthe, G., Hedin, D., Zanella Béguelin, S., Grégoire, B., Heraud, S.: A machine-checked formalization of sigma-protocols. In: CSF, pp. 246–260. IEEE Computer Society (2010)
6. Basin, D.A., Lochbihler, A., Sefidgar, S.R.: CryptHOL: game-based proofs in higher-order logic. IACR Cryptology ePrint Archive, p. 753 (2017)
7. Butler, D., Aspinall, D., Gascón, A.: How to simulate it in Isabelle: towards formal proof for secure multi-party computation. In: Ayala-Rincón, M., Muñoz, C.A. (eds.) ITP 2017. LNCS, vol. 10499, pp. 114–130. Springer, Cham (2017). https://doi.org/10.1007/978-3-319-66107-0_8
8. Damgard, I.: On Σ-protocols. Lecture Notes, University of Aarhus, Department for Computer Science (2002)
9. Damgård, I.: Commitment schemes and zero-knowledge protocols. In: Damgård, I.B. (ed.) EEF School 1998. LNCS, vol. 1561, pp. 63–86. Springer, Heidelberg (1999). https://doi.org/10.1007/3-540-48969-X_3
10. Gordon, M.J.C., Melham, T.F.: Introduction to HOL a Theorem Proving Environment for Higher Order Logic. Cambridge University Press, New York (1993)
11. Haagh, H., Karbyshev, A., Oechsner, S., Spitters, B., Strub, P.-Y.: Computer-aided proofs for multiparty computation with active security. In: CSF, pp. 119–131. IEEE Computer Society (2018)
12. Halevi, S.: A plausible approach to computer-aided cryptographic proofs. IACR Cryptology ePrint Archive 2005:181 (2005)
13. Kunčar, O., Popescu, A.: A consistent foundation for Isabelle/HOL. In: Urban, C., Zhang, X. (eds.) ITP 2015. LNCS, vol. 9236, pp. 234–252. Springer, Cham (2015). https://doi.org/10.1007/978-3-319-22102-1_16
14. Lochbihler, A.: CryptHOL. Archive of Formal Proofs (2017)
15. Lochbihler, A.: Probabilistic functions and cryptographic oracles in higher order logic. In: Thiemann, P. (ed.) ESOP 2016. LNCS, vol. 9632, pp. 503–531. Springer, Heidelberg (2016). https://doi.org/10.1007/978-3-662-49498-1_20
16. Lochbihler, A., Sefidgar, S.R., Bhatt, B.: Game-based cryptography in HOL. Archive of Formal Proofs (2017)
17. Metere, R., Dong, C.: Automated cryptographic analysis of the Pedersen commitment scheme. In: Rak, J., Bay, J., Kotenko, I., Popyack, L., Skormin, V., Szczypiorski, K. (eds.) MMM-ACNS 2017. LNCS, vol. 10446, pp. 275–287. Springer, Cham (2017). https://doi.org/10.1007/978-3-319-65127-9_22
18. Petcher, A., Morrisett, G.: The foundational cryptography framework. In: Focardi, R., Myers, A. (eds.) POST 2015. LNCS, vol. 9036, pp. 53–72. Springer, Heidelberg (2015). https://doi.org/10.1007/978-3-662-46666-7_4

19. Schneider, J., Eberl, M., Lochbihler, A.: Monad normalisation. Archive of Formal Proofs (2017)
20. Smart, N.P.: Cryptography Made Simple. Information Security and Cryptography. Springer, Cham (2016). https://doi.org/10.1007/978-3-319-21936-3. https://www.cs.umd.edu/~waa/414-F11/IntroToCrypto

Check for updates

Orchestrating Layered Attestations

John D. Ramsdell[1(✉)], Paul D. Rowe[1], Perry Alexander[2], Sarah C. Helble[3], Peter Loscocco[4], J. Aaron Pendergrass[3], and Adam Petz[2]

[1] The MITRE Corporation, Bedford, USA
ramsdell@mitre.org
[2] The University of Kansas, Lawrence, USA
[3] John Hopkins University Applied Physics Laboratory, Laurel, USA
[4] National Security Agency, Fort Meade, USA

Abstract. We present COPLAND, a language for specifying layered attestations. Layered attestations provide a remote appraiser with structured evidence of the integrity of a target system to support a trust decision. The language is designed to bridge the gap between formal analysis of attestation security guarantees and concrete implementations. We therefore provide two semantic interpretations of terms in our language. The first is a denotational semantics in terms of partially ordered sets of events. This directly connects COPLAND to prior work on layered attestation. The second is an operational semantics detailing how the data and control flow are executed. This gives explicit implementation guidance for attestation frameworks. We show a formal connection between the two semantics ensuring that any execution according to the operational semantics is consistent with the denotational event semantics. This ensures that formal guarantees resulting from analyzing the event semantics will hold for executions respecting the operational semantics. All results have been formally verified with the Coq proof assistant.

1 Introduction

It is common to ask a particular target system whether it is trustworthy enough to engage in a given activity. Remote attestation is a useful technique to support such trust decisions in a wide variety of contexts. Fundamentally, remote attestation consists in generating *evidence* of a system's integrity via *measurements*, and *reporting* the evidence to a remote party for appraisal. Depending on their interpretation of the evidence, the remote appraiser can adjust their decision according to the level of risk they are willing to assume.

Others have recognized the insufficiency of coarse-grained measurements in supporting trust decisions [8,10,20,22]. Integrity evidence is typically either too broad or too narrow to provide useful information to an appraiser. Very broad evidence—such as patch levels for software—easily allows compromises to go undetected by attestation. Very narrow evidence—such as a combined hash of the complete trusted computing base—does not allow for natural variation across systems and over time.

F. Nielson and D. Sands (Eds.): POST 2019, LNCS 11426, pp. 197–221, 2019.
https://doi.org/10.1007/978-3-030-17138-4_9

An alternative approach is to build a global picture of system integrity by measuring a subset of system components and reasoning about their integrity individually and as a coherent whole. This approach can give an appraiser a more nuanced view of the target system's state because it can isolate integrity violations, telling the appraiser exactly which portions of the system can or cannot be trusted. We call this approach *layered attestation* because protected isolation frequently built into systems (e.g. hypervisor-enforced separation of virtual machines) allows the attestation to build the global picture of integrity from the bottom up, one layer at a time. A layered attestation whose structure mimics the layered dependency structure of a target system can provide strong trust guarantees. In prior work, we have formally proved that "bottom-up" strategies for layered attestation force an adversary to either corrupt well-protected components or work within small time-of-check-time-of-use windows [17,18].

The "bottom-up" principle has been embodied in many attestation systems (e.g. [2,6,7,10,22]). A common tactic in these papers is to design the target system and the attestation protocol in tandem to ensure the structure of the attestation corresponds to the structure of the system. This results in solutions that are too rigid and overly prescriptive. The solutions do not translate to other systems with different structures.

In previous work, members of our team have taken a different approach. Maat is a policy-based measurement and attestation (M&A) framework which provides a centralized, pluggable service to gather and report integrity measurements [16]. Maat listens for attestation requests and can act as both an appraiser and an attester, depending on the needs of the current scenario. After a request for appraisal is received, the Maat instance on the appraiser system contacts and negotiates with the attesting system's Maat instance to agree upon the set of evidence that must be provided for the scenario. Thus Maat provides a flexible set of capabilities that can be tailored to the needs of any given situation. It is therefore a much more extensible attestation framework.

In early development of Maat, the negotiation was entirely based on a set of well-known UUIDs and was limited in flexibility, especially when Maat instances did not share a core set of measurement capabilities. We discovered that this approach to negotiation severely limited the extensibility of Maat. It is not sufficient to have a flexible set of attestation mechanisms—a flexible language for specifying layered attestations is crucial. This paper introduces such a language.

Contribution. We present Copland, a language and formal system for orchestrating layered attestations. Copland provides domain specific syntax for specifying attestation protocols, an operational semantics for guiding implementations, and a denotational semantics for reasoning and negotiation. We designed Copland with Maat in mind aiming to address three main requirements.

First, it must be flexible enough to accommodate the wide diversity of capabilities offered by Maat. Copland is parametric with respect to the basic actions that generate and process evidence (i.e. measurement and bundling). Since we cannot expect all platforms and architectures to have the same set of capabilities, Copland focuses instead on specifying the ways in which these pieces fit together. COPLAND programs, which we call *phrases* or *terms*, are built out of a small set of operators designed to orchestrate the activities of measurement agents across several layers of a target system.

Second, the language must have an unambiguous execution semantics. We provide a formal, operational semantics allowing a target to know precisely how to manage the flow of control and data throughout the attestation. This operational semantics serves as a correctness constraint for implementations, and generates traces of events that record the order in which actions occurred.

Finally, it must enable static analysis to determine the trust properties guaranteed by alternative phrases. For this purpose we provide a denotational semantics relating phrases to a partially ordered set of events. This semantics is explicitly designed to connect with our prior work on analytic principles of layered attestation [17,18]. By applying those principles in static analysis, both target and appraiser can write policies determining which phrases may be used in which situations based on the trust guarantees they provide.

Critically, we prove a strong connection between the operational execution semantics and the denotational event semantics. We show that any trace generated by the operational semantics is a linearization of the event partial ordering given by the denotational semantics. This ensures that any trust conclusions made from the event partial order are guaranteed to hold over the concrete execution. In particular, our previous work [17,18] characterizes what an adversary must do to avoid detection given a specific partial order of events, identifying strategies to force an adversary to work quickly in short time-of-check-time-of-use windows, or dig deeper into more protected layers of the system. This connection is particularly important in light of the flexibility of the language. Since our basic tenet is that a more constrained language is inherently of less value, it is crucial that we provide a link to analytic techniques that help people distinguish between good and bad ways to perform a layered attestations. We discuss this connection to our previous work in much more detail in Sect. 7.

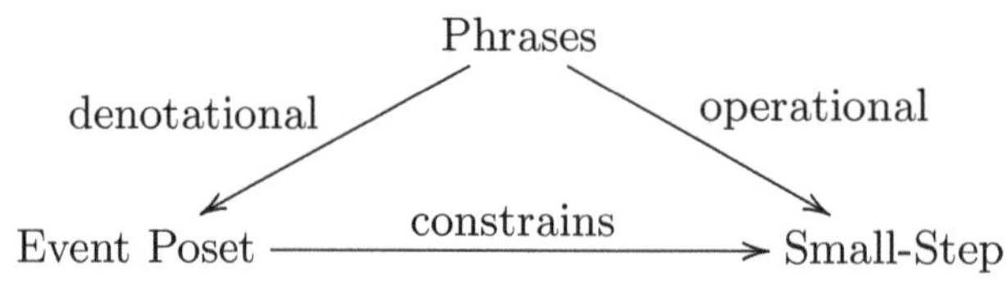

Fig. 1. Semantic relations

Figure 1 depicts the connections among our various contributions. It also provides a useful outline of the paper. Section 3 describes the syntax of COPLAND corresponding to the apex of the triangle in Fig. 1. Section 4 introduces events. Events are the foundation for both semantic notions depicted in Fig. 1. Each semantic notion constrains the event ordering in its own way. The denotational semantics of the left leg of the triangle is presented in Sect. 5, and the operational semantics of the right leg is given in Sect. 6. The crucial theorem connecting the two semantic notions is sketched in Sect. 7.

All lemmas and theorems stated in this paper have been formally verified using the Coq proof assistant [1]. The Coq proofs are available at https://ku-sldg.github.io/copland/. The notation used in this paper closely follows the Coq proofs. The tables in Appendix B link figures and formulas with their definitions in the Coq proofs.

Before jumping into the formal details of the syntax and semantics of Copland, however, we present a sequence of simple examples designed to give the reader a feel for the language and its purpose.

2 Examples of Layered Attestations

Consider an example of a corporate gateway that appraises machines before allowing them to join the corporate network. A simple attestation might entail a request for the machine to perform an asset inventory to ensure all software is up-to-date. For purposes of exposition, we may view this as an abstract userspace measurement USM that takes an argument list $\bar{a}_1$ of the enterprise software to inventory. We can express a request for a particular target p to perform this measurement with the following Copland phrase:

$$@_p\, \mathsf{USM}\ \bar{a}_1 \tag{1}$$

This says the measurement capability identifiable as USM should be executed at location identified by p using arguments $\bar{a}_1$. The request results in evidence of the form $\mathsf{U}_p(\xi)$ indicating the type of measurement performed, the target of the measurement p, and any previously generated evidence (in this case the empty evidence ξ) it received and combined with the newly generated evidence.

If the company is concerned with the assets in the inventory being undermined by a rootkit in the operating system kernel, it might require additional evidence that no such rootkit exists. This could be done by asking for a kernel integrity measurement KIM to be taken of the place p in addition to the userspace measurement. The request could be made with the following phrase:

$$@_p\, (\mathsf{KIM}\ p\ \bar{a}_2 \overset{(\bot,\bot)}{\sim} \mathsf{USM}\ \bar{a}_1) \tag{2}$$

In this notation, KIM $p\ \bar{a}_2$ represents a request for the KIM measurement capability to be applied to the target place p with arguments $\bar{a}_2$. The symbol $\overset{(\ell,r)}{\sim}$ indicates the two measurements may be taken concurrently. The annotation ℓ defines how evidence accumulated so far is transformed for use by the phrase on the left, and r for the one on the right. In the case of $(\bot, \bot)$, no evidence is sent in either direction. The evidence resulting from the two composed measurements has the form $\mathsf{K}^p_p(\xi) \parallel \mathsf{U}_p(\xi)$, where $\parallel$ indicates the measurements were invoked concurrently.

If the enterprise has configured their machines to have two layers of different privilege levels (say by virtualization), then they may wish to request that the kernel measurement be taken from a more protected location q. This results in the following request.

$$@_q\,(\mathsf{KIM}\ p\ \bar{a}_2 \overset{(\bot,\bot)}{\sim} @_p\,\mathsf{USM}\ \bar{a}_1) \tag{3}$$

Notice the kernel measurement target is still the kernel at p, but the request is now being made of the measurement capability located at q. The kernel measurement of p taken from q and the request for p to take a userspace measurement of its own environment can occur concurrently. The resulting evidence has the form $\mathsf{K}^p_q(\xi) \parallel \mathsf{U}_p(\xi)$, where the subscript q indicates the kernel measurement was taken from the vantage point of q, and the superscript p indicates the location of the kernel measurer's target. The subscript p in the second occurrence of the @ sign indicates that the userspace measurement is taken from location p.

Finally, consider two more changes to the request that makes the evidence more convincing. By measuring the kernel at p *before* the userspace measurement occurs, the appraiser can learn that the kernel was uncompromised at the time of the userspace measurement. This bottom-up strategy is common in approaches to layered attestation [17,22]. Additionally, an appraiser may wish each piece of evidence to be signed as a rudimentary chain of evidence. These can both be specified with the following phrase.

$$@_q\,((\mathsf{KIM}\ p\ \bar{a}_2 \rightarrow \mathsf{SIG}) \overset{(\bot,\bot)}{\prec} @_p\,(\mathsf{USM}\ \bar{a}_1 \rightarrow \mathsf{SIG})) \tag{4}$$

In this phrase, the $\prec$ symbol is used to request that the term on the left complete its execution before starting execution of the term on the right. The $\rightarrow$ symbol routes data from the term on the left to the term on the right, similar to function composition. In this case evidence coming from KIM and USM is routed to two separate instances of a digital signature primitive. Since these signatures occur at two different locations, they will use two different signing keys. The resulting evidence has the form $[\![\mathsf{K}^p_q(\xi)]\!]_q \;;;\; [\![\mathsf{U}_p(\xi)]\!]_p$, where ;; indicates the evidence was generated in sequence, and the square brackets represent signatures using the private key associated with the location identified by the subscript.

Copland provides a level of flexibility and explicitness that can be leveraged for more than the prescription of the evidence to be gathered. Using this common semantics, appraisers and attesters have the ability to negotiate *specific* measurement agents and targets to utilize to prove integrity. For example, if the measurement requested is computationally intensive, an attester may prefer to provide a cached version of the evidence. The appraiser may be willing to accept this cached version, depending on local policy. In this scenario, a negotiation would take place between the two systems to determine an agreeable set of terms. The appraiser could begin by requesting that Eq. (4) be performed by the target, which would then counter with a different phrase specifying cached instead of fresh measurement. Depending on the implementation, this difference could utilize an entirely separate measurement primitive (e.g., C_USM instead of USM) or merely a separate set of arguments to the primitive. The ability to specify the collection of previously generated evidence is especially important when gathering evidence created via a measured boot.

The actions taken to appraise evidence can also be defined by phrases and negotiated before the attestation takes place. If the target is willing to perform a measurement action but doesn't trust the appraiser with the result, the two parties could agree upon a mutually trusted third party to act as the appraiser.

3 Phrases

We begin with the basic syntax of phrases in COPLAND. Figure 2 defines the grammar of phrases (T) parameterized by atomic actions (A) and the type (E) of evidence they produce when evaluated. Figure 3 defines phrase evaluation. Each phrase specifies what measurements are taken, various operations on evidence, and where measurements and operations are performed. Phrases also specify orderings and dependencies among measurements and operations.

$$
\begin{aligned}
A &\leftarrow \mathsf{CPY} \mid \mathsf{USM}\ \bar{a} \mid \mathsf{KIM}\ P\ \bar{a} \mid \mathsf{SIG} \mid \mathsf{HSH} \mid \cdots \\
T &\leftarrow A \mid @_P\, T \mid (T \rightarrow T) \mid (T \overset{\pi}{\prec} T) \mid (T \overset{\pi}{\sim} T) \\
E &\leftarrow \xi \mid \mathsf{U}_P(E) \mid \mathsf{K}_P^P(E) \mid [\![E]\!]_P \mid \#_P\, E \mid (E \mathbin{;;} E) \mid (E \parallel E) \mid \cdots
\end{aligned}
$$

where $\pi = (\pi_1, \pi_2)$ is a pair of splitting functions.

Fig. 2. Phrase and evidence grammar

The atomic phrases either produce evidence via measurement, or transform evidence via computation. Some actions, like $\mathsf{USM}\ \bar{a}$, perform measurements of their associated place, while others, such as $\mathsf{KIM}\ q\ \bar{a}$, measure another place. A *userspace measurement*, $\mathsf{USM}\ \bar{a}$, measures the local environment. The term $@_p\, \mathsf{USM}\ \bar{a}$ requests that place p perform some measurement $\mathsf{USM}\ \bar{a}$ of its userspace. Such measurements may range from a simple file hash to complex run time analysis of an application. A *kernel integrity measurement*, $\mathsf{KIM}\ q\ \bar{a}$, measures another place. The term $@_p\, \mathsf{KIM}\ q\ \bar{a}$ requests that p perform a kernel measurement on place q. Such measurements measure one place from another and perform integrity measurements such as LKIM [14]. Starting from a trusted place p, $@_p\, \mathsf{KIM}\ q\ \bar{a}$ can gather evidence for establishing trust in q and transitively construct chains of trusted enclaves.

The COPLAND phrase $@_p\, t$ corresponds to the essential function of remote attestation—making a request of place p to execute a protocol term t. Places correspond with attestation managers that are capable of responding to attestation requests. Places may be as simple as an IoT device that returns a single value on request or as complicated as a full SELinux installation capable of complex protocol execution.

Evidence produced by $@_p\, \mathsf{USM}\ \bar{a}$ and $@_p\, \mathsf{KIM}\ q\ \bar{a}$ have types $\mathsf{U}_p(e)$ and $\mathsf{K}_p^q(e)$ respectively where p is the place performing measurement, q is the target place, and e is the type of incoming evidence. Place p is obtained from context specified by the $@_p\, t$ phrase invoking $\mathsf{KIM}\ q\ \bar{a}$. Notice that we work with dependent types.

The phrases $(t_1 \rightarrow t_2)$, $(t_1 \overset{\pi}{\prec} t_2)$, and $(t_1 \overset{\pi}{\sim} t_2)$ specify sequential and parallel composition of subterms. Phrase $(t_1 \rightarrow t_2)$ evaluates two terms in sequence, passing the evidence output by the first term as input to the second term. The phrase $(t_1 \overset{\pi}{\prec} t_2)$ is similar in that the first term runs to completion before the second term begins. It differs in that evidence is not sent from the first term as input to the second term. Instead, each term receives some filtered version of the evidence accumulated thus far from the parent phrase. This evidence is split between the two subterms according to the splitting functions $\pi = (\pi_1, \pi_2)$ that specify the filter used before passing evidence to each subterm. The resulting evidence has the form $(e_1 \;;; e_2)$ indicating evidence gathered in sequence. Finally, $(t_1 \overset{\pi}{\sim} t_2)$ specifies its two subterms execute in parallel with data splitting specified by $\pi = (\pi_1, \pi_2)$. The evidence term $(e_1 \parallel e_2)$ captures that subterm evaluation occurs in parallel.

Two common filters are identity and empty. $id\, e = e$ returns its argument, producing a copy of the filtered evidence while $\perp e = \xi$ always returns empty evidence regardless of input. For example, $\pi = (\perp, \perp)$ passes empty evidence to both subterms, $\pi = (\perp, id)$ sends all evidence to the right subterm, and $\pi = (id, id)$ sends all evidence to both subterms.

A collection of operator terms specifies various operations over evidence. SIG, HSH, and CPY generate a signature, a hash and a copy of evidence previously gathered. The evidence forms generated by SIG and HSH are $[\![e]\!]_p$ and $\#_p\, e$, respectively. A place identifies itself in a hash by including its identity in the data being hashed. Unlike a cryptographic signature, this serves only to identify the entity performing the hash. It does not provide protection against forgery. Our choice to use hashes in this way is not critical to achieving the Copland design goals. Replacing it with more standard hashes would cause no problem. Other operator terms are anticipated, but these are sufficient for this exposition and for most phrases used in our examples.

$$
\begin{aligned}
\mathcal{E}(\mathsf{CPY}, p, e) &= e \\
\mathcal{E}(\mathsf{USM}\ \bar{a}, p, e) &= \mathsf{U}_p(e) \\
\mathcal{E}(\mathsf{KIM}\ q\ \bar{a}, p, e) &= \mathsf{K}_p^q(e) \\
\mathcal{E}(\mathsf{SIG}, p, e) &= [\![e]\!]_p \\
\mathcal{E}(\mathsf{HSH}, p, e) &= \#_p\, e \\
\mathcal{E}(@_q\, t, p, e) &= \mathcal{E}(t, q, e) \\
\mathcal{E}(t_1 \rightarrow t_2, p, e) &= \mathcal{E}(t_2, p, \mathcal{E}(t_1, p, e)) \\
\mathcal{E}(t_1 \overset{\pi}{\prec} t_2, p, e) &= \mathcal{E}(t_1, p, \pi_1(e)) \;;;\; \mathcal{E}(t_2, p, \pi_2(e)) \text{ where } \pi = (\pi_1, \pi_2) \\
\mathcal{E}(t_1 \overset{\pi}{\sim} t_2, p, e) &= \mathcal{E}(t_1, p, \pi_1(e)) \parallel \mathcal{E}(t_2, p, \pi_2(e)) \text{ where } \pi = (\pi_1, \pi_2)
\end{aligned}
$$

Fig. 3. Evidence semantics

4 Events

Events are observable effects associated with phrase execution. For example, a userspace measurement event occurs when a USM term executes; a remote request event occurs when $@_p t$ begins executing; and a sequence of split and join events occur when the various sequential and parallel composition terms execute. The events resulting from executing a phrase characterize that phrase.

The events associated with a subphrase t_1 within phrase t_0 is determined by the position in t_0 at which the subphrase occurs. For example, the term $(t \to t)$ has two occurrences of t that will be associated with some events. It is essential that the set of events associated with the left occurrence is disjoint from the set of events associated with the right occurrence. For this reason, each event has an associated natural number that is unique to that event.

$$
\begin{array}{ll}
[t]_i^{i+1} \in T_i^{i+1} & \text{if } t \text{ is atomic} \\
[@_p\, t]_i^{j+1} \in T_i^{j+1} & \text{if } t \in T_{i+1}^j \\
[t_1 \to t_2]_i^k \in T_i^k & \text{if } t_1 \in T_i^j \text{ and } t_2 \in T_j^k \\
[t_1 \overset{\pi}{\prec} t_2]_i^{k+1} \in T_i^{k+1} & \text{if } t_1 \in T_{i+1}^j \text{ and } t_2 \in T_j^k \\
[t_1 \overset{\pi}{\sim} t_2]_i^{k+1} \in T_i^{k+1} & \text{if } t_1 \in T_{i+1}^j \text{ and } t_2 \in T_j^k
\end{array}
$$

Fig. 4. Annotated terms

Annotated terms enable the generation of a unique number for each event in the Coq proofs. An annotated term, $[t]_i^j$, adds bounds, i and j to term t, where i and j are natural numbers. By construction each event related to $[t]_i^j$ has a unique natural number k such that $i \le k < j$. The set of all annotated terms is defined by $\bar{T} = \bigcup_{i,j=0}^{\infty} T_i^j$, where T_i^j is defined in Fig. 4. The number of events associated with $[t]_i^j$ is $j - i$.

As examples, two terms from $\bar{T}$ are:

$$
[[\mathsf{KIM}\ p\ \bar{a}]_0^1 \to [\mathsf{SIG}]_1^2]_0^2 \qquad\qquad [@_p\, [\mathsf{USM}\ \bar{a}]_1^2]_0^3
$$

The annotations on KIM and SIG indicate that the event associated with KIM is numbered 0 while the event associated with SIG is numbered 1. The entire sequence term includes numbers for both KIM and SIG. Similarly the $@_p\, \mathsf{USM}\ \bar{a}$ term allocates the number 1 for USM, and adds 0 and 2 for a request and reply event respectively associated with $@_p t$. For details of annotation generation, see Fig. 9 in Appendix A, which presents a simple function that translates terms into annotated terms.

Figure 5 presents event syntax while Fig. 6 relates phrases to events. The relation between annotated term t, place p, evidence e, and the associated event v, is written $t \diamond_e^p v$. Given some term t and current evidence e in place p, $t \diamond_e^p v$ relates event v to t in p. Note that each event has a natural number whose purpose is to uniquely identify the event as required by the Coq proofs.

$$
\begin{aligned}
V \leftarrow\ & \mathsf{CPY}(\mathbb{N}, P, E) \mid \mathsf{USM}(\mathbb{N}, P, L, E, E) \mid \mathsf{KIM}(\mathbb{N}, P, L, E, E) \\
\mid\ & \mathsf{SIG}(\mathbb{N}, P, E, E) \mid \mathsf{HSH}(\mathbb{N}, P, E, E) \mid \mathsf{REQ}(\mathbb{N}, P, P, E) \\
\mid\ & \mathsf{RPY}(\mathbb{N}, P, P, E) \mid \mathsf{SPLIT}(\mathbb{N}, P, E, E, E) \mid \mathsf{JOIN}(\mathbb{N}, P, E, E, E)
\end{aligned}
$$

Fig. 5. Event grammar

$$
\begin{aligned}
[\mathsf{CPY}]_i^{i+1} &\ \diamond_e^p\ \mathsf{CPY}(i, p, e) \\
[\mathsf{USM}\ \bar{a}]_i^{i+1} &\ \diamond_e^p\ \mathsf{USM}(i, p, \bar{a}, e, \mathsf{U}_p(e)) \\
[\mathsf{KIM}\ q\ \bar{a}]_i^{i+1} &\ \diamond_e^p\ \mathsf{KIM}(i, p, \bar{a}, e, \mathsf{K}_p^q(e)) \\
[\mathsf{SIG}]_i^{i+1} &\ \diamond_e^p\ \mathsf{SIG}(i, p, e, [\![e]\!]_p) \\
[\mathsf{HSH}]_i^{i+1} &\ \diamond_e^p\ \mathsf{HSH}(i, p, e, \#_p\, e) \\[1ex]
[@_q\, t]_i^j &\ \diamond_e^p\ \mathsf{REQ}(i, p, q, e) \\
[@_q\, t]_i^j &\ \diamond_e^p\ v \text{ if } t \diamond_e^q v \\
[@_q\, t]_i^j &\ \diamond_e^p\ \mathsf{RPY}(j-1, p, q, \bar{\mathcal{E}}(t, q, e)) \\[1ex]
[t_1 \to t_2]_i^j &\ \diamond_e^p\ v \text{ if } t_1 \diamond_e^p v \\
[t_1 \to t_2]_i^j &\ \diamond_e^p\ v \text{ if } t_2 \diamond_{\bar{\mathcal{E}}(t_1, p, e)}^p v \\[1ex]
[t_1 \overset{\pi}{\prec} t_2]_i^j &\ \diamond_e^p\ \mathsf{SPLIT}(i, p, e, \pi_1(e), \pi_2(e)) \\
[t_1 \overset{\pi}{\prec} t_2]_i^j &\ \diamond_e^p\ v \text{ if } t_1 \diamond_{\pi_1(e)}^p v \\
[t_1 \overset{\pi}{\prec} t_2]_i^j &\ \diamond_e^p\ v \text{ if } t_2 \diamond_{\pi_2(e)}^p v \\
[t_1 \overset{\pi}{\prec} t_2]_i^j &\ \diamond_e^p\ \mathsf{JOIN}(j-1, p, e_1, e_2, e_1 \;;;\; e_2) \\
\text{where } e_1 = \bar{\mathcal{E}}&(t_1, p, \pi_1(e)) \text{ and } e_2 = \bar{\mathcal{E}}(t_2, p, \pi_2(e)) \\[1ex]
[t_1 \overset{\pi}{\sim} t_2]_i^j &\ \diamond_e^p\ \mathsf{SPLIT}(i, p, e, \pi_1(e), \pi_2(e)) \\
[t_1 \overset{\pi}{\sim} t_2]_i^j &\ \diamond_e^p\ v \text{ if } t_1 \diamond_{\pi_1(e)}^p v \\
[t_1 \overset{\pi}{\sim} t_2]_i^j &\ \diamond_e^p\ v \text{ if } t_2 \diamond_{\pi_2(e)}^p v \\
[t_1 \overset{\pi}{\sim} t_2]_i^j &\ \diamond_e^p\ \mathsf{JOIN}(j-1, p, e_1, e_2, e_1 \parallel e_2) \\
\text{where } e_1 = \bar{\mathcal{E}}&(t_1, p, \pi_1(e)) \text{ and } e_2 = \bar{\mathcal{E}}(t_2, p, \pi_2(e))
\end{aligned}
$$

Fig. 6. Events of terms

Each atomic term has exactly one associated event that records execution details of the term including resulting evidence. Each $@_p\, t$ term is associated with a request event, a reply event, and the events associated with term t. Each $(t_1 \to t_2)$ term is associated with the events of its subterms. Both $(t_1 \overset{\pi}{\prec} t_2)$ and $(t_1 \overset{\pi}{\sim} t_2)$ are associated with the events of their subterms as well as a split and a join event. The evidence function $\bar{\mathcal{E}}$ is the same as $\mathcal{E}$ except it applies to annotated terms instead of terms.

Essential properties of the annotations are expressed in Lemmas 1–3. In each lemma, let ι be a projection from an event to its number.

Lemma 1. *$[t]_i^j \diamond_e^p v$ implies $i \le \iota(v) < j$.*

Each event associated with a term has a number in the range of the term's annotation. This is critical to the way that subterm annotations are composed to form term annotations.

Lemma 2. *$t \diamond_e^p v_1$ and $t \diamond_e^p v_2$ and $\iota(v_1) = \iota(v_2)$ implies $v_1 = v_2$.*

Event numbers are unique to events. If two events have the same number, they must be the same event.

Lemma 3. *$i \le k < j$ implies for some v, $[t]_i^j \diamond_e^p v$ and $\iota(v) = k$.*

There is an event associated with every number in an annotation range. There are no unassigned numbers in the range of an annotation.

5 Partial Order Semantics

The previous mapping of phrases to evidence types defines a denotational semantics for evaluation. The $t \diamond_e^p v$ relation defines visible events that result when a phrase executes. Here we add a partial order to define correct orderings of events associated with an execution. In Definition 5, we define strict partial order $\mathcal{R}(t, p, e)$ over the set $\{v \mid t \diamond_e^p v\}$, for some term t, place p, and initial evidence e. It defines requirements on any event trace produced by evaluating t at p with e.

The relation $\mathcal{R}(t, p, e)$ is defined by first introducing a language for representing strict partial orders, then representing semantics of language terms as event partial orders. The grammar defining the objects used to represent strict partial orders is

$$O \leftarrow V \mid (O \rhd O) \mid (O \bowtie O).$$

Events are ordered with the precedes relation. We write $o{:}v \prec v'$ when event v *precedes* another v' in partial order o. We write $v \in o$ if event v occurs in o.

Definition 4 (Precedes). *$o : v \prec v'$ is the smallest relation such that:*

1. *$o = o_1 \rhd o_2$ implies $v \in o_1$ and $v' \in o_2$ or $o_1 : v \prec v'$ or $o_2 : v \prec v'$*
2. *$o = o_1 \bowtie o_2$ implies $o_1 : v \prec v'$ or $o_2 : v \prec v'$*

The set of events associated with o is the set $\{v \mid v \in o\}$, and o represents the poset that orders that set.

If o_1 and o_2 represent disjoint posets, then $o_1 \rhd o_2$ represents the poset that respects the orders in o_1 and o_2 and for which every event in o_1 is before every event in o_2. Therefore, $\rhd$ is called the *before* operator. Additionally, $o_1 \bowtie o_2$ represents the poset which simply retains the orders in both o_1 and o_2, and so $\bowtie$ is called the *merge* operator. When applied to mutually disjoint posets, $\rhd$ and $\bowtie$ are associative.

Definition 5 (Strict Partial Order)

$$\mathcal{R}(t,p,e)(v,v') = \mathcal{V}(t,p,e) : v \prec v'$$

where $\mathcal{V}(t,p,e)$ *is defined in Fig. 7.*

The definition of $\mathcal{V}(t,p,e)$ is carefully crafted so that the posets combined by $\rhd$ and $\bowtie$ are disjoint.

For the phrase $@_q \, \mathsf{USM}\ \bar{a}$, the strict partial order term starting with 0 is

Example 6. $\mathcal{V}([@_q\,[\mathsf{USM}\ \bar{a}]_1^2]_0^3, p, e) = \mathsf{REQ}(0,\ldots) \rhd \mathsf{USM}(1,\ldots) \rhd \mathsf{RPY}(2,\ldots)$.

$$\begin{aligned}
\mathcal{V}([\mathsf{CPY}]_i^{i+1}, p, e) &= \mathsf{CPY}(i,p,e)\\
\mathcal{V}([\mathsf{USM}\ \bar{a}]_i^{i+1}, p, e) &= \mathsf{USM}(i,p,\bar{a},e,\mathsf{U}_p(e))\\
\mathcal{V}([\mathsf{KIM}\ q\ \bar{a}]_i^{i+1}, p, e) &= \mathsf{KIM}(i,p,\bar{a},e,\mathsf{K}_p^q(e))\\
\mathcal{V}([\mathsf{SIG}]_i^{i+1}, p, e) &= \mathsf{SIG}(i,p,e,[\![e]\!]_p)\\
\mathcal{V}([\mathsf{HSH}]_i^{i+1}, p, e) &= \mathsf{HSH}(i,p,e,\#_p\,e)\\
\mathcal{V}([@_q\,t]_i^j, p, e) &= \mathsf{REQ}(i,p,q,e) \rhd \mathcal{V}(t,q,e) \rhd \mathsf{RPY}(j-1,p,q,\bar{\mathcal{E}}(t,q,e))\\
\mathcal{V}([t_1 \to t_2]_i^j, p, e) &= \mathcal{V}(t_1,p,e) \rhd \mathcal{V}(t_2,p,\bar{\mathcal{E}}(t_1,p,e))\\
\mathcal{V}([t_1 \overset{\pi}{\prec} t_2]_i^j, p, e) &= \mathsf{SPLIT}(i,p,e,\pi_1(e),\pi_2(e)) \rhd \mathcal{V}(t_1,p,\pi_1(e)) \rhd \mathcal{V}(t_2,p,\pi_2(e)) \rhd\\
&\quad\ \mathsf{JOIN}(j-1,p,e_1,e_2,e_1 \;;\; e_2)\\
\text{where } e_1 &= \bar{\mathcal{E}}(t_1,p,\pi_1(e)) \text{ and } e_2 = \bar{\mathcal{E}}(t_2,p,\pi_2(e))\\
\mathcal{V}([t_1 \overset{\pi}{\sim} t_2]_i^j, p, e) &= \mathsf{SPLIT}(i,p,e,\pi_1(e),\pi_2(e)) \rhd (\mathcal{V}(t_1,p,\pi_1(e)) \bowtie \mathcal{V}(t_2,p,\pi_2(e))) \rhd\\
&\quad\ \mathsf{JOIN}(j-1,p,e_1,e_2,e_1 \parallel e_2)\\
\text{where } e_1 &= \bar{\mathcal{E}}(t_1,p,\pi_1(e)) \text{ and } e_2 = \bar{\mathcal{E}}(t_2,p,\pi_2(e))
\end{aligned}$$

Fig. 7. Event semantics

The $\mathcal{R}(t,p,e)$ relation is verified to be both irreflexive and transitive, demonstrating it is a strict partial order.

Lemma 7 (Irreflexive). $\neg\mathcal{V}(t,p,e) : v \prec v$.

Lemma 8 (Transitive). $\mathcal{V}(t,p,e) : v_1 \prec v_2$ *and* $\mathcal{V}(t,p,e) : v_2 \prec v_3$ *implies* $\mathcal{V}(t,p,e) : v_1 \prec v_3$.

Evaluating t is shown to include v if and only if v is associated with t. This ensures that all events associated with t are accounted for in the evaluation relation and that the evaluation relation does not introduce events not associated with t. Thus $\mathcal{R}(t,p,e)$ is a strict partial order for the set $\{v \mid t \diamond_e^p v\}$.

Lemma 9 (Correspondence). $v \in \mathcal{V}(t,p,e)$ *iff* $t \diamond_e^p v$.

Figure 7 defines event semantics in terms of the term being processed, the place managing execution, and the initial evidence. Measurement terms and evidence operations trivially translate into their corresponding atomic events whose output is the corresponding measurement or calculated result.

Simple sequential execution $t = (t_1 \rightarrow t_2)$ is defined using the canonical method where output evidence from the first operation is used as input to the second. The before operator ($\triangleright$) ensures that all events from t_1 complete in the order specified by $\mathcal{R}(t, p, e)$ before events from t_2 start. Note the appearance of evidence semantics in the definition to calculate event output in the canonical fashion.

Sequential execution with data splitting $t = (t_1 \overset{\pi}{\prec} t_2)$ is defined by again using the before operator to ensure t_1 events complete as specified by $\mathcal{R}(t, p, e)$ before events from t_2 begin. The distinction from simple sequential execution is using π_1 and π_2 from π to split evidence between t_1 and t_2. The SPLIT event routes evidence to t_1 and t_2 while JOIN composes results indicating sequential execution.

Parallel execution with data splitting $(t_1 \overset{\pi}{\sim} t_2)$ is defined using split and join events. Again π_1 and π_2 determine how evidence is routed to the composed posets. The merge operator ($\bowtie$) specifies parallel composition while respecting the orders specified for t_1 and t_2. The final $\triangleright$ operator ensures that both posets are ordered before JOIN.

The $@_p\, t$ operation responsible for making requests of other places is defined using communication events. The protocol term $@_q\, t$ evaluated by p results in an event poset where: (i) p and q synchronize on a request for q to perform t; (ii) q runs t; (iii) p and q synchronize on the reply back to p sending the resulting evidence. The before operator ($\triangleright$) ensures that each sequential step completes before moving to the next.

Definition 10. *The* output evidence *associated with an event is the right-most evidence used to construct the event.*

Lemma 11. *$\mathcal{V}(t, p, e)$ always has a unique maximal event e_{max}, and the output of e_{max} is $\bar{\mathcal{E}}(t, p, e)$.*

Lemma 11 shows that evaluating a term with the evidence semantics of Fig. 3 produces the same evidence as evaluating the same term with the event semantics of Fig. 7. Every annotated term has a unique maximal event as defined by $\mathcal{V}(t, p, e)$ implying that each finite sequence of events must have a last event. The evidence associated with that maximal event represents evidence produced by any event sequence satisfying the partial order. Additionally, that evidence is equal to the evidence produced by $\bar{\mathcal{E}}(t, p, e)$ for the same term, place and evidence. Lemma 11 proves that evaluating t in place p results in the same evidence using both the evidence and event semantics. Specifically, that $\bar{\mathcal{E}}(t, p, e)$ and $\mathcal{V}(t, p, e)$ are weakly bisimilar, producing the same result.

6 Small-Step Semantics

The small-step semantics for Copland is defined as a labeled transition system whose states represent protocol execution states and whose labels represent events interacting with the execution environment. The single-step transition relation is

$s_1 \overset{\ell}{\rightsquigarrow} s_2$, where s_1 and s_2 are states and ℓ is either an event or τ denoting a silent transition. The transition $s_1 \overset{\ell}{\rightsquigarrow} s_2$ says that a system in state s_1 will transition in one step to state s_2 engaging in the observable event, v, or no event when $\ell = \tau$. The relation $s_1 \overset{c}{\rightsquigarrow}{}^* s_2$ is the reflexive, transitive closure of the single-step relation. c is called an event trace and is the sequence of events resulting from each state transition. The transition $s_1 \overset{c}{\rightsquigarrow}{}^* s_2$ says that a system in state s_1 will transition to state s_2 in zero or more steps engaging in the event sequence c.

The grammar defining the set of states, S, is

$$\begin{aligned} S \leftarrow\ & \mathcal{C}(\bar{T}, P, E) \mid \mathcal{D}(P, E) \mid \mathcal{A}(\mathbb{N}, P, S) \mid \mathcal{LS}(S, \bar{T}) \\ \mid\ & \mathcal{BS}^{\ell}(\mathbb{N}, S, \bar{T}, P, E) \mid \mathcal{BS}^{r}(\mathbb{N}, E, S) \mid \mathcal{BP}(\mathbb{N}, S, S), \end{aligned}$$

where P is the syntactic category for places, E is for evidence, and $\bar{T}$ is for annotated terms. The transition relation for phrases is presented in Fig. 8.

State $\mathcal{C}(t, p, e)$ is a configuration state defining the start of evaluating t at p with initial evidence e. Its complement is the stop state $\mathcal{D}(p, e')$ defining the end of evaluation in p with final evidence e'. Assertion $\mathcal{C}(t, p, e) \overset{c}{\rightsquigarrow}{}^* \mathcal{D}(p, e')$ represents evaluating t at p resulting in evidence e' and event trace c.

A configuration for an atomic term transitions in one step to a done state containing measured or computed evidence after executing an event. For example, the state $\mathcal{C}([\mathsf{USM}\ \bar{a}]_i^{i+1}, p, e)$ transitions to $\mathcal{D}(p, \mathsf{U}_p(e))$ after the single event $\mathsf{USM}(i, p, \bar{a}, e, \mathsf{U}_p(e))$ performs the represented measurement. Similarly, the state $\mathcal{C}([\mathsf{CPY}]_i^{i+1}, p, e)$ transitions to $\mathcal{D}(p, e)$ after the single event $\mathsf{CPY}(i, p, e)$ copies the evidence.

The state $\mathcal{A}(j-1, p, s)$ occurs while evaluating an $[@_q\, t]_i^j$ term and is used to remember the number to be used to construct a reply event and the place to send the result of evaluating t at q after the reply event. A configuration state $\mathcal{C}(@_q\, t, p, e)$ starts the evaluation of $@_q\, t$ by p and transitions immediately to $\mathcal{A}(j-1, p, \mathcal{C}(t, q, e))$ after executing the request event $\mathsf{REQ}(i, p, q, e)$. The nested state $\mathcal{C}(t, q, e)$ represents remote term execution. Evaluation proceeds with $\mathcal{A}(j-1, p, s)$ transitioning to $\mathcal{A}(j-1, p, s')$ when $s \overset{v}{\rightsquigarrow} s'$. Any event v associated with $s \overset{v}{\rightsquigarrow} s'$ is also associated with the transition $\mathcal{A}(j-1, p, s) \overset{v}{\rightsquigarrow} \mathcal{A}(j-1, p, s')$ and will contribute to the trace. When a state $\mathcal{A}(j-1, p, \mathcal{D}(q, e'))$ results, remote execution completes and the result of q evaluating t as requested by p is $\mathcal{D}(p, e')$ after event $\mathsf{RPY}(j-1, p, q, e')$.

The state $\mathcal{LS}(s_1, t_2)$ is associated with evaluating $(t_1 \to t_2)$. State s_1 represents the current state of term t_1 and t_2 is the second term waiting for evaluation. The state $\mathcal{C}([t_1 \to t_2]_i^j, p, s)$ transitions to $\mathcal{LS}(\mathcal{C}(t_1, p, e), t_2)$ representing t_1 ready for evaluation and t_2 waiting. The annotation is ignored in this transition because the transitions are silent. Subsequent transitions evaluate $\mathcal{C}(t_1, p, e)$ until reaching state $\mathcal{LS}(\mathcal{D}(p, e_1), t_2)$ after producing event trace v_1. This state silently transitions to $\mathcal{C}(t_2, p, e_1)$ configuring t_2 for evaluation using e_1 as initial evidence. t_2 evaluates in a similar fashion resulting in e_2 and trace v_2. State $\mathcal{D}(p, e_2)$ is the final state with e_2 as evidence having engaged in the concatenation of v_1 and v_2, $v_1 * v_2$.

For atomic terms:

$$\begin{array}{rl}
\mathcal{C}([\mathsf{CPY}]_i^{i+1}, p, e) \overset{v}{\rightsquigarrow} \mathcal{D}(p, e) & [v = \mathsf{CPY}(i, p, e)] \\
\mathcal{C}([\mathsf{USM}\ \bar{a}]_i^{i+1}, p, e) \overset{v}{\rightsquigarrow} \mathcal{D}(p, \mathsf{U}_p(e)) & [v = \mathsf{USM}(i, p, \bar{a}, e, \mathsf{U}_p(e))] \\
\mathcal{C}([\mathsf{KIM}\ q\ \bar{a}]_i^{i+1}, p, e) \overset{v}{\rightsquigarrow} \mathcal{D}(p, \mathsf{K}_p^q(e)) & [v = \mathsf{KIM}(i, p, \bar{a}, e, \mathsf{K}_p^q(e))] \\
\mathcal{C}([\mathsf{SIG}]_i^{i+1}, p, e) \overset{v}{\rightsquigarrow} \mathcal{D}(p, [\![e]\!]_p) & [v = \mathsf{SIG}(i, p, e, [\![e]\!]_p)] \\
\mathcal{C}([\mathsf{HSH}]_i^{i+1}, p, e) \overset{v}{\rightsquigarrow} \mathcal{D}(p, \#_p\, e) & [v = \mathsf{HSH}(i, p, e, \#_p\, e)]
\end{array}$$

For $@_q\, t$:

$$\begin{array}{rl}
\mathcal{C}([@_q\, t]_i^j, p, e) \overset{v}{\rightsquigarrow} \mathcal{A}(j-1, p, \mathcal{C}(t, q, e)) & [v = \mathsf{REQ}(i, p, q, e)] \\
\mathcal{A}(i, p, s_1) \overset{v}{\rightsquigarrow} \mathcal{A}(i, p, s_2) & \text{if } s_1 \overset{v}{\rightsquigarrow} s_2 \\
\mathcal{A}(i, p, \mathcal{D}(q, e)) \overset{v}{\rightsquigarrow} \mathcal{D}(p, e) & [v = \mathsf{RPY}(i, p, q, e)]
\end{array}$$

For $t_1 \rightarrow t_2$:

$$\begin{array}{rl}
\mathcal{C}([t_1 \rightarrow t_2]_i^j, p, e) \overset{\tau}{\rightsquigarrow} \mathcal{LS}(\mathcal{C}(t_1, p, e), t_2) & \\
\mathcal{LS}(s_1, t_2) \overset{v}{\rightsquigarrow} \mathcal{LS}(s_2, t_2) & \text{if } s_1 \overset{v}{\rightsquigarrow} s_2 \\
\mathcal{LS}(\mathcal{D}(p, e), t) \overset{\tau}{\rightsquigarrow} \mathcal{C}(t, p, e) &
\end{array}$$

For $t_1 \overset{s}{\prec} t_2$:

$$\begin{array}{rl}
\mathcal{C}([t_1 \overset{s}{\prec} t_2]_i^j, p, e) \overset{v}{\rightsquigarrow} \mathcal{BS}^\ell(j-1, \mathcal{C}(t_1, p, \pi_1(e)), t_2, p, \pi_2(e)) & \\
 & [v = \mathsf{SPLIT}(i, p, e, \pi_1(e), \pi_2(e))] \\
\mathcal{BS}^\ell(i, s_1, t, p, e) \overset{v}{\rightsquigarrow} \mathcal{BS}^\ell(i, s_2, t, p, e) & \text{if } s_1 \overset{v}{\rightsquigarrow} s_2 \\
\mathcal{BS}^\ell(i, \mathcal{D}(p, e), t, p', e') \overset{\tau}{\rightsquigarrow} \mathcal{BS}^r(i, e, \mathcal{C}(t, p', e')) & \\
\mathcal{BS}^r(i, e, s_1) \overset{v}{\rightsquigarrow} \mathcal{BS}^r(i, e, s_2) & \text{if } s_1 \overset{v}{\rightsquigarrow} s_2 \\
\mathcal{BS}^r(i, e_1, \mathcal{D}(p, e_2)) \overset{v}{\rightsquigarrow} \mathcal{D}(p, e_1 ;; e_2) & [v = \mathsf{JOIN}(i, p, e_1, e_2, e_1 ;; e_2)]
\end{array}$$

For $t_1 \overset{s}{\sim} t_2$:

$$\begin{array}{rl}
\mathcal{C}([t_1 \overset{s}{\sim} t_2]_i^j, p, e) \overset{v}{\rightsquigarrow} \mathcal{BP}(j-1, \mathcal{C}(t_1, p, \pi_1(e)), \mathcal{C}(t_2, p, \pi_2(e))) & \\
 & [v = \mathsf{SPLIT}(i, p, e, \pi_1(e), \pi_2(e))] \\
\mathcal{BP}(i, S, s_1) \overset{v}{\rightsquigarrow} \mathcal{BP}(i, S, s_2) & \text{if } s_1 \overset{v}{\rightsquigarrow} s_2 \\
\mathcal{BP}(i, s_1, S) \overset{v}{\rightsquigarrow} \mathcal{BP}(i, s_2, S) & \text{if } s_1 \overset{v}{\rightsquigarrow} s_2 \\
\mathcal{BP}(i, \mathcal{D}(p, e_1), \mathcal{D}(p, e_2)) \overset{v}{\rightsquigarrow} \mathcal{D}(p, e_1 \parallel e_2) & [v = \mathsf{JOIN}(i, p, e_1, e_2, e_1 \parallel e_2)]
\end{array}$$

Fig. 8. Labeled transition system

States $\mathcal{BS}^\ell(j-1, s, t, p, e)$ and $\mathcal{BS}^r(j-1, e, s)$ are associated with evaluating the left and right subterms of $[t_1 \overset{\pi}{\prec} t_2]_i^j$ respectively. Recall that $t_1 \overset{\pi}{\prec} t_2$ differs from $t_1 \rightarrow t_2$ because the initial evidence for $t_1 \overset{\pi}{\prec} t_2$ is split between t_1 and t_2 and the resulting evidence is the sequential composition of evidence from t_1 and t_2. The configuration state $\mathcal{C}([t_1 \overset{\pi}{\prec} t_2]_i^j, p, e)$ transitions immediately to $\mathcal{BS}^\ell(j-1, \mathcal{C}(t_1, p, \pi_1(e)), t_2, p, \pi_2(e))$ after the split event $\mathsf{SPLIT}(i, p, e, \pi_1(e), \pi_2(e))$, where $\pi = (\pi_1, \pi_2)$. This state captures the initial configuration of t_1 ready to evaluate with evidence $\pi_1(e)$ along with t_2 waiting to execute with evidence $\pi_2(e)$ after t_1 completes. Evaluation proceeds with state $\mathcal{BS}^\ell(j-1, s, t_2, p, \pi_2(e))$ transitioning to $\mathcal{BS}^\ell(j-1, s', t_2, p, \pi_2(e))$ after event v when $s \overset{v}{\leadsto} s'$. After one or more such transitions a state $\mathcal{BS}^\ell(j-1, \mathcal{D}(p, e_1'), t, p, e_2)$ is reached after event sequence v_1 indicating that evaluating t_1 has ended and t_2 should begin. This state transitions to $\mathcal{BS}^r(j-1, e_1', s)$ with s initially $\mathcal{C}(t_2, p, \pi_2(e))$ and e_1' being the evidence from t_1. This state will transition repeatedly until a state $\mathcal{BS}^r(j-1, e_1', \mathcal{D}(p, e_2'))$ results after trace v_2 representing completion of t_2. Both t_1 and t_2 are complete with evidence e_1' and e_2' and evidence must be composed. The final state transitions to $\mathcal{D}(p, e_1 ;; e_2)$ after the join event $\mathsf{JOIN}(j-1, p, e_1, e_2, e_1 ;; e_2)$ where $e_n = \bar{\mathcal{E}}(t_n, p, \pi_n(e))$.

State $\mathcal{BP}(j-1, s_1, s_2)$ is associated with parallel evaluation of t_1 and t_2. The configuration state $\mathcal{C}([t_1 \overset{\pi}{\sim} t_2]_i^j, p, e)$ immediately transitions to $\mathcal{BP}(j-1, \mathcal{C}(t_1, p, \pi_1(e)), \mathcal{C}(t_2, p, \pi_2(e)))$ after the split event $\mathsf{SPLIT}(i, p, e, \pi_1(e), \pi_2(e))$. Note that in the state $\mathcal{BP}(j-1, \mathcal{C}(t_1, p, \pi_1(e)), \mathcal{C}(t_2, p, \pi_2(e)))$ configuration states for both t_1 and t_2 can evaluate. More generally in any state $\mathcal{BP}(j-1, s_1, s_2)$ evaluating either s_1 and s_2 may cause the state to transition. When evaluation reaches a term of the form $\mathcal{BP}(j-1, \mathcal{D}(p, e_1'), \mathcal{D}(p, e_2'))$ both term evaluations are complete. This final state transitions to $\mathcal{D}(p, e_1 \parallel e_2)$ after the join event $\mathsf{JOIN}(j-1, p, e_1, e_2, e_1 \parallel e_2)$.

We prove Correctness, Progress, and Termination with respect to this transition system. Correctness defines congruence between the small-step operational semantics and the denotational evidence semantics. Specifically, if the multi-step evaluation relation maps state $\mathcal{C}(t, p, e)$ to $\mathcal{D}(p, e')$ then $\bar{\mathcal{E}}(t, p, e) = e'$.

Lemma 12 (Correctness). *If* $\mathcal{C}(t, p, e) \overset{c}{\leadsto}{}^* \mathcal{D}(p, e')$ *then* $\bar{\mathcal{E}}(t, p, e) = e'$.

Progress states that every state is either a stop state of the form $\mathcal{D}(p, e)$ or it can be evaluated. With the Progress lemma we know that there exist no "stuck" states in the operational semantics.

Lemma 13 (Progress). *Either* $s_1 = \mathcal{D}(p, e)$ *for some* p *and* e *or* $s_1 \overset{v}{\leadsto} s_2$ *for some* v *and* s_2.

Termination states that any configuration state will transition to a done state of the form $\mathcal{D}(p, e)$ in a finite number of steps. This is a strong condition that assures evaluation of any well-formed term will terminate.

Lemma 14 (Termination). *For some* n, $\mathcal{C}(t, p, e) \overset{c}{\leadsto}{}^n \mathcal{D}(p, e')$.

7 Proof Summary

The ordering of events is a critically important property of attestation systems. Even when measurement events properly execute individually, their ordering is what establishes trust chains. If a component performs measurement before being measured, any trust in that component and subsequent components is lost.

Figure 1 shows phrases denoted as event posets and defined operationally as a labeled transition system. The event posets define legal orderings of events in traces while the LTS defines traces associated with phrase evaluation. The remaining theoretical result is proving that the small-step semantics produces traces compatible with the partial order semantics.

To present event sequences we use the classical notation $\langle v_1, v_2, \ldots, v_n\rangle$ for sequence construction and $c \downarrow i$ to select the ith element from sequence c. The concatenation of c_1 and c_2 is $c_1 * c_2$. Event v is *earlier* than event v' in trace c, written $v \ll_c v'$, iff there exists an i and j such that $i < j$ and $c \downarrow i = v$ and $c \downarrow j = v'$.

The main correctness theorem states that if some term t evaluates to evidence e' after trace c and two events v and v' from c are ordered by the event semantics, then that order is guaranteed in c. Said differently, if the event semantics constrains two events, then the small-step LTS semantics respects that constraint. This theorem is stated formally in Theorem 15.

Theorem 15 (Correctness). *If* $\mathcal{C}(t, p, e) \overset{c}{\leadsto}{}^{*} \mathcal{D}(p, e')$ *and* $\mathcal{V}(t, p, e) : v \prec v'$, *then* $v \ll_c v'$.

The proof is done in two steps using a big-step semantics defining traces for individual phrases as an intermediary. The inductive structure of the big-step semantics more closely matches the inductive structure of the partial order semantics, easing the proofs about the relation between the two.

The intermediate big-step semantics is specified as a relation between annotated term t, place p, evidence e, and trace c, written $t \Box^p_e c$. The structure of the definition is similar to the structure of the $\Diamond$ relation in Fig. 6. Most cases of the definition are straightforward event sequences taken from the small-step semantics.

For atomic actions, the associated sequence is a single event implementing the action. As an illustrative example, $\mathsf{USM}\ \bar{a}$ is associated with

$$[\mathsf{USM}\ \bar{a}]_i^{i+1} \Box^p_e \langle \mathsf{USM}(i, p, \bar{a}, e, \mathsf{U}_p(e))\rangle.$$

For remote actions, $@_q\, t$, the associated trace starts with a request event followed by the trace c executed remotely and ending with a reply event:

$$[@_q\, t]_i^j \Box^p_e \langle \mathsf{REQ}(i, p, q, e)\rangle * c * \langle \mathsf{RPY}(j-1, p, q, \bar{\mathcal{E}}(t, q, e))\rangle \qquad \text{if } t \Box^q_e c.$$

For sequential actions, $(t_1 \rightarrow t_2)$, the associated trace starts with the trace c_1 associated with t_1 and ends with the trace c_2 associated with t_2 starting with evidence e_1 from c_1:

$$[t_1 \rightarrow t_2]_i^j \Box^p_e c_1 * c_2 \qquad \text{if } t_1 \Box^p_e c_1 \text{ and } t_2 \Box^p_{e_1} c_2,$$

where $e_1 = \bar{\mathcal{E}}(t_1, p, e)$.

For sequential branching, $(t_1 \overset{\pi}{\prec} t_2)$, the associated trace starts with a split event and continues with trace c_1 associated with t_1 starting with $\pi_1(e)$ followed by trace c_2 associated with t_2 starting with $\pi_2(e)$:

$$[(t_1 \overset{\pi}{\prec} t_2)]_i^j \,\Box_e^p\, \langle v_1\rangle * c_1 * c_2 * \langle v_2\rangle \qquad \text{if } t_1 \,\Box_{\pi_1(e)}^p\, c_1 \text{ and } t_2 \,\Box_{\pi_2(e)}^p\, c_2,$$

where

$$\begin{aligned} v_1 &= \mathsf{SPLIT}(i, p, e, \pi_1(e), \pi_2(e)) \\ v_2 &= \mathsf{JOIN}(j-1, p, e_1, e_2, e_1 \;;;\; e_2) \\ e_1 &= \bar{\mathcal{E}}(t_1, p, \pi_1(e)) \\ e_2 &= \bar{\mathcal{E}}(t_2, p, \pi_2(e)). \end{aligned}$$

The case for parallel branching, $(t_1 \overset{\pi}{\sim} t_2)$, requires additional work to capture parallel execution semantics using trace interleaving. We write $il(c, c', c'')$ to assert that trace c is a result of interleaving c' with c''.

Definition 16 (Interleave). *$il(c, c', c'')$ is the smallest relation such that*

1. *$il(c, \langle\rangle, c)$ and $il(c, c, \langle\rangle)$;*
2. *$il(\langle v\rangle * c, \langle v\rangle * c', c'')$ if $il(c, c', c'')$; and*
3. *$il(\langle v\rangle * c, c', \langle v\rangle * c'')$ if $il(c, c', c'')$.*

When c is an interleaving of c' and c'', $v_1 \ll_{c'} v_2$ implies $v_1 \ll_c v_2$ and $v_1 \ll_{c''} v_2$ implies $v_1 \ll_c v_2$, but the order of events in c is otherwise unconstrained.

With interleaving defined, the trace for $(t_1 \overset{\pi}{\sim} t_2)$ begins with a split operation and continues with an interleaving of c_1 and c_2 associated with t_1 and t_2 starting with $\pi_1(e)$ and $\pi_2(e)$ respectively. The trace ends with a join event when both interleaved traces end:

$$[t_1 \overset{\pi}{\sim} t_2]_i^j \,\Box_e^p\, \langle v_1\rangle * c * \langle v_2\rangle \quad \text{if } t_1 \,\Box_{\pi_1(e)}^p\, c',\ t_2 \,\Box_{\pi_2(e)}^p\, c'', \text{ and } il(c, c', c''),$$

where

$$\begin{aligned} v_1 &= \mathsf{SPLIT}(i, p, e, \pi_1(e), \pi_2(e)) \\ v_2 &= \mathsf{JOIN}(j-1, p, e_1, e_2, e_1 \parallel e_2) \\ e_1 &= \bar{\mathcal{E}}(t_1, p, \pi_1(e)) \\ e_2 &= \bar{\mathcal{E}}(t_2, p, \pi_2(e)). \end{aligned}$$

The following two lemmas show that every trace in the big-step semantics contains the correct events. Lemma 17 asserts that the right number of events occurs and Lemma 18 asserts that all events do in fact occur in the trace.

Lemma 17. *$[t]_i^j \,\Box_e^p\, c$ implies the length of c is $j - i$.*

Lemma 18. *$t \,\Box_e^p\, c$ implies $t \,\Diamond_e^p\, v$ iff for some i, $v = c \downarrow i$.*

The first step in the proof of Theorem 15 is to show that a trace of the small-step semantics is also a trace of the big-step semantics as shown in Lemma 19. The lemma asserts that any trace c resulting from evaluating t is also related to t in the big-step semantics.

Lemma 19. *$\mathcal{C}(t, p, e) \overset{c}{\leadsto}{}^* \mathcal{D}(p, e')$ implies $t \,\Box^p_e\, c$.*

The next step is to show that if c is a trace of the big-step semantics, then that trace is compatible with the partial order semantics.

Lemma 20. *If $t \,\Box^p_e\, c$ and $\mathcal{V}(t, p, e) : v \prec v'$, then $v \ll_c v'$.*

The proof of Theorem 15 follows from a transitive composition of Lemmas 19 and 20.

The real value of Theorem 15 is that it triangulates specifications, implementations, and formal analysis as depicted in Fig. 1. On one hand, the operational semantics is immediately implementable. This allows us to explicitly test and experiment with alternative options as specified in Copland. On the other hand, however, simple testing is not sufficient to understand the trust properties provided by alternative options. It is better to offer potential users the ability to analyze Copland phrases to establish (or refute) desired trust properties. This is the primary purpose of the event poset semantics. Our prior work on the analytic principles of layered attestation [17,18] is based on partially ordered sets of measurement and processing events. That work details how to characterize what an adversary would have to do in order to escape detection by a given collection of events. In particular, it establishes the fact that bottom-up strategies for measurement and evidence bundling force an adversary to perform either recent or deep corruptions. Recent corruptions must occur within a small time window, so it intuitively raises the bar for an adversary. Similarly, deep corruptions burrow into lower (and presumably better protected) systems layers also raising the bar for the adversary.

Although the event posets in Copland's denotational semantics are somewhat richer than those in [17,18], the reasoning principles can easily be adapted to this richer setting. This enables a verification methodology in which Copland phrases are compiled to event posets, then analyzed according to these principles. In this way, the relative strength of Copland phrases could be directly compared according to the trust properties they guarantee. Theorem 15 ensures that any conclusions made on the basis of this static analysis must also hold for dynamic executions conforming to the operational semantics. It essentially transfers formal guarantees into the world of concrete implementations. We are currently exploring methods to more explicitly leverage such formal analysis to help Maat users write local policies based on the relative strength of Copland phrases.

8 Related Work

The concept of adapting an attestation to the layered structure of a target system is not new. The concept is already present in attestation systems like trusted boot [15] and Integrity Measurement Architecture (IMA) [19] which leverage a layered architecture to create static, boot-time or load-time measurements of system components. Other solutions have designed layered architectures to enable attestation of the runtime state of a system [10,22]. A major focus is on information flow integrity properties since this allows fine-grained, local measurements to be composed without having to measure the entire system [20]. The main contrast between this line of research and our work is that they fix the structure of an attestation based on the structure of the target architecture, whereas in our work, we support extensible attestation specifications that can be altered to suit many different architectures and many different contexts for trust decisions.

Coker et al. [4] present a general approach for using virtualization to achieve a layered architecture, and it presents generic principles for remote attestation suggesting the possibility of diverse, policy-based orchestrations of attestations. These principles have recently been extended in [13] in the context of cloud systems built with Trusted Platform Modules (TPMs) and virtual TPMs [9].

Several implementations of measurement and attestation (M&A) frameworks have been proposed to address the need for a central service to manage policies for the orchestration and collection of integrity evidence. The Maat framework, as described in Sect. 2, is being utilized by the authors as a testing ground for COPLAND. Maat provides a pluggable interface for Attestation Service Providers (ASPs), functional units of measurement which are executed by Attestation Protocol Blocks (APBs) after a negotiation between an attester and appraiser machine [16]. Another architecture, given in [8], implements a policy mechanism designed to allow the appraiser to ask for different conditions to be satisfied by the target for different types of interactions. The main focus is on determining suitability of the target system to handle sensitive data. Negotiation between systems and frameworks, and the supporting policy specification, are examples of places where COPLAND can be leveraged to provide a common language and understanding of attestation guarantees.

Another line of research has focused on hardware/software co-design for embedded devices to enable remote attestation on platforms that are constrained in various ways [2,6,7]. For example, the absence of a TPM can increase an adversary's ability to forge evidence. A careful co-design of hardware and software allows them to tailor attestation protocols to the particular structure of a target device. More recently, Multiple-Tier Remote Attestation (MTRA) extends this work with a protocol that is specifically targeted for the attestation of heterogeneous IoT networks [21]. This protocol uses a preparation stage to configure attestations where more-capable devices (those with TPMs, for example) provide a makeshift root of trust for less-capable devices and measurement of the entire network is distributed across the more-capable devices. We believe that COPLAND would be beneficial in specifying the complex set of actions required of these heterogeneous networks.

Finally, there has been some work on the semantics of attestation. Datta et al. [5] introduces a formal logic for trusted computing systems. Its semantics is similar to our operational semantics in that it works as a transition system on state configurations. The underlying programming language was designed specifically for the logic, and is considerably more complex than COPLAND. It was not designed to be used by implementations as part of a negotiation. Also, it seems the logic has only been applied to static measurements such as trusted boot. We also previously developed a formal approach to the semantics of dynamic measurement [17,18]. In this work we characterize the benefit of a bottom-up measurement strategy as constraining the adversary to corrupt quickly or deeply. These results are obtained based on a partial order of events consisting of measurements and evidence bundling. As discussed above, this basis is similar to our partially ordered event semantics. We explicitly provide such a semantics to leverage the formal results that can be obtained by such analysis. While our set of events is richer, we expect the methods of this line of research to apply.

9 Conclusion and Ongoing Work

COPLAND serves as a basis for discussing the formal properties of attestation protocols under composition. We have described the denotational semantics of COPLAND by mapping phrases to evidence and to partially ordered event sets describing events associated with a phrase and constraints on event ordering. While the denotational semantics does not specify unique traces, it specifies event orderings mandatory for believing evidence resulting from evaluation.

We have described the operational semantics of COPLAND by associating phrases with a labeled transition system. States capture evidence and order execution while labels on transitions describe resulting events. The transitive closure of the LTS transition function describes traces associated with LTS execution.

We then show the small-step semantics generates traces that obey partial orderings specified by the denotational semantics. Furthermore, we show those orderings are preserved under protocol composition. This result is vital to the correctness of attestation outcomes whose validity is equally dependent on resulting evidence and the proper ordering of evidence gathering events.

Beyond the correctness proof, the most impactful contribution of COPLAND semantics is a foundation for testing and experimenting with layered attestation protocols, pushing the bounds of complexity and diversity of application. We are actively exploring advanced attestation scenarios between Maat Attestation Managers (AMs). Recall from the introduction that Maat is a policy-based measurement and attestation (M&A) framework which provides a centralized, pluggable service to gather and report integrity measurements [16]. The Maat team is leveraging COPLAND to test attestation scenarios involving the configuration of multiple instances of Maat in multi-realm and multi-party scenarios. In addition to its application to traditional Linux platforms, the Maat framework has been applied to IoT device platforms, where different configurations due to limited resources were explored [3]. We believe frameworks such as Maat provide a rich testing ground for the application of COPLAND as the basis of policy specification and negotiation across many kinds of system architectures, and are feeding the lessons learned in this application back into the on-going COPLAND research.

The authors are also using COPLAND as an implementation language for remote attestation protocols in other systems. A collection of COPLAND interpreters written in Haskell, F# and CakeML [12] running on Linux, Windows 10 and seL4 [11] provide a mechanism for executing COPLAND phrases. Each interpreter forms the core of an AM that receives phrases, calls the interpreter, and returns evidence. Additionally, the AMs maintain and protect keys associated places and policies mapping USM and KIM instances to specific implementations. Policies are critically important as they describe details of measurers held abstract within a phrase. Policies will eventually play a central role in negotiating attestation protocols among the various AMs implementing complex, layered attestations. A common JSON exchange format allows exchange of phrases and evidence among AMs running on different systems.

Of particular note, the CakeML interpreter targeting the seL4 platform will be formally verified with respect to the formal COPLAND semantics. CakeML implements a formally verified fragment of ML in the HOL4 proof system while seL4 provides a verified microkernel with VMM support. Verifying the COPLAND CakeML implementation and individual COPLAND phrases requires embedding the CakeML semantics in Coq. The COPLAND implementation will then be verified with respect to the formal semantics. Additionally, the Coq semantics supports proof search techniques for synthesizing COPLAND phrases. Running the CakeML implementation on the seL4 platform with formally synthesized phrases provides a verified attestation platform that may be retargeted to any environment supporting seL4.

As we continue exploring the richness of layered attestation we are also developing type systems and static checkers that determine correctness of specific protocols and protocol interpreters and compilers that produce provably correct results relative to COPLAND semantics. We are considering extensions to COPLAND that include nonces, lambda expressions, keys, and TPM interactions to represent a richer set of protocols. Without this formal semantics, it would be impossible to consider the correctness of such extensions.

A Annotated Terms

As noted in Sect. 4, when t is annotated by i and j, we write $[t]_i^j$. The annotations are used in the Coq proofs to construct sequences of unique events associated with collecting the evidence specified by the term.

$$
\begin{aligned}
&\mathsf{anno}(i, \mathsf{CPY}) = (i+1, [\mathsf{CPY}]_i^{i+1})\\
&\mathsf{anno}(i, \mathsf{KIM}\ p\ \bar{a}) = (i+1, [\mathsf{KIM}\ p\ \bar{a}]_i^{i+1})\\
&\mathsf{anno}(i, \mathsf{USM}\ \bar{a}) = (i+1, [\mathsf{USM}\ \bar{a}]_i^{i+1})\\
&\mathsf{anno}(i, \mathsf{SIG}) = (i+1, [\mathsf{SIG}]_i^{i+1})\\
&\mathsf{anno}(i, \mathsf{HSH}) = (i+1, [\mathsf{HSH}]_i^{i+1})\\
&\mathsf{anno}(i, @_p\, t) =\\
&\quad \mathsf{let}\ (j, a) \leftarrow \mathsf{anno}(i+1, t)\ \mathsf{in}\\
&\quad \mathsf{anno}(j+1, [@_p\, a]_i^{j+1})\\
&\mathsf{anno}(i, t_1 \to t_2) =\\
&\quad \mathsf{let}\ (j, a_1) \leftarrow \mathsf{anno}(i, t_1)\ \mathsf{in}\\
&\quad \mathsf{let}\ (k, a_2) \leftarrow \mathsf{anno}(j, t_2)\ \mathsf{in}\\
&\quad \mathsf{anno}(k, [a_1 \to a_2]_i^k)\\
&\mathsf{anno}(i, t_1 \overset{s}{\prec} t_2) =\\
&\quad \mathsf{let}\ (j, a_1) \leftarrow \mathsf{anno}(i+1, t_1)\ \mathsf{in}\\
&\quad \mathsf{let}\ (k, a_2) \leftarrow \mathsf{anno}(j, t_2)\ \mathsf{in}\\
&\quad \mathsf{anno}(k+1, [a_1 \overset{s}{\prec} a_2]_i^{k+1})\\
&\mathsf{anno}(i, t_1 \overset{s}{\sim} t_2) =\\
&\quad \mathsf{let}\ (j, a_1) \leftarrow \mathsf{anno}(i+1, t_1)\ \mathsf{in}\\
&\quad \mathsf{let}\ (k, a_2) \leftarrow \mathsf{anno}(j, t_2)\ \mathsf{in}\\
&\quad \mathsf{anno}(k+1, [a_1 \overset{s}{\sim} a_2]_i^{k+1})
\end{aligned}
$$

Fig. 9. Term annotation

Terms are annotated using the function displayed in Fig. 9. An annotated term for $t = \mathsf{KIM}\ p\ \bar{a} \to \mathsf{SIG}$ is

$$\mathsf{anno}(0, t) = (2, [[\mathsf{KIM}\ p\ \bar{a}]_0^1 \to [\mathsf{SIG}]_1^2]_0^2),$$

and when $t = @_p\, \mathsf{USM}\ \bar{a}$,

$$\mathsf{anno}(0, t) = (3, [@_p\, [\mathsf{USM}\ \bar{a}]_1^2]_0^3).$$

Lemma 21. $\mathsf{anno}(i, t) \in T_i$.

B Coq Cross Reference

Table 1 matches the contents of a figure with its definition in the Coq proofs. Table 2 does the same for lemmas, definitions, and the theorem.

Table 1. Coq figure cross reference

Fig. 2: `Term.Term`	Fig. 3: `Term.eval`	Fig. 4: `Term.well_founded`
Fig. 5: `Term.Ev`	Fig. 6: `Term.events`	Fig. 7: `Term_system.ev_evsys`
Fig. 8: `LTS.step`	Fig. 9: `Term.anno`	

Table 2. Coq cross reference

Lem. 1:	`Term.event_range`
Lem. 2:	`Term.events_injective`
Lem. 3:	`Term.events_range_event`
Def. 4:	`Event_system.prec`
Lem. 7:	`Event_system.evsys_irreflexive`
Lem. 8:	`Event_system.evsys_transitive`
Lem. 9:	`Term_system.evsys_events`
Def. 10:	`Term_system.out_ev`
Lem. 11:	`Term_system.max_eval`
Lem. 12:	`LTS.steps_preserve_eval`
Lem. 13:	`LTS.never_stuck`
Lem. 14:	`LTS.steps_to_stop`
Thm. 15:	`Main.ordered`
Def. 16:	`Trace.shuffle`
Lem. 17:	`Trace.trace_length`
Lem. 18:	`Trace.trace_events`
Lem. 19:	`Main.lstar_trace`
Lem. 20:	`Trace.trace_order`

References

1. The Coq proof assistant reference manual (2018). Version 8.0. http://coq.inria.fr
2. Carpent, X., Tsudik, G., Rattanavipanon, N.: ERASMUS: efficient remote attestation via self-measurement for unattended settings. In: 2018 Design, Automation & Test in Europe Conference & Exhibition, DATE 2018, Dresden, Germany, 19–23 March 2018, pp. 1191–1194 (2018)
3. Clemens, J., Paul, R., Sherrell, B.: Runtime state verification on resource-constrained platforms. In: Military Communications Conference (MILCOM) 2018, October 2018
4. Coker, G., et al.: Principles of remote attestation. Int. J. Inf. Secur. **10**(2), 63–81 (2011)
5. Datta, A., Franklin, J., Garg, D., Kaynar, D.: A logic of secure systems and its application to trusted computing. In: 2009 30th IEEE Symposium on Security and Privacy, pp. 221–236. IEEE (2009)
6. Eldefrawy, K., Rattanavipanon, N., Tsudik, G.: HYDRA: hybrid design for remote attestation (using a formally verified microkernel). In: Proceedings of the 10th ACM Conference on Security and Privacy in Wireless and Mobile Networks, WiSec 2017, Boston, MA, USA, 18–20 July 2017, pp. 99–110 (2017)
7. Francillon, A., Nguyen, Q., Rasmussen, K.B., Tsudik, G.: A minimalist approach to remote attestation. In: Design, Automation & Test in Europe Conference & Exhibition, DATE 2014, Dresden, Germany, 24–28 March 2014, pp. 1–6 (2014)

8. Gopalan, A., Gowadia, V., Scalavino, E., Lupu, E.: Policy driven remote attestation. In: Prasad, R., Farkas, K., Schmidt, A.U., Lioy, A., Russello, G., Luccio, F.L. (eds.) MobiSec 2011. LNICSSITE, vol. 94, pp. 148–159. Springer, Heidelberg (2012). https://doi.org/10.1007/978-3-642-30244-2_13
9. Trusted Computing Group: TPM Main Specification Level 2 version 1.2 (2011)
10. Jaeger, T., Sailer, R., Shankar, U.: PRIMA: policy-reduced integrity measurement architecture. In: Proceedings of the 11th ACM Symposium on Access Control Models and Technologies, SACMAT 2006, Lake Tahoe, California, USA, 7–9 June 2006, pp. 19–28 (2006)
11. Klein, G., et al.: seL4: formal verification of an operating-system kernel. Commun. ACM **53**(6), 107–115 (2010)
12. Kumar, R., Myreen, M.O., Norrish, M., Owens, S.: CakeML: a verified implementation of ML. In: Proceedings of the 41st ACM SIGPLAN-SIGACT Symposium on Principles of Programming Languages, POPL 2014, pp. 179–191. ACM, New York (2014)
13. Lauer, H., Ahmad Salehi, S., Rudolph, C., Nepal, S.: User-centered attestation for layered and decentralized systems. In: Workshop on Decentralized IoT Security and Standards (DISS) 2018, February 2018
14. Loscocco, P., Wilson, P.W., Aaron Pendergrass, J., Durward McDonell, C.: Linux kernel integrity measurement using contextual inspection. In: Proceedings of the 2nd ACM Workshop on Scalable Trusted Computing, STC 2007, Alexandria, VA, USA, 2 November 2007, pp. 21–29 (2007)
15. Maliszewski, R., Sun, N., Wang, S., Wei, J., Qiaowei, R.: Trusted boot (tboot). http://sourceforge.net/p/tboot/wiki/Home/
16. Pendergrass, A., Helble, S., Clemens, J., Loscocco, P.: A platform service for remote integrity measurement and attestation. In: Military Communications Conference (MILCOM) 2018, October 2018
17. Rowe, P.D.: Bundling evidence for layered attestation. In: Franz, M., Papadimitratos, P. (eds.) Trust 2016. LNCS, vol. 9824, pp. 119–139. Springer, Cham (2016). https://doi.org/10.1007/978-3-319-45572-3_7
18. Rowe, P.D.: Confining adversary actions via measurement. In: Kordy, B., Ekstedt, M., Kim, D.S. (eds.) GraMSec 2016. LNCS, vol. 9987, pp. 150–166. Springer, Cham (2016). https://doi.org/10.1007/978-3-319-46263-9_10
19. Sailer, R., Zhang, X., Jaeger, T., van Doorn, L.: Design and implementation of a TCG-based integrity measurement architecture. In: Proceedings of the 13th USENIX Security Symposium, San Diego, CA, USA, 9–13 August 2004, pp. 223–238 (2004)
20. Shi, E., Perrig, A., van Doorn, L.: BIND: a fine-grained attestation service for secure distributed systems. In: 2005 IEEE Symposium on Security and Privacy (S&P 2005), Oakland, CA, USA, 8–11 May 2005, pp. 154–168 (2005)
21. Tan, H., Tsudik, G., Jha, S.: MTRA: multiple-tier remote attestation in IoT networks. In: 2017 IEEE Conference on Communications and Network Security (CNS). IEEE, October 2017
22. Xu, W., Ahn, G.-J., Hu, H., Zhang, X., Seifert, J.-P.: DR@FT: efficient remote attestation framework for dynamic systems. In: Gritzalis, D., Preneel, B., Theoharidou, M. (eds.) ESORICS 2010. LNCS, vol. 6345, pp. 182–198. Springer, Heidelberg (2010). https://doi.org/10.1007/978-3-642-15497-3_12

Verifying Liquidity of Bitcoin Contracts

Massimo Bartoletti[1](✉) and Roberto Zunino[2]

[1] Università degli Studi di Cagliari, Cagliari, Italy
bart@unica.it
[2] Università degli Studi di Trento, Trento, Italy

Abstract. A landmark security property of smart contracts is *liquidity*: in a non-liquid contract, it may happen that some funds remain frozen. The relevance of this issue is witnessed by a recent liquidity attack to the Ethereum Parity Wallet, which has frozen $\sim 160M$ USD within the contract, making this sum unredeemable by any user. We address the problem of verifying liquidity of Bitcoin contracts. Focussing on BitML, a contracts DSL with a computationally sound compiler to Bitcoin, we study various notions of liquidity. Our main result is that liquidity of BitML contracts is decidable, in all the proposed variants. To prove this, we first transform the infinite-state semantics of BitML into a finite-state one, which focusses on the behaviour of any given set of contracts, abstracting the context moves. With respect to the chosen contracts, this abstraction is sound and complete. Our decision procedure for liquidity is then based on model-checking the finite space of states of the abstraction.

Keywords: Bitcoin · Smart contracts · Verification

1 Introduction

Decentralized ledgers like Bitcoin and Ethereum [19,32] enable the trustworthy execution of *smart contracts*—computer protocols which regulate the exchange of assets among mutually untrusted users. The underlying protocols used to update the ledger (which defines the state of each contract) ensure that, even without trusted intermediaries, the execution of contracts is correct with respect to the contract rules. However, it may happen that the rules themselves are not correct with respect to the behaviour expected by the users. Indeed, all the attacks to smart contracts successfully carried out so far, which have plundered or frozen millions of USD in Ethereum [1–3,8,27,30], exploit some discrepancy between the intended and the actual behaviour of a contract.

To counteract these attacks, the research community has recently started to formalize smart contracts and their security properties [22–24], and to develop automated verification tools based on these models [21,27,31,35]. As a matter of fact, most of this research is targeted to Ethereum, the most widespread (and attacked) platform for smart contracts: for this reason, the security properties addressed by current tools focus on specific features of Solidity, the high-level language for smart contracts in Ethereum. For instance, some vulnerability patterns

F. Nielson and D. Sands (Eds.): POST 2019, LNCS 11426, pp. 222–247, 2019.
https://doi.org/10.1007/978-3-030-17138-4_10

checked by these tools are reentrancy and mishandled exceptions, whose peculiar implementation in Solidity has led to attacks, like to one to the DAO [1]. Only a few tools verify *general* security properties of smart contracts, that would be meaningful also outside the realm of Ethereum. Among these works, [35] checks a property called *liquidity*, which holds when the contract always admits a trace where its balance is decreased (so, the funds stored within the contract do not remain frozen). This has been inspired from a recent attack to Ethereum [2], which has frozen ~160M USD within a contract, exploiting a bug in a library. While being capable of classifying this particular contract as non-liquid, any contract where the adversary can lock some funds and redeem them at a later moment would be classified as liquid. Stronger notions of liquidity may rule out these unsafe contracts, e.g. by checking that funds are never frozen *for all* possible strategies of the adversary. Studying liquidity in a more general setting would be important for various reasons. First, taking into account adversaries would allow to detect more security issues w.r.t. those checked by the current verification tools. Second, platform-agnostic notions of liquidity could be applied to the forthcoming blockchain technologies, e.g. [20,34]. Third, studying liquidity in simpler settings than Ethereum could simplify the verification problem, which is undecidable in Turing-powerful languages like those supported by Ethereum.

Contributions. We study several notions of liquidity for smart contracts, in a general setting where their behaviour is defined as a transition system. We then consider the special case where contracts are expressed in BitML, a high-level DSL for smart contracts which compiles into Bitcoin [14]. In such setting, we develop a verification technique for liquidity of smart contracts. We can summarise our main contributions as follows:

1. We formalize a notion of liquidity (Definition 2), and we illustrate several meaningful variants. Our notion of liquidity takes into account both the contract and the *strategy* that a participant follows to perform contract actions. Roughly, a strategy is liquid when following it ensures that funds do not remain frozen within the contract, even in the presence of adversaries.
2. We introduce an abstraction of the semantics of BitML which is finite-state (Theorem 1), and sound and complete w.r.t. the concrete (infinite-state) semantics, given a set of contracts under observation (Theorems 2 and 3).
3. We devise a verification technique for liquidity in BitML. Our technique can establish whether a strategy is liquid for a given contract, and also to synthesise a liquid strategy, when it exists (Theorem 4).

Our finite-state abstraction is general-purpose: verifying liquidity is only one of its possible applications (some other applications are discussed in Sect. 6).

Related Works. Several recent works study security issues related to Ethereum smart contracts. A few papers address EVM, the bytecode language which is the target of compilation of Solidity. Among them, [27] introduces an operational semantics of a simplified version of EVM, and develops Oyente, a tool to detect some vulnerability patterns of EVM contracts through symbolic execution. Securify [35] checks vulnerability patterns by analysing dependency graphs extracted from EVM code. As mentioned before, this tool also addresses a form of liquidity, which essentially assumes a cooperating adversary. EtherTrust [21] is a framework for the static verification of EVM contracts, which can establish e.g. the absence of reentrancy vulnerabilities. This tool is based on the detailed formalisation of EVM provided in [22], which is validated against the official Ethereum test suite. The work [23] introduces an executable semantics of EVM, specified in the $\mathbb{K}$ framework. The tool in [18] translates Solidity and EVM code into F^*, and use its verification tools to detect vulnerabilities of contracts; further, the tool verifies the equivalence between a Solidity program and an alleged compilation of it into EVM. The work [24] verifies EVM code through the Isabelle/HOL proof assistant [33], proving that, upon an invocation of a specific contract, only its owner can decrease the balance.

Smart contracts in Bitcoin have a completely different flavour compared to Ethereum, since they are usually expressed as cryptographic protocols, rather than as programs. Despite the limited expressiveness of the scripts in Bitcoin transactions [10], several kinds of contracts for Bitcoin have been proposed [9]: they range from lotteries [6,7,13,29], to general multiparty computations [4,17,26], to contingent payments [11,28], etc. All these works focus on proving the security of a *fixed* contract, unlike the above-mentioned works on Ethereum, where the goal is to verify arbitrary contracts. As far as we know, only a couple of works pursue this goal for Bitcoin. The tool in [25] analyses Bitcoin scripts, in order to find under which conditions the enclosing transaction can be redeemed. Compared to [25], our work verifies contracts spanning among many transactions, rather than single scripts. The work [5] models contracts as timed automata, and then uses the Uppaal model checker [16] to verify their properties. The contracts modelled as in [5] cannot be directly translated to Bitcoin, while in our approach we can exploit the BitML compiler to translate contracts to standard Bitcoin transactions. Note also that the properties considered in [5] are specific to the modelled contract, while in this work we are interested in verifying general properties of contracts, like liquidity.

2 Overview

In this section we briefly overview BitML; we then give some intuition about liquidity and our verification technique. Because of space limits, we refer to [14] for a detailed treatment of BitML, and to [12] for a more gentle introduction.

We assume a set of *participants*, ranged over by $\mathsf{A}, \mathsf{B}, \ldots$, and a set of names, of two kinds: $x, y, \ldots$ denote *deposits* of ₿, while $a, b, \ldots$ denote *secrets*. We write $\boldsymbol{x}$ (resp. $\boldsymbol{a}$) for a finite sequence of deposit (resp. secrets) names.

2.1 BitML in a Nutshell

BitML is a domain-specific language for Bitcoin smart contracts, which allows participants to exchange cryptocurrency according to pre-agreed contract rules. In BitML, any participant can broadcast a *contract advertisement* $\{G\}C$, where

$G ::=$	precondition	$D ::=$	guarded contract
$\mathsf{A}:!\,v\,@\,x$	persistent deposit	$\mathtt{withdraw}\ \mathsf{A}$	transfer balance to A
$\mid \mathsf{A}:?\,v\,@\,x$	volatile deposit	$\mid \mathtt{split}\ \boldsymbol{v} \to C$	split balance ($\lvert\boldsymbol{v}\rvert = \lvert C\rvert$)
$\mid \mathsf{A}:\mathtt{secret}\ a$	committed secret	$\mid \mathsf{A} : D$	wait A's authorization
$\mid G \mid G'$	composition	$\mid \mathtt{after}\ t : D$	wait until time t
$C ::= \sum_{i \in I} D_i$	contract	$\mid \mathtt{put}\ \boldsymbol{x}\ \&\ \mathtt{reveal}\ \boldsymbol{a}\ \mathtt{if}\ p.\,C$	collect deposits/secrets

Fig. 1. Syntax of BitML contracts and preconditions.

$p ::=$	predicate
$true$	truth
$\mid p \wedge p$	conjunction
$\mid \neg p$	negation
$\mid E \circ E$	($\circ \in \{=, <\}$)

$E ::=$	expression
N	32-bit constant
$\mid \lvert a \rvert$	length of a secret
$\mid E \circ E$	($\circ \in \{+, -\}$)

Fig. 2. Syntax of predicates.

C is the actual contract, specifying the rules to transfer bitcoins (₿), while G is a set of *preconditions* to its execution.

Preconditions (Fig. 1, left) may require participants to deposit some ₿ in the contract (either upfront or at runtime), or to commit to some secret. More in detail, $\mathsf{A}:!\,v\,@\,x$ requires A to own v₿ in a deposit x, and to spend it for stipulating a contract C. Instead, $\mathsf{A}:?\,v\,@\,x$ only requires A to pre-authorize the spending of x, which can be gathered by the contract at run-time. The precondition $\mathsf{A}:\mathtt{secret}\ a$ requires A to commit to a secret a before C starts.

After $\{G\}C$ has been advertised, each participant can choose whether to accept it, or not. When all the preconditions G have been satisfied, and all the involved participants have accepted, the contract C becomes *stipulated.* The contract starts its execution with a balance, initially set to the sum of the !-deposits required by its preconditions. Running C will affect this balance, when participants deposit/withdraw funds to/from the contract.

A contract C is a *choice* among zero or more branches. Each branch is a *guarded contract* (Fig. 1, right) which enables an action, and possibly proceeds with a continuation C'. The guarded contract $\mathtt{withdraw}\ \mathsf{A}$ transfers the whole balance to A, while $\mathtt{split}\ v_1 \to C_1 \mid \cdots \mid v_n \to C_n$ decomposes the contract into n parallel components C_i, each one with balance v_i. The guarded contract $\mathtt{put}\ \boldsymbol{x}\ \&\ \mathtt{reveal}\ \boldsymbol{a}\ \mathtt{if}\ p$ atomically performs the following: (i) spend all the ?-deposits $\boldsymbol{x}$, adding their values to the contract balance; (ii) check that all the secrets $\boldsymbol{a}$ have been revealed and satisfy the predicate p (Fig. 2). When enabled, the above-mentioned actions can be fired by anyone, at anytime. To restrict *who* can execute actions and *when*, one can use the decoration $\mathsf{A} : D$, which requires the authorization of A, and the decoration $\mathtt{after}\ t : D$, which requires to wait until time t.

A Basic Example. As a first example, we express in BitML the *timed commitment* [6], a basic protocol to construct more complex contracts, like e.g. lotteries and other games [7]. In the timed commitment, a participant A wants to choose a secret, and promises to reveal it before some time t. The contract ensures that if A does not reveal the secret in time, then she will pay a penalty of 1₿ to B (e.g., the opponent player in a game). In BitML, this is modelled as follows:

$$\{\mathsf{A}:!\,1@x \mid \mathsf{A}:\mathtt{secret}\,a\}\ (\mathtt{reveal}\,a.\,\mathtt{withdraw}\,\mathsf{A}\ \ +\ \ \mathtt{after}\,t:\mathtt{withdraw}\,\mathsf{B})$$

The precondition requires A to pay upfront 1₿, and to commit to a secret a. The contract (hereafter, named TC) is a non-deterministic choice between two branches. Only A can choose the first branch, by performing $\mathtt{reveal}\,a$ (syntactic sugar for $\mathtt{put}\,[]\,\&\,\mathtt{reveal}\,a\,\mathtt{if}\,\mathit{true}$). Subsequently, anyone can transfer 1₿ to A. Only after t, if the `reveal` has not been fired, any participant can fire `withdraw` B in the second branch, moving 1₿ to B. So, before t, A has the option to reveal a (avoiding the penalty), or to keep it secret (paying the penalty). If no branch is taken by t, the first one who fires its `withdraw` gets 1₿.

2.2 BitML Semantics

We briefly recall from [14] the semantics of BitML. The semantics is a labelled transition system between configurations of the following form:

- $\{G\}C$, representing the advertisement of contract C with preconditions G;
- $\langle C, v\rangle_x$, representing a stipulated contract, holding a current balance of v₿. The name x uniquely identifies the contract in a configuration;
- $\langle \mathsf{A}, v\rangle_x$ representing a fund of v₿ owned by A, and with unique name x;
- $\mathsf{A}[\chi]$, representing A's *authorizations* to perform some operation χ. We refer to [14] for the syntax of authorizations (some of them are exemplified below);
- $\{\mathsf{A} : a\#N\}$, representing that A has committed to a random secret a with (secret) length N;
- $\mathsf{A} : a\#N$, representing that A has revealed her secret a (with its length N).
- $\Gamma \mid \Delta$ is the parallel composition of two configurations (with identity 0);
- $\Gamma \mid t$ is a *timed* configuration, where $t \in \mathbb{N}$ is a global time.

We now illustrate the BitML semantics by examples; when time is immaterial, we only show the steps of the untimed semantics. We omit labels on transitions.

Deposits. When A owns a deposit $\langle \mathsf{A}, v\rangle_x$, she can use it in various ways: she can divide the deposit into two smaller deposits, or join it with another deposit of hers to form a larger one; the deposit can also be transferred to another participant, or destroyed. For instance, to donate a deposit x to B, A must first issue the authorization $\mathsf{A}[x \rhd \mathsf{B}]$; then, anyone can transfer the money to B:

$$\langle \mathsf{A}, v\rangle_x \mid \cdots \rightarrow \langle \mathsf{A}, v\rangle_x \mid \mathsf{A}[x \rhd \mathsf{B}] \mid \cdots \rightarrow \langle \mathsf{B}, v\rangle_y \mid \cdots \qquad (y\,\text{fresh})$$

We assume that whenever a participant authorizes an operation on some deposit x, then she is also authorising a self-donation $\mathsf{A}[x \rhd \mathsf{A}]$ of such deposit.[1]

[1] This assumption, while helpful to simplify the subsequent technical development, does not allow an adversary to steal money; at worst, the adversary can use the authorization to transfer the money back to the original owner.

Advertisement. Any participant can advertise a new contract C (with preconditions G). This is obtained by performing the step $\Gamma \rightarrow \Gamma \mid \{G\}C$.

Stipulation. Stipulation turns a contract advertisement into an active contract. For instance, let $G = \mathsf{A}\texttt{:!}\,1\,\texttt{@}\,x \mid \mathsf{A}\texttt{:?}\,1\,\texttt{@}\,y \mid \mathsf{A}\texttt{:secret}\,a$. Given a contract C, the stipulation of $\{G\}C$ is done in a few steps:

$$\langle \mathsf{A}, 1\rangle_x \mid \langle \mathsf{A}, 1\rangle_y \mid \{G\}C \ \rightarrow^* \ \langle \mathsf{A}, 1\rangle_y \mid \langle C, 1\rangle_z \mid \{\mathsf{A} : a\#N\}$$

Above, the funds in the deposit x are transferred to the newly created contract, to fulfill the precondition $\mathsf{A}\texttt{:!}\,1\,\texttt{@}\,x$. Instead, the deposit y remains in the configuration, to be possibly spent after some time. The component $\{\mathsf{A} : a\#N\}$ represents the secret committed to by A, with its length N.

Withdraw. Executing `withdraw` A terminates the contract, and transfers its whole balance to A by creating a fresh deposit owned by A:

$$\langle \texttt{withdraw}\ \mathsf{A} + C', v\rangle_x \ \rightarrow \ \langle \mathsf{A}, v\rangle_y \qquad (y \text{ fresh})$$

Above, `withdraw` A is executed as a branch within a choice: as usual, taking a branch discards the other ones (denoted as C').

Split. The `split` primitive can be used to spawn several new concurrent contracts, dividing the balance among them. For instance:

$$\langle(\texttt{split}\ v_1 \rightarrow C_1 \mid v_2 \rightarrow C_2), v_1 + v_2\rangle_x \rightarrow \langle C_1, v_1\rangle_y \mid \langle C_2, v_2\rangle_z \qquad (y, z \text{ fresh})$$

Put & Reveal. A prefix $\texttt{put}\ z\,\texttt{\&}\,\texttt{reveal}\ a\ \texttt{if}\ p$ can be fired when the previously committed secret a (satisfying the predicate p) has been revealed, and the deposit z is available in the configuration. For instance:

$$\begin{aligned}
&\langle \texttt{put}\ z\,\texttt{\&}\,\texttt{reveal}\ a\ \texttt{if}\ |a| = N.\,C, v\rangle_x \mid \langle \mathsf{A}, v'\rangle_z \mid \{\mathsf{A} : a\#N\}\\
\rightarrow\ &\langle \texttt{put}\ z\,\texttt{\&}\,\texttt{reveal}\ a\ \texttt{if}\ |a| = N.\,C, v\rangle_x \mid \langle \mathsf{A}, v'\rangle_z \mid \mathsf{A} : a\#N\\
\rightarrow\ &\langle C, v + v'\rangle_y \mid \mathsf{A} : a\#N
\end{aligned}$$

In the first step, A reveals her secret a. In the second step, any participant fires the prefix; doing so rakes the deposit z within the contract.

Authorizations. When a branch is decorated by $\mathsf{A} : \cdots$ it can be taken only after A has provided her authorization. For instance:

$$\begin{aligned}
&\langle \mathsf{A} : \texttt{withdraw}\ \mathsf{B} + \mathsf{A} : \texttt{withdraw}\ \mathsf{C}, v\rangle_x\\
\rightarrow &\langle \mathsf{A} : \texttt{withdraw}\ \mathsf{B} + \mathsf{A} : \texttt{withdraw}\ \mathsf{C}, v\rangle_x \mid \mathsf{A}[x \triangleright \mathsf{A} : \texttt{withdraw}\ \mathsf{B}] \ \rightarrow \ \langle \mathsf{B}, v\rangle_y
\end{aligned}$$

In the first step, A authorizes to take the branch `withdraw` B. After that, any participant can fire such branch.

Time. We always allow time t to advance by a delay $\delta > 0$, through a transition $\Gamma \mid t \rightarrow \Gamma \mid t + \delta$. Advancing time can enable branches decorated with $\texttt{after}\, t$. For instance, if $t_0 + \delta \geq t$, we have the following computation:

$$\begin{aligned} &\langle (\texttt{after}\, t : \texttt{withdraw}\ \mathsf{B}) + C', v \rangle_x \mid t_0 \\ \rightarrow\ &\langle (\texttt{after}\, t : \texttt{withdraw}\ \mathsf{B}) + C', v \rangle_x \mid t_0 + \delta \ \rightarrow\ \langle \mathsf{B}, v \rangle_y \mid t_0 + \delta \end{aligned}$$

Runs and Strategies. A *run* $\mathcal{R}$ is a (possibly infinite) sequence:

$$\Gamma_0 \mid t_0 \xrightarrow{\ell_0} \Gamma_1 \mid t_1 \xrightarrow{\ell_1} \cdots$$

where ℓ_i are the transition labels, Γ_0 contains only deposits, and $t_0 = 0$. If $\mathcal{R}$ is finite, we write $\Gamma_{\mathcal{R}}$ for its last untimed configuration, and $\delta_{\mathcal{R}}$ for its last time. A *strategy* Σ_{A} is a PPTIME algorithm which allows A to select which actions to perform (possibly, time delays), among those permitted by the BitML semantics. The choice among these actions is controlled by the adversary strategy Σ_{Adv}, which acts on behalf of all the dishonest participants. Given the strategies of all participants (including Adv), there is a unique run *conforming* to all of them.

2.3 Liquidity

A desirable property of smart contracts is *liquidity*, which requires that the contract balance is always eventually transferred to some participant. In a non-liquid contract, funds can be frozen forever, unavailable to anyone, hence effectively destroyed. There are many possible flavours of liquidity, depending e.g. on which participants are assumed to be honest, and on which are their strategies. The simplest form of liquidity is to consider the case where everyone cooperates: i.e. a contract is liquid if there exists some strategy for each participant such that no funds are ever frozen. However, this notion does not capture the essence of smart contracts, i.e. to allow mutually untrusted participants to safely interact.

For instance, consider the following contract, where A and B contribute 1B each for a donation of 2B to either C or D (we omit the preconditions for brevity):

$$\mathsf{A} : \mathsf{B} : \texttt{withdraw}\ \mathsf{C}\ +\ \mathsf{A} : \mathsf{B} : \texttt{withdraw}\ \mathsf{D}$$

In order to unlock the funds, A and B must agree on the recipient of the donation, by giving their authorization on the same branch. This contract would be liquid only by assuming the cooperation between A and B: indeed, A alone cannot guarantee that the 2B will eventually be donated, as B can choose a different recipient, or even refuse to give any authorization. Consequently, unless A trusts B, it makes sense to consider this contract as non-liquid, from the point of view of A (and for similar reasons, also from that of B).

Consider now the timed commitment contract discussed before:

$$\texttt{reveal}\, a.\, \texttt{withdraw}\ \mathsf{A}\ +\ \texttt{after}\, t : \texttt{withdraw}\ \mathsf{B}$$

This contract is liquid from A's point of view (even if B is dishonest), because A can reveal the secret and then redeem the funds from the contract. The timed commitment is also liquid from B's point of view: if A does not reveal the secret (making the first branch stuck), the funds in the contract can be redeemed through the second branch, after time t.

In a *mutual* timed commitment contract, where A and B have to exchange their secrets or pay a 1₿ penalty, achieving liquidity is a bit more challenging. We first consider a wrong attempt:

$$\begin{aligned} &\texttt{reveal}\, a.\,\texttt{reveal}\, b.\,\texttt{split}\ (1₿ \to \texttt{withdraw}\ \mathsf{A} \mid 1₿ \to \texttt{withdraw}\ \mathsf{B}) \\ &+ \texttt{after}\, t : \texttt{withdraw}\ \mathsf{B} \end{aligned}$$

Intuitively, A has only the following strategies, according to when she decides to reveal her secret a: (i) A chooses to reveal a unconditionally, and to perform the `reveal` a action. This strategy is *not* liquid: indeed, if B does not reveal b, the contract is stuck. (ii) A chooses to reveal a only *after* B has revealed b. This strategy is *not* liquid: indeed, if B chooses not to reveal b, the contract will never advance. (iii) A chooses to wait until B reveals secret b, or until time $t' \geq t$, whichever comes first. If b was revealed, A reveals a, and splits the contract balance between A and B. Otherwise, if the deadline t' is expired, A transfers the whole balance to B. Note that, although this strategy is liquid, it is not satisfactory for A, since in the second case she will lose money.

This example highlights a crucial point: participants' strategies have to be taken into account when defining liquidity. Indeed, the mere fact that a liquid strategy exists does not imply that it is the ideal strategy for the honest participant. To fix this issue, we revise the mutual timed commitment as follows:

$$\begin{aligned} &\texttt{reveal}\, a.\,\big(\texttt{reveal}\, b.\,\texttt{split}\ (1₿ \to \texttt{withdraw}\ \mathsf{A} \mid 1₿ \to \texttt{withdraw}\ \mathsf{B}) \\ &\qquad\qquad + \texttt{after}\, t' : \texttt{withdraw}\ \mathsf{A}\big) \\ &+ \texttt{after}\, t : \texttt{withdraw}\ \mathsf{B} \end{aligned}$$

where $t < t'$. Now, A has a liquid strategy where she does not pay the penalty. First, A reveals a before time t. After that, if B reveals b, then A can execute the `split`, transferring 1₿ to herself and 1₿ to B (note that this does not require B's cooperation); otherwise, after time t', A can withdraw 2₿ by executing the `withdraw` A in the `after` $t' : \cdots$ branch.

These examples, albeit elementary, show that detecting if a strategy is liquid for a contract is not straightforward, in general. The problem of determining a liquid strategy for a given contract seems even more demanding. Automatic techniques for the verification and inference of liquid strategies can be useful tools for the developers of smart contracts.

2.4 Verifying Liquidity

One of the main contributions of this paper is a verification technique for the liquidity of BitML contracts. Our technique is based on a more general result, i.e. a strict correspondence between the semantics of BitML in [14] (hereafter, called *concrete* semantics) and a new abstract semantics, which is finite-state (Theorem 1). Our abstraction is a correct and complete approximation of the concrete semantics with respect to a given set of contracts (Theorems 2 and 3). To obtain a finite-state abstraction, we need to cope with three sources of infiniteness of the concrete semantics of BitML: the unbounded passing of time, the advertisement/stipulation of new contracts, and the operations on deposits. Our abstraction replaces the time t in concrete configurations with a finite number of time intervals $T = [t_0, t_1)$, and it disables the transitions to advertise new contracts. Further, the only operations on deposits allowed by the abstract semantics are the ones for transferring them to contracts and for destroying them. The latter is needed e.g. to properly model the situation where a participant spends a ?-deposit.

The intended use of our abstraction is to start from a configuration containing an arbitrary (but finite) set of contracts, and then analyse their possible evolutions in the presence of an honest participant and an adversary. This produces a finite set of (finite) traces, which we can model-check for liquidity. Soundness and completeness of the abstraction are exploited to prove that liquidity is decidable (Theorem 4). The computational soundness of the BitML compiler [14] guarantees that if a contract is verified to be liquid according to our analysis, this property is preserved when executing it on Bitcoin.

3 Liquidity

In this section we formalise a notion of liquidity of contracts, and we suggest some possible variants. Aiming at generality, liquidity is parameterised over (i) a set X of contract names, uniquely identifying the contracts under observation; (ii) a participant A (with her strategy Σ_{A}), which we assume to be the only honest participant in the system. Roughly, we want that the funds stored within the contracts X are eventually transferred to some participant, in any run conforming to A's strategy. The actual definition is a bit more complex, because the other participants may play against A, e.g. avoiding to reveal their secrets, or to give their authorizations for some branch.

We start by introducing an auxiliary partial function $\mathit{orig}_{\mathcal{R}_0}(\mathcal{R}, x)$ that, given a contract name x and an extension $\mathcal{R}$ of a run $\mathcal{R}_0$, determines the ancestor y of x in the last configuration of $\mathcal{R}_0$, if any. Intuitively, $\mathit{orig}_{\mathcal{R}_0}(\mathcal{R}, x) = y$ means that y has evolved into $\mathcal{R}$, eventually leading to x (and possibly to other contracts).

In BitML, there are only two ways to make a contract evolve into another contract. First, a `split` can spawn new contracts, e.g.:

$$\langle \texttt{split}\ (v_1 \rightarrow C_1 \mid v_2 \rightarrow C_2), v_1 + v_2 \rangle_x \xrightarrow{\mathit{split}(x)} \langle C_1, v_1 \rangle_{y_1} \mid \langle C_2, v_2 \rangle_{y_2}$$

Here, both y_1 and y_2 have x as ancestor. Second, `put&reveal` reduces as follows:

$$\langle \texttt{put}\ z \,\&\, \texttt{reveal}\ a . C, v \rangle_x \mid \langle \mathsf{A}, v' \rangle_z \mid \cdots \xrightarrow{\mathit{put}(z,a,x)} \langle C, v + v' \rangle_y \mid \cdots$$

In this case, the ancestor of y is x.

$$orig_{\mathcal{R}_0}(\mathcal{R}_0, x) = x \quad \text{if } x \in \text{cn}(\Gamma_{\mathcal{R}_0})$$

$$orig_{\mathcal{R}_0}(\mathcal{R}' \xrightarrow{\ell} \Gamma, x) = \begin{cases} orig_{\mathcal{R}_0}(\mathcal{R}', x) & \text{if } x \in \text{cn}(\mathcal{R}') \\ orig_{\mathcal{R}_0}(\mathcal{R}', y) & \text{if } \begin{array}{l} x \in \text{cn}(\mathcal{R}' \xrightarrow{\ell} \Gamma) \setminus \text{cn}(\mathcal{R}') \text{ and} \\ (\ell = split(y) \text{ or } \ell = put(\boldsymbol{z}, \boldsymbol{a}, y)) \end{array} \end{cases}$$

Fig. 3. Origin of a contract name within a run.

Definition 1. *Let $\mathcal{R}$ be a run extending some run $\mathcal{R}_0$, and let x be a contract name. We define $orig_{\mathcal{R}_0}(\mathcal{R}, x)$ by induction on the length of $\mathcal{R}$ in Fig. 3, where* cn(Γ) *denotes the set of contract names in Γ.*

Example 1. Let $\mathcal{R}_0$ be a run with last configuration $\Gamma_{\mathcal{R}_0} = \langle C_1, v\rangle_y \mid \langle \mathsf{A}, v\rangle_z$, and let $\mathcal{R}$ be the following extension of $\mathcal{R}_0$, where the contracts C_1 and C_2 are immaterial, but for the fact that they enable the displayed moves:

$$\begin{aligned} \langle C_1, v\rangle_y \mid \langle \mathsf{A}, v\rangle_z \rightarrow \langle C_1, v\rangle_y \mid \langle \mathsf{A}, v\rangle_z \mid \{G\}C_2 \rightarrow^* \langle C_1, v\rangle_y \mid \langle C_2, v\rangle_x \\ \xrightarrow{split(x)} \langle C_1, v\rangle_y \mid \langle C_2', v\rangle_{x'} \\ \xrightarrow{split(y)} \langle C_1', v'\rangle_{y'} \mid \langle C_1'', v - v'\rangle_{y''} \mid \langle C_2', v\rangle_{x'} \end{aligned}$$

We have that $orig_{\mathcal{R}_0}(\mathcal{R}, y') = orig_{\mathcal{R}_0}(\mathcal{R}, y'') = y$, since the corresponding contracts have been obtained through a split of the ancestor y, which was in the last configuration of $\mathcal{R}_0$. Instead, $orig_{\mathcal{R}_0}(\mathcal{R}, x')$ is undefined, because its ancestor x is not in $\mathcal{R}_0$. Further, $orig_{\mathcal{R}_0}(\mathcal{R}, y) = y$, while $orig_{\mathcal{R}_0}(\mathcal{R}, x)$ is undefined.

We now formalise liquidity. Assume that we want to observe a single contract x, occurring in the last configuration of some run $\mathcal{R}_0$ (note that x has been stipulated at some point during $\mathcal{R}_0$). A participant A wants to know if the strategy Σ_{A} allows her to make x evolve so that funds are never frozen within the contract. We require that A can do this *without* the help of the other participants, which therefore we model as a single adversary Adv. More precisely, we say that x is liquid for A when, after any extension $\mathcal{R}$ of $\mathcal{R}_0$, Σ_{A} can choose a sequence of moves so to make all the descendant contracts of x terminate, transferring their funds to some participant (possibly not A). Note that such moves can not reveal secrets of other participants, or generate authorizations for them: A must be able to unfreeze the funds on her own, using her strategy. By contrast, $\mathcal{R}$ can also involve such moves, but it must conform to A's strategy. The actual definition of liquidity generalises the above to sets X_0 of contract names.

Definition 2 (Liquidity). *Let A be an honest participant, with strategy Σ_{A}, let $\mathcal{R}_0$ be a run, and let X_0 be a set of contract names in $\Gamma_{\mathcal{R}_0}$. We say that X_0 is* liquid w.r.t. Σ_{A} in $\mathcal{R}_0$ *if, for all finite extensions $\mathcal{R}$ of $\mathcal{R}_0$ conforming to Σ_{A} and to some Σ_{Adv}, there exists an extension $\mathcal{R}' = \mathcal{R} \xrightarrow{\ell_1} \cdots \xrightarrow{\ell_n}$ of $\mathcal{R}$ such that:*

$$\forall i \in 1..n \; : \; \ell_i \in \Sigma_{\mathsf{A}}(\mathcal{R} \xrightarrow{\ell_1} \cdots \xrightarrow{\ell_{i-1}}) \tag{1}$$

$$x \in \mathrm{cn}(\Gamma_{\mathcal{R}'}) \implies orig_{\mathcal{R}_0}(\mathcal{R}', x) \notin X_0 \tag{2}$$

Condition (1) requires that all the moves after $\mathcal{R}$ can be taken by A alone, conforming to her strategy. Condition (2) checks that $\mathcal{R}'$ no longer contains descendants of the contracts X_0: since in BitML active contracts always store some funds, this is actually equivalent to checking that funds are not frozen.

We remark that, although Definition 2 is instantiated on BitML, the basic concepts it relies upon (runs, strategies, termination of contracts) are quite general. Hence, our notion of liquidity, as well as the variants proposed below, can be applied to other languages for smart contracts, using their transition semantics.

Example 2. Recall the timed commitment contract TC from Sect. 2. Assume that A's strategy is to wait until time $t - 1$ (i.e., one time unit before the deadline), then reveal the secret and fire `withdraw` A. Let $\mathcal{R}_0$ be a run with final configuration $\langle TC, 1\text{B}\rangle_x \mid \{\mathsf{A} : a\#N\}$, for some length N. We have that $\{x\}$ is liquid w.r.t. Σ_{A} in $\mathcal{R}_0$, while it is *not* liquid w.r.t. the strategy where A does not reveal the secret, or reveals it without firing `withdraw` A. Indeed, under these strategies A alone cannot make x terminate.

Example 3. Consider the following two contracts, which both require as precondition that A put a deposit of 2B and commits to a secret a, and where p is an arbitrary predicate on a:

$$C_1 = \texttt{reveal}\, a \,\texttt{if}\, p.\,\texttt{withdraw}\ \mathsf{A} + \texttt{reveal}\, a \,\texttt{if}\, \neg p.\,\texttt{withdraw}\ \mathsf{B}$$
$$C_2 = \texttt{split}\ 1\text{B} \rightarrow \texttt{reveal}\, a \,\texttt{if}\, p.\,\texttt{withdraw}\ \mathsf{A}$$
$$\mid 1\text{B} \rightarrow \texttt{reveal}\, a \,\texttt{if}\, \neg p.\,\texttt{withdraw}\ \mathsf{B}$$

Assume that A's strategy is to reveal the secret, and then fire any enabled `withdraw`. Under this strategy, C_1 is liquid, because one of the `reveal` branches is enabled, and the corresponding `withdraw` is fired, transferring 2B either to A or to B. Instead, no strategy of A can make C_2 liquid. If A does not reveal the secret, then the 2B are frozen; otherwise, if A reveals the secret, then only one of the two descendents of C_2 can fire the `reveal`, and so 1B remains frozen.

Example 4 (Lottery). Consider a lottery between two players. The preconditions require A and B to commit to one secret each (a and b, respectively), and to put a deposit of 3B each (1B as a bet, and 2B as a penalty for dishonest behaviour):

$$\begin{aligned}
&Lottery(Win) = \texttt{split}(\\
&\quad 2\text{B} \rightarrow (\texttt{reveal}\, b \,\texttt{if}\, 0 \leq |b| \leq 1.\,\texttt{withdraw}\ \mathsf{B}) + (\texttt{after}\, t : \texttt{withdraw}\ \mathsf{A})\\
&\quad \mid 2\text{B} \rightarrow (\texttt{reveal}\, a.\,\texttt{withdraw}\ \mathsf{A}) + (\texttt{after}\, t : \texttt{withdraw}\ \mathsf{B})\\
&\quad \mid 2\text{B} \rightarrow Win)\\
&Win = \texttt{reveal}\, a\, b \,\texttt{if}\, |a| = |b|.\,\texttt{withdraw}\ \mathsf{A}\\
&\quad + \texttt{reveal}\, a\, b \,\texttt{if}\, |a| \neq |b|.\,\texttt{withdraw}\ \mathsf{B}
\end{aligned}$$

The contract splits the balance in three parts, of 2B each. The first part allows B to reveal b and then redeem 2B; otherwise, after the deadline A can redeem

B's penalty (as in the timed commitment). Similarly, the second part allows A to redeem 2₿ by revealing a. To determine the winner we compare the secrets, in the subcontract *Win*: A wins if the secrets have the same length, otherwise B wins. This lottery is *fair*, since: (i) if both players are honest, then they will reveal their secrets within the deadlines (redeeming 2₿ each), and then they will have a 1/2 probability of winning[2]; (ii) if a player is dishonest, not revealing the secret, then the other player has a positive payoff, since she can redeem 4₿.

Although fair, *Lottery*(*Win*) is non-liquid w.r.t. *any* strategy of A. Indeed, if B does not reveal his secret, then the 2₿ stored in the *Win* subcontract are frozen. We can recover liquidity by replacing *Win* with the following:

$$\begin{aligned} \mathit{Win}_2 = \mathit{Win} &+ (\texttt{after}\, t' : \texttt{reveal}\, a.\ \texttt{withdraw}\ \mathsf{A}) \\ &+ (\texttt{after}\, t' : \texttt{reveal}\, b.\ \texttt{withdraw}\ \mathsf{B}) \end{aligned}$$

where $t' > t$. In this case, even if B does not reveal b, A can use a strategy firing any enabled `withdraw` at time t', to unfreeze the 2₿ stored in Win_2.

We now present some variants of the notion of liquidity presented before.

Multiparty Liquidity. A straightforward generalisation of liquidity is to assume a set of honest participants (rather than just one). In this case, we can extend Definition 2 by requiring that the run $\mathcal{R}$ conforms to the strategies of all honest participants, and the moves in (1) can be taken by any honest participant.

We illustrate this notion through the following escrow contract between two participants A and B, where the precondition requires A to deposit 1₿:

$$\begin{aligned} \mathit{Escrow} &= \mathsf{A} : \texttt{withdraw}\ \mathsf{B} + \mathsf{B} : \texttt{withdraw}\ \mathsf{A} + \mathsf{A} : \mathit{Resolve} + \mathsf{B} : \mathit{Resolve} \\ \mathit{Resolve} &= \texttt{split}(0.1₿ \rightarrow \texttt{withdraw}\ \mathsf{M} \\ &\qquad\quad \mid 0.9₿ \rightarrow \mathsf{M} : \texttt{withdraw}\ \mathsf{A} + \mathsf{M} : \texttt{withdraw}\ \mathsf{B}) \end{aligned}$$

After the contract has been stipulated, A can choose to pay B, by authorizing the first branch. Similarly, B can allow A to take her money back, by authorizing the second branch. If they do not agree, any of them can invoke a mediator M to resolve the dispute, invoking a *Resolve* branch. There, the 1₿ deposit is split in two parts: 0.1₿ go to the mediator, while 0.9₿ are assigned either to A and B, depending on M's choice.

Assuming that only A is honest, this contract does not admit any liquid strategy for A, according to Definition 2. This is because B can invoke the mediator, who can refuse to act, freezing the funds within the contract. Similarly, B alone has no liquid strategy, as well as M. Instead, *Escrow* admits a liquid multiparty strategy for any pair of honest participants. For instance, if A and M are honest, their strategies could be the following. A chooses whether to authorize

[2] Note that B could increase his probability to win the lottery by choosing a secret with length $N > 1$. However, doing so will make B lose his 2₿ deposit in the first part of `split`, and so B's *average* payoff would be negative.

the first branch or not; in the first case, she fires `withdraw` B; otherwise, if B gives his authorization within a certain deadline, then A withdraws 1฿; if not, after the deadline A invokes M. The strategy of M is to authorize some participant to redeem the 0.9฿, and to fire all the `withdraw` within *Resolve*.

Strategyless Liquidity. Another variant of liquidity can be obtained by inspecting only the contract, neglecting A's strategy. In this case, we consider the contract as liquid when there exists some strategy of A which satisfies the constraints in Definition 2. For instance, the contract B : `withdraw` A is non-liquid from A's point of view, according to this notion, while it would be liquid for B.

Quantitative Liquidity. Definition 2 requires that no funds remain frozen within the contract. However, in some cases A could accept the fact that a portion of the funds remain frozen, especially when these funds would be ideally assigned to other participants. Following this intuition, we could define a contract *v-liquid* w.r.t. Σ_{A} if at least v bitcoins are guaranteed to be redeemable. If the contract uses only !-deposits, the special case where v is the sum of all these deposits corresponds to the notion in Definition 2. For instance, *Lottery*(*Win*) from Example 4 is non-liquid for any strategy of A, but it is 4฿-liquid if A's strategy is to reveal her secret, and perform all the enabled `withdraw`. Instead, *Lottery*(Win_2) is 6฿-liquid, and then also liquid, under this strategy.

A refinement of this variant could require that at least v฿ are transferred to A, rather than to any participant. Under this notion, both *Lottery*(*Win*) and *Lottery*(Win_2) would be 2฿-liquid for A. Further, *Lottery*(Win_2) would be 4฿-liquid in case A wins the lottery.

Liquidity with Unknown Secrets. All the notions of liquidity proposed so far depend on the initial run $\mathcal{R}_0$, which contains the lengths of the committed secrets. For instance, consider the run ending with the following configuration:

$$\{\mathsf{B} : b\#0\} \mid \langle(\texttt{reveal}\, b \;\texttt{if}\; |b| = 1.\ \mathsf{B} : \texttt{withdraw}\ \mathsf{A}) + \texttt{withdraw}\ \mathsf{A}, 1฿\rangle_x$$

Since the length of b is zero, the `reveal` branch cannot be taken, so A has a liquid strategy (e.g., fire the `withdraw` A). Instead, in an alternative initial run where B chooses a secret of length 1, A has no liquid strategy, since B can reveal the secret and then deny his authorization, freezing 1฿.

In practice, when A performs the liquidity analysis, she does not know the secrets of other participants. To be safe, A should use a worst-case analysis, which would regard the contract (`reveal` b `if` $|b| = 1$. B : `withdraw` A) + `withdraw` A as non-liquid. We can obtain such worst-case analysis by verifying liquidity (in the flavour of Definition 2) for all possible choices of the lengths of Adv's secrets. Although there is an infinite set of such lengths, each contract only checks a finite set of `if` conditions. Hence, the infinite set of lengths can be partitioned into a finite set of regions, which can be used as samples for the analysis. In this way, the basic liquidity analysis is performed a finite number of times.

Similar worst-case analyses can be obtained for all the other above-mentioned variants of liquidity. An average-case analysis can be obtained by assuming to know the probability distribution of A's secrets lengths, partitioning secrets lengths like in the worst-case analysis.

Other Variants. Mixing multiparty and strategyless liquidity, we obtain the notion of liquidity used in [35], in the context of Ethereum smart contracts. This notion considers a contract liquid if there exists a collaborative strategy of all participants that never freezes funds. Other variants may take into account the time when funds become liquid, the payoff of strategies (e.g., ruling out irrational adversaries), or fairness issues. Note indeed that Definition 2 already assumes a sort of fairness, by effectively forbidding the adversary to interfere when the honest participant attempts to unfreeze some funds. Technically, this is implemented in item (1) of Definition 2, requiring that the moves $\ell_1 \dots \ell_n$ are performed atomically. Atomicity might be realistic in some settings, but not in others. For instance, in Ethereum a sequence $\ell_1 \dots \ell_n$ of method calls can be performed atomically: this requires to deploy a new contract with a suitable method which performs the calls $\ell_1 \dots \ell_n$ in sequence, and then to invoke it. BitML, instead, does not allow participants to perform an atomic sequence of moves: an honest participant could start to perform the sequence, but at some point in the middle the adversary interferes. To make the contract liquid, the honest participant must still have a way to unfreeze the funds from the contract. Of course, the adversary could interfere once again, and so on. This could lead to an infinite trace where each attempt by the honest player is hindered by the adversary. However, this is not an issue in BitML, for the following reason. Since the moves $\ell_1 \dots \ell_n$ make the contract terminate, we can safely assume that each of these moves makes the contract progress (as moves which do not affect the contract can be avoided). Since a BitML contract can not progress forever without terminating (and unfreezing its funds), the honest participant just needs to be able to make a step at a time (with possible interferences by the adversary, which may affect the choice of the next step). Defining liquidity beyond BitML and Ethereum may require to rule out unfair runs, where the adversary prevents honest participants to perform the needed sequences of moves.

4 A Finite-State Semantics of BitML

The concrete BitML semantics is infinite-state because participants can always create new contracts and deposits, and can advance the current time (a natural number). In this section we introduce an abstract semantics for BitML, which focuses on both these features so to reduce the state space to a finite one. More specifically, for a concrete configuration $\Gamma \mid t$:

- we abstract Γ as an *abstract configuration* $\alpha_X(\Gamma)$, where X is the (finite) set of contract names under observation. Roughly, $\alpha_X(\Gamma)$ represents only the part of Γ needed to run the contracts X, discarding the other parts;
- we abstract t as a time interval $\alpha_{\mathcal{T}}(t) = [t_0, t_1)$, where $t_0, t_1 \in \mathcal{T} \cup \{0, +\infty\}$. The parameter $\mathcal{T}$ is a finite set of naturals, which intuitively represents all the deadlines occurring in the contracts X.

$$\alpha_{X,Z}(\langle C, v\rangle_x) = \begin{cases} \langle C, v\rangle_x & \text{if } x \in X \\ 0 & \text{otherwise} \end{cases} \qquad \alpha_{X,Z}(\{\mathsf{A} : a\#N\}) = \begin{cases} \{\mathsf{A} : a\#N\} & \text{if } a \in Z \\ 0 & \text{otherwise} \end{cases}$$

$$\alpha_{X,Z}(\langle \mathsf{A}, v\rangle_x) = \begin{cases} \langle \mathsf{A}, v\rangle_x & \text{if } x \in Z \\ 0 & \text{otherwise} \end{cases} \qquad \alpha_{X,Z}(\mathsf{A} : a\#N) = \begin{cases} \mathsf{A} : a\#N & \text{if } a \in Z \\ 0 & \text{otherwise} \end{cases}$$

$$\alpha_{X,Z}(\mathsf{A}[\chi]) = \begin{cases} \mathsf{A}[\chi] & \text{if } \chi = x \rhd D \text{ and } x \in X \\ \mathsf{A}[x, 0 \rhd y^\star] & \text{if } \chi = x \rhd \mathsf{B} \text{ and } x \in Z \\ 0 & \text{otherwise} \end{cases}$$

$$\alpha_{X,Z}(\{G\}C) = 0 \qquad \alpha_{X,Z}(\Delta \mid \Delta') = \alpha_{X,Z}(\Delta) \mid \alpha_{X,Z}(\Delta')$$

Fig. 4. Abstraction of configurations.

We start by defining the abstraction of configurations.

Definition 3 (Abstraction of configurations). *We define the function $\alpha_{X,Z}$ on concrete configurations in Fig. 4, where $y^\star$ denotes a fixed name not present in any concrete configuration. We write $\alpha_X(\Gamma)$ for $\alpha_{X,\mathcal{N}(X,\Gamma)}(\Gamma)$, where:*

$$\mathcal{N}(X, \Gamma) = \{z \mid \exists x, C, v, \Gamma' : \Gamma = \langle C, v\rangle_x \mid \Gamma' \ \wedge\ x \in X \ \wedge\ z \in \mathrm{dn}(C) \cup \mathrm{sn}(C)\}$$

where we denote with $\mathrm{dn}(C)$ *the set of deposit names in some* `put` *within* C*, and with* $\mathrm{sn}(C)$ *the set of secrets names in some* `reveal` *within* C*.*

The abstraction removes from Γ all the deposits not in Z, all the (committed or revealed) secrets not in Z, and all the authorizations enabling branches of some contracts not in Z. All the other authorizations—but the deposit authorizations, which are handled in a special way—are removed. This is because, in the concrete semantics, deposits move into fresh ones which are no longer relevant for the contracts X. Note that if we precisely tracked such irrelevant deposits and their authorizations, our abstract semantics would become infinite-state. To cope with this issue, the abstract semantics will render deposit moves as "destroy" moves, removing the now irrelevant deposits from the configuration. As anticipated in Sect. 2.2, an authorization of a deposit move can only be performed after a "self-donate" authorization $\mathsf{A}[x \rhd \mathsf{A}]$, which lets A transfer the funds in x to another of her deposits. Our abstraction maps such $\mathsf{A}[x \rhd \mathsf{A}]$ into an "abstract destroy" authorization $\mathsf{A}[x, 0 \rhd y^\star]$. In this way, in abstract configurations, deposits can be destroyed when, in concrete configurations, they are no longer relevant.

The abstraction of time $\alpha_{\mathcal{T}}$ is parameterised over a finite set of naturals $\mathcal{T}$, which partitions $\mathbb{N}$ into a finite set of non-overlapping intervals[3]. Each time t is abstracted as $\alpha_{\mathcal{T}}(t)$, which is the unique interval containing t.

[3] A specific choice of $\mathcal{T}$, which considers all the deadlines in the contracts X under observation, is defined later on (Definition 8).

Definition 4 (Abstraction of time). *Let* $\mathcal{T} \in \wp_{fin}(\mathbb{N})$*. We define the function* $\alpha_{\mathcal{T}} : \mathbb{N} \to \wp(\mathbb{N})$ *as* $\alpha_{\mathcal{T}}(t) = [t_0, t_1)$ *where:*

$$t_0 = \max\left(\{t' \in \mathcal{T} \mid t' \leq t\} \cup \{0\}\right) \quad t_1 = \min\left(\{t' \in \mathcal{T} \mid t' > t_0\} \cup \{+\infty\}\right)$$

Lemma 1. *If* $\mathcal{T} \in \wp_{fin}(\mathbb{N})$*, then: (i)* $\forall t \in \mathbb{N} : t \in \alpha_{\mathcal{T}}(t)$*; (ii)* $\operatorname{ran} \alpha_{\mathcal{T}}$ *is finite.*

Abstract Semantics. We now describe the abstract semantics of BitML (the detailed formalisation is deferred to Definition 7 in Appendix A). An *abstract configuration* is a term of the form $\Gamma \mid T$, where Γ is a concrete untimed configuration, and $T \in \operatorname{ran} \alpha_{\mathcal{T}}$. We then define the relation $\to_\sharp$ between abstract configurations by differences w.r.t. the concrete relation $\to$:

1. the rule to advertise contracts is removed.
2. the rules for deposits are replaced by two rules, which authorize and perform the destroy of deposits. In these rules we use the fixed name $y^\star$, unlike the fresh names in the concrete semantics, so to avoid infinite branching.
3. the rule for delays is replaced by a new rule, which allows for transitions $\Gamma \mid T \xrightarrow{\delta}_\sharp \Gamma \mid T'$. The delay δ is the least positive integer which makes T (in the earliest moment) step to T', i.e. $\delta = \min T' - \min T$.
4. the rule for making a contract $\langle \texttt{withdraw}\ \mathsf{A}, v\rangle_x$ reduce to a deposit $\langle \mathsf{A}, v\rangle_y$ is replaced so that $\langle \texttt{withdraw}\ \mathsf{A}, v\rangle_x$ reduces to 0 (the empty configuration).
5. the rule for making branches $\texttt{after}\, t : D$ evolve is adapted to time intervals. The new rule requires that the current time interval T is later than t.

Abstract Runs. Given an arbitrary abstract configuration $\Gamma_0 \mid T_0$, an *abstract run* $\mathcal{R}^\sharp$ is a (possibly infinite) sequence $\Gamma_0 \mid T_0 \to_\sharp \Gamma_1 \mid T_1 \to_\sharp \cdots$. While concrete runs always start (at time 0) from configurations which contain only deposits, abstract runs can start from arbitrary configurations.

Abstract Strategies. An *abstract strategy* $\Sigma^{\#}_{\mathsf{A}}$ is a PPTIME algorithm which allows A to select which actions to perform, among those permitted by the abstract semantics. Conformance between abstract runs and strategies is defined similarly to the concrete case [14].

Concretisation of Strategies. Each abstract strategy $\Sigma^{\#}_{\mathsf{A}}$ can be transformed into a concrete strategy $\Sigma_{\mathsf{A}} = \gamma(\Sigma^{\#}_{\mathsf{A}})$ as follows. The transformation is parameterised over a concrete run $\mathcal{R}_0$ and a set of contract names $X_0 \subseteq \operatorname{cn}(\Gamma_{\mathcal{R}_0})$: intuitively, $\mathcal{R}_0$ is the concrete counterpart of the initial abstract configuration $\Gamma_0 \mid T_0$, and X_0 is the set of contracts under observation. The strategy Σ_{A} receives as input a concrete run $\mathcal{R}$, and it must output the next actions. If $\mathcal{R}$ is a prefix of $\mathcal{R}_0$, the next move is chosen as in $\mathcal{R}_0$. The case where $\mathcal{R}$ is not an extension of $\mathcal{R}_0$ is immaterial. Assuming that $\mathcal{R}$ extends $\mathcal{R}_0$, we first abstract the part of $\mathcal{R}$ exceeding $\mathcal{R}_0$, so to obtain an abstract run $\mathcal{R}^\sharp$. This is done by abstracting every configuration in the run: times are abstracted with $\alpha_{\mathcal{T}_0}$, while untimed configurations are abstracted with α_X, where X is the set of the descendants of X_0 in the configuration at hand. The moves of $\mathcal{R}$ are mapped to abstract moves in a natural way: moves not affecting the descendents of X_0, nor their relevant deposits or secrets, are not represented in the abstract run. Once the abstract run $\mathcal{R}^\sharp$ has been constructed, we apply $\Sigma^\#_{\mathsf{A}}(\mathcal{R}^\sharp)$ to obtain the next abstract actions. $\Sigma_{\mathsf{A}}(\mathcal{R})$ is defined as the concretisation of these actions. The concretisation of the adversary strategy $\Sigma^\#_{\mathsf{Adv}}$ can be defined in a similar way.

Theorem 1. *Starting from any abstract configuration, the relation $\rightarrow_\sharp$ is finitely branching, and it admits a finite number of runs.*

A direct consequence of Theorem 1 is that the abstract semantics is *finite-state*, and that *each abstract run is finite*. This makes the abstract LTS amenable to model checking.

Correspondence Between the Semantics. We now establish a correspondence between the abstract and the concrete semantics of BitML. Assume that we have a concrete run $\mathcal{R}_0$, representing the computation done so far. We want to observe the behaviour of a set of contracts X_0 in $\Gamma_{\mathcal{R}_0}$ (the last untimed configuration of $\mathcal{R}_0$). To this purpose, we run the abstract semantics, starting from an initial configuration $\Gamma^\sharp_0$, whose untimed component is $\alpha_{X_0}(\Gamma_{\mathcal{R}_0})$. The time component is obtained by abstracting the last time $\delta_{\mathcal{R}_0}$ in the concrete run. The parameter $\mathcal{T}_0$ used to abstract time is any finite superset of the deadlines occurring in contracts X_0 within $\Gamma_{\mathcal{R}_0}$. Hereafter we denote this set of deadlines as $\mathit{ticks}_{X_0}(\Gamma_{\mathcal{R}_0})$ (see Definition 8 in Appendix A).

When the contracts in X_0 evolve, the run $\mathcal{R}_0$ is extended to a run $\mathcal{R}$, which contains the descendents of X_0, i.e. those contracts whose *origin* belongs to X_0. These descendents are denoted with $\mathit{desc}_{\mathcal{R}_0}(\mathcal{R}, X_0)$.

Definition 5. *For all concrete runs $\mathcal{R}_0, \mathcal{R}$ such that $\mathcal{R}$ extends $\mathcal{R}_0$, and set of deposit names X_0, we define the set of deposit names $\mathit{desc}_{\mathcal{R}_0}(\mathcal{R}, X_0)$ as follows:*

$$\mathit{desc}_{\mathcal{R}_0}(\mathcal{R}, X_0) \;=\; \{x \mid \exists \Gamma', C, v : \Gamma_{\mathcal{R}} = \langle C, v\rangle_x \mid \Gamma' \text{ and } \mathit{orig}_{\mathcal{R}_0}(\mathcal{R}, x) \in X_0\}$$

The following theorem states that the abstract semantics is a sound approximation of the concrete one. Every abstract run (conforming to A's abstract strategy $\Sigma^\#_{\mathsf{A}}$) has a corresponding concrete run (conforming to the concrete strategy derived from $\Sigma^\#_{\mathsf{A}}$). More precisely, each configuration $\Gamma^\sharp \mid T$ in the abstract run has a corresponding configuration in the concrete run, containing the concretization Γ of $\Gamma^\sharp$, besides a term Δ containing the parts unrelated to X_0. Further, each move in the abstract run corresponds to an analogous move in the concrete run.

Theorem 2 (Soundness). *Let $\mathcal{R}_0$ be a concrete run, let $X_0 \subseteq \mathrm{cn}(\Gamma_{\mathcal{R}_0})$, let $Z_0 \supseteq \mathcal{N}(X_0, \Gamma_{\mathcal{R}_0})$, let $\mathcal{T}_0 \in \wp_{\mathit{fin}}(\mathbb{N})$, let $\Gamma^\sharp_0 = \alpha_{X_0,Z_0}(\Gamma_{\mathcal{R}_0}) \mid \alpha_{\mathcal{T}_0}(\Gamma_{\mathcal{R}_0})$. Let $\Sigma^\#_{\mathsf{A}}$ and $\Sigma^\#_{\mathsf{Adv}}$ be the abstract strategies of A and of Adv, and let $\Sigma_{\mathsf{A}} = \gamma(\Sigma^\#_{\mathsf{A}})$ and $\Sigma_{\mathsf{Adv}} = \gamma(\Sigma^\#_{\mathsf{Adv}})$ be the corresponding concrete strategies. For each abstract run $\Gamma^\sharp_0 \rightarrow^*_\sharp \Gamma^\sharp \mid T$ conforming to $\Sigma^\#_{\mathsf{A}}$ and $\Sigma^\#_{\mathsf{Adv}}$, there exists a concrete run:*

$$\mathcal{R} \;=\; \mathcal{R}_0 \;\rightarrow^*\; \Gamma \mid \Delta \mid \min T$$

such that: (i) $\mathcal{R}$ *conforms to* Σ_{A} *and* Σ_{Adv}*; (ii)* Δ *contains all the subterms of* $\Gamma_{\mathcal{R}_0}$ *which are mapped to* 0 *when evaluating* $\alpha_{X_0,Z_0}(\Gamma_{\mathcal{R}_0})$*; (iii)* $\alpha_{X,Z_0}(\Gamma \mid \Delta) = \Gamma^\sharp$*, where* $X = desc_{\mathcal{R}_0}(\mathcal{R}, X_0)$*; (iv)* $\alpha_{\mathcal{T}_0}(\min T) = T$*; (v) the labels in* $\mathcal{R}$ *are the same as in* $\mathcal{R}^\sharp$*, except for the occurrences of* $y^\star$*.*

Note that soundness only guarantees the existence of some concrete runs, which are a strict subset of all the possible concrete runs. For instance, the concrete semantics also allows the non-observed part Δ to progress, and it contains configurations with a time $t \neq \min T$, for any T in any abstract run. Still, these concrete runs have an abstract counterpart, as established by the following completeness result (Theorem 3). This is almost dual to our soundness result (Theorem 2). Completeness maps concrete configurations to abstract ones using our abstraction functions for untimed configurations and time. Moreover, this run correspondence holds when the concrete strategy of A is derived from an abstract strategy, while no such restriction is required for the adversary strategy.

Theorem 3 (Completeness). *Let* $\mathcal{R}_0$ *be a concrete run, let* $X_0 \subseteq \mathrm{cn}(\Gamma_{\mathcal{R}_0})$*, let* $Z_0 \supseteq \mathcal{N}(X_0, \Gamma_{\mathcal{R}_0})$*, let* $\mathcal{T}_0 \supseteq ticks_{X_0}(\Gamma_{\mathcal{R}_0})$*, and let* $\Gamma_0^\sharp = \alpha_{X_0,Z_0}(\Gamma_{\mathcal{R}_0}) \mid \alpha_{\mathcal{T}_0}(\Gamma_{\mathcal{R}_0})$*. Let* $\Sigma_{\mathsf{A}}^{\#}$ *be the abstract strategy of* A*, and let* $\Sigma_{\mathsf{A}} = \gamma(\Sigma_{\mathsf{A}}^{\#})$ *be the corresponding concrete strategy. For each concrete run* $\mathcal{R} = \mathcal{R}_0 \to^* \Gamma \mid t$ *conforming to* Σ_{A} *and to some* Σ_{Adv}*, there exists an abstract run:*

$$\mathcal{R}^\sharp \;=\; \Gamma_0^\sharp \to_\sharp^* \alpha_{X,Z_0}(\Gamma) \mid \alpha_{\mathcal{T}_0}(t)$$

such that: (i) $\mathcal{R}^\sharp$ *conforms to* $\Sigma_{\mathsf{A}}^{\#}$ *and to some* $\Sigma_{\mathsf{Adv}}^{\#}$*; (ii)* $X = desc_{\mathcal{R}_0}(\mathcal{R}, X_0)$*; (iii) if* $\mathcal{R} = \mathcal{R}_0 \to^* \Gamma' \mid t' \xrightarrow{\ell} \cdots$ *and* $\ell \in \Sigma_{\mathsf{A}}(\mathcal{R}_0 \to^* \Gamma' \mid t')$*, then there exists* ℓ' *such that* $\mathcal{R}^\sharp = \Gamma_0^\sharp \to_\sharp^* \Gamma^\sharp = \alpha_{X',Z_0}(\Gamma') \mid \alpha_{\mathcal{T}_0}(t') \xrightarrow{\ell'}_\sharp \cdots$ *where* $\ell' \in \Sigma_{\mathsf{A}}^{\#}(\Gamma_0^\sharp \to_\sharp^* \Gamma^\sharp)$ *and* $X' = desc_{\mathcal{R}_0}(\mathcal{R}_0 \to^* \Gamma' \mid t', X_0)$*.*

Example 5. Let C = `reveal` a.`withdraw` A + `put` y.`withdraw` B, and let $\mathcal{R}$ be the following concrete run, where the prefix $\cdots$ is immaterial (for simplicity, we also omit labels, times, and participants' strategies):

$$\begin{aligned}
\cdots &\to \langle C, 1\text{₿}\rangle_x \mid \langle \mathsf{B}, 1\text{₿}\rangle_y \mid \langle \mathsf{A}, 2\text{₿}\rangle_z \mid \{\mathsf{A} : a\#10\} \;= \Gamma_0 \\
&\to \langle C, 1\text{₿}\rangle_x \mid \langle \mathsf{B}, 1\text{₿}\rangle_y \mid \langle \mathsf{A}, 2\text{₿}\rangle_z \mid \{\mathsf{A} : a\#10\} \mid \mathsf{B}[y \rhd \mathsf{B}] \\
&\to \langle C, 1\text{₿}\rangle_x \mid \langle \mathsf{B}, 1\text{₿}\rangle_y \mid \langle \mathsf{A}, 2\text{₿}\rangle_z \mid \{\mathsf{A} : a\#10\} \mid \mathsf{B}[y \rhd \mathsf{B}] \mid \mathsf{B}[y \rhd \mathsf{C}] \\
&\to \langle C, 1\text{₿}\rangle_x \mid \langle \mathsf{B}, 1\text{₿}\rangle_y \mid \langle \mathsf{A}, 2\text{₿}\rangle_z \mid \mathsf{A} : a\#10 \mid \mathsf{B}[y \rhd \mathsf{B}] \mid \mathsf{B}[y \rhd \mathsf{C}] \\
&\to \langle \texttt{withdraw}\ \mathsf{A}, 1\text{₿}\rangle_{x'} \mid \langle \mathsf{B}, 1\text{₿}\rangle_y \mid \langle \mathsf{A}, 2\text{₿}\rangle_z \mid \mathsf{A} : a\#10 \mid \mathsf{B}[y \rhd \mathsf{B}] \mid \mathsf{B}[y \rhd \mathsf{C}] \;= \Gamma \\
&\to \langle \texttt{withdraw}\ \mathsf{A}, 1\text{₿}\rangle_{x'} \mid \langle \mathsf{C}, 1\text{₿}\rangle_{y'} \mid \langle \mathsf{A}, 2\text{₿}\rangle_z \mid \mathsf{A} : a\#10 \mid \mathsf{B}[y \rhd \mathsf{B}] \mid \mathsf{B}[y \rhd \mathsf{C}] \\
&\to \langle \mathsf{A}, 1\text{₿}\rangle_{x''} \mid \langle \mathsf{C}, 1\text{₿}\rangle_{y'} \mid \langle \mathsf{A}, 2\text{₿}\rangle_z \mid \mathsf{A} : a\#10 \mid \mathsf{B}[y \rhd \mathsf{B}] \mid \mathsf{B}[y \rhd \mathsf{C}]
\end{aligned}$$

By Theorem 3, this concrete run has the following corresponding abstract run w.r.t. $X_0 = \{x\}$. The initial configuration Γ_0 is abstracted w.r.t. X_0 and $Z_0 = \mathcal{N}(X_0, \Gamma_0) = \{a, y\}$. This causes deposit z to be neglected in the abstraction.

$$
\begin{aligned}
& \langle C, 1\text{B}\rangle_x \mid \langle \mathsf{B}, 1\text{B}\rangle_y \mid \{\mathsf{A} : a\#10\} \quad = \Gamma_0^\sharp \\
\rightarrow_\sharp\ & \langle C, 1\text{B}\rangle_x \mid \langle \mathsf{B}, 1\text{B}\rangle_y \mid \{\mathsf{A} : a\#10\} \mid \mathsf{B}[y, 0 \rhd y^\star] \\
\rightarrow_\sharp\ & \langle C, 1\text{B}\rangle_x \mid \langle \mathsf{B}, 1\text{B}\rangle_y \mid \mathsf{A} : a\#10 \mid \mathsf{B}[y, 0 \rhd y^\star] \\
\rightarrow_\sharp\ & \langle \texttt{withdraw}\ \mathsf{A}, 1\text{B}\rangle_{x'} \mid \langle \mathsf{B}, 1\text{B}\rangle_y \mid \mathsf{A} : a\#10 \mid \mathsf{B}[y, 0 \rhd y^\star] \quad = \Gamma^\sharp \\
\rightarrow_\sharp\ & \langle \texttt{withdraw}\ \mathsf{A}, 1\text{B}\rangle_{x'} \mid \mathsf{A} : a\#10 \\
\rightarrow_\sharp\ & \mathsf{A} : a\#10
\end{aligned}
$$

We now compare the two runs. The concrete authorization for a self-donate of y is abstracted as an authorization for destroying y. Instead, the concrete authorization for donating y to C has no abstract counterpart. The concrete reveal of secret a and the subsequent contract move have identical abstract moves, which reach the abstract configuration $\Gamma^\sharp$. Technically, $\Gamma^\sharp$ is the result of abstracting the concrete configuration Γ w.r.t. $X' = \{x'\}$ and Z_0: here, we no longer abstract w.r.t. X_0, but instead use the set of its descendents X'. By contrast, the set Z_0 is unchanged. Note that, if we instead abstracted with respect to X_0, we would discard the contract x', in which case we could not perform the abstract step, because the abstract semantics does not discard x'. Similarly, if we instead used $Z' = \mathcal{N}(X', \Gamma) = \emptyset$ we would discard the secret a and the deposit y, invalidating the abstract steps. When Γ performs the next move (a donation) this is abstracted as a destroy move. Finally, the last concrete `withdraw` move is mapped to an abstract `withdraw` move, which does not create the deposit x''.

5 Verifying Liquidity

In this section we devise a verification technique for liquidity of BitML contracts, exploiting our abstract semantics. The first step is to give an abstract counterpart of liquidity: this is done in Definition 6, which mimics Definition 2, replacing concrete objects with abstract ones.

Definition 6 (Abstract liquidity). *Let* A *be an honest participant, with abstract strategy* $\Sigma^\#_{\mathsf{A}}$, *let* $\mathcal{R}^\sharp_0$ *be an abstract run, and let* X_0 *be a set of contract names in* $\Gamma_{\mathcal{R}^\sharp_0}$. *We say that* X_0 *is* $\sharp$-liquid w.r.t. $\Sigma^\#_{\mathsf{A}}$ in $\mathcal{R}^\sharp_0$ *if for all extensions* $\mathcal{R}^\sharp$ *of* $\mathcal{R}^\sharp_0$ *conforming to* $\Sigma^\#_{\mathsf{A}}$ *and to some* $\Sigma^\#_{\mathsf{Adv}}$, *there exists an extension* $\dot{\mathcal{R}}^\sharp = \mathcal{R}^\sharp \xrightarrow{\ell_1} \cdots \xrightarrow{\ell_n}$ *of* $\mathcal{R}^\sharp$ *such that:*

$$
\forall i \in 1..n : \ell_i \in \Sigma^\#_{\mathsf{A}}(\mathcal{R}^\sharp \xrightarrow{\ell_1}_\sharp \cdots \xrightarrow{\ell_{i-1}}_\sharp) \tag{3}
$$

$$
x \in \mathrm{cn}(\Gamma_{\dot{\mathcal{R}}^\sharp}) \implies \mathit{orig}_{\mathcal{R}^\sharp_0}(\dot{\mathcal{R}}^\sharp, x) \notin X_0 \tag{4}
$$

To verify liquidity of a set of contracts X_0 in a concrete run $\mathcal{R}_0$, we will choose $\mathcal{R}^\sharp_0$ to be the run containing a single configuration $\Gamma^\sharp_0$, obtained by abstracting with α_{X_0} the last configuration of $\mathcal{R}_0$. In such case, the condition (4) above can be simplified by just requiring that $\mathrm{cn}(\Gamma_{\dot{\mathcal{R}}^\sharp}) = \emptyset$.

The following lemma states that abstract and concrete liquidity are equivalent. For this, it suffices that the abstraction is performed with respect to the contract names X_0, and to the set of deadlines occurring in the contracts X_0.

Lemma 2 (Abstract vs. concrete liquidity). *Let $\mathcal{R}_0$ be a concrete run, let $X_0 \subseteq \mathrm{cn}(\Gamma_{\mathcal{R}_0})$, and let $\mathcal{T}_0 = ticks_{X_0}(\Gamma_{\mathcal{R}_0})$. Let $\Gamma_0^\sharp = \alpha_{X_0}(\Gamma_{\mathcal{R}_0}) \mid \alpha_{\mathcal{T}_0}(\delta_{\mathcal{R}_0})$. Let $\Sigma_{\mathsf{A}}^{\#}$ be an abstract strategy (w.r.t. $\mathcal{T}_0$ and $\Gamma_0^\sharp$), and let $\Sigma_{\mathsf{A}} = \gamma_{\mathcal{R}_0}(\Sigma_{\mathsf{A}}^{\#})$. Let $\mathcal{R}_0^\sharp = \Gamma_0^\sharp$ (i.e., the run with no moves). Then:*

$$X_0 \, is \, liquid \, w.r.t. \, \Sigma_{\mathsf{A}} \, in \, \mathcal{R}_0 \iff X_0 \, is \, \sharp\text{-}liquid \, w.r.t. \, \Sigma_{\mathsf{A}}^{\#} \, in \, \mathcal{R}_0^\sharp.$$

The following lemma states that if a contract is liquid w.r.t. some concrete strategy, then is also liquid w.r.t. some abstract strategy, and *vice versa*. Intuitively, this holds since if it is possible to make a contract evolve with a sequence of moves conforming to any concrete strategy, then the same moves can be also be generated by an abstract strategy.

Lemma 3. *Let $\mathcal{R}_0$ be a concrete run, and let $X_0 \subseteq \mathrm{cn}(\Gamma_{\mathcal{R}_0})$. X_0 is liquid w.r.t. some Σ_{A} in $\mathcal{R}_0$ iff X_0 is liquid w.r.t. $\gamma(\Sigma_{\mathsf{A}}^{\#})$ in $\mathcal{R}_0$, for some $\Sigma_{\mathsf{A}}^{\#}$.*

Our main technical result follows. It states that liquidity is decidable, and that it is possible to automatically infer liquid strategies for a given contract.

Theorem 4 (Decidability of liquidity). *Liquidity is decidable. Furthermore, for any $\mathcal{R}_0$ and X_0, it is decidable whether there exists a strategy Σ_{A} such that X_0 is liquid w.r.t. Σ_{A} in $\mathcal{R}_0$. If such strategy exists, then it can be automatically inferred given $\mathcal{R}_0$ and X_0.*

Proof. Let A be an honest participant with strategy Σ_{A}, let $\mathcal{R}_0$ be a concrete run, and let X_0 be a set of contract names in $\Gamma_{\mathcal{R}_0}$. By Lemma 3, X_0 is liquid w.r.t. Σ_{A} iff there exists some abstract strategy $\Sigma_{\mathsf{A}}^{\#}$ such that X_0 is liquid w.r.t. $\Sigma'_{\mathsf{A}} = \gamma(\Sigma_{\mathsf{A}}^{\#})$. By Lemma 2, X_0 is liquid w.r.t. Σ'_{A} iff X_0 is $\sharp$-liquid w.r.t. $\Sigma_{\mathsf{A}}^{\#}$. By Theorem 1, the abstract semantics is finite, and so the possible abstract strategies are finite. Therefore, $\sharp$-liquidity is decidable, and consequently also liquidity is decidable. Note that this procedure also finds a liquid strategy, if there exists one. □

6 Conclusions

We have developed a theory of liquidity for smart contracts, and a verification technique which is sound and complete for contracts expressed in BitML. Our finite-state abstraction can be applied, besides liquidity, to verify other properties of smart contracts. For instance, we could decide whether a strategy allows a participant to always terminate a contract within a certain deadline. Additionally, we could infer a strategy which guarantees that the contract terminates before a certain time (if any such strategy exists), or infer the strategy that terminates in the shortest time, etc. Although our theory is focussed on BitML, the various notions of liquidity we have proposed could be applied to more expressive languages for smart contracts, like e.g. Solidity (the high-level language used by Ethereum). To the best of our knowledge, the only form of liquidity verified so far in Ethereum is the "strategyless multiparty" variant, which only requires the existence of a cooperative strategy to unfreeze funds (this property is analysed, e.g., by the Securify tool [35]). Since Ethereum contracts are Turing-powerful, verifying their liquidity is not possible in a sound and complete manner; instead, the reduced expressiveness of BitML makes liquidity decidable in that setting.

Acknowledgements. Massimo Bartoletti is partially supported by Aut. Reg. of Sardinia projects *Sardcoin* and *Smart collaborative engineering*. Roberto Zunino is partially supported by MIUR PON *Distributed Ledgers for Secure Open Communities*.

A Appendix

Lemma 4. *Let* $\mathcal{R}_0, \mathcal{R}_1, \mathcal{R}_2$ *be such that* $\mathcal{R}_1$ *extends* $\mathcal{R}_0$ *and* $\mathcal{R}_2$ *extends* $\mathcal{R}_1$. *Then:*

$$orig_{\mathcal{R}_0}(\mathcal{R}_1, orig_{\mathcal{R}_1}(\mathcal{R}_2, x)) \;=\; orig_{\mathcal{R}_0}(\mathcal{R}_2, x)$$

Proof of Lemma 4 (sketch). By induction on $\mathcal{R}_1$.

Definition 7 (Abstract semantics). *Let* $\mathcal{T} \in \wp_{fin}(\mathbb{N})$. *An* abstract configuration *is a term of the form* $\Gamma \mid T$, *where* Γ *is a concrete untimed configuration, and* $T \in \operatorname{ran} \alpha_{\mathcal{T}}$. *We then define the relation* $\rightarrow_\sharp$ *between abstract configurations by differences w.r.t. the concrete relation* $\rightarrow$:

1. *the rule* [C-Advertise] *is removed.*
2. *the rules for deposits are replaced by the following two rules:*

$$\frac{}{\langle \mathsf{A}, v\rangle_x \mid \Gamma \xrightarrow{\mathsf{A}:x,0,y^\star}_\sharp \langle \mathsf{A}, v\rangle_x \mid \mathsf{A}[x, 0 \triangleright y^\star] \mid \Gamma} \text{[Dep-AbsAuthDestroy]}$$

$$\frac{}{\langle \mathsf{A}, v\rangle_x \mid \mathsf{A}[x, 0 \triangleright y^\star] \mid \Gamma \xrightarrow{destroy(x,y^\star)}_\sharp \Gamma} \text{[Dep-AbsDestroy]}$$

3. *the rule* [Delay] *is replaced by the following:*

$$\frac{\delta = \min T' - \min T > 0}{\Gamma \mid T \xrightarrow{\delta}_\sharp \Gamma \mid T'} \text{[AbsDelay]}$$

4. *the rule* [C-Withdraw] *is replaced by the following:*

$$\frac{}{\langle \mathtt{withdraw}\ \mathsf{A}, v\rangle_y \mid \Gamma \xrightarrow{withdraw(\mathsf{A},v,y)} 0} \text{[C-AbsWithdraw]}$$

5. *the rule* [TIMEOUT] *is replaced by the following:*

$$\frac{D \equiv \texttt{after}\, t_1 : \cdots : \texttt{after}\, t_m : D' \quad D' \not\equiv \texttt{after}\, t' : \cdots \qquad \langle D, v\rangle_x \mid \Gamma \xrightarrow{\ell}_{\sharp} \Gamma' \quad x \in cv(\ell) \qquad \min T \geq t_1, \ldots, t_m}{\langle D + C, v\rangle_x \mid \Gamma \mid T \xrightarrow{\ell}_{\sharp} \Gamma' \mid T} \text{[AbsTimeout]}$$

Definition 8. *We define the function ticks from contracts to* $\wp_{fin}(\mathbb{N})$ *as follows:*

$$\begin{array}{ll} \mathit{ticks}(\sum_{i\in I} D_i) = \bigcup_{i \in I} \mathit{ticks}(D_i) & \mathit{ticks}(\mathsf{A} : D) = \mathit{ticks}(D) \\ \mathit{ticks}(\texttt{withdraw}\ \mathsf{A}) = \emptyset & \mathit{ticks}(\texttt{after}\, t : D) = \{t\} \cup \mathit{ticks}(D) \\ \mathit{ticks}(\texttt{split}\ \boldsymbol{v} \to \boldsymbol{C}) = \bigcup \mathit{ticks}(\boldsymbol{C}) & \mathit{ticks}(\texttt{put}\ \boldsymbol{x}\ \&\ \texttt{reveal}\ \boldsymbol{a}\ \texttt{if}\ p.\, C) = \mathit{ticks}(C) \end{array}$$

Then, for any set of names X, we define the function ticks_X *from concrete untimed configurations to* $\wp_{fin}(\mathbb{N})$ *as follows:*

$$\begin{array}{l} \mathit{ticks}_X(\{G\}C) = \emptyset \\ \mathit{ticks}_X(\langle C, v\rangle_x) = \begin{cases} \mathit{ticks}(C) & \text{if } x \in X \\ \emptyset & \text{otherwise} \end{cases} \\ \mathit{ticks}_X(\langle \mathsf{A}, v\rangle) = \mathit{ticks}_X(\mathsf{A}[\chi]) = \mathit{ticks}_X(\{\mathsf{A} : a\#N\}) = \mathit{ticks}_X(\mathsf{A} : a\#N) = \emptyset \\ \mathit{ticks}_X(\Gamma \mid \Gamma') = \mathit{ticks}_X(\Gamma) \cup \mathit{ticks}_X(\Gamma') \end{array}$$

Lemma 5. *If* $\mathcal{R} = \mathcal{R}_0 \to^* \Gamma \mid t$*, then* $\mathit{ticks}_{X_0}(\Gamma_{\mathcal{R}_0}) \supseteq \mathit{ticks}_{desc_{\mathcal{R}_0}(\mathcal{R}, X_0)}(\Gamma)$.

Proof of Lemma 5 (sketch). When a move is performed, a contract becomes syntactically smaller, hence the set of deposit names and secret names within the contract becomes a subset.

Definition 9 (Abstract strategies). *For any* $\mathcal{T} \in \wp_{fin}(\mathbb{N})$ *and initial abstract configuration* $\Gamma_0 \mid T_0$ *with* $T_0 \in \operatorname{ran} \alpha_{\mathcal{T}}$*, we define an* abstract strategy $\Sigma^{\#}_{\mathsf{A}}$ *as a PPTIME algorithm which takes as input an abstract run starting from* $\Gamma_0 \mid T_0$ *and a randomness source, and gives as output a finite sequence of actions. Abstract strategies are subject to same constraints imposed to concrete ones.*

Note that, since $\Sigma^{\#}_{\mathsf{A}}$ can only output moves according to the abstract semantics, it can only choose delays δ which jump from an interval T to a subsequent interval T', i.e. $\delta = \min T' - \min T$.

Proof of Theorem 1 (sketch). The theorem immediately follows from the definition of our abstract semantics, which, compared to the concrete semantics, removes or abstracts all the BitML rules which can violate the statement. More precisely, using rule induction we observe that each abstract step makes the configuration syntactically "smaller", ensuring termination. Further, we have a finite amount of rules, and each rule can only cause a finite amount of branches.

Proof of Theorem 2 (sketch). Essentially, the concrete run can perform the same moves of the abstract run, with the following minor changes. The abstract rules for destroying deposits (and the related authorizations) involve the name $y^\star$, which are replaced by fresh names y in the concrete run. Further, abstract delay moves change the abstract time T to T': in the concrete run, instead, we make time move from $\min T$ to $\min T'$. This makes the concrete and abstract timeout rules to agree on which branches $\texttt{after}\, t : D$ are enabled.

Proof of Theorem 3 (sketch). Each concrete move corresponds to zero or more abstract moves: in the latter case, the concrete and abstract moves are related as follows: (i) contract moves are unchanged; (ii) all authorizations are unchanged, but for $\mathsf{A} : x, \mathsf{B}$ (generated by [Dep-AuthDonate]) which is abstracted as $\mathsf{A} : x, 0, y^\star$; (iii) deposit moves affecting a set Y of deposits are transformed to a sequence of [Dep-AbsDestroy] moves, destroying those deposits in Y which are present in the abstract configuration; (iv) reveal moves are unchanged; (v) delay moves are mapped to delay moves (not necessarily of the same duration).

Proof of Lemma 2. See [15].

Proof of Lemma 3 (sketch). The lemma holds since $\Sigma^{\#}_{\mathsf{A}}$ can be defined in terms of Σ_{A}, in such a way to preserve the following invariant: each conforming run to $\Sigma^{\#}_{\mathsf{A}}$ can be transformed into a concrete run conforming to Σ_{A}. Upon receiving a (conforming) abstract run, if some descendent of X_0 is still present, $\Sigma^{\#}_{\mathsf{A}}$ computes a corresponding concrete run and queries $\Sigma^{\#}_{\mathsf{A}}$ with it, learning the next concrete moves. Since X_0 is liquid, the concrete strategy eventually must perform a move which is relevant for the contracts X_0, and that move can then be chosen by $\Sigma^{\#}_{\mathsf{A}}$. If such move is then taken by the abstract adversary, the invariant is clearly preserved. If instead the adversary takes another move, we can extend the concrete run accordingly, and still preserve the invariant.

Liquidity for Finite LTS. We now give an alternative characterization of liquidity, which corresponds to Definition 2 on transition systems with finite traces, like the one obtained through the abstraction introduced in Sect. 4.

Definition 10 (Maximal run). *We say that a run* $\mathcal{R}$ *is maximal w.r.t. a set of strategies* $\mathbf{\Sigma}$ *when* $\mathcal{R} \xrightarrow{\ell}$ *implies* $\ell \notin \mathbf{\Sigma}(\mathcal{R})$.

Definition 11 (Liquidity for finite LTS). *Assume that* A *is the only honest participant, with strategy* $\Sigma^{\#}_{\mathsf{A}}$. *We say that* X_0 *is* $\sharp_{\mathit{fin}}$-liquid w.r.t. $\Sigma^{\#}_{\mathsf{A}}$ in $\mathcal{R}^{\sharp}_0$ *when, for all extensions* $\mathcal{R}^{\sharp}$ *of* $\mathcal{R}^{\sharp}_0$ *conforming to* $\Sigma^{\#}_{\mathsf{A}}$ *(and to some* $\Sigma^{\#}_{\mathsf{Adv}}$*), if* $\mathcal{R}^{\sharp}$ *is maximal w.r.t.* $\Sigma_{\mathsf{A}}, \Sigma_{\mathsf{Adv}}$ *and* $x \in \mathrm{cn}(\Gamma_{\mathcal{R}^{\sharp}})$, *then* $\mathit{orig}_{\mathcal{R}^{\sharp}_0}(\mathcal{R}^{\sharp}, x) \notin X_0$.

Lemma 6. *X_0 is $\sharp$-liquid w.r.t. $\Sigma^{\#}_{\mathsf{A}}$ in $\mathcal{R}^{\sharp}_0$ iff X_0 is $\sharp_{\mathit{fin}}$-liquid w.r.t. $\Sigma^{\#}_{\mathsf{A}}$ in $\mathcal{R}^{\sharp}_0$.*

Proof. For the "only if part", assume that X_0 is $\sharp$-liquid w.r.t. $\Sigma^{\#}_{\mathsf{A}}$ in $\mathcal{R}^{\sharp}_0$, and let $\mathcal{R}^{\sharp}$ be a maximal extension (w.r.t. $\Sigma^{\#}_{\mathsf{A}}, \Sigma^{\#}_{\mathsf{Adv}}$) of $\mathcal{R}^{\sharp}_0$ conforming to $\Sigma^{\#}_{\mathsf{A}}, \Sigma^{\#}_{\mathsf{Adv}}$. By Definition 6, condition (3) can only hold for $\dot{\mathcal{R}}^{\sharp} = \mathcal{R}^{\sharp}$. Hence, for all $x \in \mathrm{cn}(\Gamma_{\mathcal{R}^{\sharp}})$, by condition (4) it follows that $\mathit{orig}_{\mathcal{R}^{\sharp}_0}(\mathcal{R}^{\sharp}, x) \notin X_0$.

For the "if part", assume that X_0 is $\sharp_{fin}$-liquid w.r.t. $\Sigma^{\#}_{\mathsf{A}}$ in $\mathcal{R}^{\sharp}_0$, and let $\mathcal{R}^{\sharp}$ be an extension of $\mathcal{R}^{\sharp}_0$ conforming to $\Sigma^{\#}_{\mathsf{A}}, \Sigma^{\#}_{\mathsf{Adv}}$. There are two cases:

- If $\mathcal{R}^{\sharp}$ is maximal w.r.t. $\Sigma^{\#}_{\mathsf{A}}, \Sigma^{\#}_{\mathsf{Adv}}$, then by Definition 11 it follows that $x \in \text{cn}(\Gamma_{\mathcal{R}^{\sharp}})$ implies $orig_{\mathcal{R}^{\sharp}_0}(\mathcal{R}^{\sharp}, x) \notin X_0$. Hence, conditions (3)–(4) of Definition 6 follow by choosing $\dot{\mathcal{R}}^{\sharp} = \mathcal{R}^{\sharp}$.
- If $\mathcal{R}^{\sharp}$ is *not* maximal w.r.t. $\Sigma^{\#}_{\mathsf{A}}, \Sigma^{\#}_{\mathsf{Adv}}$, let $\dot{\mathcal{R}}^{\sharp}$ be the longest extension of $\mathcal{R}^{\sharp}$ made only by moves conforming to $\Sigma^{\#}_{\mathsf{A}}$. Let $\dot{\Sigma}^{\#}_{\mathsf{Adv}}$ be the strategy which (i) is equal to $\Sigma^{\#}_{\mathsf{Adv}}$ on the prefix $\mathcal{R}^{\sharp}$, (ii) permits A's action on the extension, (iii) forbids any action after $\dot{\mathcal{R}}^{\sharp}$. By this construction, $\dot{\mathcal{R}}^{\sharp}$ is maximal w.r.t. $\Sigma^{\#}_{\mathsf{A}}, \dot{\Sigma}^{\#}_{\mathsf{Adv}}$. So, by Definition 11 we have $orig_{\mathcal{R}^{\sharp}_0}(\dot{\mathcal{R}}^{\sharp}, x) \notin X_0$ for all $x \in \text{cn}(\Gamma_{\dot{\mathcal{R}}^{\sharp}})$. Conditions (3)–(4) of Definition 6 follow by choosing $\dot{\mathcal{R}}^{\sharp}$. □

References

1. Understanding the DAO attack, June 2016. http://www.coindesk.com/understanding-dao-hack-journalists/
2. Parity Wallet security alert, July 2017. https://paritytech.io/blog/security-alert.html
3. A Postmortem on the Parity Multi-Sig library self-destruct, November 2017. https://goo.gl/Kw3gXi
4. Andrychowicz, M., Dziembowski, S., Malinowski, D., Mazurek, Ł.: Fair two-party computations via Bitcoin deposits. In: Böhme, R., Brenner, M., Moore, T., Smith, M. (eds.) FC 2014. LNCS, vol. 8438, pp. 105–121. Springer, Heidelberg (2014). https://doi.org/10.1007/978-3-662-44774-1_8
5. Andrychowicz, M., Dziembowski, S., Malinowski, D., Mazurek, Ł.: Modeling Bitcoin contracts by timed automata. In: Legay, A., Bozga, M. (eds.) FORMATS 2014. LNCS, vol. 8711, pp. 7–22. Springer, Cham (2014). https://doi.org/10.1007/978-3-319-10512-3_2
6. Andrychowicz, M., Dziembowski, S., Malinowski, D., Mazurek, L.: Secure multiparty computations on Bitcoin. In: IEEE S & P, pp. 443–458 (2014). First appeared on Cryptology ePrint Archive. http://eprint.iacr.org/2013/784
7. Andrychowicz, M., Dziembowski, S., Malinowski, D., Mazurek, L.: Secure multiparty computations on Bitcoin. Commun. ACM **59**(4), 76–84 (2016)
8. Atzei, N., Bartoletti, M., Cimoli, T.: A survey of attacks on Ethereum Smart Contracts (SoK). In: Maffei, M., Ryan, M. (eds.) POST 2017. LNCS, vol. 10204, pp. 164–186. Springer, Heidelberg (2017). https://doi.org/10.1007/978-3-662-54455-6_8
9. Atzei, N., Bartoletti, M., Cimoli, T., Lande, S., Zunino, R.: SoK: unraveling bitcoin smart contracts. In: Bauer, L., Küsters, R. (eds.) POST 2018. LNCS, vol. 10804, pp. 217–242. Springer, Cham (2018). https://doi.org/10.1007/978-3-319-89722-6_9
10. Atzei, N., Bartoletti, M., Lande, S., Zunino, R.: A formal model of Bitcoin transactions. In: Meiklejohn, S., Sako, K. (eds.) FC 2018. LNCS, vol. 10957, pp. 541–560. Springer, Heidelberg (2018). https://doi.org/10.1007/978-3-662-58387-6_29

11. Banasik, W., Dziembowski, S., Malinowski, D.: Efficient zero-knowledge contingent payments in cryptocurrencies without scripts. In: Askoxylakis, I., Ioannidis, S., Katsikas, S., Meadows, C. (eds.) ESORICS 2016. LNCS, vol. 9879, pp. 261–280. Springer, Cham (2016). https://doi.org/10.1007/978-3-319-45741-3_14
12. Bartoletti, M., Cimoli, T., Zunino, R.: Fun with Bitcoin smart contracts. In: Margaria, T., Steffen, B. (eds.) ISoLA 2018. LNCS, vol. 11247, pp. 432–449. Springer, Cham (2018). https://doi.org/10.1007/978-3-030-03427-6_32
13. Bartoletti, M., Zunino, R.: Constant-deposit multiparty lotteries on Bitcoin. In: Brenner, M., et al. (eds.) FC 2017. LNCS, vol. 10323, pp. 231–247. Springer, Cham (2017). https://doi.org/10.1007/978-3-319-70278-0_15
14. Bartoletti, M., Zunino, R.: BitML: a calculus for Bitcoin smart contracts. In: ACM SIGSAC CCS, pp. 83–100. ACM (2018)
15. Bartoletti, M., Zunino, R.: Verifying liquidity of Bitcoin contracts. Cryptology ePrint Archive, Report 2018/1125 (2018). https://eprint.iacr.org/2018/1125
16. Behrmann, G., David, A., Larsen, K.G.: A tutorial on Uppaal. In: Bernardo, M., Corradini, F. (eds.) SFM-RT 2004. LNCS, vol. 3185, pp. 200–236. Springer, Heidelberg (2004). https://doi.org/10.1007/978-3-540-30080-9_7. http://www.it.uu.se/research/group/darts/papers/texts/new-tutorial.pdf
17. Bentov, I., Kumaresan, R.: How to use Bitcoin to design fair protocols. In: Garay, J.A., Gennaro, R. (eds.) CRYPTO 2014. LNCS, vol. 8617, pp. 421–439. Springer, Heidelberg (2014). https://doi.org/10.1007/978-3-662-44381-1_24
18. Bhargavan, K., et al.: Formal verification of smart contracts. In: PLAS (2016)
19. Buterin, V.: Ethereum: a next generation smart contract and decentralized application platform (2013). https://github.com/ethereum/wiki/wiki/White-Paper
20. Gilad, Y., Hemo, R., Micali, S., Vlachos, G., Zeldovich, N.: Algorand: scaling byzantine agreements for cryptocurrencies. In: Symposium on Operating Systems Principles, pp. 51–68 (2017)
21. Grishchenko, I., Maffei, M., Schneidewind, C.: Foundations and tools for the static analysis of Ethereum smart contracts. In: Chockler, H., Weissenbacher, G. (eds.) CAV 2018. LNCS, vol. 10981, pp. 51–78. Springer, Cham (2018). https://doi.org/10.1007/978-3-319-96145-3_4
22. Grishchenko, I., Maffei, M., Schneidewind, C.: A semantic framework for the security analysis of Ethereum smart contracts. In: Bauer, L., Küsters, R. (eds.) POST 2018. LNCS, vol. 10804, pp. 243–269. Springer, Cham (2018). https://doi.org/10.1007/978-3-319-89722-6_10
23. Hildenbrandt, E., et al.: KEVM: a complete formal semantics of the Ethereum Virtual Machine. In: IEEE Computer Security Foundations Symposium (CSF), pp. 204–217. IEEE Computer Society (2018)
24. Hirai, Y.: Defining the Ethereum Virtual Machine for interactive theorem provers. In: Brenner, M., et al. (eds.) FC 2017. LNCS, vol. 10323, pp. 520–535. Springer, Cham (2017). https://doi.org/10.1007/978-3-319-70278-0_33
25. Klomp, R., Bracciali, A.: On symbolic verification of Bitcoin's script language. In: Garcia-Alfaro, J., Herrera-Joancomartí, J., Livraga, G., Rios, R. (eds.) DPM/CBT -2018. LNCS, vol. 11025, pp. 38–56. Springer, Cham (2018). https://doi.org/10.1007/978-3-030-00305-0_3
26. Kumaresan, R., Bentov, I.: How to use Bitcoin to incentivize correct computations. In: ACM CCS, pp. 30–41 (2014)
27. Luu, L., Chu, D.H., Olickel, H., Saxena, P., Hobor, A.: Making smart contracts smarter. In: ACM CCS, pp. 254–269 (2016)

28. Maxwell, G.: The first successful zero-knowledge contingent payment (2016). https://bitcoincore.org/en/2016/02/26/zero-knowledge-contingent-payments-announcement/
29. Miller, A., Bentov, I.: Zero-collateral lotteries in Bitcoin and Ethereum. In: EuroS&P Workshops, pp. 4–13 (2017)
30. Miller, A., Cai, Z., Jha, S.: Smart contracts and opportunities for formal methods. In: Margaria, T., Steffen, B. (eds.) ISoLA 2018. LNCS, vol. 11247, pp. 280–299. Springer, Cham (2018). https://doi.org/10.1007/978-3-030-03427-6_22
31. Mythril (2018). https://github.com/ConsenSys/mythril
32. Nakamoto, S.: Bitcoin: a peer-to-peer electronic cash system (2008). https://bitcoin.org/bitcoin.pdf
33. Nipkow, T., Paulson, L.C., Wenzel, M.: Isabelle/HOL: A Proof Assistant for Higherorderlogic, vol. 2283. Springer Science & Business Media, Heidelberg (2002). https://doi.org/10.1007/3-540-45949-9
34. Rocket, T.: Snowflake to avalanche: a novel metastable consensus protocol family for cryptocurrencies (2018). https://avalanchelabs.org/avalanche.pdf
35. Tsankov, P., Dan, A.M., Drachsler-Cohen, D., Gervais, A., Bünzli, F., Vechev, M.T.: Securify: practical security analysis of smart contracts. In: ACM CCS, pp. 67–82 (2018)

Author Index

www.ingramcontent.com/pod-product-compliance
Lightning Source LLC
LaVergne TN
LVHW082126200926
848484LV00008B/2012

* 9 7 8 1 0 1 3 2 7 1 2 9 8 *